THE EEC
AND
INTELLECTUAL PROPERTY

AUSTRALIA
The Law Book Company Ltd.
Sydney : Melbourne : Brisbane

CANADA AND U.S.A.
Oceana Publications Inc.
New York

INDIA
N.M. Tripathi Private Ltd.
Bombay
and
Eastern Law House Private Ltd.
Calcutta
M.P.P. House
Bangalore

ISRAEL
Steimatzky's Agency Ltd.
Jerusalem : Tel Aviv : Haifa

MALAYSIA : SINGAPORE : BRUNEI
Malayan Law Journal (Pte.) Ltd.
Singapore

NEW ZEALAND
Sweet & Maxwell (N.Z.) Ltd.
Auckland

PAKISTAN
Pakistan Law House
Karachi

THE EEC
AND
INTELLECTUAL PROPERTY

by
DIANA GUY

M.A. (Oxon.)
Solicitor of the Supreme Court

and

GUY I. F. LEIGH

B.A., J.D. (University of Pennsylvania)
Dip. Int. Law (Cantab.)
Solicitor of the Supreme Court

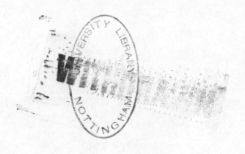

LONDON
SWEET & MAXWELL
1981

Published in Great Britain by
Sweet & Maxwell Ltd. of
11, New Fetter Lane, London
Computerset by
MFK Graphic Systems (Typesetting) Ltd.
Saffron Walden, Essex
Printed in Great Britain
by Page Bros (Norwich) Ltd

British Library Cataloguing in Publication Data

Guy, Diana
   The EEC and intellectual property.
   1.   Intellectual property—European   Economic   Community
   countries
   I. Title   II. Leigh, Guy
   346. 04′8   [Law]

ISBN   0–421–23420–2

PREFACE

In this book we have considered the effect of EEC law on intellectual property and, more particularly, on the way in which intellectual property is used and dealt with. We have not been concerned with national intellectual property as such, but rather with the extent to which EEC law affects the traditional exercise of national intellectual property rights, whether the party exercising those rights does so as owner, licensee, or assignee. Similar questions are also considered in the context of the European Patent, and, in so far as one is able to speculate at this stage, in the context of the Community Patent and the Community Trade Mark.

Throughout, we have sought to isolate the common thread which runs through virtually all the judgments of the Court of Justice and decisions of the Commission concerned with intellectual property. This common thread is the distinction which the Court and the Commission have drawn between the "existence" of intellectual property, which is not affected by EEC law, and the "exercise" of rights in intellectual property, which may be affected by EEC law. More particularly, the exercise of such rights may be affected by the provisions of the EEC Treaty dealing with competition and the free movement of goods and, though as yet only peripherally, by the provisions dealing with free movement of services.

Our approach has been to deal first with the effect of EEC law on intellectual property generally, and then to indicate the extent to which these generalisations require qualification in the context of a particular type of intellectual property.

We adopted this approach both because we believe it to be the natural approach to intellectual property from the perspective of EEC law, and because the practitioner is most often faced with transactions involving a combination of intellectual property rights, rather than a single type of intellectual property in isolation.

Finally, we would express our thanks to all those who assisted us in writing this book including, in particular, Michael Wisher and Donald Turner, who kindly commented in detail on the manuscript, Margaret Fothergill and Paul Haines who laboriously assisted with proof reading and footnoting, our librarian, Lynn Orsborn, who went to extraordinary efforts to procure for us material not generally available in the closing days of 1980, our secretaries, Eileen Tyrer and Julie Dryhurst-Roberts and, last but not least, our respective spouses, who endured this labour with patience and understanding. The responsibility for inaccuracies and omissions is, of course, ours alone.

The law is stated as at December 31, 1980.

16 *St. Martin's-Le-Grand*
London

Diana Guy
Guy I. F. Leigh

CONTENTS

TABLE OF CASES

xiii

TABLE OF CASES

ALPHABETICAL TABLE OF CASES

NATIONAL COURTS

Germany

United Kingdom

TABLE OF COMMUNITY TREATIES

TABLE OF COMMUNITY
SECONDARY LEGISLATION

TABLE OF UNITED KINGDOM LEGISLATION

Part I

General Introduction

CHAPTER 1

SCOPE AND PURPOSE

I. *PRELIMINARY COMMENTS*

1.01 It is intended in this book to examine the effect of EEC law on intellectual property, in particular patents, trade marks, copyright, know-how and plant breeders' rights.

II. *ORGANISATION*

1.02 The next six chapters will provide a general introduction to the relevant provisions of Community law. Then, in Parts II, III and IV the effects of Community law on national intellectual property will be considered. This will be done in three separate contexts, namely where:

(1) the intellectual property is owned outright by one or more enterprises within the Community;

(2) the intellectual property is licensed;

(3) ownership of the intellectual property is disposed of, whether by way of assignment or otherwise.

1.03 Finally, to complete the picture, Part V will deal with the effects of EEC law on patents governed by the two Patents Conventions,[1] and on trade marks granted under the proposed Community Trade Mark Regulation.[2]

III. *LEGISLATIVE BACKGROUND*

A. OBJECTIVES OF THE EUROPEAN ECONOMIC COMMUNITY

1.04 The Treaty Establishing the European Economic Community[3] ("the Treaty") was signed by the six original Member States[4] on March 25, 1957 and came into force on January 1, 1958.

---

[1] Convention on the Grant of European Patents (European Patent Convention) reprinted in, *e.g.* European Patent Handbook (by the Chartered Institute of Patent Agents (1978), Chap. 51). Convention of December 15, 1975 for the European Patent for the Common Market (Community Patent Convention) (O.J. 1976, L17/1).

[2] O.J. 1980, C351; [1981] 1 C.M.L.R. 365.

[3] On the Treaty Establishing the European Economic Community (Cmnd. 4864), see generally Chap. 2. For a consolidated version of the Treaty as amended, see *Sweet & Maxwell's European Community Treaties* (4th ed., 1980).

[4] Belgium, the Federal Republic of Germany, France, Italy, Luxembourg and the Netherlands.

1.05   The aims of the Community are set out in Article 2 which provides:
"The Community shall have as its task, by establishing a common
market and progressively approximating the economic policies of
Member States, to promote throughout the Community a harmonious development of economic activities, a continuous and
balanced expansion, an increase in stability, an accelerated raising of
the standard of living and closer relations between the States belonging to it."

1.06   The concern in this book is merely with the effect of the Treaty on
intellectual property within the Member States and not with its effect on
the whole range of economic and political activities which, prior to the
establishment of the Community, were within the exclusive sovereign
competence of the national governments. It is, however, difficult, if not
impossible, to understand the impact of Community law on intellectual
property unless the aim underlying the Treaty, and motivating much of the
activity of the Commission, is understood. That aim is the creation of a
single Community among the ten Member States.[4a] As expressed in the
Treaty, the Community is primarily economic in nature, but economics can
never entirely be divorced from politics.

1.07   Superficially the Community may manifest itself simply as a customs
union, that is to say, as a group of countries which have abolished customs
duties between each other, while applying a common customs tariff *vis-à-
vis* the rest of the world.[5] Whilst, however, the customs union is the
foundation on which the Community is built, the activities of the Community are far more extensive and include the establishment of common
policies in the fields of agriculture and transport, approximation of the laws
of the Member States in certain areas, and the so-called "four freedoms":
free movement of goods, persons, services and capital.[6]

B. PRINCIPLES OF COMMUNITY LAW AFFECTING INTELLECTUAL PROPERTY

(1) *General*

1.08   The aims of the Treaty as a whole are set out in Article 2, but the activities
entrusted to the Community are contained in Article 3. It is here that one
first finds expressed the two principles which again and again conflict with

---

[4a] The original six Member States were joined by Denmark, Eire and the United Kingdom
on January 1, 1973, and by Greece on January 1, 1981.
[5] The general objective of achieving a customs union is contained in Arts. 3 (*a*) and 3 (*b*) of
the Treaty (Appendix 1). The general subject of the establishment of the customs union is
outside the scope of this book.
[6] These general objectives are assigned to the Community by Art. 3 (*a*), (*c*), (*d*) (*e*) and (*h*)
(Appendix 1). The provisions of the Treaty relating to the free movement of goods, in so far
as relevant to intellectual property, will be referred to subsequently in the text, and are set out
in full in the Appendix. The other topics are outside the scope of this book.

the traditional exercise of intellectual property rights within national boundaries, namely:

1. the free movement of goods across national frontiers within the Community, and
2. the need to ensure that competition within the Community is not distorted.

1.09   Thus, Article 3 of the Treaty states: "... the activities of the Community shall include, as provided in this Treaty and in accordance with the timetable set out therein:

(*a*) the elimination, as between Member States, of customs duties and of quantitative restrictions on the import and export of goods, and of all other measures having equivalent effect;

(*f*) the institution of a system ensuring that competition in the common market is not distorted."

(2) *Provisions on Free Movement of Goods*

1.10   Although perhaps not self-evident from the wording, Article 3 (*a*) is concerned with the free movement of goods. The link between this and intellectual property is to be found in the innocuous phrase "all other measures having equivalent effect." For, although such a development would hardly have been anticipated on the birth of the Community in 1958, it is now firmly established that the enforcement of an intellectual property right can, in certain circumstances, constitute a "measure having equivalent effect,"[7] to a quantitative restriction.

1.11   The substantive provisions of the Treaty are to be found in Title I of Part Two of the Treaty, which is itself headed "Free movement of goods" and, particularly, in Articles 9 and 30 to 37.[8]

(3) *Competition Provisions*

1.12   If it is not immediately apparent from its wording that Article 3 (*a*) is concerned generally with the principle of free movement of goods, Article 3 (*f*) is quite clearly concerned with the establishment of "a system ensuring that competition in the common market is not distorted." The relevant Articles of the Treaty dealing with competition are Articles 85 to 90,[9] and particularly Articles 85 and 86.

---

[7] See, *e.g. Deutsche-Grammophon Gesellschaft GmbH* v. *Metro-SB-Grossmärkte GmbH & Co. KG* [1971] E.C.R. 487; [1971] C.M.L.R. 631 discussed, *infra,* at paras. 8–07 *et seq*.

[8] Arts. 30–37 are in fact contained in Pt. Two, Title I, Chap. 2 of the Treaty, entitled "Elimination of Quantitative Restrictions between Member States." These Articles are set out in full in App. 1.

[9] Arts. 85–90 are set out in Chap. 1 of Title I of Part Three of the Treaty and are reproduced in full in App. 1. Part Three is entitled "Policy of the Community," while Title I is headed "Common Rules." Not surprisingly, Chap. 1 is entitled "Rules on Competition."

1.13   Broadly, Article 85 is concerned with distortions of competition within the Community resulting from restrictive agreements, decisions or concerted practices between two or more parties. It therefore can, and frequently does, affect agreements dealing with intellectual property.

1.14   By contract, Article 86 is directed at any "abuse by one or more undertakings of a dominant position within the Common Market or in a substantial part of it." This can affect domestic intellectual property rights to the extent that those rights (as a matter of Community law) help to create a dominant position, or are involved in an abuse of it.

(4) *Provisions on Free Movement of Services*

The provisions of the Treaty concerned with "Free Movement of Services" may also be relevant to intellectual property in the particular context of performing rights as an element of copyright. The provisions in question are Articles 3 (*c*), 59 and 60, and these will be discussed in the text where relevant.

C. The Inherent Conflict between Intellectual Property and the EEC

1.15   It will by now be apparent that conflicts are inevitable between the provisions of the Treaty already mentioned, and the traditional exercise of national intellectual property rights. For one thing is common to such statutory protection as is afforded in the ten Member States to different types of intellectual property: the statutory protection is national in scope. For example, a United Kingdom patent is valid throughout the United Kingdom of Great Britain and Northern Ireland and the Isle of Man,[10] and it is normally assumed that, provided the patent owner does not infringe any applicable law (whether concerned with patents or otherwise), he may exploit his patent as he sees fit. Similarly, registration of a trade mark is national in scope,[10a] and, again, it is assumed that, provided the owner complies with the relevant national legislation, he will be entitled to use his trade mark for the territory in respect of which it has been registered, assigning it, licensing it and/or simply using it as he sees fit. Yet, since the emergence of Community law, this is no longer the case.

1.16   For example, in the patent context, it is now clearly established that the mere grant of an exclusive patent licence between enterprises in different Member States may infringe the prohibition against restrictive agreements in Article 85 (1) where there is an effect on trade (as there almost in-

---

[10] A U.K. patent does not, however, extend to the Channel Islands. See s. 21 of the Patents Act 1949 (not repealed by the Patents Act 1977).

[10a] In this context Benelux constitutes a single territory. Furthermore, the possibility of registrations under the Arrangement of Madrid for the International Registration of Marks of April 14, 1891 (as revised), should be borne in mind.

variably will be).[11] Perhaps more surprisingly, from the point of view of the British practitioner, it has now repeatedly been held that where the patentee and the licensee are established in different Member States, a clause in a patent licence prohibiting the licensee from challenging the validity of the patent will also infringe Article 85 (1).[12] This is all the more unexpected because as a matter of British patent law the licensee is estopped from challenging the validity of the patent which has been licensed to him.[13] To date, the European Court of Justice has not been asked to consider the effect of EEC law on this particular aspect of the doctrine of estoppel, although the possibility that it may one day be called upon to do so is by no means far-fetched.

1.17   Equally, significant developments have taken place affecting other types of intellectual property. Thus, it is now established that where an identical trade mark is owned in Member State A by Company X, and in Member State B by Company Y, both companies belonging to the same corporate group, Y will not be able to rely on its exclusive right to use the trade mark in Member State B in order to prevent a third party importing into that state goods bearing the trade mark and acquired by that third party in Member State A, after they have been marketed there by Company X.[14]

1.18   In 1968, the European Court of Justice recognised the source of the conflict between Community law and national intellectual property when it suggested that as long as national laws in the individual Member States have not been harmonised, the resulting differences are bound to give rise to obstacles both to the free movement of goods and to competition within the EEC.[15]

D. THE TREATY AND THE PROTECTION OF INTELLECTUAL PROPERTY

(1) *General*

1.19   Even though the Treaty contains the basis of inherent conflict between intellectual property rights as traditionally exercised within the individual Member States and the objectives of the Treaty, it also guarantees the continued existence of those rights within the Community. In particular,

---

[11] *Re Kabelmetal's Agreement*, decision of July 18, 1975 [1975] 2 C.M.L.R. D. 40 at paras. 22–28; *Zuid-Nederlandsche Bronbemaling en Grondboringen BV* v. *Heidemaatschappi*; *Beheer NV*, decision of July 25, 1975 [1975] 2 C.M.L.R. D. 67 at para. 14 (*d*).

[12] *Re Agreement of Davidson Rubber Co.*, decision of June 9, 1972 [1972] C.M.L.R. D. 52.

[13] Falconer, Aldous, Young and Terrell, *The Law of Patents* (1971), p. 256.

[14] *Centrafarm BV* v. *Winthrop BV*, October 31, 1974 [1974] E.C.R. 1183; [1974] 2 C.M.L.R. 480. The position is similar under English trade mark law. See in this connection s. 4 (3) (*a*) Trade Marks Act 1938, and note *Revlon Inc.* v. *Cripps Lee Ltd. and Others* [1980] F.S.R. 85.

[15] *Parke Davis & Co.* v. *Probel and Others*, judgment of February 29, 1968 [1968] E.C.R. 55; [1968] C.M.L.R. 47 at p. 58.

Article 222 of the Treaty states: "This Treaty shall in no way prejudice the rules in Member States governing the system of property ownership."

1.20   How, it may be asked, can the provisions of Articles 30 to 36, 85 and 86 in certain circumstances prevent the continued use of national intellectual property rights in ways which before the establishment of the European Community were perfectly acceptable, when Article 222 expressly guarantees those rights? The way in which the European Commission and the European Court of Justice have sought to resolve this question will occupy a large part of this book. The Court articulated its approach to this problem in its decision in the *Grundig-Consten* case.[16-17] In that case, it drew a distinction between the "existence" and the "exercise" of a national intellectual property right.

(2) *Resolution of the Conflict between Intellectual Property Rights and the Treaty*

1.21   This is not the place to consider either the facts or the reasoning of the Grundig decision in detail. It is enough to mention here that the European Court was considering an appeal against a decision of the Commission that certain distribution and trade mark arrangements between the German company, Grundig, and its distributor in France, infringed Article 85 (1). One of the questions with which the Court had to deal was whether Article 222[17] of the Treaty prevented the application of Article 85 to the exercise of national intellectual property rights in the circumstances of that case.[18] The Court concluded on this point:

> "Article 222 is limited to stating that the 'Treaty shall in no way prejudice existing systems and incidents of ownership' in the Member States. The injunction in . . . the [Commission's] attacked decision not to use national law relating to trade marks to obstruct parallel imports, without touching the grant of those rights, limits their *exercise*[19] to the extent necessary for the attainment of the prohibition deriving from Article 85 (1)."[20]

Thus the Court, though affirming the continued existence of national intellectual property rights, held that the exercise of those rights is circumscribed by Community law.

[16-17] *Etablissement Consten SA and Grundig-Verkaufs GmbH* v. *EC Commission* [1966] E.C.R. 299 [1966] C.M.L.R. 418 and p. 476; see also *Italy* v. *EEC Council and Commission* [1966] E.C.R. 389; [1969] C.M.L.R. 39.
[18] At p. 475. The European Court had, in fact, to consider the same question with regard to Arts. 36 and 234.
[19] Emphasis supplied.
[20] At p. 476.

(3) *The Distinction between "Existence" and "Exercise"*

1.22 The distinction between "existence" and "exercise" is easily criticised on the grounds that it is merely a semantic distinction which has no basis in fact. Certainly, in traditional terms the existence and the exercise of an intellectual property right are opposite sides of the same coin, and cannot easily be separated. The owner of a patent, for example, is free to license it exclusively or otherwise, as he sees fit. From this point of view, it is nonsense to suggest that the ownership of a patent is a characteristic of its *existence* and is protected under EEC law, whereas the grant of a licence is a feature of the *exercise* of the patent which, depending on its terms, may well infringe the prohibition in Article 85 (1) of the Treaty; and, further, that the grant of an exclusive patent licence will normally infringe that prohibition.[21]

1.23 Whatever the merits of the distinction between existence and exercise of intellectual property rights in terms of national law, the fact remains that the distinction is one which has frequently been drawn both by the European Court of Justice and the European Commission. It has been used by the Court as a means of reconciling the guaranteed existence of national intellectual property on the one hand, and the need to ensure the free movement of goods and the competition provisions of the Treaty on the other hand. In these circumstances, and whatever the weaknesses of the distinction, it is unhelpful in the extreme simply to disregard it on the grounds that it is not one which can properly be drawn. It must be accepted that, whether or not in terms of national law it can be made, the distinction between existence and exercise of intellectual property rights in the EEC has now been firmly established by the European Court of Justice.

---

[21] *Parke Davis & Co. supra*, n. 15, at pp. 58 *et seq.*; *re Kabelmetal's Agreement, supra*, n. 11, at paras. 23 and 29.

CHAPTER 2

NATURE AND SOURCES OF COMMUNITY LAW
AND THE COMMUNITY INSTITUTIONS

I. *INTRODUCTION*

2.01 EEC law is the law stemming from the Treaty itself, the secondary legislation[1] of the Council and the Commission (*i.e.* regulations, directives and decisions under Article 189), and certain related Conventions entered into by the Member States.[2] It is, therefore, a system of law in its own right, albeit one whose scope is limited by the primarily economic nature of the objectives of the Treaty bringing it into existence.[3] Although the legal systems of the individual Member States inevitably exercise a substantial influence on the form of secondary legislation[4] and, indeed, on the whole context within which Community law operates,[5] Community law is in no sense a branch of comparative law.

II. *NATURE OF COMMUNITY LAW*

2.02 The unique nature of Community law was strikingly described by the European Court in its judgment in the *Van Gend en Loos* case,[6] where it said:

"The purpose of the E.E.C. Treaty—to create a Common Market, the functioning of which directly affects the citizens of the Community—implies that this Treaty is more than an agreement creating only mutual obligations between the contracting parties. This interpretation is confirmed by the preamble to the Treaty which, in addition to mentioning governments affects individuals ... we must

---

[1] See *infra*, paras. 2.24 *et seq.*
[2] *e.g.* Convention of December 15, 1975 for the European Patent for the Common Market (Community Patent Convention) (O.J. 1976, L17/1)
[3] See Case 36/74 *Walrave and Koch* v. *Association Union Cycliste Internationale* [1974] E.C.R. 1405; [1975] 1 C.M.L.R. 320, where the European Court held that the practice of sport is subject to Community law only so far as it constitutes an economic activity within the meaning of Art. 2.
[4] *e.g.* the requirement under German company law for a supervisory board ("Aufsichtsrat") is reflected in the proposed fifth Directive on the harmonisation of company law, submitted by the Commission to the Council on October 9, 1972 (Bull. No. 10/72).
[5] See *infra*, paras. 2.14 *et seq.*
[6] Case 26/62 *N.V. Algemene Transport en Expeditie Onderneming Van Gend en Loos* v. *Nederlandse Tariefcommissie* [1963] E.C.R.I.; [1963] C.M.L.R. 105.

conclude from this that the Community constitutes *a new legal order*[7] in international law for whose benefit the States have limited their sovereign rights, albeit within limited fields."[8]

2.03 Again, in its decision in *Costa* v. *ENEL,*[9] the Court said:

"As opposed to other international treaties, the Treaty instituting the E.E.C. has created its own order which was integrated with the national order of the Member States the moment the Treaty came into force; as such it is binding upon them. In fact, by creating a Community of unlimited duration having its own institutions, its own personality and its own capacity in law, apart from having international standing and more particularly, *real powers*[10] resulting from a limitation of competence or a transfer of powers from the States to the Community, the Member States albeit within limited spheres have restricted their sovereign rights and created a body of law applicable both to their nationals and to themselves."[11]

2.04 From these statements emerge two points of fundamental importance. First, the Court confirms the status of Community law as an entirely new legal system, one brought into existence by each of the Member States abandoning a part of its traditional sovereign powers in certain defined areas of activity. Henceforth in the areas covered by the Treaty, the Member States are not merely to co-ordinate their activities,[12] but are to act as one. Common policies are to replace national policies.[13]

2.05 Secondly, the Court characterises the position of the Community as that of a quasi-sovereign body in its own right, with its own legal personality,[14] exercising "real powers." Those powers are rendered effective because certain acts of the Community are made binding on the Member States[15] and, in some cases, on the individual citizens of the Member States.

2.06 As in other developed legal systems, where there are obligations, there are corresponding rights. Thus, the Treaty gives rights to the Member States, both against the Community[16] and the other Member States.[17] In some instances, private individuals, too, have the right under Community

---

[7] Emphasis supplied.

[8] *Van Gend en Loos, supra,* n. 6 at p. 129.

[9] *Costa* v. *Ente Nazionale per l'Energia Elettrica (ENEL)* [1964] E.C.R. 585; [1964] C.M.L.R. 425.

[10] Emphasis supplied.

[11] *Costa* v. *ENEL, supra,* n. 9 at p. 455.

[12] As, for example, under the General Agreement on Trade and Tariffs (GATT).

[13] Among many examples are the Common Agricultural Policy (Arts. 38–47), the Common Customs Tariff (Arts. 18–29) and the control of dumping by non-Member States (Reg. 3017/79).

[14] Note also Art. 210.

[15] Art. 189.

[16] Art. 173.

[17] Art. 170.

law to take action against the Community,[18] their own[19] and other Member States[20] and private individuals.[21]

III. *SOURCES OF COMMUNITY LAW*

A. GENERAL

2.07   As membership of the Community requires a partial surrender by the Member States of certain of their traditional sovereign powers in favour of the Community, it is clearly important that the legitimacy of every act of the Community institutions can be traced to a specific provision of the Treaty or to some other primary source of Community law. For this purpose, a primary source of Community law is defined as one which does not derive from another Community enactment, but which exists independently. Apart from the Treaty itself, the other primary sources are certain of the Conventions concluded between Member States, and the general principles of law and fundamental rights which are common to and recognised by the Member States.

2.08   In addition to the primary sources of Community law, there are also:
  (i) secondary sources, *i.e.* regulations, directives, decisions and judgments of the Court of Justice (as well as other acts of the Court); and
  (ii) other "sources," such as opinions and recommendations of the Council and the Commission.

B. PRIMARY SOURCES

(1) *The Treaty*

2.09   The pre-eminent source of Community law is, of course, the Treaty itself.[22] In *Application des Gaz SA* v. *Falks Veritas Limited*,[23] Lord Denning M.R. commented on Articles 85 and 86 in terms which are equally appropriate to describe most of the substantive provisions of the Treaty:
  "Those provisions are framed in a style very different from an English statute. They state general principles. They lay down broad policies. But they do not go into detail. The words and phrases are not defined.

---

[18] Arts. 173 (2), 175 (3).
[19] See, *e.g. Gabrielle Defrenne* v. *Belgian State* [1971] E.C.R. 445; [1974] 1 C.M.L.R. 494; and *Re: an illness in France* [1976] 1 C.M.L.R. 243.
[20] See, *e.g. Van Duyn* v. *Home Office* [1974] E.C.R. 1337; [1975] 1 C.M.L.R.; *Reyners* v. *The Belgian State* [1974] E.C.R. 631; [1974] 2 C.M.L.R. 305.
[21] For a general discussion of direct applicability, see *infra,* Chap. 3, paras. 3.08 *et seq.*
[22] In addition to the EEC Treaty, numerous other Treaties have been concluded between the Member States, *e.g.* the Treaty establishing the European Coal and Steel Community (1951), the Treaty establishing the European Atomic Energy Community (1957), the Treaty of Accession (1972). A discussion of those Treaties is outside the scope of this book. For the full text of the Treaties, see *Encyclopedia of European Community Law,* Vols. B. I and II.
[23] [1974] 2 C.M.L.R. 75.

There is no interpretation clause. Much is left unsaid. So much, indeed, that a great deal has to be filled in by the Courts of Law. If you read through the Common Market Law Reports you will find that case after case is referred to the European Court at Luxembourg so as to find out the meaning of those Articles.[24] The European Court interprets them according to the 'wording and spirit of the Treaty.' "[25]

2.10 The spirit of the Treaty referred to here by Lord Denning may, more mundanely, be described as the aims and objectives of the Community created by the Treaty and the general principles on which that Community is based.[26] The Treaty also, of course, sets up the institutions and the legal machinery needed to enable the Community to achieve these aims and objectives.[27]

(2) *Conventions*

2.11 Conventions entered into by the Member States of the EEC are, broadly speaking, of three different types:
> (i) Conventions to which only the Member States are a party[28];
> (ii) Conventions between the Community on the one hand and another State or group of States on the other hand[29]; and
> (iii) Conventions to which a number of States are a party, including all the Member States of the EEC.[30]

2.12 Of these, only the first can truly be categorised as a primary source of Community law. The second type is usually incorporated into Community law by means of a Decision or a Regulation of the Council of Ministers (both of which are examples of secondary Community legislation)[31] and the third type is not, strictly speaking, a part of Community law at all.

2.13 As far as the first type—the true Community Convention—is concerned, some Conventions are more closely related to the Treaty than others,[32] but

---

[24] *i.e.* Arts. 85 and 86 EEC.   [25] *Application des Gaz, supra*, n. 23 at p. 82.

[26] See *supra*, para. 1.04.   [27] See *infra*, paras. 2.58 *et seq.*

[28] *e.g.* Convention of December 15, 1975 for the European Patent for the Common Market (Community Patent Convention) (O.J. 1976, L17/1); Convention of September 27, 1968 on jurisdiction and the enforcement of Civil and Commercial Judgments (Bull. Supp. 2 1969; O.J. 1075, L204/28); and see generally Pt. 11, Vol. B of *Encyclopedia of European Community Law*.

[29] *e.g.* second ACP-EEC Convention of Lomé of October 31, 1979 (O.J. 1980, L347, Cmnd. 7895); and see generally Pt. 12, Vol. B of *Encyclopedia of European Community Law* (Sweet & Maxwell). See also Arts. 113 and 114 EEC.

[30] *e.g.* Convention on the Grant of European Patents (European Patent Convention) of October 5, 1973.

[31] See also Art. 228 EEC.

[32] See Art. 220 EEC. To date, only two Conventions have been signed under Art. 220, the Convention of February 29, 1968 on the mutual recognition of companies and bodies corporate (Bull. Supp. 2 1969) and the Convention of September 27, 1968 on jurisdiction and the enforcement of Civil and Commercial Judgments (Bull. Sup. 2 1969; O.J. 1975, L204/23), as amended by Convention of October 9, 1978 on the accession of Denmark, Ireland and the U.K. (O.J. 1978, L304/1).

it is not essential that there should be a specific reference in the Treaty to the particular subject, to enable a Convention to be concluded between Member States. The Community Patent Convention, for instance, states in its Preamble, amongst the reasons for its existence that:

> "The High Contracting Parties to the Treaty establishing the European Economic Community ... anxious to establish a Community patent system which contributes to the attainment of the objectives of the Treaty ... and in particular to the elimination within the Community of the distortion of competition which may result from the territorial aspect of national protection rights ... have decided to conclude this Convention. ..."

(3) *General Principles Common to the Member States and Fundamental Rights*

2.14   This third primary source of Community law is quite different in character to the Treaty and Conventions and is, almost entirely, the creation of the Court of Justice. The Treaty only once makes specific reference to "general principles," in the relatively limited context of Article 215 (2), dealing with the non-contractual liability of the Community where it provides:

> "In the case of non-contractual liability, the Community shall, *in accordance with the general principles common to the laws of the Member States,*[33] make good any damage caused by its institutions or its servants in the performance of their duties."

2.15   Although this may be the only specific reference in the Treaty to "general principles," it is clear that the concept underlies the whole approach of the Court of Justice to its task. Indeed, Article 164 lays down as the primary duty of the Court to "ensure that in the interpretation and application of this Treaty the law is observed."

2.16   In one of the earliest cases to come before the Court under the Coal and Steel Treaty,[34] the Advocate-General pointed out that the Court was not excused from giving judgment simply because of a lacuna in Community law. Clearly, where such lacunae exist there is a tendency to fill them by looking to the general principles of law common to the Member States, in so far as such general principles may exist. It is a statement of the obvious, no doubt, but the judges of the Court cannot help but be influenced in carrying out their duties by their own legal training and experience, and by the legal systems with which they are familiar.

---

[33] Emphasis supplied.
[34] Case 8/55 *Fédération Charbonnière de Belgique* v. *High Authority* [1954–1955] E.C.R. 245.

2.17   Once acknowledged by the Court as a general principle common to the Member States, that principle then becomes part of the jurisprudence of the Court, and thus itself a part of Community law.[35]

Legal certainty

2.18   One important principle which has been invoked very frequently is that of "legal certainty" or "certainty of law." Although of general application, it has played a particularly important role in the development of competition law, where it has been invoked on either side of the argument as to what exactly is meant by the words "automatically void" in Article 85 (2).[36]

Legitimate expectation

2.19   A slightly different formulation of this principle is to be found in the principle of "legitimate expectation" which has, for instance, successfully been used as the basis for a claim against the Commission under Article 215 (2) where a trader's "legitimate expectation" that certain compensatory amounts would be maintained was disappointed.[37]

2.20   The Court made clear in that case, as it has on several other occasions, that for an individual to be able to invoke Article 215 (2) some "superior rule of law" must have been violated:

> "Since the disputed measure is of a legislative nature and constitutes a measure taken in the sphere of economic policy, the Community cannot be liable for any damage suffered by individuals as a consequence of that measure under the provisions of the second paragraph of Article 215 of the Treaty, unless a sufficiently flagrant violation of a superior rule for the protection of the individual has occurred."[38]

Fundamental rights

2.21   This quotation from the Court's judgment in the *CNTA* case usefully points the link between the "general principles common to the laws of the

---

[35] For a fuller discussion of this topic see J. A. Usher, "The Influence of National Concepts on Decisions of the European Court" [1976] E.L.Rev. 359.

[36] See *Portelange SA* v. *Smith Corona Marchant International SA and Others* [1969] E.C.R. 309; [1974] 1 C.M.L.R. 397 at p. 418, where the Court was thought by some commentators at the time to have held that a duly notified agreement was "provisionally valid." But contrast *Brasserie de Haecht* v. *Wilkin (No. 2)* [1973] E.C.R. 77; [1973] C.M.L.R. 287 at p. 302, where it became clear that "provisional validity" only applied to duly notified "old Agreements," *i.e.* Agreements in existence at the date Reg. 17/62 came into force.

[37] *Comptoir National Technique Agricole (CNTA) SA* v. *EC Commission* [1976] E.C.R. 797; [1977] 1 C.M.L.R. 171.

[38] *Ibid.* at p. 188.

member states" and the broader concept of "fundamental rights" to which the heading of this section also refers.

2.22   The Court's thinking on this subject was further developed in the *Nold* case[39] when it held:

"As this Court has already held, fundamental rights form an integral part of the general principles of law which it enforces. In assuring the protection of such rights, this Court is required to base itself on the constitutional traditions common to the Member States and therefore could not allow measures which are incompatible with the fundamental rights recognised and guaranteed by the constitutions of such States. The international treaties on the protection of human rights in which the Member States have co-operated or to which they have adhered can also supply indications which may be taken into account within the framework of Community law."[40]

2.23   The Court further clarified its reasoning in the *Hauer* case[40a] where it said:

"The introduction of special criteria for assessment stemming from the legislation or constitutional law of a particular member-State would, by damaging the substantive unity and efficacy of Community law, lead inevitably to the destruction of the unity of the Common Market and the jeopardising of the cohesion of the Community.... Fundamental rights form an integral part of the general principles of the law, the observance of which it [*i.e.* the Court] ensures, that in safeguarding those rights, the Court is bound to draw inspiration from constitutional traditions common to the member-States, so that measures which are incompatible with the fundamental rights recognised by the constitutions of those States are unacceptable in the Community."[40b]

Thus, fundamental rights are recognised by the Court not because they are in some cases guaranteed by the constitution of a particular Member State, but because they form part of Community law itself.

C. SECONDARY SOURCES

(1) *General*

2.24   Primary sources of Community law have been defined above[41] as those which do not derive from some other Community enactment, but which exist independently. Secondary sources are those which derive their validity solely from some provision of the Treaty. If the Treaty did not exist, they

---

[39] *Firma J. Nold KG* v. *EC Commission* [1974] E.C.R. 491; [1974] 2 C.M.L.R. 338.
[40] *Ibid.* at p. 354.
[40a] Case 44/79 *Liselotte Hauer* v. *Land Rheinland-Pfalz* [1979] E.C.R. 3727; [1980] 3 C.M.L.R. 42.
[40b] *Ibid.* at p. 64.
[41] *Supra,* para. 2.07.

could not exist. In that sense, therefore, they are secondary. Nevertheless, in acting in the manner provided for in the Treaty, the Community institutions are carrying out a true law-making function, and are not merely exercising a power delegated to them by the Member States. It follows from this that, once in being, a Community enactment can only be amended or repealed by the institution which created it in the first place, or, in certain circumstances by the Court of Justice. The Member States themselves have no power to do so.

2.25   The principal secondary sources are the Regulations, Directives and Decisions enacted by the Council and the Commission under Article 189 and the judgments and rulings of the Court of Justice, promulgated under various Articles detailing the Court's powers.

(2) *Regulations*

(a) General

2.26   Article 189 (2) provides as follows: "A regulation shall have general application. It shall be binding in its entirety and directly applicable in all Member States."

2.27   Article 190 then goes on to provide that, in common with Directives and Decisions: "Regulations . . . shall state the reasons on which they are based and shall refer to any proposals or opinions which were required to be obtained pursuant to this Treaty."

2.28   Finally, Article 191 (1) requires that: "Regulations shall be published in the *Official Journal* of the Community. They shall enter into force on the date specified in them or, in the absence thereof, on the twentieth day following their publication."

2.29   These few, deceptively simple, sentences belie the true importance of the Regulation in Community law. The key to its unique character is to be found in the second sentence of Article 189 (2), namely that it is "binding in its entirety," and that it is "directly applicable." Thus, a regulation has the same effect at the Community level, as a national law at the national level.

(b) Binding in its entirety and directly applicable

2.30   No action is required on the part of the national authorities to bring a Regulation into force and any such actions are precluded if they "would . . . have the result of creating an obstacle to the direct effect of Community Regulations and of jeopardising their simultaneous and uniform application in the whole of the Community."[42]

2.31   Indeed, if a national law, whether already in existence or subsequently enacted, is incompatible with a Community Regulation, then the pro-

---

[42] Case 39/72 *EC Commission* v. *Re Provision for Reducing Dairy Production* [1973] E.C.R. 101; [1973] C.M.L.R. 439 at p. 456.

visions of the Regulation automatically prevail.[43] This was made clear by the European Court in the *Politi* case[44] as follows:

> "... by reason of their very nature and their function in the system of sources of Community law, [Regulations] are immediately effective, and, as such, are capable of conferring upon individual persons rights which the national courts are bound to protect. Consequently, the effect of Regulations as laid down in Article 189, is to prevent the application of any legislative measure, even enacted subsequently, which is incompatible with their provisions."[45]

2.32   It is clear that without the machinery of the Regulation, the Community would be unable effectively to exercise those "real powers" which it was intended by the founders of the Community to enjoy.[46]

(c) Further characteristics of a Regulation

2.33   The other features of the Regulation which should perhaps be mentioned are the need for reasons to be given[47] and the need for publication.[48] It is also plain from the first sentence of Article 189 (2) that a Regulation applies "generally," that is to say throughout the territory of the Community, and to all natural and legal persons who are subject to the laws of the individual Member States. A Regulation does not cease to be such merely because the persons who will, in practice, be affected by it can be identified with a fair degree of precision. This was made clear by the European Court[49] when it said:

> "... the nature of a measure as a Regulation is not called in question by the possibility of determining more or less precisely the number or even the identity of the persons to whom it applies at a given moment as long as it is established that it is applied by virtue of an objective legal or factual situation defined by the measure in relation to the objective of the latter. Moreover, the fact that a legal provision may have different actual effects for the various persons to whom it applies is not inconsistent with its nature as a Regulation when that situation is objectively defined."[50]

2.34   The important practical consequence of knowing whether a particular measure is a Regulation or not, stems from Article 173 (2) of the Treaty which provides:

---

[43] For a fuller discussion of the relationship between Community law and national law, see Chap. 3.
[44] Case 43/71 *Politi SAS* v. *Ministero delle Finanze* [1973] C.M.L.R. 60.
[45] *Ibid.* at p. 70.
[46] See *supra*, para. 2.05.
[47] See Art. 190, *infra,* para. 2.47.
[48] See Art. 191 (1).
[49] Case 101/76 *Koninklijke Scholten Honig NV* v. *Council and Commission of the European Communities* [1977] E.C.R. 797; [1980] 2 C.M.L.R. 669.
[50] *Ibid* at pp. 680–681.

"Any natural or legal person may ... institute proceedings against a Decision addressed to that person or against a Decision which, although in the form of a Regulation or a Decision addressed to another person is of direct and individual concern to the former."[51]

2.35 The right to institute proceedings under this Article is not available in respect of a "true" Regulation, although the legality of a Regulation may always, of course, be challenged before the European Court by a Member State, the Council or the Commission "on grounds of lack of competence, infringement of an essential procedural requirement, infringement of [this] Treaty or of any rule of law relating to its application, or misuse of powers."[52]

(3) *Directives*

2.36 Article 189 (3) provides:
"A directive shall be binding as to the result to be achieved, upon each Member State to which it is addressed, but shall leave to the national authorities the choice of form and methods."

2.37 A Directive thus defines the objective, but leaves it to each individual Member State to decide, within the context of its own legal and factual situation, how best to achieve it. On the face of it, therefore, it might seem that a Directive cannot be directly applicable in the sense of a Regulation. In fact, on several occasions, the Court of Justice has stated that a Directive may nonetheless produce direct effects in a similar way to a Regulation.

2.38 In *Van Duyn* v. *Home Office*,[53] for instance, the Court said:
"If, however, by virtue of the provisions of Article 189 regulations are directly applicable and, consequently, may by their very nature have direct effects, it does not follow from this that other categories of acts mentioned in that Article can never have similar effects. It would be incompatible with the binding effect attributed to a directive by Article 189 to exclude, in principle, the possibility that the obligation which it imposes may be invoked by those concerned. In particular, where the Community authorities have, by directive, imposed on Member States the obligation to pursue a particular course of conduct, the useful effect of such an act would be weakened if individuals were prevented from relying on it before their national courts and if the latter were prevented from taking it into consideration as an element of Community law ... It is necessary to examine, in every case, whether the nature, general scheme and wording of the pro-

---

[51] See also Art. 184 where, in the special circumstances mentioned, a Reg. may be challenged outside the time limits provided in Art. 173 (3).

[52] Art. 173 (1).

[53] *Van Duyn* v. *Home Office* [1974] E.C.R. 1337; [1975] 1 C.M.L.R. 1.

vision in question are capable of having direct effects on the relations between Member States and individuals."[54,55,55a]

2.39   Every Directive lays down a time limit within which the Member States to which it is addressed must comply with its provisions. Clearly, it is of great importance that this time limit is adhered to for "such acts would lose all effectiveness if the objectives in view were not attained within the prescribed time limits."[56,57] Like a Regulation, a Directive must state the reasons for its introduction, and must refer to any proposals or opinions which it was necessary to obtain under any relevant Article of the Treaty.[58] Also, like a Regulation a Directive can be challenged before the European Court by a Member State, the Council or the Commission on the grounds set out in Article 173 (1).

2.40   Unlike a Regulation, a Directive does not have to be published in the *Official Journal* although, as a matter of practice, the Commission frequently publishes the more important Directives. It is, however, by virtue of Article 191 (2) necessary for a Directive to be notified to the Member States to which it is addressed and it takes effect immediately upon notification.

(4) Decisions

2.41   Article 189 (4) provides: "A decision shall be binding in its entirety upon those to whom it is addressed."

2.42   Decisions are, in fact, of two types: those addressed to one or more of the Member States, and those addressed to private individuals.

(a) Decisions addressed to the Member States

2.43   Decisions addressed to the Member States are sometimes used as an alternative to Directives where more detailed provisions are needed than can, effectively, be incorporated in a Directive. Like a Directive, a Decision addressed to the Member States can sometimes produce direct effects, as in the *Grad* case[59] where the European Court said:

---

[54] *Ibid.* at pp. 15–16.

[55] See also Case 33/70 *S.A.C.E.* v. *Italian Ministry of Finance* [1970] E.C.R. 1213; [1971] C.M.L.R. 123 at p. 132.

[55a] See also Case 148/78 *Pubblico Ministero* v. *Tullio Ratti* [1979] E.C.R. 1629; [1980] 1 C.M.L.R. 96.

[56] Case 79/72 *Re Forestry Reproductive Material: EC Commission* v. *Italy* [1973] E.C.R. 667; [1973] C.M.L.R. 773 at p. 781.

[57] Failure to comply with a Directive within the time limits laid down exposes a Member State to the risk of proceedings against it by the Commission under Art. 169 or another Member State under Art. 170. A Member State may not rely on domestic difficulties or provisions of its national legal system, even its constitutional system, to justify a failure to implement a Directive within the time limits. See Case 100/77 *Re Measuring Instruments: EC Commission* v. *Italy* [1978] E.C.R. 879; [1979] 2 C.M.L.R. 655.

[58] See Art. 190.

[59] Case 9/70 *Franz Grad.* v. *Finanzamt Traunstein* [1970] E.C.R. 285; [1971] C.M.L.R. 1.

"Although the effects of a decision may be different from those of a provision contained in a Regulation this difference does not prevent the end result, namely the right of the individual to invoke the measure in the courts, from being the same in a given case as that in the case of a directly applicable provision of a Regulation."[60]

(b) Decisions addressed to individuals

2.44   Decisions addressed to individuals clearly produce legal effects only for those individuals. Where financial penalties are imposed, as in the case of some of the Decisions of the Commission under Regulation 17/62, finding infringements of Articles 85 or 86, those decisions are enforceable under Article 192 of the Treaty. Enforcement is carried out by the courts of the Member States, in accordance with their own national procedures. Apart from verifying that a decision is authentic, the national courts cannot question its validity and must give effect to it.

2.45   Like a Directive, a Decision does not have to be published in the *Official Journal,* but merely has to be notified to the person to whom it is addressed.[61] It takes effect upon notification. Decisions addressed to the Member States are often published, as a matter of information in the same way as Directives, and the Commission also usually publishes its Decisions in cases involving Articles 85 and 86, again as a matter of information.

2.46   In the same way as Regulations and Directives, a Decision must state the reasons on which it is based and must refer to any proposals or opinions which had to be obtained prior to its being issued.[62] This need to state reasons applies even where a Decision is not expressed in a formal manner.[63] The crucial factor is not the formality or informality of its presentation, but whether or not it changes the legal position of the addressee. If it does, it is a decision and reasons must be given.

2.47   The need to give reasons is, of course, linked to the provisions in Article 173 giving powers of review to the Court of Justice, which apply to Decisions just as to other legally binding acts of the Community institutions. Without reasons, it would, clearly, be much more difficult for the Court to carry out its task under that Article.

(5) *Judgments and other Acts of the Court of Justice*

2.48   Despite the general admonition to the Court of Justice in Article 164 "to ensure that in the interpretation and application of this Treaty the law is observed," the areas in which the Court is empowered to act are only those

---

[60] *Ibid.* at p. 23.
[61] See Art. 191 (2).
[62] See Art. 190.
[63] Case 8-11/66 *Re Noordwijks Cement Accoord* [1967] E.C.R. 75; [1967] C.M.L.R. 77.

specifically laid down by the various Articles of the Treaty. Except where the Treaty so provides, the Court has no jurisdiction.[64]

2.49   The nature of the Court's jurisdiction varies widely, depending upon the Treaty article under which it is acting. Among the roles it is called upon to play are those of an administrative court,[65] an employment tribunal,[66] a constitutional court,[67] an arbitration tribunal[68] and an advisory court.[69] It has jurisdiction in disputes between the Member States, both where jurisdiction is conferred upon it by agreement,[70] and where a breach of a Treaty obligation is alleged.[71] Indeed, it has a general power to act where breach of the Treaty is alleged, either on the part of a Member State[72] or on the part of the Council or the Commission.[73] Clearly, therefore, the Court's role is crucial in the application and enforcement of the Treaty, and, more generally, in the development of Community law.[74]

2.50   The legal effects of the Court's decisions also vary, depending upon the circumstances. The European Court does not recognise the doctrine of strictly binding precedent in the English sense, but, as already mentioned,[75] it takes into account general principles common to the laws of the Member States. Among those general principles is that of legal certainty, a similar, though much broader and less formalised, concept to the English doctrine of *"stare decisis."*

2.51   A decision of the European Court generally, therefore, has only persuasive effect in a subsequent case on the same point. Although not definitive, earlier decisions clearly give useful guidance.

2.52   Where, however, a directly applicable act of the Council or the Commission is declared a nullity[76] that declaration changes the legal situation, not only for the parties to the particular case, but also for everyone else affected by the act in question. In order to avoid the problem which could

---

[64] In addition to the powers conferred on it by the EEC Treaty (and also the ECSC and Euratom Treaties), the Court is empowered to give preliminary rulings on points of interpretation of certain conventions concluded between the Member States. See, *e.g.* Art. 73 of Convention for the European Patent for the Common Market (Community Patent Convention) O.J. 1976, L17/1; and the Protocol of June 3, 1972 to the Convention of September 27, 1968 on Jurisdiction and the Enforcement of Civil and Commercial Judgments (Bull. Supp. 2 1969: O.J. 1975, L205/28).
[65] Art. 173.
[66] Art. 179.
[67] Art. 177, and see Chap. 3 .
[68] Art. 181.
[69] Art. 228.
[70] Art. 182.
[71] Art. 170.
[72] Art. 169.
[73] Art. 175.
[74] For a fuller discussion of the Court's role, see Brinkhorst and Schermers, *Judicial Remedies in the European Communities* (2nd ed., 1978); Parry and Hardy, *EEC Law*, Pt. III; and Lipstein, *The Law of the European Economic Community*, Chaps. 19 and 20.
[75] See *supra*, para. 2.14.
[76] See Art. 174, EEC.

arise where a regulation is declared void the Court has power, under Article 174 (2) to "state which of the effects of the regulation which it has declared void shall be considered as definitive."

2.53   A declaration of nullity may occur, not only where the Court is considering the legality of a measure under Article 173 but also where the Court is giving a ruling on a point referred to it by a national court under Article 177.[77]

2.54   A ruling under Article 177 is, of course, binding on the Court which made the reference, and must be given effect in that Court's eventual judgment in the case before it. Where a decision of the Council or the Commission imposing a "pecuniary obligation," is upheld by the Court, the decision is enforceable under Article 192. An appeal to the Court does not, of itself, have suspensory effect on the original decision although the Court may, under Article 192 (4) order enforcement to be suspended.

2.55   There is no machinery for enforcement of other decisions of the Court, although, to date, its decisions have always been implemented even if after a delay. A Decision of the European Court cannot be the subject of an appeal to any higher Court.

D. Other "Sources" of Community Law

(1) Recommendations and Opinions

2.56   Article 189 envisages that not all acts of the Council and Commission will produce legal effects. As well as Regulations, Directives and Decisions, Article 189 (1) empowers the Council and the Commission, "in order to carry out their task" to "make recommendations or deliver opinions." Article 189 (5) specifically provides: "Recommendations and opinions shall have no binding force."

(2) Notices and Replies to Questions from the European Parliament

2.57   As well as formal recommendations and opinions under Article 189, the Commission also makes known its policies and views in a variety of other ways.[78] These include notices published in the *Official Journal* and other documents published by the Commission; and a further useful source of information on Community policy is sometimes to be found in replies given

---

[77] See Cases 114, 116, 119, 120/76 *Bela-Müle Gmbh KG Landforden* v. *Grows-Farm GmbH & Co. KG*; *Granaria BV, Rotterdam* v. *Hoofproduktschap voor Akkerbouwprodukten,* the Hague; *Olmuhle Hamburg AG* v. *HZA Hamburg-Waltershof*; *Kurt A. Brecherg Bremen* v. *HZA Bremen-Nord* [1977] E.C.R. 1211; [1979] 2 C.M.L.R. 83.

[78] See, *e.g.* Notice of July 29, 1968 on Co-operation Agreements (O.J. 1968, C75/3); Notice of December 19, 1977 concerning agreements of minor importance (O.J. 1977, C313/3); Commission's Annual Reports on Competition Policy; Bulletin of the European Communities, published monthly.

to questions raised by members of the European Parliament. Replies to written questions are regularly published in the "Information and Notices" section of the *Official Journal*.

IV. *INSTITUTIONS OF THE COMMUNITY*

A. GENERAL

2.58   The three principal institutions[79] which between them exercise the powers granted to the Community are the Council, the Commission and the Court of Justice. Of these, the main lawmaking body is the Council which, unlike the Commission or the Court of Justice, is composed of members of the national governments of the Member States, whose primary allegiance is to their own States and not to the Community. It is perhaps a reflection of the very limited degree of sovereignty which the Member States have in practice abandoned that the major legislative organ of the Community should be so often unable to act because of the failure of the Member States to reach agreement.[80]

B. THE COUNCIL

2.59   Article 145 describes the role of the Council in the following terms:
"To ensure that the objectives set out in this Treaty are attained, the Council shall, in accordance with the provisions of this Treaty:
—ensure co-ordination of the general economic policies of the Member States;
—have power to take decisions."

C. THE COMMISSION

2.60   By contrast, the role of the Commission as the "civil service" of the Community, is laid down in Article 155 in terms which emphasise the "day

---

[79] The other main institutions established by the Treaty are the Assembly of European Parliament (Arts. 4 (1), 137-144), the Economic and Social Committee (Arts. 4 (2), 193-198) and the European Investment Bank (Arts. 3 (*j*), 129-130). In addition, there are various advisory bodies such as the Monetary Committee (Art. 105) and the Advisory Committee on Transport (Art. 83).

[80] Although the Treaty provides in Art. 148 for majority voting in the Council, in practice, since The Luxembourg Accords of January 29, 1966 (1966 Bull. 3, p. 8), the Council only acts as if its Members are unanimous where a Member State considers its fundamental national interests are involved.

to day" operation of the Community, as compared with the longer-term objectives to be pursued by the Council. Article 155 provides:

"In order to ensure the proper functioning and development of the Common Market, the Commission shall:

—ensure that the provisions of this Treaty and the measures taken by the institutions pursuant thereto are applied;

—formulate recommendations or deliver opinions on matters dealt with in this Treaty, if it expressly so provides or if the Commission considers it necessary;

—have its own power of decision and participate in the shaping of measures taken by the Council and by the Assembly in the manner provided for in this Treaty;

—exercise the powers conferred on it by the Council for the implementation of the rules laid down by the latter."

2.61   The members of the Commission are people "chosen on the grounds of their general competence and whose independence is beyond doubt."[81,82] They are required "in the general interest of the Community [to] be completely independent in the performance of their duties ... they shall neither seek nor take instructions from any Government or other body."[83]

D. The Court of Justice

2.62   Similar criteria are laid down for the appointment of the Judges and Advocates-General of the Court of Justice:

"The Judges and Advocates-General shall be chosen from persons whose independence is beyond doubt and who possess the qualifications required for appointment to the highest judicial offices in their respective countries or who are jurisconsults of recognised competence."[84]

2.63   The specific tasks allocated to the Court are wide-ranging and varied, but its over-riding responsibility is to "ensure that in the interpretation and application of this Treaty the law is observed."[85]

---

[81] See Art. 157.

[82] In practice, each of the larger Member States (*i.e.* France, Italy, West Germany and the U.K.) selects two Commissioners, and each of the smaller Member States (*i.e.* Belgium, Denmark, Eire, Greece, Luxembourg and the Netherlands) selects one. The appointment of the people so selected is then confirmed by "common accord of the Governments of the Member States" (Art. 158 EEC).

[83] Art. 157 (2).

[84] Art. 167.

[85] Art. 164.

CHAPTER 3

RELATIONSHIP BETWEEN COMMUNITY LAW
AND DOMESTIC LAW

I. *INTRODUCTION*

3.01   As has already been pointed out,[1] EEC law is a system of law in its own right. It cannot, however, operate in a vacuum, but only within the framework of the legal systems of the individual Member States of the Community. Inevitably, therefore, questions arise as to the relationship between the two.

3.02   In this chapter, three separate aspects of that relationship will be considered:

(1) certain fundamental concepts which have been developed by the European Court, and which constitute the basic ground rules for resolving potential conflicts between national and Community law;

(2) the reception of Community law at the national level; and

(3) the procedure in Article 177 of the Treaty, by means of which national courts and tribunals can obtain rulings from the European Court on questions of interpretation of Community law.

II. *FUNDAMENTAL CONCEPTS OF COMMUNITY LAW*

A. GENERAL

3.03   Over the years since the creation of the European Economic Community in 1958, the European Court has developed two basic concepts which are crucial in defining the status of Community law within the legal systems of the Member States. These concepts are:

—supremacy of community law over national laws, and

—"direct applicability"

B. SUPREMACY OF COMMUNITY LAW

3.04   The concept of the supremacy of Community law can be stated in very simple terms. If a directly applicable rule of Community law conflicts with a rule of domestic law, Community law prevails, and it is irrelevant whether the domestic law was enacted before or after the Community law.

---

[1] See Chap. 2.

3.05   This principle has been restated by the Court of Justice on numerous occasions.[2] Perhaps one of the clearest statements is to be found in the Court's judgment in a case in 1969, *Wilhelm and Others* v. *Bundeskartellamt*[3] where the Court was dealing with the relationship between Community rules on competition and national law on the same subject:

"Article 87 (2) (e), in attributing to an institution of the Community the power to define the relations between the national laws and the Community law on competition, confirms the *pre-eminent character*[4] of Community law. The EEC Treaty instituted its own legal order, integrated into the legal systems of the Member States and which has priority before their courts. It would be contrary to the nature of such a system to accept that the Member States may take or maintain in force measures liable to compromise the useful effect of the Treaty. The imperative force of the Treaty and of the acts issued in implementation of it could not vary from State to State by the effect of internal acts, without the functioning of the Community system being obstructed and the attainment of the aims of the Treaty being placed in peril.

Consequently, conflicts between the Community rule and the national rules on competition should be resolved by the application of the principle of the primacy of the Community rule.[5]

3.06   This quotation from the Court's judgment in the *Wilhelm* case, also neatly summarises the justification for the supremacy of Community law. Although many theories have been advanced in justification of the rule,[6] they all amount to very much the same. If Community law did not prevail over domestic law, the "Common Market" would no longer be truly "common," in the sense that its rules would be interpreted and applied differently in the different Member States.

3.07   This concept of the supremacy of Community law over domestic law is not, however, confined to imposing obligations upon the Member States to act or refrain from acting in a certain way. One of the crucial differences between the EEC Treaty and most other international treaties is that, in certain circumstances, individual citizens of the Member States have enforceable rights, even if the Member States themselves have purported to act contrary to the Treaty. Such rights exist where the relevant provision of the Treaty or secondary legislation is "directly applicable," or where, as

---

[2] See, *e.g. Costa* v. *ENEL* [1964] C.M.L.R. 425; Case 11/70 *Internationale Handelsgesellschaft GmbH* v. *Einfuhr & Vorratsstelle fur Getreide & Futtermittel* [1970] E.C.R. 1125; [1972] C.M.L.R. 255; *Amministrazione delle Finance dello Stato* v. *Simmenthal SpA (No. 2)* [1978] E.C.R. 629; [1978] 3 C.M.L.R. 263.
[3] [1969] C.M.L.R. 100.
[4] Emphasis added.
[5] *Wilhelm and Others* v. *Bunderkartellant, supra,* n. 3 at p. 119.
[6] See, *e.g.* Parry & Hardy, *EEC Law,* pp. 132–138.

with some Directives even though not directly applicable they produce "direct effects."[6a]

C. DIRECT APPLICABILITY

(1) *General*

3.08   If a provision of the Treaty (or indeed of secondary legislation of the Community) is "directly applicable," rights are automatically created for individual citizens, without any legislative or administrative act being needed on the part of the Member States.[7]

3.09   The phrase "directly applicable" is used only once in the Treaty, in Article 189, dealing with the effects of a Regulation.[8] The Court of Justice has, however, frequently resorted to this concept when defining the effects of certain provisions of the Treaty, and it is as much a fundamental concept as that of the supremacy of Community law.

(2) *The Criteria for Direct Applicability*

3.10   The criteria for judging whether or not a particular provision of the Treaty is directly applicable are not easy to define. It is, however, clear from the decided cases, that a provision will only be declared "directly applicable" if its terms are sufficiently clearcut to be capable of operating without the need for implementing legislation. In addition to this practical pre-condition, the Court has developed a number of other criteria for deciding whether a provision which meets the pre-condition is, in fact, then directly applicable.

3.11   Thus, in one of its earliest decisions on this point,[9] the European Court said that, in order to decide whether a particular provision is directly applicable "it is necessary to look at its spirit, its economic aspect and the terms used."[10] Applying those guidelines to the question before it in that case, the Court stated: "The text of Article 12[11] sets out a clear and

---

[6a] See, *e.g.* Case 148/78 *Pubblico Ministero* v. *Tullio Ratti* [1979] E.C.R. 1629; [1980] 1 C.M.L.R. 96; see also "The Direct Effect of Directives" by J. A. Usher [1979] 4 E.L. Rev. 268, where he concludes that the Court's judgment in *Ratti* means that a Directive only produces direct effects for individuals where a Member State has failed to implement a Directive in the time limits, and where the obligations imposed on a Member State fulfil the tests of being clear, unconditional and leaving no discretion.

[7] See, *e.g.* Case 83/78 *Pigs Marketing Board* (*Northern Ireland*) v. *Redmond* [1979] E.C.R. 2347; [1979] 1 C.M.L.R. 177.

[8] See *supra*, Chap. 2, para. 2.24.

[9] *N.V. Algemene Transport En Expeditie Onderneming Van Gend En Loos* v. *Nederlandse Tariefcommissie* [1963] E.C.R. 1; [1963] C.M.L.R. 105.

[10] *Ibid.* at p. 129.

[11] Art. 12: "Member States shall refrain from introducing between themselves any new customs duties on imports or exports or any charges having equivalent effect, and from increasing those which they already apply in their trade with each other."

unconditional prohibition, which is not a duty to act but a duty not to act."[12]

3.12   Although provisions which impose "a clear and unconditional prohibition" lend themselves to being considered directly applicable, it must not, however, be assumed that those are the only Articles of the Treaty which are capable of being "directly applicable." This said, it is probably true that the majority of such Articles are, in fact, directly applicable.

3.13   The category of directly applicable Articles of the Treaty was considerably extended as a result of the Court's decision in the *Reyners* case.[13] The Court's ruling in that case clearly shows that the reference in the *Van Gend en Loos* case to "spirit," refers not only to the "spirit" of the particular Article under consideration, but also to the "spirit" of the whole Treaty.

3.14   The *Reyners* case itself was concerned with Article 52[14] on freedom of establishment, one of the four freedoms enshrined in the Treaty. In deciding that that Article was, as from the end of the transitional period, directly applicable, the Court referred back to Article 7 of the Treaty,[15] on the basis that "the rule on equal treatment with nationals is one of the fundamental legal provisions of the Community."[16] The fact that the "general programme for the abolition of existing restrictions on freedom of establishment within the Community" referred to in Article 54 has not yet been implemented did not, in the Court's view, prevent the basic right in Article 52 from being directly applicable as from the end of the transitional period. In its own words:

> "In laying down that freedom of establishment shall be attained at the end of the transitional period, Article 52 thus imposes an obligation to attain a precise result, the fulfilment of which had to be made easier by, but not made dependent on, the implementation of a programme of progressive measures."[17]

3.15   Whilst it is unarguable that equal treatment for all Common Market nationals is a basic principle of the Community, and that the free right of

---

[12] [1963] C.M.L.R. 105 at p. 130.

[13] Case 2/74 *Reyners* v. *Belgian State* [1974] E.C.R. 631; [1974] 2 C.M.L.R. 305.

[14] Art. 52: "Within the framework of the provisions set out below, restrictions on the freedom of establishment of nationals of a Member State in the territory of another Member State shall be abolished by progressive stages in the course of the transitional period. Such progressive abolition shall also apply to restrictions on the setting up of agencies, branches or subsidiaries by nationals of any Member States established in the territory of any Member State. Freedom of establishment shall include the right to take up and pursue activities as self-employed persons and to set up and manage undertakings, in particular companies or firms within the meaning of the second paragraph of Article 58, under the conditions laid down for its own nationals by the law of the country where such establishment is effected, subject to the provisions of the Chapter relating to capital."

[15] Art. 7: "Within the scope of application of this Treaty, and without prejudice to any special provisions contained therein, any discrimination on grounds of nationality shall be prohibited."

[16] *Reyners* v. *Belgian State*, *supra*, n. 13 at p. 326.

[17] *Ibid.* at p. 327.

establishment is one of the four fundamental freedoms enshrined in the Treaty, it is perhaps less clear that Article 119[18] providing for equal pay as between men and women, is of the same importance. Nevertheless, the Court has held that Article too to be directly applicable.[19] It reached that conclusion by looking at two separate aspects of the Treaty: first, the need to ensure competition in the Common Market is not distorted,[20] as it might well be if only some of the Member States had implemented the principle of equal pay, and, secondly, the place of Article 119 among the social objectives of the Community.[21]

3.16   In deciding, therefore, whether or not a particular provision of the Treaty is directly applicable, it is necessary to look both at the terms of the particular provision, and at its "spirit" and "economic aspect" in the context of the Treaty as a whole.[22]

III. *RECEPTION OF COMMUNITY LAW AT THE NATIONAL LEVEL*

A. MEMBERSHIP OF THE COMMUNITY

3.17   Although the twin concepts of the supremacy of Community law and direct applicability are crucial in the relationship between Community law and national law, that relationship can only come into existence, in the first place, once a state has become a member of the Community. Merely signing the Treaty[23] is not enough; before it can come into force it must have been ratified by the signatory States "in accordance with their respective constitutional requirements."[24]

---

[18] Art. 119: "Each Member State shall during the first stage assume and subsequently maintain the application of the principle that men and women should receive equal pay for equal work.

For the purpose of this Article, 'pay' means the ordinary basic or minimum wage or salary and any other consideration, whether in cash or in kind, which the worker receives, directly or indirectly, in respect of his employment from his employer. Equal pay without discrimination based on sex means:

  (*a*) that pay for the same work at piece rates shall be calculated on the basis of the same unit of measurement;
  (*b*) that pay for work at time rates shall be the same for the same job."

[19] Case 43/75 *Defrenne* v. *Sabena* [1976] E.C.R. 455; [1976] 2 C.M.L.R. 98.

[20] See Art. 3 (f).

[21] See Art. 2 and Art. 3 (i).

[22] Secondary legislation of the Community can also be "directly applicable." See *supra*, Chap. 2, paras. 2–24 *et seq.*

[23] *i.e.* in the case of the original six Member States, the Treaty establishing the European Economic Community signed at Rome on March 25, 1957; in the case of the three new Member States, the Treaty concerning the Accession of the Kingdom of Denmark, Ireland, the Kingdom of Norway and the United Kingdom of Great Britain and Northern Ireland to the European Economic Community signed at Brussels on January 22, 1972; and in the case of Greece, the Treaty concerning the Accession of the Hellenic Republic to the European Economic Community signed at Athens on May 28, 1979.

[24] See Art. 247 of the EEC Treaty and Art. 2 of the Treaty of Accession.

3.18   From the Community's standpoint, it does not matter how the individual Member States achieve ratification, provided that, at the end of the day, Community law has the same effect in all the Member States.[25]

3.19   As far as the United Kingdom was concerned, for example, the Treaty of Accession was ratified by means of the European Communities Act 1972, a surprisingly short and succinct Act for such a major constitutional innovation.[26] The vital step in relinquishing the necessary part of the United Kingdom's sovereignty was achieved, effectively, by one subsection, *viz.* subsection 2 (1):

> "All such rights, powers, liabilities, obligations and restrictions from time to time created or arising by or under the Treaties, as in accordance with the Treaties are without further enactment to be given legal effect or used in the United Kingdom shall be recognised and available in law, and be enforced, allowed and followed accordingly; and the expression "enforceable Community right" and similar expressions shall be read as referring to one to which this subsection applies."

3.20   These words led Lord Denning to make his famous and colourful remark, that:

> "... the Treaty is like an incoming tide. It flows into the estuaries and up the rivers. It cannot be held back. Parliament has decreed that the Treaty is henceforward to be part of our law. It is equal in force to any statute."[27]

B. Application of Community Law by Domestic Courts

3.21   The main burden of applying Community law and of ensuring that it is observed, falls upon the courts and tribunals of the Member States. The concepts of the supremacy of Community law and direct applicability have been developed to assist them in carrying out this task.

3.22   Whilst a remedy may exist in a Community forum,[28] Community law frequently provides a remedy—or, indeed, a defence—which can be pursued, either at the same time or in isolation, before a domestic court or tribunal. Were this not so, the whole basis of the system set up by the Treaty

---

[25] See Parry & Hardy, *EEC Law,* Chap. 19; and Lipstein, *The Law of the European Economic Community*, Chap. 2, Pt. X.

[26] The European Communities Act 1972 consists of a preamble, twelve sections and four Schedules.

[27] *H. P. Bulmer Ltd. and Another* v. *J. Bollinger SA and Another* [1974] 2 C.M.L.R. 91 at p. 111.

[28] *e.g.* in cases of a breach of Arts. 85 or 86 a complaint can be filed with the Commission under art. 3 of Reg. 17/62.

would be in jeopardy, and, indeed, in a practical sense, it would be largely unworkable.

3.23   The existence of a dual remedy is perhaps, most commonly found in competition matters. Frequently, the status of an Agreement under Article 85 of the Treaty, or the legality of a particular course of conduct in relation to Article 86 of the Treaty, is in issue in proceedings before a domestic court. At the same time, a complaint may well have been made to the Commission under Article 3 of Regulation 17/62, or the Agreement in question may have been notified to the Commission under Article 4 or Article 5 of Regulation 17/62. Since the European Court's decision in the *SABAM* case,[29] it is clear that, with one exception,[30] a domestic court is not precluded from dealing with a matter involving Articles 85 or 86, simply because the Commission may be dealing with the same matter.

3.24   As Lord Denning pointed out in one of the first cases to come before the English Court of Appeal in which Articles 85 and 86 were involved, it would be tantamount to a denial of justice to make the remedy available from the domestic court and the remedy available from the Commission mutually exclusive:

"One remedy is set out in Article 3 of Regulation 17. If a person has a 'justified interest,' he can request the Commission at Brussels to investigate the matter ... It was suggested that this was the *only* proper procedure in cases of an infringement of Articles 85 and 86. But it is obvious that it might take months and even years. By the time that the Commission completed an investigation, much damage might have been done, and done irreparably. So there is much to be said for a remedy to be given in the national courts. It seems likely that there is one."[31]

3.25   In that same case, Lord Denning went on to speculate on the nature of the remedy which, as a matter of English law, was available for infringements of Articles 85 and 86:

"So we reach this important conclusion: Articles 85 and 86 are part of our law. They create new torts or wrongs. Their names are 'undue restriction of competition within the Common Market,' and 'abuse of a dominant position within the Common Market.' "[32]

---

[29] Case 127/73 *Belgische Radio en Televisie* v. *Société Belge Des Auteurs, Compositeurs et Editeurs (SABAM) and N. V. Fonior* [1974] E.C.R. 313; [1974] 2 C.M.L.R. 238.

[30] The only exception to this principle is where the domestic court or tribunal is one of "the authorities of the Member States" referred to in Art. 88, when Art. 9 (3) of Reg. 17/62 gives exclusive jurisdiction to the Commission once it has initiated a procedure in the particular case. "The authorities of the Member States" are those directly concerned with competition law and policy "*à titre principal*," *e.g.* in the U.K., the Office of Fair Trading, but not those authorities which only deal with such matters as "*à titre incident*," *i.e.* as ancillary to other issues.

[31] *Application des Gaz SA* v. *Falks Veritas Ltd.* [1974] 2 C.M.L.R. 75 at p. 84.

[32] *Ibid.* at p. 84.

3.26   These statements were criticised by Lord Justice Roskill in later proceedings involving the same dispute,[33] and cannot be accepted, at present, as necessarily a correct view of the position.

3.27   Again, in the same judgment, Lord Denning went on to draw the vital distinction between *applying* Community law and interpreting it:

"It is for our courts to find the facts, to apply the law, and to use the remedies which we have available. If it should turn out, after finding the facts, that it is necessary to seek the opinion of the European Court on a point of interpretation of the Treaty, the English courts can refer that point to the European Court. But the eventual decision of the case is for our English courts. It is for us to give the judgment and to enforce it. It is a task worthy of our mettle."[34]

IV. *ARTICLE 177 AND INTERPRETATION BY THE EUROPEAN COURT*

A. GENERAL

3.28   The role of the European Court in giving an interpretation of a doubtful point of Community law at the request of a domestic court or tribunal, is provided for in Article 177. That Article plays a vital part in ensuring that, in carrying out their task of applying Community law, the courts and tribunals of the Member States are applying the same law throughout the Community, and are not, by interpreting the law in their own way, destroying the common application of that law in the Member States.

3.29   Article 177 is of such importance in the relationship between domestic law and Community law that it merits quotation in full. It provides:

"The Court of Justice shall have jurisdiction to give preliminary rulings concerning:

(*a*) The interpretation of this Treaty;

(*b*) The validity and interpretation of acts of the institutions of the Community;

(*c*) The interpretation of the statutes of bodies established by an act of the Council, where those statutes so provide.

Where such a question is raised before any court or tribunal of a Member State, that court or tribunal may, if it considers that a decision on the question is necessary to enable it to give judgment, request the Court of Justice to give a ruling thereon. Where any such question is raised in a case pending before a court or tribunal of a Member State, against whose decision there is no judicial remedy under national law, that court or tribunal shall bring the matter before the Court of Justice."

---

[33] *Valor International Ltd.* v. *Application des Gaz* [1978] 3 C.M.L.R. 87 at p. 99.
[34] *Application des Gaz* v. *Falks Veritas, supra,* n. 31 at p. 85.

3.30   The first paragraph of the Article thus defines the limits of the Court's jurisdiction to give rulings, and the second and third paragraphs specify the bodies which either may invoke that jurisdiction voluntarily, or are bound to do so.

B. THE COURT AND JURISDICTION

3.31   The European Court itself has frequently emphasised that its role is to interpret the Treaty, and not to apply it. In the *Van Gend en Loos* case[35] in 1963, for instance the Court said:

> "The Court is here not called upon to give a decision on the application of the Treaty according to the principles of Dutch internal law, which fall within the sphere of national jurisdiction, but is asked in accordance with Article 177 (1) (*a*) of the Treaty only to interpret the meaning of Article 12 of the said Treaty within the framework of Community law and in the light of its incidence on individuals."[36]

3.32   In providing for this particular solution to the problem of ensuring the uniform application of Community law throughout the Member States, the authors of the Treaty were opting for a rather less radical solution than they might have chosen. A more effective answer to the problem might well have been to have provided for an appeal to the Court of Justice from a decision of a national court, where a point of Community law was involved. The European Court would then have been able to rule on the conformity of that decision with established Community law, and to ensure, by direct rather than indirect means, the uniform application of Community law. The system set up by Article 177 provides a reduced role for the European Court and one which depends entirely on the willingness of courts and tribunals of the Member States to co-operate in making it workable. It can, however, be very effective.

3.33   A good illustration of the effectiveness of the Article 177 procedure in appropriate circumstances was provided by a series of cases in 1975 between EMI Records Limited and various European subsidiaries of the American Corporation, CBS Inc., all of which were concerned with the trade mark "Columbia."[37] CBS held the rights to the mark in the United States, and the European rights belonged to EMI. EMI was trying to prevent the importation into Europe by CBS subsidiaries of records manufactured in the United States bearing the "Columbia" mark. In each case,

---

[35] *Van Gend en Loos* [1963] C.M.L.R. 105.
[36] *Ibid.* at p. 128.
[37] Case 51/75 *EMI Records Ltd.* v. *CBS United Kingdom Ltd.*; Case 86/75 *The Same* v. *CBS Grammofon A/S* and Case 96/75 *The Same* v. *CBS Schallplatten GmbH* [1976] E.C.R. 811, 871, 913; [1976] 2 C.M.L.R. 235.

the defence of CBS's subsidiaries turned on Community law, and, in particular, on the provisions of Article 36.[38]

3.34   Requests under Article 177 for a preliminary ruling were made by courts in three Member States—the United Kingdom, Denmark and Germany—as parallel proceedings were in progress before each of them, involving the same question.[39] The three references were all heard at the same time, and the possibility that the English, Danish and German courts might each reach a different conclusion was, by means of this procedure, eliminated.

3.35   Some national courts are obviously more skilful than others in framing questions for the European Court, but the Court will always try to extract from the wording actually used, points on which it can rule as a matter of interpretation and not of application.[40] For example, in the *Pigs Marketing Board* (*Northern Ireland*) case,[41] the Court said:

> "As regards the division of jurisdiction between national courts and the Court of Justice under Article 177 of the Treaty the national court, which is alone in having a direct knowledge of the facts of the case and of the arguments put forward by the parties, and which will have to give judgment in the case, is in the best position to appreciate, with full knowledge of law raised by the dispute before it, the reference of the questions of law raised by the dispute before it and the necessity for a preliminary ruling so as to enable it to give judgment. However, in the event of questions having been improperly formulated or going beyond the scope of the powers conferred on the Court of Justice by Article 177, the Court is free to extract from all the factors provided by the national court and in particular from the statement of grounds contained in the reference, the elements of Community law requiring an interpretation—or, as the case may be, an assessment of validity—having regard to the subject matter of the dispute."[42]

---

[38] Although that Article permits "prohibitions or restrictions on imports, exports or goods in transit justified on grounds of . . . the protection of industrial and commercial property," such a departure from the general principle of the free movement of goods is not acceptable where it would "constitute a means of arbitrary discrimination or a disguised restriction on trade between Member States." The jurisprudence of the Court of Justice at that time (notably Case 192/73 *Van Zuylen Frères* v. *Hag AG* [1974] E.C.R. 2, C.M.L.R. 127 731) left open the possibility that where two trade marks had a common origin, as in this case, an attempt to invoke the first part of Art. 36 would be considered an "arbitrary discrimination or a disguised restriction on trade between Member States," and thus would be prohibited.

[39] In the event, the Court ruled that provided no Agreement or concerted practice which might infringe Art. 85 was involved, the proprietor of a mark in all the Member States of the Community was entitled to exercise his trade-mark rights to prevent importation of products bearing the same mark, where it was owned by a third party based in a country outside the Community.

[40] See, *e.g. Costa* v. *ENEL* [1964] C.M.L.R. 425; *Albatros SARL* v. *SOPECO* [1963] E.C.R. 29; [1966] C.M.L.R. 159; *Simmenthal SpA* (*No. 2)* [1978] 3 C.M.L.R. 263.

[41] *Pigs Marketing Board* (*Northern Ireland*) [1979] 1 C.M.L.R. 177.

[42] *Ibid.* at pp. 198–199.

3.36 In that case, among a large number of questions, the Resident Magistrate, County Armagh, specifically asked whether the Pigs Marketing Scheme in Northern Ireland contravened Community law. If the Court had answered the question, as put to it, it would have exceeded its powers under Article 177, as it would have been ruling directly upon the validity of the Pigs Marketing Scheme in Northern Ireland. The answer given was, therefore, couched in abstract terms and referred only to "a marketing system on a national or regional scale" with powers such as those enjoyed by the Pigs Marketing Board, being incompatible with the Treaty and the relevant Regulation on the common organisation of the market in pig meat.[43]

3.37 The extent of the Court's jurisdiction under the first paragraph of Article 177 is, ultimately, a matter for the Court itself to decide. As part of the Treaty, interpretation of Article 177, like any other Article of the Treaty, must fall within the scope of that paragraph.

3.38 As well as interpreting the Treaty, the Court is also empowered by virtue of sub-paragraph (b) to rule on "the validity and interpretation of acts of the institutions of the Community." Those acts would appear to include all legally binding acts of the Community institutions. It would, for instance, include a decision in relation to Articles 85 or 86 of the Treaty issued by the Commission under Regulation 17/62, where a national court found itself unable to give judgment without clarification of the Commission's decision.

3.39 The procedure for reviewing "validity" is not in any sense a duplication of the Court's powers under Articles 173 and 174 to review the legality of acts of the Council and Commission and, in appropriate cases, to declare such acts void. Under Article 177, the Court's ruling on a question of validity applies, as a matter of legal theory, only to the particular case before the national court and has no general application. In practice, where a ruling of the Court is given in sufficiently clear terms, another national court faced with the same point, would apply the Court's ruling in the earlier case, on the basis that the Community question had already been settled, so that nothing would be gained by a further reference under Article 177. One such example of the Court giving a clear-cut ruling was the series of cases in 1976/77 involving the Commission's scheme for disposing of surplus skimmed milk powder,[44] where the Court ruled that the Regulation in question was "null and void."[45]

3.40 Sub-paragraph (c) of Article 177 (1) empowers the Court to rule on "the interpretation of the statutes of bodies established by an Act of the Council where those statutes so provide." Such a provision is frequently found in

---

[43] Reg. 2759/75.
[44] Reg. 563/76.
[45] Case 114/76 *Bela-Mühle Josef Bergmann KG* v. *Grows-Farm GmbH & Co. KG*: Case 116/76 *Granaria BV* v. *Hoofproduktschap Voor Akkerbouwprodukten*; Case 119/76 *Olmuhle Hamburg AG* v. *Hauptzollamt Hamburg-Waltershof*; Case 120/76 *Firma Kurt A. Brecherg* v. *Hauptzollamt Bremen-Nord* [1977] E.C.R. 1211; [1979] 2 C.M.L.R. 83.

Conventions and Protocols concluded between the Member States, including, for example, the Community Patent Convention.[46]

C. The Courts and Tribunals Entitled to make a Reference

(1) *General*

3.41 The second and third paragraphs of Article 177 are both concerned with the institutions of the Member States which have the right to invoke Article 177, namely "any court or tribunal." In the final analysis, the meaning of this phrase is for the Court of Justice to decide as a matter of interpretation of the Treaty under Article 177 (1) (*a*). It is clear, however, that all courts of law, in the normally understood sense, and permanently constituted tribunals[47] fall within the definition.

(2) *Article 177 (2): Optional References*

3.42 It is for the court or tribunal making the reference to decide whether or not it is "necessary," and the Court of Justice has shown itself as reluctant to investigate reasons for a reference, as it has been anxious to extract a suitable question for interpretation, from an inappropriately phrased request.[48]

3.43 Although the parties to an action may request the national court to make a reference, it is for that court itself to decide within the framework of Article 177 whether or not to do so, subject to a right of appeal, if any, under national law.[49] It is also open to the parties to suggest the form in which the question might be put to the Court of Justice, and although the judge is not obliged to accept the parties' wording, it seems to be the usual practice of the English High Court to do so.[50]

3.44 It is clear that the guidelines laid down by Lord Denning in *Bulmer* v. *Bollinger*[51] to assist courts in deciding whether or not to make a reference under Article 177 (2), have, as a matter of Community law, no binding force. He attempted there to deal not only with the exercise of the court's discretion, but also with what he described as "the condition precedent"[52]

---

[46] Convention for the European Patent for the Common Market, Art. 63.

[47] *i.e.* as opposed to tribunals established for a particular purpose. Examples of such tribunals in the U.K. are the Employment Appeal Tribunal and the National Insurance Commissioner.

[48] Para. 3.35. See further Case 104/79 *Foglia* [1981] 1 C.M.L.R. 45

[49] *e.g.* in the U.K., R.S.C., Ord. 114. It appears that the European Court will allow a reference to be withdrawn if the court making the reference is overruled on appeal. See note on Case 813/79 *Dymo Industries Inc.* v. *Etiketten Service Arnhem BV* in [1980] E.C.R. 128.

[50] *e.g. EMI Records Ltd.* v. *CBS U.K. Ltd.* [1975] 1 C.M.L.R. 285.

[51] *H. P. Bulmer Ltd. and Another* v. *J. Bollinger SA and Another* [1974] 2 C.M.L.R. 91.

[52] *Ibid.* at p. 114.

to that discretion, namely that the reference should be "necessary." He interpreted "necessary" in the context of Article 177 (2) as being synonymous with "conclusive." In the words of the judgment:

"The judge must have got to the stage when he says to himself: 'This clause of the Treaty is capable of two or more meanings. If it means *this*, I give judgment for the plaintiff. If it means *that*, I give judgment for the defendant.' In short, the point must be such that, whichever way the point is decided, it is conclusive of the case."[53]

3.45 Although in such a situation the judge would almost certainly wish to make a reference,[54] there is nothing in the jurisprudence of the European Court to support such a restricted view, and it seems to be of doubtful validity.

3.46 The other, less controversial, guidelines laid down by Lord Denning are: first, to see whether there has been a previous ruling on the point, in which case a reference will, presumably, not be "necessary" (although, as the European Court is not subject to the doctrine of strictly binding precedent, the national court might want to give it the opportunity to change its mind)[55]: secondly, to establish whether the point is reasonably clear and free from doubt[56]: thirdly, to decide the facts first, as it may be that when all the facts are clear a reference is not needed.[57]

(3) *Article 177 (3): Mandatory Reference*

3.47 Although any court or tribunal of a Member State is entitled to make a reference if it so wishes, certain courts are, by virtue of Article 177 (3), obliged to do so. Those are courts "against whose decisions there is no judicial remedy under national law." This is not necessarily confined to the highest appellate court,[58] but can apply to any court where, in the particular circumstances, no further appeal lies. One exception to this general rule is in the case of interlocutory proceedings where, even though no appeal lies against the interlocutory order, the Court is not bound to make a reference

---

[53] *Ibid.* at p. 115.
[54] See, *e.g. Van Duyn* v. *The Home Office* [1974] 1 C.M.L.R. 347.
[55] See, e.g. Cases 28, 29 and 30/62, *Da Costa en Schaake N.V. and Others* v. *Nederlandse Belastingadministratie* [1963] E.C.R. 31; [1963] C.M.L.R. 224.
[56] *i.e.* the French doctrine of "L'acte claire."
[57] Having established that a reference *is* necessary, the guidelines for the exercise of the discretion are set out on pp. 116–118 of the judgment. They are:
  . (i) the time required to obtain a reference, which may make it undesirable in situations such as injunction proceedings, where speed is important;
  (ii) the need not to overload the European Court;
  (iii) the importance of formulating the question clearly;
  (iv) the difficulty and importance of the question;
  (v) the expense;
  (vi) the wishes of the parties.
[58] *e.g.* in the U.K. the House of Lords. See, *e.g. DPP* v. *Henn and Darby* [1979] 2 C.M.L.R. 495.

if the question on which a ruling is required can be raised by the parties at the hearing of the substantive issues.[59]

3.48   Whilst, therefore, Article 177 does not provide a watertight solution to the problem of ensuring the uniform application of Community law by the courts of the Member States, in that a court may wrongly decide that a matter is clearcut when it is not, or may misunderstand the Court's ruling, it nevertheless provides a relatively cheap and speedy method of ensuring that, at least on major points, uniformity will, in large measure, be achieved.

---

[59] Case 107/76 *Hoffmann-La Roche AG* v. *Centrafarm Vertriebsgesellschaft Pharmazeutischer Erzeugniss GmbH* [1977] E.C.R. 957; [1977] 2 C.M.L.R. 334.

CHAPTER 4

RESTRAINTS ON COMPETITION WITHIN THE
COMMON MARKET

(Article 85 and its implementation under Council Regulation 17/62)

I. *INTRODUCTION*

A. GENERAL

4.01 Broadly, Article 85 is concerned with distortions of competition within the Community resulting from restrictive arrangements between two or more parties. In consequence, it can and frequently does affect Agreements concerned with intellectual property.

4.02 Article 85 is one of the Articles of the Treaty which gives rise to the inherent conflict between national intellectual property rights, and the various provisions of the Treaty which regulate and may, indeed, curtail the traditional use of those rights. The Commission and the European Court have attempted to resolve this conflict by drawing a distinction between the existence of intellectual property rights, which both have repeatedly proclaimed sacrosanct in reliance upon Article 222,[1] and the exercise of those rights, which both have repeatedly held to be the subject to the various other relevant provisions of the Treaty.

4.03 The distinction is of practical importance in the context of Article 85 because a number of restrictive provisions in agreements have been held to relate to the *existence* of intellectual property rights, rather than to their *exercise*. As a result, those restrictions have been held to fall outside the scope of Article 85 (1).[2]

4.04 It is not, however, helpful to discuss the distinction between existence and exercise in the abstract. It is a difficult one to draw, and one which, if meaningful at all, is so primarily when considering the application of

---

[1] Art. 222: "This Treaty shall in no way prejudice the rules in Member States governing systems of property ownership."
[2] See the discussion *infra*, Chap. 11, paras. 11.05 *et seq.*

particular provisions of the Treaty to given factual situations involving intellectual property rights.[3]

B. The Three Paragraphs of Article 85

4.05 Article 85 consists of three paragraphs and must be considered in conjunction with Council regulation 17/62 ("Regulation 17"), by which it was implemented.[4] Article 85 (1) contains the basic prohibition against restrictions on competition. Article 85 (2) then specifies one of the two primary consequences for an agreement, decision or concerted practice which infringes that basic prohibition, namely that the infringing agreement, decision or concerted practice will be "automatically void."[5]

4.06 Finally, Article 85 (3) enables the Commission to declare Article 85 (1) inapplicable to a given agreement, decision or concerted practice provided that it meets specified criteria.[6] Such a declaration is known as an "exemption." With certain relatively insignificant exceptions,[7] the Commission is only empowered to grant an exemption in one of two ways:

(i) on an individual basis, after a particular agreement, decision or concerted practice has been duly "notified" to it by the parties[8]; or

(ii) by a so-called "block exemption," whereby agreements are exempted by category, so that the exemption applies to any agreement falling within the specified category without notification being necessary.[9]

---

[3] This is so, at least in part, because the distinction is one which has been superimposed by the Commission and the Court of Justice on the domestic law of patents, trade marks and other intellectual property in response to the inevitable conflict between industrial property rights and, *inter alia*, Art. 222 of the Treaty on the one hand, and the provisions of the Treaty concerning competition and the free movement of goods on the other hand. It is not a distinction which is native to the domestic law governing the various intellectual property rights. In consequence, from the vantage point of those schooled in the domestic law of such rights, the distinction appears at first glance artificial, if not meaningless.

[4] Reg. 17/62 was adopted by the Council pursuant to Art. 87 of the Treaty, which requires the Council in the manner and circumstances specified in that Article to "... adopt any appropriate regulations or directives to give effect to the principles set out in Articles 85 and 86."

[5] The other possible consequence is the imposition by the Commission of substantial fines on each of the parties to the infringing agreement, decision or concerted practice, in appropriate circumstances. The nature of the fines which the Commission may impose and the circumstances in which it may do so are discussed in Chap. 6, at para. 6.48. The Commission may not impose fines, in respect of acts taking place between the date of a "notification" to the Commission pursuant to Art. 85 (3) and the date of the Commission's Decision.

[6] Art. 85 (3) and art. 9 (1) of Reg. 17/62.

[7] Broadly, agreements, decisions and concerted practices of the types described in Arts. 4 (2) and 5 (2) of Reg. 17. See discussion *infra,* para. 4.107.

[8] *i.e.* pursuant to the relevant article of Reg. 17. See in this connection Arts. 4, 5, 7 and 25 of that Reg. See also discussion *infra,* paras. 4.101 *et seq.*

[9] The Commission must be specifically empowered to issue a block exemption by the Council of Ministers, pursuant to Art. 87 of the Treaty.

C. NEGATIVE CLEARANCE

4.07   By way of introductory comment, mention should also be made of the Commission's power to declare, on application, that a particular agreement, decision or concerted practice does not infringe Article 85 (1) (*i.e.* to grant a "negative clearance"). This procedure is designed to provide a means of obtaining a definitive ruling in doubtful cases.[10]

4.08   In this chapter the three paragraphs of Article 85 will be discussed separately.

II. *ARTICLE 85 (1)—THE BASIC PROHIBITION*

A. ARTICLE 85 (1): THREE REQUIREMENTS FOR ITS APPLICATION

4.09   Article 85 (1) provides:
"1. The following shall be prohibited as incompatible with the common market: all agreements between undertakings, decisions by associations of undertakings and concerted practices which may affect trade between Member States and which have as their object or effect the prevention, restriction or distortion of competition within the common market, and in particular those which:

(*a*) directly or indirectly fix purchase or selling prices or any other trading conditions;

(*b*) limit or control production, markets, technical development, or investment;

(*c*) share markets or sources of supply;

(*d*) apply dissimilar conditions to equivalent transactions with other trading parties, thereby placing them at a competitive disadvantage;

(*e*) make the conclusion of contracts subject to acceptance by the other parties of supplementary obligations which, by their nature or according to commercial usage, have no connection with the subject of such contracts."

4.10   The Article thus takes the form of a general prohibition, followed by a non-exclusive list of specific prohibited practices. The general prohibition itself may conveniently be divided into three separate parts or requirements, all of which must be present. Thus:

(i) there must be an agreement between undertakings, a decision by an association of undertakings or a concerted practice between undertakings;

(ii) there must be the possibility that the agreement, decision or concerted practice in question will affect trade between two or more Member States of the EEC;

---

[10] Art. 2 of Reg. 17/62. See discussion, *infra,* paras. 4.101 *et seq.*

(iii) the object or effect of the agreement, decision or concerted practice must be the prevention, restriction or distortion of competition within the EEC.

B. AGREEMENTS BETWEEN UNDERTAKINGS, DECISIONS BY ASSOCIATIONS OF UNDERTAKINGS AND CONCERTED PRACTICES

(1) *General*

4.11 It has long been established that mere reliance on intellectual property rights cannot, in and of itself, give rise to an infringement of Article 85 (1). There can be no such infringement in the absence of an agreement, decision or concerted practice. This point was settled by the European Court in the first case to come before it involving the rights of a patent holder, namely the *Parke Davis* case, decided in 1968.[11]

4.12 One of the issues which the Court was required to consider in that case was whether the concept of a prohibited practice under Article 85 (1) might include a patent infringement action, instituted by the owner of a patent in a Member State when, on the basis of his patent, the patentee is seeking to prevent commercial dealing in that Member State of similar products imported from another Member State where no patent protection was available.

4.13 In the course of considering this question, the Court reasoned that the specific wording of Article 85 (1) suggests that conduct will only constitute a prohibited practice within the meaning of Article 85 (1) if it can be traced to an agreement, decision or concerted practice and, further, that clearly a patent in and of itself, does not come within any of these three categories.[12] Indeed, in giving its answer to the questions referred to it in the *Parke Davis* case the Court succinctly summarised its views on the question of whether Article 85 (1) can affect the rights of a patent holder in the absence of an agreement, decision or concerted practice. It stated:

> "... the rights granted by a member-State to the holder of a patent are not affected as regards their existence by the prohibitions of Articles 85 (1) and 86 of the Treaty.... The exercise of those rights would fall under neither Article 85 (1) in the absence of any agreement, decision or concerted practice mentioned by that provision, nor Article 86 in the absence of any abuse of dominant position."[13]

4.14 Clearly, then, the mere ownership by an original patentee of his patent cannot be affected by Article 85 (1), because such ownership is an integral

---

[11] *Parke Davis & Co.* v. *Probel and Others* [1968] E.C.R. 55; [1968] C.M.L.R. 47. The facts of this case are fully set out *infra*, para. 8.81.

[12] *Ibid.* at p. 59.

[13] *Ibid.* at p. 60.

part of the *existence* of intellectual property and as such is outside the ambit of Article 85 (1). While action taken by a patentee in reliance on his patent will involve the *exercise* of the patentee's rights, that *exercise* will only risk infringing Article 85 (1) if it takes place in the context of an agreement, decision or concerted practice. The same is true, of course, in the case of other types of intellectual property.[14]

(2) *The Nature of Agreements, Decisions and Concerted Practices*

(a) Agreements

4.15   The term "agreement" is not defined in the Treaty. Obviously, it will include all duly executed written agreements, but the term undoubtedly also includes any oral agreement which would be enforceable as a matter of domestic law.

4.16   How far the term may be extended beyond these two categories is uncertain, particularly as to date there is no decision of the European Court in point. In *Re the Franco-Japanese Ballbearings Agreement,*[15] however, the European Commission construed "agreement" quite broadly. The Commission was concerned, in that case, with a series of meetings and an exchange of correspondence which took place in 1972 between certain of the main French and Japanese ballbearing manufacturers and at which there were also present representatives of their trade associations. The principal concern of the French ballbearing manufacturers was that the Japanese should curtail their exports to France and increase their prices, and certain undertakings were, indeed, given by the Japanese side in this regard. Various price increases were subsequently made by the Japanese manufacturers when selling to their French distributors. The Commission instituted proceedings on its own initiative in 1973 and, eventually concluded that an agreement existed between the Japanese and French trade associations which infringed Article 85 (1). In the course of its decision the Commission stated:

> "... for Article 85 (1) of the EEC Treaty to apply it is not essential that this agreement should take the form of a contract having all the elements required by civil law: it is sufficient that one of the parties voluntarily undertakes to limit its freedom of action with regard to the other."[16]

---

[14] See, *e.g.* in the trade marks context *Etablissements Consten SA and Grundig-Verkaufs GmbH* v. *EC Commission* [1966] E.C.R. 299; [1966] C.M.L.R. 418 at p. 476; Case 40/70 *Sirena S.R.L.* v. *Eda S.R.L. and Others* [1971] E.C.R. 69; [1971] C.M.L.R. 260 at p. 273. Similarly in the copyright context see Case 78/70 *Deutsche Grammophon GmbH* v. *Metro SP GmbH & Co. KG* [1971] E.C.R. 487; [1971] C.M.L.R. 631 at p. 656.

[15] *Re the Franco-Japanese Ballbearings Agreement* (74/64/EEC) [1975] 1 C.M.L.R. D. 8.

[16] *Ibid.* D.16 at para. 25. See also *Atka A/S* v. *BP Kemi A/S* and *De Danske Spiritfabrikker* [1979] 3 C.M.L.R. 684 at p. 696, where the Commission held that an agreement which was never signed but which had been applied by both parties was an agreement for the purposes of Art. 85 (1).

4.17 This view of what constitutes an agreement is not unduly broad in the context of the Competition provisions of the Treaty[16a] nor, indeed, by comparison with the definition of an "agreement" contained in the Restrictive Trade Practices Act 1976.[17] The point is, however, probably of only academic interest because it seems likely that where the circumstances fall short of an "agreement" they will be caught by the concept of a concerted practice.

4.18 Finally, no distinction is drawn between agreements between undertakings on the same economic plain and agreements between undertakings on different economic plains. Thus, for example, it will make no difference whether the agreement in question has been entered into between two manufacturing undertakings or between a manufacturing undertaking and its distributor.[18] It is sufficient that there is an agreement between "undertakings."[19]

(b) Decisions by associations of undertakings

4.19 As its wording suggests, this phrase is directed at conduct carried out through a trade association. It follows that Article 85 (1) cannot be circumvented by the device of a trade association, if a "decision" is involved. Precisely what is meant by a decision is less than clear, but as might be expected the term is interpreted broadly. It will certainly encompass an agreement implemented through a trade association and generally adhered to by its members.[20] It has also been held that the constitution and general regulations of a trade association in themselves constitute a decision for the purposes of Article 85 (1).[21]

4.20 Although Article 85 (1) refers only to "decisions between associations of undertakings," it is clear that only one trade association needs to be involved.[22] It has also been held that an international trade association which has as its members national trade associations is itself an "association of undertakings" for the purposes of Article 85 (1).[23]

[16a] *i.e.* Arts. 3 (*a*), (*f*) and 85–90 of the Treaty. See discussion, *supra,* at paras. 1.12 *et seq.*

[17] s. 43 (1) of the Restrictive Trade Practices Act 1976 defines an agreement so as to include "... any agreement or arrangement, whether or not it is or is intended to be enforceable (apart from any provision of this Act) by legal proceedings, ..."

[18] *La Technique Minière* v. *Maschinenbau Ulm GmbH* [1966] E.C.R. 235; [1966] C.M.L.R. 357 at p. 374; *Etablissements Consten SA*, *supra*, 14, at p. 470.

[19] *La Technique Minière* v. *Maschinenbau Ulm GmbH*, *supra*.

[20] See, *e.g.* Re *The Vereniging Van Vernis En Verffabrikanten in Nederland (VVVF)* [1970] C.M.L.R. D.1; Re *The Discount Agreement of the Interessengemeinschaft der Deutschen Keramischen Wand Und Bodenfliesenwerke* [1971] C.M.L.R. D.6.

[21] Re *The Association Syndicale Belge de la Parfumerie* [1970] C.M.L.R. D.25 at D.28, para. 14; see also *Donck* v. *Central Bureau voor de Ritwielhandel* [1978] 2 C.M.L.R. 194 at p. 203.

[22] See, *e.g. The Vereniging Van Vernis En Verffabrikanten in Nederland (VVVF)*, *supra*, n. 20; Re *The Discount Agreement of the Interessengemeinschaft der Deutschen Keramischen Wand Und Bodenfliesenwerke*, *supra*, n. 20, and Re *The Association Syndicale Belge de la Parfumerie*, *supra*, n. 21.

[23] Re *The Comité Européan de Cooperation des Industries de la Machine-Outil (CECIMO)* [1967] C.M.L.R. D.1 at D.16, para. 13.

4.21   Finally, although Article 85 (1) refers to agreements between undertakings and to decisions by associations of undertakings, the European Court has confirmed that an agreement between associations of undertakings will also be covered.[24]

4.22   To summarise, using the words of the Court in the same case: "Article 85 (1) applies to associations insofar as their own activities or those of the undertakings belonging to them are calculated to produce the results to which it refers."[25]

(c) Concerted practices

4.23   The European Court of Justice considered the meaning of this term in the *Aniline Dyestuffs* case.[26] At issue were three general and uniform price increases which took place between January 1964 and October 1967, in respect of most dye-stuffs based on aniline. Following information supplied to it, the European Commission instituted proceedings for a suspected violation of Article 85 (1)[27] against 17 dye-stuffs manufacturers established both within the EEC and outside it, as well as against various subsidiary companies and their representatives. In due course, the Commission found that the price increases in question were the result of concerted practices infringing Article 85 (1), and imposed substantial fines on 10 of the manufacturers. Subsequently, all but one of those fined appealed to the European Court. The appeals failed and in the course of its judgment the Court stated:

> "If Article 85 distinguishes the concept of 'concerted practice' from that of 'agreements between enterprises' or 'decisions of associations of enterprises,' this is done with the object of bringing under the prohibitions of this Article a form of co-ordination between undertakings which, without going so far as to amount to an agreement properly so called, knowingly substitutes a practical co-operation between them for the risks of competition.
>
> By its very nature, then, the concerted practice does not combine all the elements of an agreement but may, inter alia, result from a co-ordination which becomes apparent from the behaviour of the participants.
>
> Although a parallelism of behaviour cannot by itself be identified with a concerted practice, it is nevertheless liable to constitute a strong indication of such a practice when it leads to conditions of competition which do not correspond to the normal conditions of the

---

[24] *Nederlandse Vereniging voor de Fruit en Groentenimporthandel and Nederlandse Bond van Grossiers in Zuidvruchten en Ander Geimporteerd Fruit "Frubo"* v. *EC Commission* [1975] E.C.R. 563; [1975] 2 C.M.L.R. 123 at p. 146.

[25] *Ibid.* p. 124.

[26] Case 48/69 *Imperial Chemical Industries Ltd. and Others* v. *EC Commission* [1972] E.C.R. 619; [1972] C.M.L.R. 557.

[27] Pursuant to Art. 3 of Reg. 17.

market, having regard to the nature of the products, the importance and number of the undertakings and the volume of the said market. Such is the case especially where the parallel behaviour is such as to permit the parties to seek price equilibrium at a different level from that which would have resulted from competition, and to crystallise the status quo to the detriment of effective freedom of movement of the products in the Common Market and free choice by consumers of their suppliers."[28]

4.24 More recently, in 1975, in the *Sugar Cartel* case,[29] the European Court substantially re-stated this definition of a concerted practice, though modifying it in such a way as to suggest that the existence of co-operation (in place of competition) is not merely a strong indication but an integral part of a concerted practice. The Court said:

"The concept of a 'concerted practice' refers to a form of co-ordination between undertakings which, without having been taken to the stage where an agreement properly so-called has been concluded, knowingly substitutes for the risks of competition, co-operation in practice between them which leads to conditions of competition which do not correspond to the normal conditions of the market, having regard to the nature of the products, the importance and number of the undertakings as well as the size and nature of the said market."[30]

4.25 Indeed, in the *Sugar Cartel* case, the Court provided some insight into its view of a concerted practice by emphasising that the concept could not be understood without first appreciating that the principle underlying the rules of competition embodied in the Treaty is that "each economic operator must determine independently the policy which he intends to adopt on the Common Market ..."[31] The Court continued:

"Although it is correct to say that this requirement of independence does not deprive economic operators of the right to adapt themselves intelligently to the existing and anticipated conduct of their competitors, it does however strictly preclude any direct or indirect contact between such operators, the object or effect whereof is either to influence the conduct of the market of an actual or potential competitor or to disclose to such a competitor the course of conduct which they themselves have decided to adopt or contemplate adopting on the market."[31]

4.26 Clearly, then, the concept of a concerted practice is extremely broad, and

---

[28] *ICI* v. *EC Commission, supra,* n. 26 at pp. 622–623, para. 64/67.
[29] *Co-operatieve Vereniging "Suiker Unie" UA (SU) and Others* v. *EC Commission Unione Nazionale Consumation* [1975] E.C.R. 1663; [1976] 1 C.M.L.R. 295. For a detailed survey of this case, see Dashwood, Guy, Laddie, & Leigh, "The Sugar Industry Marathon" [1976] 1 E.L. Rev. 470.
[30] *Ibid.* at p. 405.
[31] *Ibid.* at p. 425.

will encompass much which would not amount to an agreement, even if defined in the broad terms used by the Commission in the *Franco-Japanese Ballbearings* case.[32] At the same time, it is probably fair to say that the concept is as yet relatively under-developed and that its precise scope is unclear.

(3) *Meaning of Undertaking*

(a) **General**

4.27   It is clear from the wording of Article 85 (1), that at least two undertakings must be involved. The term "undertaking" is a wide one, and one which has not been exhaustively defined either by the Commission or the Court.

4.28   The term does, however, apply to both public and private undertakings, as well as to state-owned corporations.[33] The Commission was required to consider whether the term applied to an individual in the *AOIP* case.[34] A Mr. Beyrard was a self-employed inventor resident in Paris, and he had, in his individual capacity, licensed his patents to the *Association des Ouvriers en Instruments de Précision* (AOIP), a French *Société Anonyme*. The Commission concluded that Mr. Beyrard was an "undertaking" for the purposes of Article 85 (1) because "by licensing his patents he has commercially exploited his invention."[35] It has similarly been held that leading opera singers are "undertakings" when commercially exploiting their artistic performances.[36] This line of reasoning suggests that virtually any legal or natural person may be treated as an undertaking, provided that they are engaged in a form of commercial activity. Whether in given circumstances it could be successfully argued that an entity which is not engaged in normal commercial activity, for example, a charity, is for that reason alone immune from the application of Article 85 (1) remains to be seen.

(b) **Geographical location of undertaking**

4.29   The geographical location of an undertaking is immaterial. The requirement in Article 85 (1) that at least two undertakings must be involved will be satisfied, irrespective of whether one or more of the undertakings in question happens to be established outside the EEC.[37]

---

[32] *Ibid.* See para. 4.16. See also, *e.g. Re "Pioneer" Hi-Fi Equipment* [1980] 1 C.M.L.R. 457.

[33] As to state owned corporations see, *e.g. The State* v. *Sacchi* [1974] 2 C.M.L.R. 177, concerned with Art. 86 but, no doubt, also relevant to the definition of an undertaking in the context of Art. 85.

[34] *Association des Ouvriers en Instruments de Précision (AOIP)* v. *Beyrard* [1976] 1 C.M.L.R. D.14; see also *Reuter* v. *B.A.S.F. AG* [1976] 2 C.M.L.R. D.44 and D.55; *H. Vaessen BV* v. *Moris* [1979] 1 C.M.L.R. 511.

[35] *Association des Ouvriers en Instruments de Précision (AOIP) supra*, at D.22, para. 17.

[36] Case 516/78 *Re Unitel Film—Und Fernseh-Produktionsgesellschaft mbH & Co.* [1978] 3 C.M.L.R. 306.

[37] *Re Béguelin Import Co. and Another* v. *G.L. Import Export SA and Others* [1972] C.M.L.R. 81 at p. 95; *Tepea BV* v. *EC Commission* [1978] E.C.R. 1391; [1978] 3 C.M.L.R. 392.

(c) Subsidiary and associated undertakings—the concept of "enterprise entity"

4.30   To date, neither the Commission nor the Court has ever concluded that an agreement between a parent and its wholly owned subsidiary infringed Article 85 (1), although the door has invariably been left open for such a finding should the facts warrant it. For example, in the *Christiani and Nielsen* case[38] a Danish company had a wholly owned subsidiary in Holland and various other wholly owned subsidiaries, including one in France and one in Germany. An agreement existed between the Danish company and the Dutch subsidiary whereby the Danish company undertook to put at the disposal of the Dutch company its experience, patents, inventions and know-how, and generally to co-operate with it. The Danish company retained the right to nominate directors to the Dutch company's Board. The Danish company undertook not to operate in Holland and the Dutch company not to operate outside Holland except with the express approval of its parent. The agreement included various other restrictive provisions. Faced with this agreement, the Commission concluded that in the case of an agreement between a parent company and its wholly owned subsidiary, where as a matter of fact the subsidiary has no effective autonomy, the two legally separate entities will for the purposes of Article 85 (1) be regarded as a single economic unit.[39]

4.31   The Commission implied that if, in given circumstances, a subsidiary operated with a sufficient degree of autonomy, an agreement between it and its parent might infringe Article 85 (1). In reaching its conclusion, the Commission reasoned that before Article 85 (1) can be infringed there must exist "... competition which is capable of being restricted ... in that respect it is imperative to know whether, on the factual level, autonomous activity of the subsidiary with regard to the parent company is possible on the economic plane."[40]

4.32   This has become known as the concept of "enterprise entity," and the rationale behind it has been variously expressed.[41] The underlying idea would appear to be that, at least in the context of a parent/subsidiary relationship, one is not really dealing with two undertakings, but, rather

---

[38] Case 69/195 *Christiani & Nielsen NV* [1969] C.M.L.R. D. 36.
[39] *Ibid.* at D. 39 (para. 10.13).
[40] *Ibid.* at D. 38/39 (para. 11).
[41] See, *e.g.* Case 70/332 *Re Kodak* [1970] C.M.L.R. D. 19 at D. 21–22, in which the Commission reasoned that there could be no agreement or concerted practice in circumstances in which a parent company exercises its power of control by issuing precise instructions to its various subsidiaries, and that Art. 85 (1) could not apply because of this deficiency; also *Imperial Chemical Industries Ltd.* [1972] C.M.L.R. 557 at p. 629 (paras. 132–136); Case 22/71 *Béguelin Import Co. and Another* v. *G.L. Import Export SA and Others* [1971] E.C.R. 949 [1972] C.M.L.R. 81.

with a group or single economic entity. In these circumstances, therefore, it is nonsense to speak of an agreement between undertakings. Thus, for example, in the *Sterling Drug* case,[42] the European Court said:

> "Article 85 of the Treaty does not apply to agreements or concerted practices between undertakings belonging to the same group in the form of parent company and subsidiary, if the undertakings form an economic unit within which the subsidiary does not have real autonomy in determining its lines of conduct on the market and if the agreements or practices have the aim of establishing an internal distribution of tasks between the undertakings."[43]

4.33   It is doubtful whether there would ever be a situation in which a wholly owned subsidiary would be found to enjoy such a rare degree of autonomy as to justify it being treated as a separate undertaking from its parent for the purposes of Article 85 (1).[43a] Obviously, the position is far less clear-cut when the shareholding in the affiliated undertaking is less than 100 per cent.[44] Presumably, much would then depend on the precise relationship between the two companies and upon whether one could be said to "control" the other, so that the latter did not conduct its affairs with "real autonomy."

4.34   Finally, the concept of enterprise entity is not restricted to arrangements existing between a parent company and its subsidiary. It will also apply to arrangements between two subsidiaries which are beneficially owned by the same parent company.[45]

---

[42] Case 15/74 *Centrafarm BV* v. *Sterling Drug Inc.* [1974] E.C.R. 1183; [1974] 2 C.M.L.R. 480.

[43] *Ibid.* at pp. 507–508. See also Case 16/74 *Centrafarm BV* v. *Winthrop BV* [1974] E.C.R. 1183; [1974] 2 C.M.L.R. 480 at p. 511.

[43a] Note, however, Cases 32 & 36–82/78 *BMW Belgium SA and Others* v. *EC Commission* [1979] E.C.R. 2435; [1980] 1 C.M.L.R. 370, where the wholly-owned Belgian subsidiaries of a German car manufacturer entered into restrictive agreements with third-party dealers against the express instructions of its German parent. The European Court held that "the bond of economic dependence existing between a parent company and the subsidiary does not preclude a divergence in conduct or even a divergence in interests between the two companies." The Court concluded that the subsidiary had independently entered into agreements with third-party dealers which infringed Art. 85 (1), and upheld a Commission decision imposing fines on the subsidiary; at p. 399.

[44] In the context of Art. 86, a U.S. company owning 51 per cent. of the shares in its Italian subsidiary (and otherwise having control over its subsidiary) has been held to constitute a "single economic unit," so that the two companies were held to be jointly and severally responsible for the conduct complained of: *Zoja* v. *Commercial Solvents Corporation* [1973] C.M.L.R. D. 50; *Commercial Solvents Corporation* v. *EC Commission* [1974] E.C.R. 223; [1974] 1 C.M.L.R. 309. Note *Johnson & Johnson*, O.J. 1980, L377/17.

[45] *Re Kodak* [1970] C.M.L.R. D. 19 at D. 21–22.

C. The Object or Effect of Preventing, Restricting or Distorting Competition within the Common Market

1. *General*

4.35   Article 85 (1) states that before an agreement can come within its scope, that agreement must both potentially "affect trade between Member States" and have as its "object or effect the prevention, restriction or distortion of competition within the Common Market." Each of these two requirements is independent of the other, and both must be present.[46] There is nonetheless a degree of overlap between the two, so that in practice they are at times virtually inseparable from each other.[47] The former requirement, that the agreement, decision or concerted practice in question must be such as "may affect trade between Member States," will be discussed in the next section.

2. *"Object or Effect"*

4.36   Before an agreement between undertakings can infringe Article 85 (1), it must have as its "object or effect the prevention, restriction or distortion of competition within the Common Market." The meaning of this requirement, and particularly of the phrase "object or effect" was discussed by the European Court in the *Technique Minière* case ("LTM").[48]

4.37   The facts of the case were straightforward. In 1961, LTM purchased from a German enterprise, Maschinenbau Ulm, 37 levellers for delivery over a two-year period. The contract granted LTM exclusive sales rights in France and obliged it not to distribute equipment of other manufacturers in competition with Maschinenbau Ulm's equipment. Litigation eventually ensued between the parties before the French Courts in the context of which LTM pleaded that the contract was "absolutely void" as infringing Article 85 (1). The French Court duly made a reference to the European Court under Article 177, and one of the issues which the European Court was required to consider was the relationship which must exist between an agreement and competition in order for Article 85 (1) to apply. Referring to the requirement that an agreement must have either the object or effect of preventing, restricting or distorting competition, the Court reasoned that the phrase "object or effect" clearly envisages that the requirement may be satisfied in either of two ways. In consequence, the Court suggested that to decide whether an agreement satisfies this requirement its "object" should first be considered, by reference to the particular provisions in the agree-

---

[46] *Re Béguelin Import Co. & Another* [1972] C.M.L.R. 81 at p. 96.
[47] See in this connection the Commission's Notice Concerning Agreements of Minor Importance, discussed *infra* at para. 4.66. As is there pointed out, the Notice draws no distinction between the two requirements.
[48] *La Technique Minière* v. *Maschinenbau Ulm GmbH* [1966] C.M.L.R. 357.

ment, and of course, in the light of the economic context in which it will operate. If on its face the agreement does not appear to be restrictive, one must then go on to consider whether the "effect" of the agreement is to prevent, restrict or distort competition in the economic context in which the agreement will operate. The relevant passage in the Court's decision was as follows:

> "The fact that these are not cumulative but alternative conditions, indicated by the conjunction 'or' suggests first the need to consider the very object of the agreement, in the light of the economic context in which it is to be applied. The alterations in the play of competition envisaged by Art. 85 (1) should result from all or part of the clauses of the agreement itself. Where, however, an analysis of the said clauses does not reveal a sufficient degree of harmfulness with regard to competition, examination should then be made of the effects of the agreement and, if it is to be subjected to the prohibition, the presence of those elements which establish that competition has in fact been prevented, restricted or distorted to a noticeable extent should be required. The competition in question should be understood within the actual context in which it would occur in the absence of the agreement in question."[49]

4.38   Obviously, it is a relatively easy matter to ascertain whether an agreement by its terms infringes Article 85 (1), *i.e.* whether it has the *object* of so doing. By contrast, the effect of the agreement in the broader economic context will usually be more difficult to ascertain, and any conclusion as to whether a restriction on competition is involved may depend to a greater or lesser extent on a subjective judgment.

3. *"Appreciable" Prevention, Restriction or Distortion of Competition*

(a) Relevant factors
4.39   Among the factors which must be borne in mind in deciding whether an agreement is restrictive for the purposes of Article 85 (1) are: the nature and quantity of the products with which the agreement is concerned; the position and size of each of the parties on the relevant product market; whether the agreement is one of a series of agreements; the actual provisions of the agreement; the degree to which those provisions are in themselves restrictive and the degree to which competition remains possible in the type of products covered by the agreement, both within the relevant territory and outside it, for example, by similar products being imported into the territory or exported from it.[49]

---

[49] *Ibid.* at p. 375.

(b) The role of intellectual property

4.40 Obviously, the existence of intellectual property rights and the manner in which those rights are exercised may also be of critical importance. This, like so many other cornerstones of Community competition law, has been apparent since the *Consten and Grundig* case,[50] decided by the Court in 1966. The case is of sufficient importance to warrant setting out the facts at some length.

The Grundig-Consten case

4.41 In 1957, the German Company, Grundig GmbH, appointed Consten SA as its exclusive distributor in France for the sale of radios, tape recorders, dictating machines, and televisions manufactured by Grundig. Consten undertook not to sell competing goods and not to export Grundig products outside France. Grundig, for its part, in addition to granting Consten exclusive distribution rights for France, undertook not to export Grundig products either directly or indirectly to France. Grundig imposed similar restrictions on its distributors in other EEC countries. In addition, Consten was authorised to use the trade mark "GRUNDIG" and the Grundig emblem in France, and to register the trade mark "GINT" in France in its own name.[51] Consten undertook, however, to transfer or cancel the "GINT" registration on termination of its sole distributorship. The "GINT" mark, it transpired, appeared on all goods manufactured by Grundig, including those sold in Germany.

4.42 In 1961, a French company, UNEF, bought Grundig appliances from German traders and re-sold them in France to retailers, undercutting Consten's prices. Consten instituted proceedings before the French Courts for unfair competition and infringement of the "GINT" trade mark. It succeeded at first instance whereupon UNEF appealed and, in 1962, lodged a complaint with the Commission that the 1957 agreement between Grundig and Consten infringed Article 85 (1). The Appeal Court thereupon suspended its proceedings pending the Commission's decision. This was made in 1964, when the Commission condemned the agreement between Grundig and Consten on the grounds that it infringed Article 85 (1). Moreover, and of particular concern for present purposes, the Commission in effect prohibited Consten from using the "GINT" trade mark in conjunction with national trade mark law to prevent "parallel imports" of Grundig products into France.[52]

4.43 Grundig and Consten appealed against that decision to the European Court. The Court substantially endorsed the Commission's conclusions. It

---

[50] *Etablissements Consten SA* [1966] C.M.L.R. 418 at p. 476.
[51] The "GINT" mark owned by Grundig was the subject of an international registration under the Madrid Agreement, see, *supra*, Chap. 1, n. 10a.
[52] *Re the Agreement of Grundig Verkaufs GmbH* [1964] C.M.L.R. 489.

held that Article 85 (1) is infringed by an agreement imposing on a distributor an obligation not to make deliveries outside its allotted territory, and on the manufacturer an obligation not to supply in that territory, at least when combined with the grant to the distributor of trade mark rights intended to ensure absolute territorial protection for the distributor. The Court also upheld the Commission's refusal to grant an exemption under Article 85 (3), and its injunction against the use by Consten of national intellectual property to prevent "parallel imports" from Germany.[53]

4.44   With the benefit of hindsight, it is hard to believe that one of the contentions advanced before the Court in an attempt to have the Commission's decision annulled, was that the Commission had improperly restricted its analysis *solely* to Grundig products, and that a restriction on competition within the meaning of Article 85 (1) could exist only where there is a restriction between different brands of similar products. Not surprisingly, the Court rejected this narrow interpretation of a restriction on competition.[54]

4.45   More directly relevant for present purposes, the Court also declined to condemn the Commission for failing to carry out a factual analysis of the effect of the Grundig/Consten agreement on competition in the relevant product market generally (*i.e.* the market for radios, televisions and the like), in the light of the clear restriction on competition contained in the Grundig/Consten agreement. No such broader analysis was necessary, in the Court's view, because once it is clear that an agreement has the object of restricting competition, it is unnecessary to enquire further into its effect.[55] This assertion, while in broad principle correct, requires two qualifications. First, and as will be seen below, an agreement will only be caught by Article 85 (1) if it prevents, restricts or distorts competition within the Common Market to an appreciable extent. Second, an agreement will not infringe Article 85 (1) unless it may actually or potentially affect trade between Member States, again to an "appreciable" extent.[56]

(c) The nature of a prevention, restriction or distortion of competition

4.46   It is not proposed now to discuss in any detail the type of provision which will constitute a prevention, restriction or distortion of competition within the meaning of Article 85 (1) if only because much of the remainder of this book will be concerned with a detailed analysis of just such "restrictions." This being the case, it is enough to note the non-exclusive list of examples of such restrictions which is contained in Article 85 (1) itself. From this, it is apparent that many agreements involving intellectual property will poten-

---

[53] *Etablissements Consten SA* [1966] C.M.L.R. 418 at p. 476.
[54] *Ibid.* at p. 473.
[55] *Ibid.* at p. 473; see also, *inter alia, A. Bullock & Co.* v. *The Distillers Co. Ltd.* [1978] 1 C.M.L.R. 400 at p. 418.
[56] This leg of Art. 85 (1) is discussed below at paras. 4.59 *et seq.*

tially infringe Article 85 (1). It must, however, be borne in mind that the list is illustrative only, and that neither the Commission nor the Court will feel in any way constrained in considering a provision in an agreement which infringes Article 85 (1) merely because it is not referred to in the text.[57]

(d) The restriction must be appreciable

(i) *General*

4.47   Assuming now the existence of a provision which prevents, restricts or distorts competition, the effect must be "appreciable" in order to be caught by Article 85 (1).[58] In other words, there will be no infringement of Article 85 (1), even though competition is prevented, restricted or distorted, if it is *de minimis* in the context of the relevant geographical and product market.[59]

4.48   This said, in assessing whether the effects on competition are appreciable, an agreement cannot be isolated from its economic context. In the words of the European Court:

"Article 85 (1) implies that it is necessary to observe those effects in the context in which they occur, i.e. in the economic and legal context in which such agreements, decisions or practices are to be found or where they might together with others amount to a cumulative effect on competition ...

To judge whether it is hit by Article 85 (1), a contract can thus not be isolated from that context, i.e. from the factual or legal circumstances resulting in its having the effect of preventing, restricting or distorting competition. With regard to that objective, the existence of similar contracts can be taken into account insofar as all the contracts of that type as a whole are such as to restrict the freedom of trade."[60]

---

[57] For example, as pointed out in Chap. 1 at para. 1.16, it is now well established that a provision in a patent licence prohibiting the licensee from challenging the validity of the relevant patent will normally infringe Art. 85 (1). See, *e.g. Re Agreement of Davidson-Rubber* [1972] C.M.L.R. D. 52; *Re Association des Ouvriers en Instruments de Précision* [1976] 1 C.M.L.R.D. 14 at D. 23; *Re the Agreement between Kabel-und Metallwerke Neumeyer AG and Les Etablissements Luchaire SA* [1975] 2 C.M.L.R. D. 40 at D. 43.

[58] Case 5/69 *Franz Völk* v. *Ets. Vervaecke S.P.R.L.* [1969] E.C.R. 295; [1969] C.M.L.R. 273, where a share of between 0.2 per cent. and 0.05 per cent. of the German washing machine market was regarded as so insignificant as to fall outside the ambit of Art. 85 (1). Note by contrast, *e.g. Re Floral Verkaufsgesellschaft* [1979] 2 C.M.L.R. 285.

[59] *Ibid.* See also *LTM* [1966] C.M.L.R. 357 at pp. 376 *et seq.*; the *Agreement of Johs Rieckerman KG and AEG-Elothern GmbH* [1968] C.M.L.R. D. 78; *Re Cement Makers' Agreement* [1969] C.M.L.R. D. 15; *Re the Société Anonyme de Fabricants de Conserves Alimentaires* [1972] C.M.L.R. D. 843. As to the importance of determining the relevant geographical and product market see, *inter alia, Kali und Salz AG and Kali-Chemie AG* v. *EC Commission* [1975] E.C.R. 499; [1975] 2 C.M.L.R. 154 at p. 171. See also in this connection *Miller International Schallplatten GmbH* v. *EC Commission* [1978] E.C.R. 131; [1978] 2 C.M.L.R. 334 at pp. 351 and 352.

[60] *Brasserie de Haecht SA* v. *Wilkin* (*No.* 1) [1967] E.C.R. 407; [1968] C.M.L.R. 26 at p. 40.

4.49   It follows that in an appropriate case a network of identical agreements may be regarded as constituting an appreciable restriction on competition even though each would, in isolation, be insignificant.[61]

4.50   The Commission has issued certain guidelines as to the circumstances in which it will treat an agreement as being insignificant, most recently in the form of its Notice Concerning Agreements of Minor Importance of December 19, 1977. This Notice will be considered in detail below as it is concerned with the *de minimis* rule both in the context of an appreciable restriction on competition and in the context of an appreciable effect on trade between Member States.[62] The Notice aside, limited guidance can be obtained from decided cases concerning the circumstances in which particular restrictions will be considered as appreciable.

(ii) *The importance of factual analysis*

4.51   Great care must, however, be taken to consider each decision carefully, having particular regard to its facts. The importance of a careful factual analysis is well illustrated by an example concerned with manufacturing exclusivity in patent licences.

4.52   The tone of two 1975 decisions[63] arguably suggested that an exclusive patent licence constituted a *per se* infringement of Article 85 (1), which therefore required to be notified to the Commission in the hope of an exemption being granted pursuant to Article 85 (3). The Commission expressly took issue with this interpretation in its Fifth Report on Competition Policy, stating with reference to its decisions on patent licences:

> "One comment has been that the Commission regards some clauses in patent licences as *per se* infringements of Article 85 (1) of the E.E.C. Treaty. This is not so. The facts of each case have to be examined before it can be decided whether Article 85 (1) has been infringed. The terms of the Article must be satisfied in each case. These in turn require the consideration of such features as the economic power of the parties, the nature of the market or business in which they are engaged, their share of the market, the number of competitors and the significance of the licensed invention or know-how."[64]

4.53   The Commission's declared position is, then, that there is no such thing as a *per se* violation of Article 85 (1), and that each case must be examined on its merits. This is no doubt the case. It is, however, a mixed blessing. It

---

[61] *Ibid.* In *Brasserie de Haecht*, the European Court was in fact required to consider whether a tied or "solus" brewery agreement could infringe Art. 85 (1); but see also *Esso Petroleum Co. Ltd.* v. *Kingswood Motors (Addlestone) Ltd.* [1973] C.M.L.R. 665.

[62] See *infra*, at para. 4.66.

[63] *Re Kabelmetal Agreement*, [1975] 2 C.M.L.R. D. 40; *Re Association des Ouvriers en Instruments de Précision*, [1976] 1 C.M.L.R. D. 14, discussed *infra*, at Chap. 11, n. 25.

[64] Fifth Rep. on Competition Policy, p. 22 at para. 10.

means, in effect, that until the case law of the Community is much more developed than it is at present, it will be imprudent to conclude that a restriction on competition is not appreciable, in circumstances in which the agreement in question is not covered by the Commission's Notice Concerning Agreements of Minor Importance, unless there is available a decided case warranting such a conclusion.

4.54   For example, while a given market share may not justify a finding of an appreciable restriction of competition simply by virtue of the grant of an exclusive manufacturing licence, a similar market share might in fact justify such a finding if the restriction in question were, say, an exclusive sales licence or a ban on exports.[65]

4. *"Within the Common Market"*

4.55   By its terms, Article 85 (1) only applies to agreements, decisions or concerted practices having the object or effect of preventing, restricting or distorting competition "within the Common Market." It follows that an agreement clearly restrictive of competition will not infringe Article 85 (1) if it is neither intended to restrict competition within the EEC nor in fact does so.

4.56   For example, a patent licence under which a French undertaking, Raymond, granted a Japanese company, Nagoya, exclusive manufacturing rights in respect of Japan and exclusive sales rights in respect of that country and certain other parts of the Far East, was held not to infringe Article 85 (1), even though the agreement included among its terms an implied prohibition on sales outside the exclusive territory and an obligation on the Japanese company not to challenge the validity of the licensor's patents.[66] It should be stressed, however, that neither the nationality of the parties to an agreement nor the territory which is the subject of that agreement are in themselves determinative on the question of whether Article 85 (1) is infringed. The sole consideration is whether there is present either the object or the effect of preventing, restricting or distorting competition within the EEC. Thus, in reaching the conclusion that the licence granted by Raymond to Nagoya did not infringe Article 85 (1), the Commission took into account the nature of the products in question, namely, plastic attachment car components such as rag buttons, door attachment fittings and the like, and the fact that these were not standardised products but suitable only for use in the particular model for which they were intended. Having regard to these and other factors, it concluded, with particular reference to the export prohibition, that "... by reason particularly of the characteristics of the products in question, the prohibi-

---

[65] See the discussion of respectively exclusivity and export bans *infra*, Chap. 11, respectively at paras. 11.11 *et seq.* and 11.45 *et seq.*
[66] *The Agreement of A. Raymond & Co.* [1972] C.M.L.R. D. 45.

tion on Nagoya exporting these articles to the Member States of the EEC cannot have a noticeable effect on the competition within the Common Market."[67]

4.57 More recently, the Commission has re-emphasised that where there is an anti-competitive effect within the EEC, albeit indirect, Article 85 (1) will apply notwithstanding that the restriction does not, by its terms, operate within the Community. In considering whether an export prohibition on sales of Junghans clocks and watches outside the EEC was caught by Article 85 (1), it stated:

> "This prohibition has no appreciable effects on competition within the Common Market and trade between Member States. Owing to the double duty borne by goods twice crossing the customs frontiers of the European Communities, there is no incentive for Junghans dealers and consumers in the Community to buy goods exported by the Junghans Dealer to a non-member country.

> However, while at present the Commission sees no reason to object to this export prohibition, this will not necessarily be the case after 1st July, 1977, as regards those States with which the E.E.C. has a free trade agreement. After that date there will be no customs duties on trade between the Community and the countries in question."[68]

4.58 No case decided since July 1, 1977, has required a decision on the effect of the abolition of customs duties on a restrictive provision prima facie operating directly only outside the EEC.[69] There can be no doubt, however, that the so called "effects" doctrine is now well established, and that a restrictive effect within the EEC will satisfy Article 85 (1), even if the restriction in question does not directly operate within the Community. Whether there is such a restrictive effect within the EEC will depend, as always, on the facts of the particular case.

D. POTENTIAL EFFECT UPON TRADE BETWEEN MEMBER STATES

(1) General

4.59 For an agreement, decision or concerted practice to infringe Article 85 (1) it must be established that it "... may affect trade between Member States."[70] Thus, there must be at least a *potential* effect on trade between at

---

[67] *Ibid.* D. 50.

[68] [1977] 1 C.M.L.R. D. 82 at D. 91; see also *Re Omega Watches* [1970] C.M.L.R. D. 49 at D. 56; *Re Kabelmetal's Agreement* [1975] 2 C.M.L.R. D. 40 at D. 46.

[69] See generally March Hunnings, "Enforceability of the EEC-EFTA Free Trade Agreements" [1977] 2 E.L. Rev.; Waelbroeck, "Enforceability of the EEC-EFTA Free Trade Agreements; A Reply" [1978] 3 E.L. Rev.; March Hunnings, "Enforceability of the EEC-EFTA Free Trade Agreements; A Rejoinder" [1978] 3 E.L. Rev.

[70] See *supra*, paras. 4.35 *et seq.*

least two Member States.[71] The critical word is, however, "may." There is no necessity that trade between Member States actually be affected, provided it can be shown that the possibility exists. Thus, in its *Technique Minière* judgment, the European Court concluded that the agreement between LTM and Maschinenbau Ulm would meet this criterion if:

"... considered on the basis of a series of objective legal or factual elements, the agreement is such as to lead to a reasonable expectation that it may be able to exercise an influence, whether direct or indirect, actual or potential, on trade between Member States capable of hindering the realisation of a single market among the said States."[72]

4.60   Moreover, it is immaterial that an agreement may affect trade between Member States beneficially in the sense of producing an increase in such trade; the question is rather whether it may hinder the realisation of a single market within the Community.[73] This said, if an agreement contains a restriction on competition within the meaning of Article 85 (1), any effect on trade between Member States which it may have can hardly fail to be in a direction capable of hindering the attainment of a single market. Certainly, this has proved the case in all decided cases to date.

(2) *Effect on Trade Between Member States must be "Appreciable"*

4.61   In order for Article 85 (1) to apply, the effect on trade between Member States, whether actual or potential, must be "appreciable."[74] Further, there is no requirement that there be a proven effect on trade between Member States, provided it can be shown that there is an appreciable *potential* effect on such trade.[75] An agreement may satisfy the requirement of a potential effect on trade between the Member States, even though, by its terms, it has no inter-community aspect. Provided such an effect is established, it is

---

[71] *Tepea BV* v. *EC Commission* [1978] E.C.R. 391; [1978] 3 C.M.L.R. 392.

[72] *LTM* [1966] C.M.L.R. 357 at p. 375 (the facts of this case are set out at para. 4.37 above); see also *Franz Volk* [1966] C.M.L.R. 273 at p. 282; *Etablissements Consten SA and Grundig-Verkaufs GmbH* v. *EC Commission* [1966] E.C.R. 299; [1966] C.M.L.R. 418 at p. 472.

[73] *Etablissements Consten SA*, *ibid*.

[74] *Beguelin Import Co.* v. *G.L. Import Export SA and Others* [1971] E.C.R. 949; [1972] C.M.L.R. 81 at p. 96; *Re the Agreement of Grundig Verkaufs-GmbH* [1964] C.M.L.R. 489, at p. 497; *Wilks* v. *Theal NV & Watts* [1977] 1 C.M.L.R. D. 44; Note also Commission Notice of December 19, 1977 Concerning Agreements of Minor Importance which do not fall under Art. 85 (1) of the Treaty establishing the European Economic Community (O.J. 1977, C313/3) in which it is stated:

"In the Commission's opinion, agreements, whose effects on trade between Member States and on competition are negligible do not fall within the prohibition on restrictive agreements in Article 85 (1) of the E.E.C. Treaty. Only those agreements are prohibited which have an appreciable impact on market conditions, in that they appreciably alter the market position."

This notice is discussed, *infra*, at paras. 4.66 *et seq*.

[75] *Miller International Schallplatten* v. *EC Commission* [1978] E.C.R. 131; [1978] 2 C.M.L.R. 334 at p. 353.

immaterial that trade between Member States actually increases during the relevant period.[75a]

The Bronbemaling case[76]

4.62   A case in point was the *Bronbemaling* case concerned exclusively with Dutch patent licences. In 1967 a Dutch Company lodged two patent applications in respect of a process for the installation of a wellpoint drainage system. Three Dutch concerns lodged opposition to the grant of the patents, and they were supported by two other Dutch concerns. The opposition proceedings were eventually settled, on the basis of an agreement under which each of the opposing undertakings withdrew their opposition in return for the grant of a licence by the applicant. Each of the five licences contained an undertaking that the Licensor would not grant licences in respect of the process in question to any other Dutch firm, without the consent of the majority of the parties involved in the opposition proceedings. On this basis the opposition proceedings were duly withdrawn, and the patents granted. Some years later, two further Dutch firms applied for licences under the relevant patents, and were refused following consultation between all the parties to the original proceedings. One of the disappointed applicants then instituted proceedings before the Dutch Courts in reliance upon Article 85, following which the original licensing agreements were notified to the Commission.

4.63   Not surprisingly, the Commission found that the undertaking in each licence regarding the grant of further licences was a restriction on competition within the meaning of Article 85 (1). Turning to the question of whether there was a sufficient actual or potential effect on trade between Member States, the Commission reasoned that the agreements

"... may affect trade between Member States in that they restrict the availability of horizontal drainage in Holland, thus preventing the process being used in work extending beyond Dutch Frontiers. The process is capital intensive and is consequently used only in major projects. The restriction is therefore appreciable."[77-78]

4.64   It is clear, therefore, that there are no hard and fast rules as to the circumstances in which an agreement may be said to satisfy the requirement of an "affect on trade between Member States." If the agreement cannot be regarded as insignificant in the light of the Commission's Notice Concerning Agreements of Minor Importance, which will be discussed next, there is no alternative but to explore the existing case law in the hope that a decided case will be relevant to the particular facts.

[75a] *Re German Ceramic Tiles* [1971] C.M.L.R. D. 6.
[76] *Zuid-Nederlandsche Bronbemaling en Grondboringen BV* v. *Heidemaatschappij Beheer NV* [1975] 2 C.M.L.R. D. 67.
[77-78] *Ibid.* at pp. D. 70–71.

[*The next paragraph is 4.66*]

E. THE COMMISSION'S NOTICE CONCERNING AGREEMENTS OF MINOR IMPORTANCE

(1) *General*

4.66 On December 19, 1977, the Commission published its second and present Notice Concerning Agreements of Minor Importance,[79] in which it sought to lay down guidelines which would, in many cases, enable undertakings to decide whether an agreement is *de minimis* and thus escapes the prohibition in Article 85 (1).

4.67 In particular, the Notice applies by its terms to "... undertakings engaged in the production or distribution of goods."[79] This wording suggests that the Notice applies only to agreements concerning goods as distinct from services.[80] There would, however, seem little reason in principle to make this distinction, given that Article 85 applies to both goods and services.[81] Indeed, it may well be that the guidelines set out in the Notice are of some relevance in the context of services as well as in that of goods.

4.68 Interestingly enough, the Notice does not lay down separate criteria for assessing whether "the restriction on competition" and "the effect on trade between the Member States" referred to in Article 85 (1) are appreciable. Rather, it lays down a single quantitative yardstick, in the following terms:

"II. The Commission holds the view that agreements between undertakings engaged in the production or distribution of goods do not fall under the prohibition of Article 85 (1) of the E.E.C. Treaty if:

—the products which are the subject of the agreement and other products of the participating undertakings considered by consumers to be similar by reason of their characteristics, price or use do not represent in a substantial part[82] of the Common Market more than 5% of the total market for such products, *and*[83] the aggregate annual turnover of the participating undertakings does not exceed 50 million units of account."[84]

---

[79] Commission Notice of December 19, 1977, *supra*, n. 74.

[80] See, *inter alia*, Barouncs Hall & James, *EEC Anti-Trust Law* (Butterworths, 1975) at p. 77.

[81] As to the application of Art. 85 to both goods and services, see, *e.g. Re Unitel* [1978] 3 C.M.L.R. 306.

[82] The phrase "substantial part" of the Common Market appears in Art. 86 of the Treaty and is discussed, *infra*, Chap. 5, at paras. 5.26 *et seq.*

[83] Authors' italics.

[84] Commission Notice of December 19, 1977, *supra*, n. 79. In the context of the competition provisions of the Treaty, a unit of account ("u.a.") refers to the European Unit of Account ("E.U.A."). The rate of exchange of the E.U.A. fluctuates daily, and is published in each edition of the Official Journal of the European Communities. On January 3, 1981, one E.U.A. was equal to £0.545668.

4.69   It should be noted that in order for an agreement to come within the terms of the Notice, it must meet *both* of these criteria. This said, an agreement will continue to be regarded as "minor," even if it exceeds either the specified turnover or the specified market share by up to 10 per cent. in two successive financial years.[84]

(2) *Undertakings*

4.70   Unfortunately, in practice the Notice all too often proves of little practical assistance. The reason for this is simply that the term "undertakings," is defined by the Notice extremely broadly so as to include the corporate groups to which the parties to an agreement belong. Indeed, brief reference to Part II of the Notice will confirm that "undertakings" for purposes of the Notice, includes not only parent and subsidiary companies, but also a variety of associated companies which might not normally be regarded as within a corporate group.[84a] The effect of this broad definition is that the criteria of turnover and/or market share are frequently not met, despite initial appearances to the contrary.

(3) *Aggregate Turnover*

4.71   In addition, in the context of the turnover criterion, it should be noted that "aggregate turnover" is defined so as to include "turnover" in all goods and services achieved during the last financial year by the participating undertakings,"[84] and not merely in the goods covered by the agreement in question. Inter-group trading is, however, excluded.[84]

(4) *General Guidance Only*

4.72   Finally, with regard to the Notice, it must be borne in mind that this is intended to provide general guidance only, and that it does not enjoy the status of "law." It is expressly stated to be ". . . without prejudice to any interpretation which may be given by the Court of Justice of the European Communities."[84]

4.73   In spite of its shortcomings, however, the Notice provides invaluable guidance to the practitioner in deciding whether or not Article 85 (1) applies, and its terms require to be kept very much in mind. It is, in effect, a sort of unofficial "block negative clearance."[85]

If the Notice does not apply, perhaps all that can be said by way of general guidance is that if the agreement, decision or concerted practice in

---

[84a] See *Putz* v. *Kawasaki* [1979] C.M.L.R. 448.
[85] As to nature of a "negative clearance" see paras. 4.07 *et seq.* and 4.101 *et seq.*

question is sufficiently insignificant in its effect upon the market, it will escape the prohibition contained in Article 85 (1).[86]

III. *ARTICLE 85 (2)—THE VALIDITY OF AN INFRINGING AGREEMENT*

A. GENERAL

4.74 As has previously been mentioned,[87] when an agreement infringes Article 85 (1) there are in principle two consequences. First, with the exception of a small class of agreements which benefit from so called "provisional validity" (discussed below), the infringing provisions will be "automatically void," which may, in turn, result in the agreement as a whole proving unenforceable. Second, the Commission has power to impose very substantial fines in respect of infringing agreements, decisions or concerted practices unless these have been duly "notified." This second consequence of infringement will be discussed in the context of "notification," in the next part of this chapter.

4.75 The concern here is with the consequences of infringement in terms of validity. It is convenient to consider first the position in terms of Community law, then the position as a matter of national law and, finally, the position with regard to a small category of agreements, decisions and concerted practices benefiting from so-called "provisional validity," a term explained below.

B. ARTICLE 85 (2)—THE PRINCIPLE OF INVALIDITY

4.76 Article 85 (2) states, quite simply, that: "Any agreements or decisions prohibited pursuant to this Article shall be automatically void."

4.77 As early as 1966, the European Court laid down that only those provisions in an agreement which infringe Article 85 (1) will be automatically void, and not the agreement as a whole unless, of course, the whole agreement infringes.[88] The point is of sufficient importance to repeat here the relevant passage from the Court's judgment in the *LTM* case. With reference to Article 85 (2), the Court said:

---

[86] *Franz Völk* v. *Ets. Vervaecke* [1969] E.C.R. 295; [1969] C.M.L.R. 273 at p. 282. Note also, however, *The Distillers Company Ltd.* v. *EC Commission* [1980] 3 C.M.L.R. 121, in which the European Court held that the "de minimis" rule did not apply to a product manufactured by a large undertaking, being responsible for the entire production of that product even if only minimal export sales are involved. The product in issue was Pimms.

[87] See *supra*, para. 4.05 (and note also n. 5).

[88] *LTM* v. *Maschinenbau Ulm, GmbH* [1966] C.M.L.R. 357 at p. 376; see also *Etablissements Consten SA and Grundig-Verkaufs* v. *EC Commission* [1966] E.C.R. 299; [1966] C.M.L.R. 418 at p. 475.

"This provision, which is aimed at ensuring respect of the Treaty, may only be interpreted in the light of its finality within the Community and should be limited to that context. The automatic nullity in question applies only to those elements of the agreement which are subject to the prohibition, or to the agreement as a whole, if those elements do not appear severable from the agreement itself. Consequently, all other contractual provisions which are not affected by the prohibition, since they do not involve the application of the Treaty, fall outside the Community law."[89]

4.78   It follows that where an agreement contains elements which infringe Article 85 (1), "automatic nullity" will apply only to those elements.

4.79   The construction and, indeed, validity of the remainder of the agreement must, therefore, be determined by the application of the relevant principles of domestic law. For example, automatic nullity might apply to a clause granting an exclusive patent licence to the extent that it grants exclusivity. It would then remain to be determined, as a matter of national law, whether the clause in question could be so construed as to survive on a non-exclusive basis and, whatever the answer to that question, whether in consequence the remainder of the agreement could survive.

C. ARTICLE 85 (2) AND RELEVANT PRINCIPLES OF ENGLISH LAW

4.80   The *Chemidus Wavin* case[90] is the leading case in English law to date on agreements containing elements which infringe Article 85 (1) and the extent to which they must, therefore, be regarded as automatically void. In April 1976 Chemidus Wavin Ltd., an English company, obtained judgment in respect of unpaid royalties due to it under a licensing agreement which it had entered into with the French defendant in 1969. After considerable delay, the defendant applied to have the judgment set aside on the basis that the licensing agreement in question, or at any rate the relevant clause in that agreement, infringed Article 85 (1). The minimum royalty clause was in fact regarded as not infringing Article 85 (1), both at first instance and before the Court of Appeal.

4.81   The judgments are, however, principally of interest on the general question of severance. In the High Court, Mr. Justice Walton had this to say:

"... Just as in any other agreement containing a number of provisions, which according to English law are unenforceable, one would have to look at what remains of the agreement after those unenforceable provisions have been struck out and then see whether on one

---

[89] *La Technique Minière*, *ibid.*
[90] *Chemidus Wavin Ltd.* v. *Société pour la Transformation et l'Exportation des Resines Industrialles SA* [1976] 2 C.M.L.R. 387, affirmed in [1978] 3 C.M.L.R. 514 (C.A.).

side or the other there was a total failure of consideration. . . . if there was a total failure of consideration, then the usual results would follow, but, in my judgment, there is no question of the application of a blue pencil test or anything of that nature.

In my view, the blue pencil test is strictly applicable and applicable only to covenants in restraint of trade where valid and invalid restrictions are merged together in the same clause and it is then sometimes possible, by striking out the invalid ones, to be left with a valid clause at the end of the day, but I do not think that this is how Article 85 works. It makes certain provisions invalid or unenforceable and one has to take what remains of the agreement after one has taken out those unenforceable provisions."[91]

4.82   The same point was considered when the case came before the Court of Appeal. Admittedly, Lord Justice Buckley did not decide on the precise way in which the law must be applied to an agreement containing clauses which infringe Article 85 (1). After reviewing the European Court's judgment in the *LTM* case, however, he concluded:

"So, the position appears clearly to be this, that when in a contract there are certain clauses which are annulled by reason of their being in contravention of Article 85, paragraph (1), of the Treaty, one must look at the contract with those clauses struck out and see what the effect of that is in the light of the domestic law which governs the particular contract . . . Whether it is right to regard the matter as one of severance of the contract or not, I do not think it necessary for us to consider now. I doubt whether it is really a question of severance in the sense in which we in these Courts are accustomed to use that term in considering whether covenants contained in contracts of employment and so forth are void as being in restraint of trade, and, if they are to any extent void, whether those covenants can be severed so as to save part of the covenant, although another part may be bad . . . In applying Article 85 . . . one may well have to consider whether, after the excisions required by the Article of the Treaty had been made from the contract, the contract could be said to fail for lack of consideration or on any other ground, or whether the contract would be so changed in its character as not to be the sort of contract that the parties intended to enter into at all."[92]

4.83   It is considered that as a matter of English law this correctly sets out the position. Thus, and while doubts exist as to whether a blue pencil test could be applied to a particular clause which is considered to infringe Article 85 (1), it is clear that an English Court would not be prepared to give effect to an agreement which could be said to have failed for lack of consideration

---

[91] *Ibid.* at p. 389.
[92] *Chemidus Wavin* (C.A.) [1978] 3 C.M.L.R. 514 at pp. 519–520.

or on any other ground. Similarly, it is unlikely that it would be prepared to save an agreement by construing it in such a way as to produce a different bargain from that which the parties had originally entered into.

4.84   Thus, and to revert to the hypothetical example mentioned above,[93] given a simple agreement granting an exclusive patent licence in respect of a particular territory and assuming that the exclusivity in question infringes Article 85 (1), there must be strong doubts whether an English Court would be prepared to uphold the agreement as conferring a valid non-exclusive licence. Of course, a great deal would depend upon the facts of the case, but it is evident that an English Court would have great difficulty upholding such a construction, at least in circumstances in which the licensee's continuing obligations appeared more appropriate to an exclusive licensee than to a non-exclusive licensee.[94]

D. PROVISIONAL VALIDITY

1. *General*

4.85   Provisional validity is inextricably bound up with Regulation 17. That Regulation distinguishes for various purposes[95] between agreements, decisions and concerted practices which were in existence at the time the Regulation came into force on March 13, 1962, and all other agreements, decisions and concerted practices.[96] The former are generally referred to as "old" agreements, and the latter as "new" agreements.

4.86   To complicate matters further, it must be borne in mind that there are two distinct types of "old" agreements, namely: old agreements requiring to be notified to the Commission in accordance with Article 5 (1) of Regulation 17, and "old" agreements not requiring to be so notified by virtue of Article 5 (2) of that Regulation, because they fall within the terms of Article 4 (2) of the Regulation.

4.87   One further classification must be mentioned. On the accession of Denmark, Ireland and the United Kingdom to the EEC on January 1, 1973, Regulation 17 was amended so as to ensure that agreements, decisions and concerted practices which had been in existence prior to the accession of those Member States and which only infringed Article 85 (1) *by virtue* of accession were given broadly analogous treatment to that which had earlier been afforded "old" agreements. Regulation 17 was further correspondingly amended on the accession of Greece to the EEC on

---

[93] *Supra*, at para. 4.79.
[94] See also Bellamy and Child, *Common Market Law of Competition* (2nd ed. 1978) at pp. 105–106, where a similar view is taken.
[95] See discussion *infra*, Pt. IV of this Chap. at paras. 4.107 *et seq.*
[96] *e.g.* contrast Arts. 4 and 6 of Reg. 17/62 with Arts. 5 and 7 of that Reg.

January 1, 1981.[97] Such agreements have, in turn, come to be referred to collectively as "accession" agreements.

4.88   Provisional validity is a concept which has its origins in the differing treatment accorded by Regulation 17 to "old" and "new" agreements, and which has been developed by the European Court to rationalise and to give effect to these differences. It applies, broadly, to both types of "old" agreements mentioned above and, therefore, by analogy, to "accession" agreements. As the phrase "provisional validity" suggests, it confers upon these categories of agreements a temporary validity pending a contrary indication by the Commission. This is a reversal of the usual position, namely that an agreement which infringes Article 85 (1) is "automatically void" by virtue of Article 85 (2), unless and until it is exempted by the Commission pursuant to Article 85 (3).

4.89   It is convenient to discuss separately the application of provisional validity to "old" agreements and "accession" agreements.

2. Provisional Validity and "Old" Agreements

4.90   Provisional validity has been applied by the European Court on various occasions[98] to "old" agreements generally, *i.e.* to agreements entered into before March 13, 1962, and infringing Article 85 (1). The Court's landmark decision was its judgment in the second *Brasserie de Haecht* case, in 1973.[99]

The second Brasserie de Haecht case

4.91   The agreements with which the Court was concerned in the second *Brasserie de Haecht* case were entered into in 1963. They were not, therefore, "old" agreements in existence at the date of entry into force of Regulation 17 at all, but rather "new" agreements which had been notified. In considering the possibility that such "new" agreements might be provisionally valid until such time as the Commission reached a contrary

---

[97] The relevant provisions are Art. 25 (1)–(4) in the cases of Denmark, Ireland and the U.K., and Art. 25 (5) in the case of Greece. Art. 25 (1)–(4) was added to the original Regulation by the Treaty of Accession, Brussels, January 22, 1972. See the Act concerning the Conditions of Accession and the Adjustments to the Treaties, Art. 29 and Annex I there referred to. Art. 25 (5) was added by the Treaty concerning the Accession of the Hellenic Republic to the European Economic Community, the European Atomic Energy Community, May 28, 1979. See Act concerning the conditions of accession of the Hellenic Republic and the adjustments to the Treaties, Art. 21 and Annex I there referred to.

[98] *Robert Bosch GmbH and Another* v. *Kleding-Verkoopbedrigf* [1962] E.C.R. 45; [1962] 1 C.M.L.R. 1; *Portelange SA* v. *Smith-Corona Marchant International* [1969] E.C.R. 309; [1974] 1 C.M.L.R. 397; *Brauerei A. Bilger Sohne GmbH* v. *Jehle & Another* [1974] 1 C.M.L.R. 382; *Brasserie de Haecht* v. *Wilkin (No. 2)* [1973] E.C.R. 77; [1973] C.M.L.R. 287; *Ets. A. de Bloos* v. *Bouyer S.C.A.* [1977] 1 C.M.L.R. 60. *Note:* Both the *Bosch* and *Bilger* judgments must now be considered as partially overruled and, in consequence, no longer being good law.

[99] *Brasserie de Haecht, supra.*

decision, the Court reviewed the concept of provisional validity generally. It first emphasised that Regulation 17 distinguishes for certain purposes between agreements in existence at the time that Regulation 17 came into force on March 13, 1962, and agreements entered into thereafter. It then went on to conclude that in considering the effect of Article 85 (2) in rendering null and void agreements which contravene Article 85 (1), it is necessary to continue to distinguish between such "old" and "new" agreements. The Court then declared:

> "As far as old agreements are concerned, certainty of law as regards contracts requires that a court cannot, particularly when an agreement has been notified in accordance with Regulation 17, establish nullity until after the Commission has made a decision under this regulation.
>
> As far as new agreements are concerned, it follows from the regulation, on the assumption that so long as the Commission has made no pronouncement the agreement can only be operated at the risk of the parties, that notifications under Article 4 (1) of Regulation 17 are without suspensory effect."[1]

4.92   The Court thus referred, particularly, to "old" agreements which had been duly notified in accordance with Regulation 17, as distinct from "old" agreements which had not been so notified, *i.e.* "old" agreements falling within the terms of article 4 (2) of Regulation 17 and, therefore, not requiring to be notified, by virtue of article 5 (2), even if they are caught by Article 85 (1).

4.93   It is submitted, however, that the Court's decision in the *Brasserie de Haecht* case applies with equal force both to "old" agreements which have been duly notified in accordance with article 5 (1) of Regulation 17 and to "old" agreements not notified because they come within the ambit of Article 5 (2), so that both categories must be regarded as valid and effective unless and until the Commission declares to the contrary. Further, a national court may not pre-empt the Decision of the Commission by itself deciding on the validity of an "old" agreement.[2]

4.93.1   The language used by the Court in its judgment in the second *Brasserie de Haecht* case suggested that provisional validity would attach to "old" agreements until the Commission rendered a formal "decision" to the contrary, in accordance with the requirements of Regulation 17. In the *S.A. Lancome and Cospar France* case,[2a] however, the Court held that such provisional validity will be terminated by the Commission writing a letter to the party that notified the agreement, stating that it is proposing to close its file on the case without taking any formal action pursuant to Article 85 (1).

---

[1] *Ibid.* at p. 302.
[2] See also *Ets. A. de Bloos* v. *Bouyer S.C.A.* [1977] 1 C.M.L.R. 60, at p. 529.
[2a] Case 99/79 *SA Lancome and Cospar France Nederland BV* v. *Etos BV and Albert Hein Supermart BV* (unreported).

The Court held further that such a letter is not a "decision" but merely an "administrative act," and that, following despatch of such a letter, a national court is free to consider the relevant agreement in the context of Article 85 (1), though in so doing it may take the Commission's letter into account as a fact.[2b]

4.93.2   Thus, the Court has further undermined the importance of the concept of provisional validity, by establishing that the Commission may bring this to an end by the relatively simple expedient of dispatching a letter indicating that it does not intend to pursue a notification through to a definitive conclusion, but rather simply proposes to regard its file on the notification in question as "closed" or, more colloquially, as "dead." In practice, however, parties to an agreement losing the benefit of provisional validity in such circumstances may find the loss of theoretical rather than practical concern. It is true that a national court will following dispatch of such a letter be entitled to consider whether the agreement infringes Article 85 (1), whereas for so long as the agreement remained provisionally valid the national court would not have been so entitled. The national court will, however, have before it a letter from the Commission indicating that in its view action pursuant to Article 85 (1) is not required with regard to the agreement in question. As the Court said in its judgment in the *Lancome and Cospar France* case:

> "The opinions expressed in such a letter are not binding on the national courts but constitute a factor which the latter may take into account in examining whether the agreements are in accordance with the provisions of Article 85."[2c]

This being the case, and in the absence of additional facts not available to the Commission when it wrote its letter, the national courts might well be reluctant to conclude that Article 85 (1) is infringed by a particular agreement when that same question has already been considered by the Commission, however informally, and been found by that body not to infringe Article 85 (1).

3. *Provisional Validity and "Accession" Agreements*

4.94   As already indicated,[3] a new article, article 25, was added to Regulation 17 to cover agreements to which Article 85 of the Treaty applied by virtue of the accession of the new Member States in 1973. Article 25 was in turn amended to cover agreements to which Article 85 of the Treaty applied by

---

[2b] *Ibid.* at paras. 10 to 17. See also Cases 253/78 and 1–3/79 *Procureur de la République* v. *Guerlain SA, Procureur de la République* v. *Parfums Rochas* v. *Lanvin Parfums SA and* v. *Nina Ricci*, July 10, 1980 (unreported); Case 37/79 *Anne Marty SA (Paris)* v. *Estée Lauder SA (Paris)* (unreported).

[2c] *Ibid.* at para. 18.

[3] See *supra* at para. 4.87.

virtue of the accession of Greece in 1981. While the language of article 25 is technical, its purpose and effect is to confer upon agreements, Decisions and Concerted Practices "... existing at the date of accession to which Article 85 of the Treaty applies by virtue of accession" the same privileges as were originally granted by Regulation 17 to "old" agreements.

4.95   The European Court has not yet had occasion to consider the application of provisional validity to "accession" agreements. It would, however, appear to follow that provided such agreements were duly notified within six months from the date of accession of the new Member States (*i.e.* by respectively June 30, 1973 or June 30, 1981) or, if not notified, were exempt from notification by virtue of article 4 (2) of that Regulation, they will be provisionally valid in the same way as are "old" agreements.[4]

4.96   It should be emphasised, however, that an agreement will not benefit from provisional validity merely because it was entered into before accession and notified within the relevant six-month period or exempt from notification by virtue of Article 4 (2) of Regulation 17. It is essential that the agreement infringes Article 85 (1) only "by virtue of accession."[5] If, therefore, the agreement would, in fact, have been caught by Article 85 (1) irrespective of the accession of the new Member States to the Community, the agreement will not benefit from provisional validity even if it was notified within the six-month period following the enlargement of the Community.

IV. NEGATIVE CLEARANCE, NOTIFICATION AND EXEMPTION

A. GENERAL

4.97   It is important to appreciate the distinction between an "application for a negative clearance" and a "notification." Negative clearance refers to a procedure whereby a ruling may be made by the Commission as to whether or not a particular agreement, decision or concerted practice infringes Article 85 (1) or Article 86 of the Treaty.[6] If the Commission concludes that there is no such infringement it may grant a negative clearance.

4.98   By contrast, notification is only relevant where there is an infringement of Article 85 (1), and no block exemption is available.[7] In such a case, it is open to the parties to "notify" the relevant agreement, decision or concerted practice to the Commission and to apply for exemption pursuant to

---

[4] See, in this connection, *Esso Petroleum Co. Ltd.* v. *Kingswood Motors (Addlestone) Ltd.* [1973] C.M.L.R. 665 at pp. 676 *et seq.*

[5] See Reg. 17/62, arts. 25 (1) and (2).

[6] Art. 2 of Reg. 17/62. See n. 4 in Pt. I of this Chap.

[7] *i.e.* an exemption granted to a category of agreements, decisions and concerted practices, with the consequence that the exemption applies to any agreement, decision or concerted practice specified in the relevant block exemption without there being any need to notify it. See discussion *supra* at para. 4.06, and *infra* at para. 4.114.

Article 85 (3). With the exception of a small category of agreements, decisions and concerted practices generally known as "article 4 (2) agreements," discussed below,[8] exemption on an individual basis can only be granted after notification.[9]

4.99 Moreover, the date of notification is significant in terms of the date from which any eventual exemption may be effective. In addition to these considerations, notification carries with it immunity from the fines which might otherwise be imposed by the Commission in respect of infringements of Article 85 (1) taking place between the date of the notification and the date of any eventual Commission decision.[10]

4.100 The Commission's power to impose fines will be discussed in detail in Chapter 6, concerned with procedure generally. In this part of this chapter, it is proposed first to discuss negative clearance and notification, and then, the criteria in Article 85 (3) for granting an exemption.

B. Negative Clearance and Notification

1. *Procedure Generally*

4.101 Commission Regulation 27 (reproduced in Appendix 3) governs the procedure by which an application for negative clearance and a notification are made. An application for negative clearance and a notification are quite distinct. An application for negative clearance is merely a request to the Commission to ". . . certify that, on the basis of the facts in its possession, there are no grounds under Article 85 (1) or Article 86 of the Treaty for action on its part in respect of an agreement, decision or concerted practice." In other words, it involves a finding of non-infringement of Article 85 (1). Notification, on the other hand, pre-supposes that Article 85 (1) is infringed, and is made with a view to seeking exemption.

4.102 This distinction notwithstanding, it is permissible to apply at the same time to the Commission for negative clearance and, in the alternative, to notify the agreement, decision or concerted practice. Indeed, for this purpose, the Commission has made available the so-called Form A/B (a copy of which is reprinted in Appendix 3).

4.103 While, obviously, there is no point in both applying for negative clearance and notifying an agreement when it is clear beyond doubt that a negative clearance will not be granted, in most cases it is advisable to complete the form in the alternative; in other words to apply both for a negative clearance and to notify the agreement.

---

[8] See *infra*, at paras. 4–107 *et seq.*

[9] See, generally, Arts. 4 (1) and 5 (1) of Reg. 17/62, *supra*, n. 4 in Pt. I, and contrast with Arts. 4 (2) and 5 (2) of that Reg.

[10] See Arts. 15 (2) and 15 (5) of Reg. 17/62 and n. 4 of Pt. I of this Chap., *supra*.

4.104   The various questions on Form A/B are largely self-explanatory, and it is not proposed here to discuss them individually, save in the general sense of the remarks which follow concerning the criteria for the application of Article 85 (3). It should be mentioned, however, that there are broadly two distinct methods of completing Form A/B, depending to some degree on the objectives of the parties. The simplest and cheapest course is simply to complete the printed form, insofar as possible providing straightforward answers to the various questions. The alternative is to complete the form partially by reference to one or more separate annexes, and to provide detailed submissions (including legal arguments) in support of a negative clearance or, in the alternative, the grant of an exemption.

4.105   Both courses of action will provide immunity from fines in respect of infringements taking place between the date of notification and the date of any Commission Decision. It is considered, however, that the prospects of obtaining a favourable ruling from the Commission are enhanced by completing Form A/B in the more comprehensive fashion, if only because there is then some prospect that the submissions made will be of assistance to the officials at the Commission dealing with the case.

4.106   The following further points should be borne in mind in completing Form A/B:

   (i) Applications for negative clearance and notifications may be made in respect of standard form contracts, by attaching the standard form contract to Form A/B. Agreements concluded thereafter which are identical to the standard form contract will enjoy the same status as the original standard form contract.[10a]

   (ii) Applications for negative clearance and notifications are only as good as the facts which they contain. Thus, a notification will not afford immunity from fines in respect of any matter not referred to in the notification.[11] This is so even where the Commission is subsequently made aware of the relevant "unnotified" facts, unless this is done in the context of amending the notification.[12] Similarly, any exemption granted by the Commission can only extend to the matters notified to it, except in the case of an Article 4 (2) agreement, decision or concerted practice discussed below.[13]

   (iii) The Commission has power to impose fines where incorrect or misleading information has been deliberately or negligently supplied to it.[14]

[10a] Case 1/70 *Parfums Marcel Rochas Vertriebs GmbH* v. *Bitsch* [1970] E.C.R. 515; [1971] C.M.L.R. 104. Note also Form A/B, paras. I and II 1 (b).

[11] Art. 2 of Reg. 17/62.

[12] *Wilkes* v. *Theal N.V. & Watts* [1977] 1 C.M.L.R. D. 44 at D. 54 *et seq.*

[13] *A. Bullock & Co.* v. *The Distillers Co. Ltd.* [1978] 1 C.M.L.R. 400 at p. 420; *The Distillers Company Ltd.* v. *EC Commission* [1980] 3 C.M.L.R. 121 at paras. 23 *et seq.*

[14] Art. 15 (1) (*a*) of Reg. 17/62.

(iv) An exemption can generally only date back to the date of the notification.[15] A potentially infringing agreement should, therefore, be notified as soon as reasonably practical after it has been entered into.

(v) One party can apply for negative clearance or notify an infringing agreement, decision or concerted practice without the agreement of the other party.[16] As will be observed, however, Question I.2. of Form A/B requires that the notifying party ". . . state what steps have been taken to inform the other undertakings." It is mandatory that the other party or parties be given notice that a notification[16a] to the Commission is proposed.

2. Special Conditions Applying to Article 4 (2) Agreements, "Old" Agreements and "Accession" Agreements

(a) Article 4 (2) agreements

4.107 Reference has repeatedly been made to "article 4 (2) agreements," by which is meant those categories of agreements, decisions and concerted practices described in art. 4 (2) of Regulation 17. Such agreements enjoy a privileged status, in that they do not require to be notified to the Commission, in order to be granted exemption, assuming that they are ultimately held to infringe Article 85 (1),[17] and are not granted an exemption. If, however, they are ultimately held to infringe Article 85 (1), they are also not entitled to any immunity from fines *as a matter of law.*[18]

4.108 As will be seen from Article 4 (2) of Regulation 17, there are essentially three categories of agreements, decisions and concerted practices by the expression "article 4 (2) agreements," namely:

(1) those having as parties only undertakings from one Member State and not relating ". . . either to imports or exports between Member States." [19] It has been held that an agreement will not be deemed to "relate either to imports or exports between Member States," merely because it contemplates marketing arrangements in respect of goods which had previously been imported into a Member State.

---

[15] Art. 6 (1) of Reg. 17/62; but see also Art. 6 (2) of that Reg. and the discussion which follows concerning old agreements.

[16] Note, however, the second sentence of Art. 7 (1) of Reg. 17/62, which is intended to protect the legal position of the party not consenting to the notification.

[16a] Art. 1 (1) of Reg. 27/62.

[17] See Arts. 4 (1) and 4 (2) of Reg. 17/62. Note also *H. Vaessen BV* [1979] 1 C.M.L.R. 511 at paras. *22 et seq.*

[18] See *H. Vaessen BV ibid.* at paras. *22 et seq.*; see also Art. 15 (5) of Reg. 17/62 and note discussion *infra* at para. 4.111.

[19] Art. 4 (2) (i) of Reg. 17/62.

It would appear, therefore, that the wording contemplates a direct relationship with imports or exports.[20]

(2) those having not more than two undertakings as parties, and in addition either:

   (a) only restricting the freedom of one of those in determining the prices or conditions on which he will resell goods obtained from the other party; or

   (b) only imposing "... restrictions on the exercise of the rights of the assignee or user of industrial property rights—in particular patents, utility models, designs or trade marks—or of the person entitled under a contract to the assignment, or grant, of the right to use a method of manufacture or knowledge relating to the use and to the application of industrial processes."[21]

This last sub-category is clearly of most interest for the purposes of this book. Unfortunately, little guidance is available concerning its proper construction. It has, however, been held that an agreement which has as its effect the prevention of both the vendor of trade-marked goods *and third parties* from freely importing and exporting those trade-marked goods within the Community will not be covered by Article 4 (2) (ii) (*b*).[22] It would thus seem that the benefit of Article 4 (2) (ii) (*b*) may only be enjoyed by agreements, decisions and concerted practices concerned with intellectual property which do not affect third parties at all. If this is so, the provision will in all probability continue to be of little practical importance.

(3) those having "as their *sole object*[23]:

   (a) The development or uniform application of standards or types;

   (b) Joint research and development;

   (c) Specialisation in the manufacture of products, including agreements necessary for the achievement thereof...."[24]

where, in addition, the total annual turnover of the participating undertakings is not in excess of 200 million units of account and the goods in question do not represent more than 15 per cent. of the market for identical and similar products[25] in a substantial part of the Common Market.

---

[20] See *Fonderies Roubaix-Wattrelos SA* v. *Société Nouvelle des Fonderies A. Roux and Another* [1976] E.C.R. 111; [1976] 1 C.M.L.R. 538 at p. 548; see also *Brauerei A. Bilger Sohne GmbH* v. *Jehle and Another* [1974] 1 C.M.L.R. 382, at p. 391; and *Re Stoves & Heaters* [1975] 2 C.M.L.R. D. 1; *Vaessen* [1979] 1 C.M.L.R. 511 at para. 22.

[21] Art. 4 (2) (ii) (*b*) of Reg. 17/62.

[22] *Re Advocaat Zwarte Kip: Soenen-Bouckaert* v. *Cinoco SA and Van Olffen VB* [1974] 2 C.M.L.R. D. 79 at D. 86; see also *Wilkes* v. *Theal N.V. & Watts* [1977] 1 C.M.L.R. D. 44; see also *H. Vaessen BV, supra*, n. 34 at para. 21.

[23] Authors' italics.   [24] Art. 4 (2) (iii) of Reg. 17/62.

[25] *i.e.* products "considered by consumers to be similar by reason of their characteristics, price and use." As to the value of E.U.A., see, *supra*, n. 84.

4.109   By its terms, Article 4 of Regulation 17 is concerned exclusively with "new" agreements. It is, however, also relevant in the context of "old" agreements.

(b) "Old" agreements

4.110   "Old" agreements falling within the categories specified in Article 4 (2) of Regulation 17 are in fact exempt from notification in the same way as "new" agreements, by virtue of Article 5 (2) of the Regulation. There are, thus, two distinct sub-categories of "old" agreements, namely those requiring to be notified to the European Commission in accordance with Article 5 (1) of Regulation 17, and those not requiring to be notified by virtue of Article 5 (2), because they are covered by the terms of Article 4 (2).[26]

(i) *"Old" Article 4 (2) agreements*

4.111   As regards "old" Article 4 (2) agreements, while such agreements are thought likely to enjoy provisional validity,[27] they do not enjoy any immunity from fines. In this respect, they are akin to "new" Article 4 (2) agreements. It would appear, therefore, that "old" Article 4 (2) agreements must be enforced by domestic courts unless and until the Commission decides to the contrary. If, however, the Commission decides that Article 85 (1) has been infringed, it would be entitled to impose a fine should it consider the circumstances to warrant it. As a matter of practice it is thought relatively unlikely that fines would be imposed.

(ii) *"Old" agreements outside the ambit of Article 4 (2)*

4.112   "Old" agreements falling outside the ambit of Article 4 (2) of course require to be notified, and only enjoy immunity from fines if they were duly notified (*i.e.* within the time limits specified in Article 5 (1)).[28] Obviously, if an "old" agreement requiring notification is eventually notified, but not within the time period specified by Article 5 (1), it would still enjoy immunity from fines in respect of acts taking place between the date of notification and the date of any Commission decision.[29] Such agreements would, however, presumably not enjoy any provisional validity, because they were not duly notified within the requisite time period.[30]

---

[26] See also the discussion of the definition of old agreements, *supra*, at paras. 4.85 *et seq.*

[27] *Brauerei A. Bilger Sohne GmbH*, v. *Jehle and Another*, *supra*; *Brasserie de Haecht*, *supra*; *Esso Petroleum Co. Ltd.*, *supra* at pp. 676 *et seq.* See also discussion of provisional validity, *supra*, paras. 4.85 *et seq.*

[28] Art. 5 (1) of Reg. 17/62. The period in question depended on whether there were only two parties or more than two parties. In the first case, notification was required to be made before February 1, 1963, and in the second case, notification was required somewhat earlier, namely before November 1, 1962.

[29] Art. 15 (5) of Reg. 17/62.

[30] This conclusion would appear warranted in the light of the European Court's judgments in, respectively, *Brasserie de Haecht* and *Ets. A. de Bloos S.P.R.L.*, both *supra*.

In the case of "old" agreements which have been duly notified the rule restricting the Commission's power to grant a retroactive exemption to the date of notification is waived, and the Commission's power to make its decision retroactive is unlimited.[31]

(c) "Accession" agreements

4.113   "Accession" agreements are agreements, decisions and concerted practices caught by Article 85 (1) solely by virtue of the accession of Denmark, Eire and the United Kingdom to the Community on January 1, 1973, or by virtue of the accession of Greece to the Community on January 1, 1981. Broadly, the status of such agreements is in every way analogous to that of "old" agreements. In particular:

(i) "Accession" agreements falling within the ambit of Article 4 (2) of Regulation 17 do not require notification,[32] are thought likely to enjoy provisional validity by analogy with "old" Article 4 (2) agreements, and probably do not enjoy any immunity from fines.

(ii) "Accession" agreements falling outside the ambit of Article 4 (2) of Regulation 17 require to be notified within six months of the date of the relevant accession, *i.e.* by June 30, 1973 or by June 30, 1981.[33] Provided they were notified within this period, it is thought likely that they enjoy provisional validity. In addition, they enjoy immunity from fines and any decision rendered by the Commission granting exemption may be made retroactive to a date earlier than their notification.[34]

C. Exemption

4.114   The Commission may declare Article 85 (1) inapplicable to any agreement, decision or concerted practice pursuant to Article 85 (3), provided that the conditions specified in Article 85 (3) for the grant of an exemption are satisfied. The Commission may grant an exemption in one of three ways:

(i) by block exemption, where a whole category of agreements, decisions or concerted practices is exempted without there being any need to make individual notifications.[35] Any agreement, decision or concerted practice coming within the terms of the relevant block exemption will automatically be exempt.

---

[31] Art. 6 (2) of Reg. 17/62. Note also Art. 7 of Reg. 17, which broadly empowers the Commission to declare that Art. 85 (1) did not apply to an old Agreement which was either determined by the parties or modified by the parties in such a way as to fall outside the prohibition contained in Art. 85 (1) or to be eligible for exemption pursuant to Art. 85 (3).
[32] Art. 6 (2) of Reg. 17/62.   [33] Art. 25 (2) and (5) of Reg. 17/62.
[34] See Art. 25 of Reg. 17/62.
[35] The Commission must be specifically empowered to promulgate a block exemption by the Council of Ministers, pursuant to Art. 87 of the Treaty.

(ii) On an individual basis, after the relevant agreement, decision or concerted practice has been notified to it in accordance with the appropriate provisions of Regulation 17.[36]

(iii) On an individual basis irrespective of whether a notification has been made, in the case of all agreements coming within the terms of Article 4 (2) of Regulation 17.[37] To date this procedure has not been adopted.[38]

4.115 There are essentially four conditions for the grant of an exemption, namely that the agreement, decision or concerted practice in question must:

(i) contribute to improving the production or distribution of goods *or* to promoting technical or economic progress, and

(ii) allow consumers a fair share of the resulting benefit, and

(iii) not impose upon the relevant undertakings any restrictions which are not indispensable to the attainment of the objectives specified in the previous two conditions, and

(iv) not afford the relevant undertakings "the possibility of eliminating competition in respect of a substantial part of the products in question."

4.116 The Commission retains a great deal of flexibility as to the manner in which it applies these conditions,[39] if only because the exercise of the Commission's powers under Article 85 (3) of necessity requires that it makes complex economic judgments. In these circumstances, judicial control is limited to considerations such as the relevance of the facts relied upon by the Commission and the validity of its reasoning.[40] The Commission is, however, required to inform the parties in good time of its proposed action and, in particular, of any conditions subject to which it intends to grant an exemption, so as to afford the parties an opportunity of presenting counter-arguments.[41]

4.117 The Commission has itself provided useful guidance with regard to its interpretation of the first condition for the application of Article 85 (3), when it stated in its decision in *Re Bayer & Gist-Brocades*[42]:

"For the agreements to contribute to the improvement of production or distribution, or to promote technical or economic progress, they must objectively constitute an improvement on the situation that

---

[36] See in this connection Arts. 4, 5, 7 and 25 of Reg. 17/62.

[37] Art. 6 (2) of Reg. 17/62 (in conjunction with Art. 5 (2) and Art. 25 (1)).

[38] But see generally *Fonderies Roubaix-Wattrelos SA* v. *Société Nouvelle des Fonderies A. Roux and Another* [1976] E.C.R. 111; [1976] 1 C.M.L.R. 538; *Vaessen* [1979] 1 C.M.L.R. 511.

[39] *Etablissements Consten SA and Grundig-Verkaufs GmbH* v. *EC Commission* [1966] E.C.R. 299; [1966] C.M.L.R. 418 at p. 477.

[40] *Ibid.*

[41] *Members of the Transocean Marine Paint Assn. No. 2* v. *EC Commission* [1974] 2 C.M.L.R. 459, at p. 477.

[42] [1976] 1 C.M.L.R. at D. 98.

would otherwise exist. The fundamental principle in this respect, established at the time the Common Market was formed, lays down that fair and undistorted competition is the best guarantee of regular supply on the best terms. Thus the question of a contribution to economic progress within the meaning of Article 85 (3) can only arise in those exceptional cases where the free play of competition is unable to produce the best result economically speaking."[43]

4.118 It follows from this that concrete evidence will have to be adduced to persuade the Commission that the economic progress would not take place without the restriction on competition for which exemption from Article 85 (1) is being requested.

4.119 Regrettably, no equally helpful guidance can readily be given with regard to the Commission's practice in applying the other conditions in Article 85 (3). The Commission's practice can only be understood from consideration of the manner in which it has applied Article 85 (3) to particular types of factual situations. For this reason no attempt will be made to discuss Article 85 (3) further at this stage. Instead, the Commission's practice in granting exemption in the context of agreements concerning intellectual property will be discussed in detail in Part III.

---

[43] *Ibid.* at D. 109.

CHAPTER 5

ARTICLE 86:ABUSE OF A DOMINANT POSITION

I. *INTRODUCTION*

A. THE RELATIONSHIP BETWEEN ARTICLES 85 AND 86

5.01 Just as Article 85 is concerned with distortions of competition resulting from restrictive arrangements between two or more parties, so Article 86 is concerned with distortions of competition resulting from the abusive behaviour of an enterprise in a dominant position. Articles 85 and 86 are, thus, each concerned with a different aspect of the same problem. The link between them is to be found in Article 3 (*f*) of the Treaty, which requires the Community to institute "a system ensuring that competition in the Common Market is not distorted." In the words of the European Court's judgment in the *Continental Can case*[1]:

> "Articles 85 and 86 are intended to achieve the same aim on different levels—the maintenance of effective competition in the Common Market. The restriction of competition, which is prohibited if it is the result of behaviour coming within Article 85, cannot be allowed by virtue of the fact that this behaviour is successful under the influence of a dominant undertaking."[2]

B. INTELLECTUAL PROPERTY AND THE EXISTENCE OF A DOMINANT POSITION

5.02 From an early stage in the development of Community competition law, it has been clear that the mere existence of a patent (or, indeed, of any other form of intellectual property) does not, in itself, give rise to a dominant position within the meaning of Article 86. Without a "dominant position," Article 86 cannot, of course, apply.

5.03 The Court's judgment in the *Parke-Davis* case[3] made this abundantly clear:

> "Under Article 86 of the Treaty it is prohibited 'insofar as trade between Member States is liable to be affected by it, for one or more undertakings to exploit in an improper manner a dominant position

---

[1] Case 6/72 *Europemballage Corpn. & Continental Can Co.Inc.* v. *EC Commission* [1973] E.C.R. 215; [1973] C.M.L.R. 199.
[2] *Ibid.* at p. 224.
[3] Case 24/67 *Parke-Davis & Co.* v. *Probel and Others* [1968] E.C.R. 55; [1968] C.M.L.R. 47.

within the Common Market or within a substantial part of it.' For an act to be prohibited it is thus necessary to find the existence of three elements: the existence of a dominant position, an improper exploitation of it, and the possibility that trade between Member States may be affected by it. Although a patent confers on its holder a special protection within the framework of a State, it does not follow that the exercise of the rights so conferred implies the existence of the three elements mentioned. It could only do so if the utilisation of the patent could degenerate into an improper exploitation of the protection."[4]

5.04   On the other hand, in assessing the factors to be taken into account in deciding whether or not a dominant position exists, the ownership of intellectual property may be very important. In the Commission's Decision in the *United Brands* case,[5] the Commission specifically referred to "other major advantages such as trade mark ownership."[6]

5.05   More generally, one very important factor always in assessing whether an undertaking is in a dominant position, is the likelihood of competition from other manufacturers. Clearly, the existence of a strong patent for a major new invention could substantially reduce the possibilities for competitors to enter the market. Similarly, but perhaps to a lesser extent, the existence of a very well-known trade mark could, in itself, reduce the likelihood of competitors entering the market, thus helping to reinforce the dominance of the leading undertaking.

5.06   In this chapter the various elements of Article 86 will be considered individually, the application of Regulation 17/62 will then be discussed, and finally the effects of a breach of Article 86 will be outlined.

II. *ARTICLE 86: GENERAL*

5.07   Article 86, which appears as part of the Treaty dealing with the "Policy of the Community," provides:

"Any abuse by one or more undertakings of a dominant position within the common market or in a substantial part of it shall be prohibited as incompatible with the common market insofar as it may affect trade between Member States. Such abuse may, in particular, consist in:

(*a*) directly or indirectly imposing unfair purchase or selling prices or other unfair trading conditions;

---

[4] *Ibid.* at p. 59.
[5] *Re United Brands Co. (Chiquita)* (O.J. 1976, L95/1) [1976] 1 C.M.L.R. D.28.
[6] *Ibid.* at D.46. In the same vein, the European Court has specifically singled out "the technological lead of an undertaking over its competitors ..." as a relevant factor in establishing the existence of a dominant position; see *Hoffmann-La Roche AG* v. *EC Commission* [1979] 3 C.M.L.R. 211 at p. 277. The technical lead enjoyed by Roche over its competitors in that case depended on its ownership of several patents *ibid.* at p. 278.

(b) limiting production, markets or technical development to the prejudice of consumers;

(c) applying dissimilar conditions to equivalent transactions with other trading parties, thereby placing them at a competitive disadvantage;

(d) making the conclusion of contracts subject to acceptance by the other parties of supplementary obligations which, by their nature or according to commercial usage, have no connection with the subject of such contracts."

5.08   Thus, for Article 86 to apply there must be shown to be:

—a dominant position in a substantial part of the Common Market;

—enjoyed by one or more undertakings;

—an abuse of that dominant position; and

—a resulting effect on trade between Member States.

III. *DOMINANT POSITION IN A SUBSTANTIAL PART OF THE COMMON MARKET*

A. GENERAL

5.09   The classic definition of a dominant position was given by the Commission in its Decision in the *United Brands* case[7] as follows:

"Undertakings are in a dominant position when they have the power to behave independently without taking into account, to any substantial extent, their competitors, purchasers and suppliers. Such is the case where an undertaking's market share, either in itself or when combined with its know-how, access to raw materials, capital or other major advantage such as trade mark ownership, enables it to determine the prices or to control the production or distribution of a significant part of the relevant goods. It is not necessary for the undertaking to have total dominance such as would deprive all other market participants of their commercial freedom, as long as it is strong enough in general terms to devise its own strategy as it wishes, even if there are differences in the extent to which it dominates individual sub markets."[8]

5.10   Whilst that definition is a useful description of dominance, no company can be dominant in the abstract; it can only be dominant in relation to a particular market. The definition is, therefore, only meaningful once the "market" for the "relevant goods" (or, indeed, services) has been established. Defining the relevant market involves an assessment of the position from two separate viewpoints: first, in terms of the products concerned,

---

[7] *Re United Brands Co.* (Chiquita) [1976] 1 C.M.L.R. D. 28.

[8] *Ibid.* at D. 46–47.

and, secondly, in terms of the geographic area involved. Once the relevant market is clear it is then necessary to decide whether or not a dominant position is enjoyed, by one, or more than one, undertakings on that market.

B. THE RELEVANT PRODUCT MARKET

(1) General

5.11   The importance of defining the relevant product market was underlined by the European Court in its decision in the *Continental Can* case,[9] when it said:

> "... the delimination of the market concerned is of crucial importance, for the possibilities of competition can only be considered in the light of the characteristics of the products in question, which reveal them to be particularly suited to satisfying a constant demand and interchangeable with other products only to a small extent."[10]

5.12   In that case, the Court overturned the Commission's decision on the grounds that the "product market" had not been correctly defined. In particular, the Court criticised the Commission's failure sufficiently to distinguish the particular product market in question from the general market for products of that type.[11]

5.13   Very rarely is the extent of the product market clear beyond any doubt, and, inevitably, in any situation where Article 86 is at issue a great deal of time will be taken in deciding this question. Almost invariably, it will be in the interests of the undertaking whose conduct is under scrutiny to have the market defined as widely as possible, and it will, equally, be in the interests of a complainant to have it defined as narrowly as possible. In the *United Brands* case itself, for instance, the United Brands Company alleged that the relevant market was the fruit market. The Commission, on the other hand, decided that the relevant market was confined to bananas, and was upheld on this point by the European Court.[12]

(2) The Essential Test: Interchangeability

5.14   Although every case ultimately depends on its own facts, some general guidance can be derived from statements of the European Court and the Commission. In describing the "product market" in other contexts,[13] the

---

[9] Case 6/72 *Europemballage Corpn. & Continental Can Co. Inc.* v. *EC Commission* [1973] E.C.R. 215; [1973] C.M.L.R. 199

[10] *Ibid.* at p. 226.

[11] *Ibid.* at p. 227. The particular market in that case was light containers for preserved meat, charcuterie, fish and shellfish, and the general market was light metal containers.

[12] *United Brands Co.* v. *EC Commission* [1978] 1 C.M.L.R. 429 at pp. 482–484.

[13] *e.g.* Reg. 2779/72 on application of Art. 85 (3) to categories of specialisation agreements (O.J. 1972, L292/23); Commission Notice of December 19, 1977 on agreements of minor importance (O.J. 1977, L313/3).

Commission has frequently referred to: "... the products considered by consumers[14] to be similar by reason of their characteristics, price or use."[15]

5.15   In other words, and harking back to the Court's judgment in the *Continental Can* case,[16] the decisive test is the extent to which the products in question are "interchangeable" with other products. Thus, a Mini and a Rolls-Royce are both used for the same purpose, but the difference in their characteristics and price would not, in the minds of most consumers, make them "interchangeable."

5.16   "Interchangeability" is also the decisive test when considering the proper market in the context of a product which has two or more uses. Thus, in the *Hoffmann-La Roche "Vitamins"* case,[17] the Court said:

> "If a product could be used for different purposes and if these different uses are in accordance with economic needs, which are themselves also different, there are good grounds for accepting that this product may, according to the circumstances, belong to separate markets which may present specific features which differ from the standpoint both of the structure and of the conditions of competition. However, this finding does not justify the conclusion that such a product together with all the other products which can replace it as far as concerns the various uses to which it may be put and with which it may compete, forms one single market. The concept of the relevant market in fact implies that there can be effective competition between the products which form part of it and this pre-supposes that there is a sufficient degree of interchangeability between all the products forming part of the same market insofar as a specific use of such products is concerned."[18]

5.17   It is also clear from the Commission's statement in the *Continental Can* case,[19] quoted above, that the relevant product market will only in very exceptional cases be co-extensive with the scope of a patent or similar right. Whilst, therefore, the existence of a patent or a trade mark may be relevant to a consideration of dominance it will only rarely be relevant to a definition of the product market.

5.18   There may be occasions when, because of particular circumstances, no interchangeability at all is possible. Such, for example, was the situation in the *General Motors* case.[20] Under Belgian law every car imported into

---

[14] "Consumers" in this context and, indeed, in EEC competition law generally, is equivalent to "customers," and does not bear the specialised meaning in, *e.g.* Supply of Goods (Implied Terms) Act 1973, Unfair Contract Terms Act 1977.
[15] Reg. 2779/72, art. 3 (1) (*a*).
[16] [1973] C.M.L.R. 199.
[17] *Hoffmann-La Roche AG* v. *EC Commission* [1979] E.C.R. 461; [1979] 3 C.M.L.R. 211.
[18] *Ibid.* at p. 272.
[19] [1973] E.C.R. 215; [1973] C.M.L.R. 199.
[20] *Re General Motors Continental NV* [1975] 1 C.M.L.R. D. 20: *General Motors Continental NV* v. *EC Commission* [1976] E.C.R. 1367; [1976] 1 C.M.L.R. 95.

Belgium has to have a "certificate of conformity" to show that it complies with the standards laid down for that type of vehicle. Only the authorised agent appointed by the manufacturer can issue the certificate; General Motors Continental NV had been appointed for Opel cars and other cars manufactured by companies in the General Motors Group. Although General Motors argued that the issue of these certificates was purely ancillary to the sale of motor cars—a market in which it clearly held no dominant position—this was rejected, both by the Commission and the European Court. The "market" was held to be the issue of certificates for Opel cars imported into Belgium, a market in which General Motors Continental NV had a complete monopoly by virtue of the requirements of Belgian law.

5.19   Similarly, in the *Hugin* case[21] there was, in practice, no interchangeability. In that case, Hugin Kassaregister AB, a Swedish manufacturer of cash registers, with a share of the market for cash registers in the EEC of around 12 per cent., was held by the Commission to have a dominant position in the supply of spare parts for its own machines. In other words, the spare parts constituted a separate market from the cash registers themselves. In the words of the Commission's decision:

> "The majority of parts for Hugin cash registers are made to Hugin design and with tools belonging to Hugin AB and are exclusive to Hugin AB. These parts are not interchangeable with the parts of other makes of cash registers and cannot otherwise be economically reproduced. Hugin cash registers cannot therefore be properly maintained, repaired or rebuilt without the use of Hugin spare parts. Hugin AB controls the supply of all Hugin spare parts throughout the world."[22, 23]

5.20   There are many factors which govern whether or not one product is "interchangeable" with another, and, thus, forms part of the same market. Price, quality, special characteristics, consumer preference, "cross elasticity of demand," and the existence of realistic alternatives may all play a part, and each case must always depend on its own facts.[24]

(3) *Product Market not always Defined by Reference to Consumers in General*

5.21   It is also clear from the decided case law of the European Court and the

---

[21] *Liptons Cash Registers and Business Equipment Ltd.* v. *Hugin Kassaregister AB and Hugin Cash Registers Ltd.* [1978] 1 C.M.L.R. D. 19.   [22] *Ibid.* at D. 33.

[23] Although the Commission's decision was annulled by the European Court (see *Hugin Kassaregister AB and Hugin Cash Registers Limited* v. *EC Commission* [1979] 3 C.M.L.R. 345), the Commission's view that spare parts could constitute a separate market was upheld by the Court.

[24] For a fuller discussion of this topic see Bellamy & Child, *Common Market Law on Competition*, pp. 159–172.

Commission, that the relevant product market is certainly not always defined in terms of consumers in general, but may well be defined in terms of a very limited group. In the *General Motors* case,[25] for example, the "consumers" in relation to that particular product market, were people who had bought Opel cars in Germany and wanted to import them to Belgium, a group which, during the relevant period covered by the Decision, consisted of five people.

C. The Relevant Geographic Market

(1) *General*

5.22　The definition of the "relevant market" for the purpose of establishing whether or not a dominant position exists, also involves consideration of geographic factors.

5.23　Clearly, the geographic area must be a "substantial part of the Common Market,"[26] in order to meet the specific requirements of Article 86, but it must also be a geographic area in which "the conditions of competition are homogeneous."[27] In the words of the Court's judgment in the *United Brands* case:

> "The conditions for the application of Article 86 to an undertaking in a dominant position presuppose the clear delimitation of the substantial part of the Common Market in which it may be able to engage in abuses which hinder effective competition and this is an area where the objective conditions of competition must be the same for all traders."[28]

5.24　In that case, United Brands was found to enjoy a dominant position in Germany, Denmark, Ireland, the Netherlands, Belgium and Luxembourg, where "although the applicable tariff provisions and transport costs are of necessity different but not discriminatory ... the conditions of competition are the same for all."[29]

5.25　In France, Italy and the United Kingdom, on the other hand, even though United Brand's market share was only slightly lower, special factors such as the system of "Commonwealth preferences" in the United Kingdom, affected the position, with the result that United Brand's bananas did not "compete on equal terms with other bananas sold in those states which benefit from a preferential system."[30]

---

[25] [1976] 1 C.M.L.R. 95.
[26] For fuller discussion of this phrase see *infra,* paras. 5.26–5.27.
[27] See *United Brands Co.* v. *EC Commission* [1978] 1 C.M.L.R. 429 at p. 484.
[28] *Ibid.* at pp. 484–485.
[29] *Ibid.* at p. 485.
[30] *Ibid.* at p. 485.

(2) *"Substantial Part of the Common Market"*

5.26 The dilemma which can arise in deciding how large an area must be to be a "substantial part of the Common Market," was highlighted by Lord Chief Justice Widgery in the *Felixstowe Dock* case[31] where he said:

> "As I see it, the plaintiffs are really in this dilemma. If they restrict the area in which they allege the Board to be dominant in order to prove dominance in that area, they will find themselves operating in an area so small that it cannot be said to be a substantial part of the Common Market at all. On the other hand, if they extend the area under review and perhaps include London and Tilbury, then ... they might very well be in trouble in that in those circumstances their own interest in the business was insufficient to be dominant."[32]

5.27 It is now clear that one Member State alone may constitute "a substantial part of the Common Market," even one of the smaller Member States.[33] In fact, even part of a Member State was found to be sufficiently "substantial" in the *Sugar Cartel* case,[34] where the southern part of Germany, comprising Bavaria, Baden-Würtemburg and parts of Hessen was held to be a "substantial part of the Common Market." This is, perhaps, not unreasonable, having regard to the fact that the land area involved there and the total population of that area is greater than the land area and population of Belgium. It seems less likely that a part of one of the smaller Member States would be sufficiently "substantial" and it must be open to doubt whether Luxembourg, as the smallest Member State of the Community, would in itself be a "substantial"part of the Common Market.

D. DOMINANCE

5.28 Having established the relevant market both in terms of the product and the geographic area, the next step is to consider whether the undertaking whose conduct is under scrutiny enjoys a "dominant position" on that market.

5.29 Unlike United Kingdom monopoly legislation, where a "monopoly situation"[35] is to be taken to exist if one company or group controls 25 per cent. or more of the relevant market, no particular market share automatically denotes dominance for the purposes of Article 86. Clearly, in some situations, where the market has been defined in such a way as to give the

---

[31] *Felixstowe Dock & Railway Co.* v. *British Transport Dock Board* [1976] 2 C.M.L.R. 405.
[32] *Ibid.* at p. 413.
[33] See, *e.g. Re General Motors Continental NV* [1975] 1 C.M.L.R. D. 20, where Belgium was held to be a substantial part of the Common Market.
[34] *Re the European Sugar Cartel* [1973] C.M.L.R. D. 65.
[35] See ss. 6, 7 and 8 of the Fair Trading Act 1973.

undertaking concerned a complete, or virtually complete, monopoly,[36] the resulting 100 per cent. market share will, in itself, be sufficient to indicate a dominant position. In most other instances, however, the size of the market share will be only one factor to be taken into consideration.

5.30 In its Eighth Report on Competition Policy,[37] the Commission considered, in some detail, the European Court's analysis of dominance in the *United Brands* case. Its comments merit quotation at some length, particularly for its assessment of the importance to be attached to a company's market share in calculating its overall dominance:

"... Article 86 can apply not only where the undertaking has such a large share of the market that it can be presumed to occupy a dominant position through its sheer size, but also in situations where the dominant position derives from a combination of several factors which, taken separately, would not necessarily be determinative. Where this appears likely, it is necessary first of all to examine the structure of the undertaking and then the situation on the relevant market as far as competition is concerned.

With regard to the structure of the undertaking ... the Court emphasised the following points in particular: UBC is an undertaking with a high degree of vertical integration, it can meet all the orders it receives, it leads the field in technical knowledge, its advertising policy hinges on the 'Chiquita' brand and guarantees a steady supply of customers, and it has control over every stage of the distribution process. Between them, these factors give UBC a considerable advantage over its competitors.

Turning to the situation with regard to competition, the Court specified that a trader can be in a dominant position on the market for a product only if he has succeeded in winning a substantial part of this market. Although it is far from negligible, a market share of between 40 per cent. and 45 per cent. does not permit the conclusion that the undertaking in question automatically controls the market. The percentage must be assessed having regard to the strength and number of the competitors. The fact that UBC's share of the market is several times larger than that of its best placed competitor, together with the structural advantages it enjoys, was seen by the Court as a very important element of proof.

... Working from the principle that a certain degree of competition is not incompatible with a dominant position the Court found that UBC gave no ground whatever in the lively competitive campaigns waged on several occasions by several producers, that it successfully

---

[36] *Re General Motors Continental NV* [1975] 1 C.M.L.R. D. 20; *General Motors Continental NV* v. *EC Commission* [1976] 1 C.M.L.R. 95; *Liptons Cash Registers and Business Equipment Ltd.* v. *Hugin Kassaregister AB and Hugin Cash Registers Ltd.* [1978] 1 C.M.L.R. D. 19.
[37] Published April 1979.

resisted new competitors attempting to establish themselves on the whole of the relevant market, that it was able to keep up its sales figures on all the relevant national markets and that customers continue to buy more bananas from UBC, even though it is the seller with the highest prices. Each of these factors constitutes evidence in support of a finding of dominance."[38]

5.31   Thus, a market share of 45 per cent. was sufficient in that case to give United Brands a dominant position, having regard to all the other advantages it enjoyed over its competitors. It should be noted that one of those advantages was its ownership of the name "Chiquita." As has already been mentioned[39] whilst the existence of intellectual property rights may well be relevant to the overall assessment of the "dominance" of an undertaking, the mere ownership of such rights will not in itself be sufficient to constitute a dominant position.

IV. *"ONE OR MORE UNDERTAKINGS"*

(1) *General*

5.32   Before Article 86 can apply, it must be shown that a dominant position is enjoyed in a substantial part of the Common Market "by one or more undertakings." The term "undertaking" has already been discussed[40] in relation to Article 85, and it has the same meaning in the context of Article 86.

(2) *Undertakings Need not be Established in the EEC*

5.33   As with Article 85, it is irrelevant whether an undertaking is based inside or outside the Community, provided that its conduct has an effect within the Community. In fact, a considerable number of the decided cases under Article 86 have involved companies established outside the EEC, operating through subsidiaries in the Community.[41]

(3) *Parent and Subsidiary in the Context of Article 86*

5.34   The interests of a parent company outside the EEC, and a subsidiary company within, were in a number of cases under Article 86 sufficiently

---

[38] *Ibid.* at pt. 22. Note: In the *Hoffman-La Roche "Vitamins"* case, at pp. 283–284, the Court expressly confirmed the relevant part of its judgment in *United Brands Hoffmann-La Roche.*

[39] See *supra,* para. 5.02.

[40] See Chap. 4, paras. 4.27 *et seq.*

[41] *e.g. Re Continental Can Co. Inc.* [1972] C.M.L.R. D. 11; *Zoja/CSC-ICI* [1973] C.M.L.R. D. 50; *United Brands Co. (Chiquita)* [1976] 1 C.M.L.R. D. 28; *The Community* v. *Hoffman-La Roche & Co. AG* [1976] 2 C.M.L.R. D. 25.

closely identified for the Commission to conclude that the "abuse" committed by the subsidiary could equally be imputed to the parent. In its decision in the *Commercial Solvents* case,[42] for example, the Commission said:

> "It may then be concluded that the Commercial Solvents Corpn. holds the power of control over Istituto Chemioterapico and exercises it in fact, at least as regards its relations with Zoja, such that in that respect there is no ground for distinguishing between the will and the acts of the Commercial Solvents Corpn. and those of Instituto Chemioterapico."[43]

5.35 A parent company and its subsidiaries are, thus, normally treated as one undertaking, even where, as in the *Commercial Solvents* case, the parent company's shareholding in the subsidiary is less than 100 per cent. The crucial test is the extent to which the parent company exercises effective control over the activities of the subsidiary.

5.36 Article 85, of course, requires an Agreement between at least two "undertakings," so that it is important in any given situation under that Article to know whether a parent and subsidiary are to be treated as one "undertaking" or not. This is, however, less important where Article 86 is concerned, as the Article refers to "any abuse *by one or more* undertakings." Thus, even if the degree of control exercised by the parent company over its subsidiary is insufficient to enable the two companies to be treated as a single undertaking, the conduct in question may still fall under Article 86 as being the conduct of more than one undertaking.

(4) *Two Separate Undertakings in the Context of Article 86*

5.37 Articles 85 and 86 are not mutually exclusive,[44] and where more than one undertaking is involved in an alleged abuse there will frequently be an agreement or concerted practice between the undertakings concerned which could also infringe Article 85. It is not clear from the decided cases whether Article 86 can apply where separate undertakings indulge in parallel conduct, without any collusion between them; in principle, there seems to be nothing to preclude the Commission taking action in such circumstances. The combined position of the undertakings in question must, of course, be one of dominance although each of them individually may well be dominant only because of the existence of the others.[45]

---

[42] *Zoja/CSC-ICI, supra*, n. 41.
[43] *Ibid.* at D. 57.
[44] See, *e.g. ibid.* at D. 62.
[45] *The European Sugar Cartel* [1973] C.M.L.R. D. 65 is the most relevant case on this question, where the Commission found that the two Dutch sugar producers had co-ordinated their conduct so closely as to "appear as a single entity." (See D. 104) This particular aspect of the Commission's Decision was not, however, dealt with in the European Court's judgment, as in the circumstances it was unnecessary for it to do so.

V. *ABUSE*

A. GENERAL

5.38 The text of Article 86 refers to four categories of conduct which may be abusive:

"... abuse may, in particular, consist in:
(a) directly or indirectly imposing unfair purchase or selling prices or other unfair trading conditions;
(b) limiting production, markets or technical development to the prejudice of consumers;
(c) applying dissimilar conditions to equivalent transactions with other trading parties, thereby placing them at a competitive disadvantage;
(d) making the conclusion of contracts subject to acceptance by the other parties of supplementary obligations which, by their nature or according to commercial usage, have no connection with the subject of such contracts."

It is, however, clear that these are merely examples, and that the list is not an exhaustive one. [46] A more generalised definition of abuse was given by the European Court in its *Hoffman-La Roche "Vitamins"* judgment:[47]

"The concept of abuse is an objective concept relating to the behaviour of an undertaking in a dominant position which is such as to influence the structure of a market where, as a result of the very presence of the undertaking in question, the degree of competition is weakened and which, through recourse to methods different from those which condition normal competition in products or services on the basis of the transaction of commercial operators, has the effect of hindering the maintenance of the degree of competition still existing in the market place."[48]

B. ABUSE AND INTELLECTUAL PROPERTY

5.39 To date, intellectual property has played only a small part in the cases involving Article 86. This will be dealt with in more detail in the relevant parts of Chapters 8 and 12. Mention can, however, here appropriately be made of the *Eurofima* case[49] which does not easily fit into either of the other chapters, yet provides a good example of how an abuse under Article 86 may involve intellectual property.

---

[46] See, *e.g. Europemballage Corpn. & Continental Can Co. Inc.* v. *EC Commission* [1973] E.C.R. 215; [1973] C.M.L.R. 199 where the "abuse" was the takeover by a company in a dominant position of another company, thus reinforcing its dominance.

[47] *Hoffmann-La Roche AG* v. *EC Commission* [1979] E.C.R. 461; [1979] 3 C.M.L.R. 211.

[48] *Ibid.* at p. 290.

[49] *Re Eurofima* [1973] C.M.L.R. D. 127.

The Eurofima case

5.40   The Commission opened proceedings against Eurofima as a result of complaints made to it, but terminated them without a formal decision. A press release was, however, published summarising the main facts and findings.[50] Basically, it found that Eurofima, as the most important buyer in the Community of a certain type of railway rolling stock, enjoyed a dominant position. Tenders had been invited by Eurofima for the manufacture of a new type of rolling stock, which was to replace the conventional type then in use. One of the terms of the tender was that contractors would allow Eurofima unlimited rights to use any patents resulting from the development, without any additional compensation being payable.

5.41   The Commission accepted that Eurofima might need the right to use the patents for maintenance and further construction, but considered it to be an abuse for it to lay claim to a licence of future patent rights, and for it to seek to grant licences to third parties, without any payment to, or consultation with, the contractor.

5.42   In the event, the offending clause was amended in the final contract and the Commission closed its file. As well as being an interesting example of how an undertaking in a dominant position can abuse that position by unjustifiably obtaining unlimited use of patent rights, the case is also an example of how Article 86 may apply not only to dominant suppliers, but also to dominant buyers.

VI. EFFECT ON TRADE BETWEEN MEMBER STATES

5.43   Both Article 85 and Article 86 require that the agreement or abuse which is at issue "may affect trade between Member States." This requirement has already been discussed in the context of Article 85,[51] and it has the same meaning in the context of Article 86. As has already been emphasised, the decisive word is "may." There is no need to show that trade between Member States has actually been affected, provided that there is a possibility of that happening and provided, moreover, that if it did, the effect would be appreciable.

5.44   Although the phrase "may affect trade between Member States" has been described as "only a criterion which goes to jurisdiction,"[52] it is nonetheless a precondition of the application of Articles 85 and 86. An expanded description of the significance of this part of Article 86 was given by the European Court in the *Hugin* case[53] as follows:

---

[50] Press release published on April 16, 1973.

[51] See *supra*, Chap. 4, paras. 4.59 *et seq.*

[52] See Advocate General's opinion in *General Motors Continental NV* v. *EC Commission* [1976] 1 C.M.L.R. 95 at p. 105.

[53] *Hugin Kassaregister AB and Hugin Cash Registers Limited* v. *EC Commission* [1979] 3 C.M.L.R. 345.

"The interpretation and application of the condition relating to effects on trade between Member States contained in Articles 85 and 86 of the Treaty must be based on the purpose of that condition which is to define, in the context of the law governing competition, the boundary between the areas respectively covered by Community law and the law of the Member States. Thus Community law covers any agreement or any practice which is capable of constituting a threat to freedom of trade between Member States in a manner which might harm the attainment of the objectives of a single market between the Member States, in particular by partitioning the national markets or by affecting the structure of competition within the Common Market. On the other hand, conduct the effects of which are confined to the territory of a single Member State is governed by the national legal order."[54]

5.45   In the *Hugin* case, the Court found that there was no potential effect on trade between Member States and, accordingly, annulled the Commission's decision. Hugin was a Swedish manufacturer of cash registers with a market share in the EEC of about 12 per cent., and the abuse for which it had been condemned was its practice of refusing to sell spare parts for its cash registers outside its own distribution network. Whilst the Court found that spare parts could constitute a separate "market," it also found that it was not, on the facts of the particular case, a market which extended beyond national frontiers. There was, thus, no trade between Member States, actual or potential, which was capable of being affected. Were it not for Hugin's policy of refusing to supply outside its own network, Liptons Cash Registers and Business Equipment Limited, the London-based company which had complained of Hugin's conduct to the Commission, would normally have been expected to have obtained supplies from Hugin's English distributor or from Hugin itself, a company based outside the Community. It would, the Court found, have been "an exceptional rather than a normal commercial transaction" for Liptons to obtain supplies from Hugin distributors in other Member States. There was, therefore, insufficient "trade between Member States" actual or potential to be capable of being affected.

5.46   In the *Commercial Solvents* case,[55] on the other hand, the Court considered it to be irrelevant that 90 per cent. of the complainant's sales were made outside the Community. In that case, Commercial Solvents, an American Corporation, and its 51 per cent. owned Italian subsidiary, were the only suppliers of a raw material required for the manufacture of an anti-tubercular drug, also manufactured by Commercial Solvents Corpora-

---

[54] *Ibid.* at pp. 372–373.
[55] *Commercial Solvents Corpn.* v. *EC Commission* [1974] E.C.R. 223; [1974] C.M.L.R. 309.

tion. Zoja, another Italian company, had been refused supplies of the raw material, and, as a result, there was a severe risk of its being eliminated as a competitor to Commercial Solvents. A small proportion of Zoja's sales were made to other Member States so that if it were to go out of business, the competitive situation in the Common Market would be affected. Presumably, if Zoja had made no sales at all in the Community and there had been no possibility of its doing so, it would have had no remedy under Article 86.

VII. APPLICATION OF REGULATION 17/62 TO ARTICLE 86

5.47 Regulation 17/62[56] applies to Article 86, just as to Article 85, with the obvious exception of the articles in the Regulation dealing with exemptions under Article 85 (3). There is, of course, no such possibility under Article 86; once it has been established that the requirements for the application of Article 86 are met, the conduct in question is automatically prohibited.[57]

5.48 It is, however, possible to apply for a "negative clearance" pursuant to Article 2 of Regulation 17, in respect of conduct which might conceivably fall under Article 86. As has already been explained[58] a "negative clearance" is a formal statement from the Commission that the requirements of the Article are not met, and that the Commission has no grounds for taking action.

5.49 No formal Decisions have been issued in respect of cases falling under Article 86, and, although informal discussions have taken place with the Commission in some instances,[58a] it is relatively unlikely that any undertaking which might possibly be found to be in a dominant position in a particular market, would voluntarily draw the Commission's attention to that fact.[59]

5.50 The article of Regulation 17/62 which has most relevance in the context of Article 86 is article 3, under which any "natural or legal persons who claim a legitimate interest" can request the Commission to take action in respect of a possible infringement of Article 86. Virtually all important cases to date, under Article 86, have come about as the result of a com-

---

[56] J.O. 1962, 204; O.J. 1959–1962, 87; and see, *supra,* Chap. 4, paras. 4.85 *et seq.*

[57] See Art. 1, Reg. 17/62.

[58] See, *supra,* Chap. 4, paras. 4.97 *et seq.*

[58a] See Ninth Report on Competition Policy published April 1980, pts. 130–133.

[59] It is, however, possible that where an undertaking which might conceivably be in a dominant position is proposing to take over a competitor, and wants to be reassured in advance that Article 86 does not apply, on the basis on which the Commission tried to apply that Article in the *Continental Can* case. Clearly, the "negative clearance" procedure under Reg. 17/62 has shortcomings as a merger control measure, and, in 1973, the Commission published a draft Reg. "on the control of concentrations between undertakings." (Submitted to the Council July 20, 1973 (O.J. 1973, C92/1)). The draft Reg. lays down clear limits beyond which prior consent to a merger would have to be obtained. The draft Reg. has, however, made virtually no progress in the Council of Ministers, and seems unlikely to be enacted in its present form.

plaint under this article of the Regulation.[60] The procedure will be discussed in detail in relation to both Articles 85 and 86 in Chapter 6.

VIII. *EFFECTS OF A BREACH OF ARTICLE 86*

5.51   The possibility of a complaint being made to the Commission under article 3 of Regulation 17/62 has already been touched on in the previous section, and will be discussed in more detail in Chapter 6. Proceedings under the Regulation can only involve not only a substantial fine[61] or periodic penalty payment[62] but also a "cease and desist" Order or, in appropriate cases, an Order to take action to remedy the abuse.[63]

5.52   The risk of action being taken under Regulation 17 is, however, only one possible effect of a breach of Article 86. Of equal, if not greater, importance are the implications under the domestic laws of the Member States, for Article 86 is a "directly applicable" provision of the Treaty.[64]

5.53   Whatever the precise remedies which may be available from a domestic court for a breach of Article 86[65] there must be some doubt whether an act prohibited by the Article is a nullity. Unlike Article 85 (2), Article 86 itself contains no reference to nullity. The reason given for this is that an abuse will not necessarily take the form of a legal act which is capable of being null and void. A refusal to supply, for example, is a "non-act," in a legal sense. There are, however, frequent occasions where the "abuse" may involve a contract and although that contract may be prohibited by virtue of Article 85 of the Treaty, that is not necessarily so. If, of course, an infringement of Article 85 is involved, the contract in question or the relevant part of it, will be void by virtue of Article 85 (2). In the *Continental Can* case,[66] however, although the takeover of Thomassen and Drijver-Verblifa involved a contract, the Commission's Decision indicates that though, in its view, the takeover constituted a breach of Article 86, the contract by which the

---

[60] *e.g. Zoja* v. *CSC-ICI* [1973] C.M.L.R. D. 50; *United Brands Co.* case [1976] 1 C.M.L.R. D. 28; *Hugin/Liptons* [1978] 1 C.M.L.R. D. 19.

[61] See Art. 15, Reg. 17/62.

[62] See Art. 16, Reg. 17/62.

[63] *e.g. Re Continental Can Co. Inc.* [1972] C.M.L.R. D. 11, where Continental Can was ordered to divest itself of the subsidiary; *Zoja/CSC-ICI,* where Commercial Solvents was ordered to supply specific quantities of the required raw material and to submit proposals for continuing supplies.

[64] For a general discussion of this phrase, see *supra.* Chap. 3, paras. 3.08 *et seq.* and for a general discussion of application of Community law by domestic courts see *supra,* Chap. 3, paras. 3.21 *et seq.*

[65] Presumably if Lord Denning's statements in *Application des Gaz SA* v. *Falks Veritas Ltd.* [1974] 2 C.M.L.R. 75 are correct as a matter of English law and breach of Art. 86 is, indeed, a tort, a remedy would be in damages. It is possible that a remedy may also lie for a breach of statutory duty, *i.e.* s. 2 (1) of the European Communities Act 1972. Finally, it would seem that an injunction or a declaration may be available see, *e.g.* note by V. Korah on *James Budgett & Son Ltd.* v. *British Sugar Corpn. Ltd.* (unreported) [1979] E.L. Rev. 417.

[66] *Continental Can Co. Inc.* [1972] C.M.L.R. D. 11.

takeover was achieved, was not a nullity. The Decision ordered Continental Can's subsidiary to divest itself of its holding which would not, presumably, have been required, if the contract by which the holding had been acquired in the first place was a legal nullity.

5.54   Ultimately it is for the national Courts of a Member State to decide on the legal consequences of an infringement of Article 86. In the *SABAM*[67] case the Court said:

> "If abusive practices are exposed, it is also for that court [*i.e.* the national court] to decide whether and to what extent they affect the interests of authors or third parties concerned, with a view to deciding the consequences with regard to the validity and effect of the contrasts in dispute or certain of their provisions."[68, 69]

---

[67] Case 127/73 *Belgische Radio en Televisie* v. *SABAM* [1974] E.C.R. 313; [1974] 2 238.
[68] *Ibid.* at p. 284.
[69] See also Case 22/79 *Greenwich Films* v. *SACEM* [1980] 1 C.M.L.R. 629, at p. 644.

CHAPTER 6

PROCEDURE

I. *INTRODUCTION*

6.01 This chapter deals with the implementation of Articles 85 and 86 under Regulation 17/62 ("Regulation 17")[1] and ancillary Regulations,[2] and with appeals to the European Court against decisions made by the Commission under the Regulations.[3] It therefore covers the powers of the Commission to investigate suspected infringements of those Articles,[4] the means by which it obtains information[5] and the procedure by which it takes its decisions.

II. *SUSPECTED INFRINGEMENTS*

6.02 Article 3 of Regulation 17 empowers the Commission to issue decisions requiring the termination of infringements of Articles 85 and 86. Its powers under this article may be exercised either on its own initiative, or as a result of complaints made to it. Complaints can be made by the Member States, or, more usually, any "natural or legal persons who claim a legitimate interest."[6] In practice, the majority of proceedings under Article 3 are started as a result of a complaint, although the Commission has certainly been prepared to act, on occasions, on its own initiative.[7]

6.03 The Commission has provided a Form C which can be used for making complaints, although, unlike Form A/B which must be used when notifying an agreement, its use is not mandatory.

6.04 Once it receives the complaint, the Commission is obliged to investigate the matter, and can be brought before the European Court under Article

---

[1] Enacted pursuant to Art. 87 (J.O. 1962, 204; O.J. 1959–1962, 87).

[2] Reg. 27 (J.O. 1962, 1118; O.J. 1959–1962 132); Reg. 99/63 (J.O. 1963, 2268; O.J. 1963–1964, 47).

[3] Reg. 17/62, Art. 17. References by national courts to the European Court for preliminary rulings under Art. 177 have already been discussed in Chap. 3, and the means by which the Commission's attempts to enforce the provisions of the Treaty concerned with the free movement of goods, including Art. 36, will be dealt with in Chap. 7. The parts of Reg. 17 which deal with applications for negative clearance and notifications with a view to obtaining an exemption under Art. 85 (3), have already been considered in Chap. 4.

[4] Reg. 17/62, Art. 3.

[5] Reg. 17/62, Arts. 11, 12, and 14.

[6] Reg. 17/62, Art. 3 (2).

[7] *e.g. Re Continental Can Co. Inc.* [1972] C.M.L.R. D.11.

175 of the Treaty if it fails to do so.[8] An action under that Article can however only be brought if the Commission has been called upon to act, and has failed to do so within two months. Although the question has not been tested in the European Court, the Commission appears to take the view that the two months' notice can only be given once a reasonable period has already elapsed since the complaint was made.

6.05 If the Commission decides that there are no grounds for proceeding in respect of the alleged infringement, it must inform the complainant of its view, and give it the opportunity to make further submissions.[9]

6.06 If, on the other hand, the Commission considers the complaint to be well founded, it then undertakes a full investigation, and the complainant ceases to be directly involved in the procedure. It is, however, entitled to be heard before the Commission's final decision is taken, if it can show a "sufficient interest."[10] Almost certainly the "legitimate interest" which it had to be able to show in order to invoke Article 3 would be a "sufficient interest" for this purpose.

III. *OBTAINING INFORMATION*

A. GENERAL

6.07 The Commission enjoys wide powers under Regulation 17 to obtain information in various ways,[11] and for various purposes.[12] Its powers are backed by the sanction of being able to impose fines[13] or periodic penalty payments[14] on those who fail to co-operate.

6.08 Although the Commission alone has the right to grant exemptions under Article 85 (3)[15] and has the right to investigate suspected infringement of Articles 85 and 86 to the exclusion of the "authorities of the Member States,"[16] Regulation 17, nevertheless, envisages "close and constant liaison"[17] between the Commission and the relevant national authorities.[18] The Commission must send copies of all notifications and complaints to the relevant authorities of all the Member States[19] and it must also send copies

---

[8] The Commission is not obliged to issue a formal decision, merely "to define its position." This may be done by letter, see Case 125/78 *GEMA* v. *Commission* [1980] 2 C.M.L.R. 177.

[9] Reg. 99/63, Art. 6.

[10] Reg. 17/62, Art. 19 (2); Reg. 99/63, Art. 5.

[11] *e.g.* written request for information under Reg. 17/62, Art. 11; on the spot investigations under Reg. 17/62, Art. 14.

[12] *e.g.* sector enquiries under Reg. 17/62, Art. 12.

[13] Reg. 17/62, Art. 15.

[14] Reg. 17/62, Art. 16.

[15] Reg. 17/62, Art. 9 (1); and see *supra*, Chap. 4, para. 4.06.

[16] Reg. 17/62, Art. 9 (3) and see *supra*, Chap. 3, n. 30. "Authorities of the Member States" does not include national courts dealing with Arts. 85 and 86 *à titre incident*.

[17] Reg. 17/62, Art. 10 (2).

[18] In the U.K. the Office of Fair Trading.

[19] Reg. 17/62, Art. 10 (1).

of all written requests for information to the relevant authorities of the Member States where the undertakings concerned are situated.[20] Before making an on the spot investigation, the Commission must consult with the authorities of the Member State concerned,[21] and it can ask for help from the national authority in carrying out the investigation.[22] The advisory committee set up by Article 10 of Regulation 17 is made up of officials from each of the Member States "competent in the matter of restrictive practices and monopolies."[23]

B. REQUESTS FOR INFORMATION

6.09 Requests for information are dealt with in article 11 of Regulation 17. Information under that article can be obtained from the Member States and from undertakings or associations of undertakings including, presumably, undertakings located outside the Community.

6.10 The request for information is normally in the form of a letter, with a specific reference to the provisions of article 15 (1) (*b*) of Regulation 17, which entitle the Commission to impose a fine from 100 to 5,000 units of account if incorrect information is supplied "intentionally or negligently." An undertaking is not, at that stage, under an obligation to respond to the request, but if it does so, the information it gives must be correct.

6.11 If an undertaking refuses to comply with the request, or only complies in part, the Commission may take a formal decision imposing a time limit for compliance.[24] An undertaking which then fails to comply with the decision not only risks a fine under Article 15 (1) (*b*), but also a periodic penalty payment under Article 16 (*c*) at a rate varying between 50 and 1,000 units of account per day.

C. ON THE SPOT INVESTIGATIONS

6.12 Under Article 14 of Regulation 17, the Commission has very wide powers to enter premises, to examine and take copies of an undertaking's business records, and to ask for oral explanations on the spot. Such investigations are carried out by Directorate A of DG IV, and the officials involved carry a written authorisation from the Commission which must be produced to the undertaking concerned. Frequently, although not always, the Commission's own officials are accompanied by an official from the relevant national authority.

---

[20] Reg. 17/62, Art. 11 (2).
[21] Reg. 17/62, Art. 14 (2).
[22] Reg. 17/62, Art. 14 (5).
[23] Reg. 17/62, Art. 10 (4).
[24] Reg. 17/62, Art. 11 (5).

6.13   Although Article 14 (2) requires that the officials' authorisation specifies "the subject matter and purpose of the investigation," this is frequently only expressed in the most general of terms, and gives very little idea of precisely what the Commission is looking for.

6.14   Although the relevant authority in the Member States concerned must be notified in good time of the proposed visit, the undertaking itself is not, under Regulation 17, entitled to prior warning, and prior notice is by no means always given.

6.15   As in the case of requests for information under Article 11 of Regulation 17, an undertaking is not bound to admit the Commission's officials or to co-operate with them unless the Commission has taken a formal decision to that effect, in this case under Article 14 (3). If, an undertaking voluntarily permits the officials to have access but then produces incomplete books or records, it runs the risk of a fine being imposed under Article 15 (1) (c).[24a]

6.16   If, however, a decision has been taken under Article 14 (3) failure to co-operate involves not only the risk of a fine under that article, but also a periodic penalty payment under Article 16 (1) (d). In some instances, the Commission will take a decision under Article 14 (3) before attempting to obtain the undertaking's voluntary co-operation.[25] The undertaking is then bound to submit to the investigation forthwith. This procedure was upheld by the European Court in the *National Panasonic* case.[25a]

D. CONFIDENTIALITY AND PRIVILEGE

6.17   Under Article 214 of the Treaty of Rome, all Community officials are required "not to disclose information of the kind covered by the obligation of professional secrecy." This is of particular importance when dealing with the sort of information likely to be disclosed by an undertaking as a result of an investigation by the Commission using its powers under Regulation 17.

6.18   Article 20 (2) of Regulation 17 extends the obligation of secrecy contained in Article 214 to all information acquired "as a result of the application of this Regulation and of the kind covered by the obligations of professional secrecy." In addition, Article 20 (1) provides that information obtained as a result of requests for information or investigations under Articles 11, 12, 13 and 14 should only be used "for the purpose of the relevant request or investigation."

6.19   Thus, whilst Commission officials are required to keep secret, information disclosed in a notification,[26] or in connection with a complaint,[27] the

---

[24a] See, *e.g. Fabbrica Pisani* [1980] O.J. L75/30; [1980] 2 C.M.L.R. 354; *Fabbrica Pietro Sciarra* [1980] O.J. L75/35; [1980] 2 C.M.L.R. 362.

[25] See Reply to Written Question 677/79 (O.J. 1979, C 310/30).

[25a] Case 136/79 *National Panasonic (U.K.) Ltd.* v. *Commission* [1980] 3 C.M.L.R. 169.

[26] Pursuant to Arts. 4 and 5 of Reg. 17/62.

[27] Pursuant to Art. 3 of Reg. 17/62.

Commission is under no duty to use such information solely for the purposes of the particular notified agreement or complaint.

6.20 Under both Article 11, dealing with requests for information, and Article 14 dealing with on the spot investigations, the Commission is only entitled to obtain "necessary information" or make "necessary investigations." It is not, however, clear whether, in using its powers under these articles of Regulation 17, the Commission is bound to observe the laws of privilege, *i.e.* either privilege against self-incrimination or normal legal professional privilege.

6.21 As far as professional privilege is concerned, the Commission's view is that "Community competition legislation does not provide for any protection for legal papers."[28] In replying to a question from a member of the European Parliament,[29] however, the Commission has stated that it will not use as evidence "any strictly legal papers written with a view to seeking or giving opinions on points of law to be observed or relating to the preparation or planning of the defence of the firm or association of firms concerned."

6.22 The Commission unequivocally takes the view that whether or not such a document should be used is a matter solely for the Commission itself, and that it is, therefore, entitled to see such documents in order to make its decision. The decision[30] in which these statements are made is currently the subject of an appeal to the European Court and the outcome of the appeal will be of great importance. This is particularly so because of the weight given by the Commission, in assessing the amount of any fine to be imposed,[31] to the fact that an undertaking knew its conduct infringed Article 85. Clearly such knowledge would, in many cases, depend on the legal advice which the undertaking concerned had obtained.[32]

IV. *INITIATION OF A PROCEDURE*

A. GENERAL

6.23 It can be important to know whether or not the Commission has formally initiated a procedure, as under Article 9 (3) of Regulation 17 the "national authorities" of the Member States remain competent to apply Articles 85 and 86 until the Commission has taken this step. The significance of this has, however, somewhat diminished since the European Court's ruling in

---

[28] *Re AM & S. Europe Ltd.* [1979] 3 C.M.L.R. 376 at p. 378.
[29] Written Questions 63/68, asked by M. Couste (O.J. 1978, C188/31).
[30] *Re AM & S. Europe Ltd., supra.*
[31] Under Art. 15 (2) of Reg. 17, fines can be imposed where undertakings "*intentionally* or *negligently*" infringe Arts. 85 or 86.
[32] See, *e.g. Re Quinine Cartel* [1969] C.M.L.R. D.41.

the *SABAM* case[33] that the ordinary courts of the Member States are not "national authorities" for this purpose. Such Courts are, thus, free to continue to deal with questions involving Articles 85 and 86 even if the Commission has initiated a procedure.

6.24 Neither Regulation 17 nor any of the related Regulations give any guidance as to when, precisely, a procedure has been initiated. In the *Brasserie de Haecht* (*No.* 2) case,[34] the European Court held that the mere acknowledgment of a notification or a complaint is *not* to be taken as the initiation of a procedure.[35]

6.25 In the same case, the Advocate General expressed the view that a procedure "is to be taken to be initiated if there has been some unequivocal and externally recognisable act towards dealing with the case."[36]

6.26 A request for information under Article 11 of Regulation 17 or a visit from the Commission's officials under Article 14 is not necessarily indicative that a procedure has been started. The Commission has used its powers under those articles in order to decide whether or not to initiate a procedure.

B. STATEMENT OF OBJECTIONS

6.27 Within the Commission, internal rules specify when a procedure has been initiated, but normally the first step as far as the parties are concerned is the receipt of a "statement of objections" from the Commission. That document is sent to the parties or to their joint agent, and is of great importance for two reasons. First, it sets out the whole basis of the Commission's case and, secondly, in its eventual decision, the Commission is *only* entitled to deal with objections in respect of which the undertakings concerned "have been afforded the opportunity of making known their views."[37]

V. *PRELIMINARY DECISIONS UNDER ARTICLE 15 (6) OF REGULATION 17*

6.28 As has already been mentioned[38] one of the benefits of notifying an agreement is that, as from the date of the notification, the Commission no longer has power to impose fines on the parties to the agreement.[39] Under Article 15 (6) of Regulation 17, however, that benefit can be lost if "the

---

[33] *Belgische Radio en Televisie* v. *SABAM* [1974] E.C.R. 313; [1974] 2 C.M.L.R. 238.
[34] *Brasserie de Haecht* v. *Wilkin* (*No.* 2) [1973] E.C.R. 77; [1973] C.M.L.R. 287.
[35] *Ibid.* at p. 303. It has also been held that a "dead letter" is not an initiating procedure. See Case 37/79 *Anne Marty SA* v. *Estée Lauder SA* (unreported).
[36] *Ibid.* at pp. 295–296.
[37] Art. 4, Reg. 99/63.
[38] See *supra*, Chap. 4, para. 4.99.
[39] Art. 15 (5), Reg. 17/62.

Commission has informed the undertakings concerned that after preliminary examination it is of opinion that Article 85 (1) of the Treaty applies and that application of Article 85 (3) is not justified."

6.29 To date, that provision has been used sparingly by the Commission, either where there is particular urgency because of proceedings before a national court[40] or where the infringement of Article 85 is almost self-evident.[41]

6.30 A communication from the Commission under Article 15 (6) produces clear legal effects for the parties concerned,[42] and is a decision within the meaning of Article 189.[43]

6.31 It appears, however, that it is not a "decision" in the sense of Article 19 of Regulation 17, so that the full procedure for hearings under Regulation 99/63 does not have to be followed.[44] The Advisory Committee on Restrictive Practices and Monopolies need not, therefore, be consulted, with the obvious result that a decision can be taken very much more quickly.

6.32 In practice, of course, the issue of a decision under Article 15 (6) is invariably the end of the matter. The agreement is then abandoned by the parties or amended so as not to infringe Article 85, and the Commission is never required to take a full formal decision.

VI. *"DEAD LETTERS"*

6.32.1 A preliminary decision under Article 15 (6) must be distinguished from a so called "dead letter." This is a letter which the Commission sometimes despatches to parties to a notified agreement stating that the Commission has concluded that no action is required under Article 85 (1), and that it is closing its file on the matter.[44a]

VII. *INTERIM MEASURES*

6.32.2 As a result of the European Court's judgment in the *Camera Care* case,[44b] it is now clear that the Commission has power to award interim measures to a complainant in an appropriate case. Since the Court's judgment the Commission has issued a practice note[44c] on the subject, from which it seems that these powers will be used very sparingly.

---

[40] *e.g. Re Sirdar/Phildar* [1975] 1 C.M.L.R. D. 93.

[41] *e.g. Re the notification by S.N.P.E. and Leafields Engineering Ltd.* [1978] 2 C.M.L.R. 758.

[42] *Re Noordwijks Cement Accoord* [1967] C.M.L.R. 77.

[43] See *supra*, Chap. 2, paras. 2.41 *et seq.*

[44] For a fuller discussion of this question see Guy I. F. Leigh, "Resurrection of the provisional decision" [1977] E.L. Rev. 91.

[44a] For a fuller discussion of "dead letters" see Chap. 4, paras. 4.92–4.93.

[44b] Case 792/79R *Camera Care Ltd.* v. *EC Commission* [1980] 1 C.M.L.R. 334.

[44c] Practice Note on Applications for Interim Measures [1980] 2 C.M.L.R. 369. See also "Interim Relief under the Rome Treaty—The European Commission's Power" by J. Ferry [1980] E.I.P.R. 330.

VIII. *PROCEDURE PRIOR TO A DECISION*

6.33 The following section applies in all respects only to "full" decisions of the Commission and not, necessarily, for example to preliminary decisions under Article 15 (6), or to decisions enforcing the Commission's right to obtain information under Articles 11 and 14.[45]

A. WRITTEN PROCEDURE

6.34 The most important procedural step before a decision is taken[46] is the issue by the Commission of its written "Statement of Objections," setting out the basis of its case against the undertakings concerned. The recipients must be given the opportunity to comment, again in writing, on the objections raised by the Commission, and of setting out the grounds of their defence.[47] A time limit for this is fixed in advance by the Commission.[48] It must be at least two weeks[49] and, frequently, in more complicated cases a considerably longer period is allowed. The Commission has power to extend the time limit,[50] and almost invariably agrees to do so if asked.

6.35 As well as the parties directly involved, other "natural or legal persons showing a sufficient interest"[51] can apply to be given the opportunity of commenting and, again, the Commission will impose a time limit for submission of their views.

6.36 Although informal meetings may have taken place with the Commission's officials, up to this stage, the formal procedure is entirely written.

B. THE ORAL HEARING

6.37 When an undertaking makes its written comments on the Commission's Statement of Objections it may request an oral hearing.[52] If the Commission is proposing to impose a fine or periodic penalty payment, it must, if requested, hold an oral hearing; in other situations, it has a discretion whether to do so.

6.38 The hearings are held in private,[53] and the parties may be assisted by lawyers or "other qualified persons." Minutes of the oral hearings are made, and the parties are entitled to approve a draft of the minutes.[54] The

---

[45] *i.e.* under Art. 11 (5) and Art. 14 (3) of Reg. 17.

[46] A statement of objections is also issued before a "decision" is taken under Art. 15 (6) of Reg. 17.

[47] Reg. 99/63, Art. 3.

[48] *Ibid.* Art. 2 (4).

[49] *Ibid.* Art. 11.

[50] *Ibid.* Art. 11 (1).

[51] *Ibid.* Art. 5.

[52] *Ibid.* Art. 7.

[53] *Ibid.* Art. 9 (3).

[54] *Ibid.* Art. 9 (4).

arrangements for the oral hearing are made by the Commission, and the Member States are entitled to send representatives to attend the hearing if they wish to do so.[55]

C. Publication of Summary

6.39 If the Commission intends to grant a negative clearance or an exemption, it must first publish a summary of the application in the *Official Journal*, and give the opportunity for "all interested third parties" to submit comments.[56] A time limit is fixed for third parties to comment, normally the minimum period of one month.

D. The Advisory Committee

6.40 After the written procedure and the oral hearing, the final stage before the Commission's decision is taken is the consultation with the Advisory Committee on Restrictive Practices and Monopolies.[57] The consultation takes place at a meeting with the Committee, and at least 14 days prior to that meeting the members of the Committee must be sent a summary of the case, an indication of the most important documents, and a preliminary draft of the decision.[58] Although the outcome of the meeting with the Advisory Committee is annexed to the final draft decision as signed by the appropriate Commissioner, it is not a public document which the parties are entitled to see.

IX. *COMMISSION'S DECISIONS*

6.41 The Commission is required by Article 21 of Regulation 17 to publish its decisions in the *Official Journal*, although, in doing so, it must protect "the legitimate interest of undertakings in the protection of their business secrets."[59]

6.42 The *Official Journal* is, of course, published in all the official languages of the Community,[60] but only the language or languages in which the decision is communicated to the parties are authentic. The *Official Journal* will always state what those languages were.

6.43 Sometimes the proceedings are settled without a formal decision of the Commission and, in those circumstances, there is no need for any publication. Frequently, however, the Commission will issue a short press release, giving the main details of the issue involved.

---

[55] *Ibid.* Art. 8 (2).
[56] Reg. 17/62, Art. 19 (3).
[57] *Ibid.* Art. 10 (3).
[58] *Ibid.* Art. 10 (5).
[59] Reg. 17, Art. 21 (2).
[60] *i.e.* French, Dutch, Italian, English, Danish, German, Greek.

6.44   Full decisions issued by the Commission are of three kinds:
(a) Negative clearance under Article 2;
(b) Exemptions under Article 6;
(c) "Cease and desist" orders under Article 3, which may be accompanied by a fine under Article 15 or a periodic penalty payment under Article 16.

A. NEGATIVE CLEARANCE

6.45   As has already been mentioned,[61] a negative clearance is a formal statement by the Commission that, on the basis of the facts in its possession, the agreement or practice in question does not involve an infringement of Article 85 (1) or Article 86.

B. EXEMPTION

6.46   As discussed in Chapter 4, an exemption means that Article 85 (1) is applicable, but that the criteria for an exemption under Article 85 (3) are met. An exemption will always be issued for a specified period[62] and will also run from a particular date, which cannot be earlier than the date of notification.[63] Almost invariably, an exemption is issued subject to conditions and the Commission has power to revoke it in certain circumstances, such as, for instance, a change in the factual situation or a breach of one of the conditions contained in the exemption.[64] On application, an exemption can be renewed, but again only for a specified period, and it is open to the Commission to amend the conditions subject to which it granted the exemption originally.[65]

C. "CEASE AND DESIST" ORDERS

6.47   Finally, the Commission may issue "cease and desist" orders under Article 3 of Regulation 17, which may also require an undertaking to take positive action such as, for example, to make supplies available where they have been withheld in breach of Article 86.[66]

D. FINES AND PERIODIC PENALTY PAYMENTS

6.48   Even where an infringement of Articles 85 or 86 is established, the Com-

---

[61] See, *supra*, Chap. 4, para. 4.101.
[62] Reg. 17/62, Art. 8 (1).
[63] *Ibid.* Art. 6 (1).
[64] *Ibid.* Art. 8 (3).
[65] See, *e.g. Transocean Marine Paint Association (No.* 2) [1975] 2 C.M.L.R. D. 75; *Re Transocean Marine Paint Association (No.* 3) [1979] 3 C.M.L.R. 430.
[66] See, *e.g. Zoja* v. *Commercial Solvents Corpn.* [1973] C.M.L.R. D. 50.

mission is not bound to impose fines and, indeed, only has power to do so where the infringement is committed "either intentionally or negligently." The amount of the fine may vary from 1,000 to 1,000,000 units of account,[67] or a sum in excess of that but not exceeding 10 per cent. of the turnover in the previous year, of the undertakings concerned.[68] In fixing the amount of the fine, the Commission is required to have regard "both to the gravity and to the duration of the infringement." Although fines have now been imposed in a number of cases, it is very difficult to obtain any general guidance on the amount of the fine likely to be imposed in any particular circumstances.[69] The Commission also has power to impose periodic penalty payments[70] of from 50 to 1,000 units of account per day.[70a]

X. APPEALS TO THE EUROPEAN COURT

A. GENERAL

6.49 An appeal lies to the European Court against decisions issued by the Commission under Regulation 17, on the general grounds set out in Article 173 of the Treaty, that is to say "on grounds of lack of competence, infringement of an essential procedural requirement, infringement of this Treaty or of any rule of law relating to its application, or misuse of powers." As well as its general powers under that Article, the Court of Justice also has unlimited jurisdiction to review decisions of the Commission which fix a fine or periodic penalty payment.[71]

B. WHO MAY BRING AN APPEAL

6.50 An appeal may be brought both by the person to whom the decision was addressed, and by a third party, if it can show that the decision, although not addressed to it, "is of direct and individual concern" to it.[72] Thus, for example, an unsuccessful intervener appealed against an exemption

---

[67] A "unit of account" is valued daily on the basis of a "basket" of currencies of the Member States. The resulting value for each individual national currency is published each day in the *Official Journal*.

[68] Art. 15 (2), Reg. 17/62.

[69] For summary of the fines imposed between 1969 and 1976 see Bellamy & Child, *Common Market Law of Competition*, pp. 363–364. See also Reply to Written Question No. 715/80 (O.J. 1980, C245/15).

[70] Art. 16, Reg. 17/62.

[70a] It should be noted that fines and periodic penalty payments have been held to be "penalties" in the meaning of s. 14 of the Civil Evidence Act 1968. This therefore is a ground for refusing to answer a question under that section and s. 3 of the Evidence (Proceedings in Other Jurisdictions) Act 1975: *Rio Tinto Zinc* v. *Westinghouse Electric (No.* 1) [1977] 2 C.M.L.R. 420.

[71] Art. 17, Reg. 17/62.

[72] Art. 173 (2).

granted by the Commission for a selective distribution system for televisions, radios and tape recorders.[73]

C. Time Limit for Appeal

6.51 The appeal must be brought within two months of the undertaking being notified of the Commission's decision, if the appellant is the recipient of the decision, or, within two months of its publication in the *Official Journal*.

D. Effects of an Appeal

6.52 In principle, the bringing of the appeal does not have any suspensory effect on the Commission's decision[74] but the Court has a discretionary power to order a stay of execution. It has indicated that it will only do so in exceptional circumstances. Presumably, therefore, it will be necessary to show that the Commission's decision, if implemented, would cause serious damage to the applicant.

6.53 The Court has, on occasions, been prepared to quash decisions of the Commission, particularly if it considers the Commission's reasoning to have been incorrect or inadequate.[75] It has also been prepared to quash fines or reduce fines.[76]

XI. *LIMITATION PERIODS*

6.54 Council Regulation 2988/74[77] which came into force on January 1, 1975 provides limitation periods in respect of the power to impose fines or penalties for infringement of the Competition rules. For most purposes the period is five years, but this period is interrupted by any "action" taken by the Commission or by a Member State on its behalf.

---

[73] *Metro-SB-Grossmärkte GmbH & Co. KG* v. *Commission* [1977] E.C.R. 1875; [1978] 2 C.M.L.R. 1.

[74] Art. 17, Reg. 17, and see Case 45/71R *GEMA* v. *EC Commission* [1971] E.C.R. 791; [1972] C.M.L.R. 694.

[75] *Europemballage Corpn. & Continental Can Co. Inc.* v. *Commission* [1973] E.C.R. 215; [1972] C.M.L.R. 690; *Hugin Kassaregister AB* v. *Commission* [1979] 3 C.M.L.R. 345.

[76] e.g. *United Brands Co. and United Brands Continental BV* v. *Commission* [1978] 1 C.M.L.R. 429.

[77] O.J. 1974, L319/1. See App. 7.

CHAPTER 7

FREE MOVEMENT OF GOODS AND SERVICES

(Introduction to Articles 30 to 36, 59 and 60)

I. *GENERAL*

7.01　Articles 30 to 36 are concerned with the "free movement of goods" within the Community, as distinct from the regulation of "competition," which is dealt with in Articles 85 and 86. Indeed, the very location of Articles 30 to 36 in Chapter 2 of Title I of Part Two of the Treaty is revealing. Part Two of the Treaty is entitled "Foundations of the Community," and Title I and Chapter 2 are headed respectively "Free Movement of Goods" and "Elimination of Quantitative Restrictions Between Member States." These headings indicate that the aim of Articles 30 to 36 is to achieve the free circulation of goods within the Community, which is one of the objectives specified in Article 3 (*a*) of the Treaty.[1]

7.02　Articles 30 to 34, in effect, lay down a "basic rule," and Article 36 grants a qualified exception to that rule. Thus, Articles 30 to 34 prohibit quantitative restrictions on the import and export of goods between Member States and "all measures having equivalent effect."[2] Article 36 then waives that prohibition in certain narrowly defined circumstances.

7.03　Article 36 is crucial to any consideration of the application to intellectual property of the provisions of the Treaty dealing with free movement of goods, because it applies expressly to measures "justified on grounds of . . . the protection of industrial and commercial property."

7.04　One crucial substantive difference between Article 85 and Articles 30 to 36 should, however, be noted at the outset. As with Article 86, Articles 30 to 36 can apply to acts carried out by only one undertaking or group of undertakings.[3] There is no requirement that there be an agreement, decision or concerted practice between two or more undertakings, as is required for the application of Article 85.

---

[1] See Art. 3 (*a*), and the discussion *supra*, Chap. 1, paras. 1.08 *et seq.*
[2] See, in particular, Art. 30 (concerned with imports) and Art. 34 (1) (concerned with exports), discussed *infra*, at paras. 7.07 *et seq.*
[3] As to the treatment of a group of undertakings in the context of Articles 30 to 36 see *infra*, Chaps. 8 and 9.

7.05   In this Chapter the general prohibition in Articles 30 to 34 will first be considered, and then the nature of the qualified exception in Article 36. Thereafter, the procedural differences between these Articles and Articles 85 and 86 will be discussed. In addition brief mention will be made at the end of this Chapter to Articles 59 and 60, which are not concerned with goods at all, but rather with services. To date, the only type of intellectual property affected by these Articles is performing rights as an element of copyright.

7.06   The application of Articles 30 to 36, 59 and 60 to specific types of intellectual property will be considered in Chapters 8, 9, and 12.

II. *ARTICLES 30 TO 34*

A. GENERAL

7.07   While all five of these Articles are, in one way or another, concerned with the general prohibition against quantitative restrictions on trade between Member States and measures having equivalent effect, the provisions which are of most relevance to intellectual property are Articles 30 and 34 (1). These two Articles complement each other. Article 30 is concerned with restrictions on imports, and Article 34 (1) with restrictions on exports. The two provisions state as follows:

Article 30

Quantitative restrictions on imports and all measures having equivalent effect shall, without prejudice to the following provisions, be prohibited between Member States.

Article 34 (1)

Quantitative restrictions on exports, and all measures having equivalent effect, shall be prohibited between Member States.

B. THE MEANING OF "MEASURES HAVING EQUIVALENT EFFECT"

7.08   In the context of intellectual property the crucial phrase is "measures having equivalent effect," which appears in both Articles 30 and 34 (1).[4]

7.09   The European Court has, in a variety of situations, held that the exercise of national intellectual property rights in such a way as to prevent the import or export of goods between Member States constitutes a "measure

---

[4] See generally Page, "The Concept of Measures Having an Equivalent Effect to Quantitative Restrictions" [1977] 2 E.L. Rev. 105. Note also that where national intellectual property rights operate as "measures having equivalent effect" to quantitative restrictions on imports and exports, Arts. 30 and 34 (1) apply to trade involving the new Member States with effect from the date of Accession: Case 15/74 *Centrafarm BV* v. *Sterling Drug Inc.* [1974] E.C.R., 1183; [1974] 2 C.M.L.R. 480 at p. 506.

having equivalent effect" to a quantitative restriction or quota,[5] and, in consequence, is prohibited.

7.10   This development was foreshadowed by an answer given by the Commission in 1967 to a question from a Member of the European Parliament, as to the meaning of the prohibition in Article 30 against "quantitative restrictions on imports and all measures having equivalent effect." Although the question was concerned specifically with Article 30, the Commission's reply is indicative of its general approach to the interpretation of Articles 30 to 36 of the Treaty. It said in part:

> "The general prohibition of Article 30 goes to the effect of measures and not their nature or content. Thus any measure, regardless of its nature or content, can, simply by reason of its effect on the free movement of goods, be a measure having the same effect to a quantitative restriction to the extent that it does not belong within the field of application of another title of the Treaty."[6]

7.11   An interesting illustration of the European Court's early willingness to apply the phrase "measures having equivalent effect" to acts which superficially do not resemble quantitative restrictions or quotas is its judgment in the *Dassonville* case.[7]

The Dassonville case

7.12   The facts of the case are relatively straightforward. Under Belgian Law it was illegal to export, sell or display for sale spirits identified with a designation of origin adopted by the Belgian Government, unless the spirits in question were accompanied by an official document from the country of origin certifying the entitlement to such designation. "Scotch Whisky" had been duly adopted as a designation of origin by the Belgian Government.

7.13   In 1970, the Dassonvilles (father and son) imported "Johnnie Walker" and "VAT 69" "Scotch Whisky" into Belgium from France, where they had purchased it from the French importers and distributors. French law did not require a certificate of origin for "Scotch Whisky." The whisky in question was then imported into Belgium after having been duly imported into France and cleared there as "Community goods," but without being accompanied by an official British document certifying the entitlement of the whisky to the designation "Scotch Whisky."

7.14   Criminal proceedings were duly instituted before the Belgian courts by the Belgian Public Prosecutor on charges relating to the violation of the Belgian Certificate of Origin requirements, while the exclusive importers

---

[5] See discussion *infra*, in Chaps. 8, 9 and 12.

[6] Answer to Written Question No. 118, submitted by Mr. Deringer to the Commission. (J.O. No. 9, January 17, 1967, p. 122, and J.O. No. 59, March 29, 1967, p. 901) (Note: the above translation is taken from the C.C.H. Common Market Reporter, since at the relevant time English was not an official Community language).

[7] *Procureur Du Roi* v. *Dassonville* [1974] E.C.R. 837; [1974] 2 C.M.L.R. 436.

and distributors of "VAT 69" and "Johnnie Walker" in Belgium instituted civil proceedings alleging damages arising from the illegal importation of the whisky by the Dassonvilles. The Dassonvilles argued in their defence that the requirements of Belgian law were incompatible with the prohibition on quantitative restrictions or measures having equivalent effect contained in the provisions of the Treaty concerning free movement of goods. Faced with this contention, the Belgian Court made a reference to the European Court of Justice.

7.15   One of the questions which the Belgian Court referred for interpretation asked whether Article 30 is infringed by a national provision which prohibits the importation of goods bearing a designation of origin unless those goods are accompanied by an official document issued by the exporting country and certifying their right to that designation. In other words, was such national provision a measure equivalent to a quantitative restriction?

7.16   It emerged from the Court's file that while a Belgian trader wishing to import whisky directly from Britain could obtain the relevant certificate with ease, it was in fact very difficult to do so when the whisky being imported into Belgium was already in free circulation in France. Thus, in practice only a direct importer could easily fulfil the Belgian requirements.

7.17   In the light of these facts the Court concluded that the Belgian requirements did indeed constitute a measure having an effect equivalent to a quantitative restriction, and that they were therefore prohibited by Article 30 of the Treaty. In the course of its judgment, the Court said:

"All trading rules enacted by Member States which are capable of hindering, directly or indirectly, actually or potentially, intra-Community trade are to be considered as measures having an effect equivalent to quantitative restrictions."[8]

7.18   In view of the uncompromising tone of this statement, it is not surprising that the enforcement of domestic intellectual property rights has, in various situations, been held to constitute a measure having an equivalent effect to a quantitative restriction. The particular cases will be discussed in detail in the next two chapters.

7.19   Where enforcement of an intellectual property right is held to be a measure having such an effect, it is then necessary to consider whether Article 36 permits the continued enforcement of that right.

---

[8] *Ibid.* at p. 453. See also generally on the interpretation of the phrase "measures having an equivalent effect" to quantitative restrictions, *e.g. Re German Sparkling Wines & Brandies* [1975] 1 C.M.L.R. 340; *Rewe-Zentralfinance GmbH* v. *Direktor Der Landwirtschaftskammer* [1975] E.C.R. 843; [1977] 1 C.M.L.R. 599; *S.A.D.M.* v. *Comitato Interministeriale Dei Prezzi* [1977] 2 C.M.L.R. 183; *Simmenthal SpA* v. *Ministero Delle Finanze* [1977] 2 C.M.L.R. 1; *Firma Joh. Eggers Sohn & Co.* v. *Freie Hansestadt Bremen* [1979] E.C.R. 1935; [1979] 1 C.M.L.R. 562; *Re the Export of Potatoes: EC Commission* v. *France* [1977] E.C.R. 515; [1977] 2 C.M.L.R. 161.

III. *ARTICLE 36*

7.20 The distinction which the European Court and the Commission have evolved between the existence and the exercise of intellectual property rights stems in particular from Article 36 of the Treaty. Article 36 states:

> "The provisions of Articles 30 to 34 shall not preclude prohibitions or restrictions on imports, exports or goods in transit justified on grounds of . . . the protection of industrial and commercial property. Such prohibitions or restrictions shall not, however, constitute a means of arbitrary discrimination or a disguised restriction on trade between Member States."

7.21 The first sentence of Article 36 therefore derogates from the prohibitions which are contained in Articles 30 to 34, where the restrictions concerned can be justified on one of the grounds specified in that sentence. For present purposes the only relevant ground is "the protection of industrial and commercial property."[9]

7.22 The second sentence of Article 36 provides that even where a restriction which would otherwise fall foul of Articles 30 to 34 is covered by the first sentence of Article 36, the restriction cannot be enforced if it would constitute either "a means of arbitrary discrimination or a disguised restriction on trade between Member States." The second sentence of Article 36 is, therefore, a proviso to the exemption conferred by the first sentence of Article 36.

7.23 Article 36 is crucial to any attempt to resolve the inherent conflict between national intellectual property rights on the one hand and provisions of the Treaty on the "free movement of goods" on the other hand.[10]

7.24 As in other contexts,[11] the European Court has sought to resolve this conflict by drawing a distinction between the *existence* of national intellectual property rights and their *exercise*. It has held that while the *existence* of national intellectual property rights is unaffected by the provisions on "free movement of goods," the manner in which those rights may be *exercised* is regulated by them.

7.25 Article 36 lends itself to this distinction, because its first and second sentences can be regarded as in themselves expressing the relationship between existence and exercise of intellectual property rights.

7.26 On this view, the first sentence of Article 36 protects those features of an intellectual property right which are essential to its "existence," while the second sentence ensures that no such protection is afforded the mere exercise of other less essential features of the right.[12]

---

[9] As to the other "grounds" specified in Art. 36, Art. 36 is reproduced in full in App. 1.

[10] See generally, Chap. I.

[11] Particularly Art. 85, as to which see Chap. 4 at paras. 4.02 *et seq.*

[12] See discussion *infra,* at para. 8.41. Note also, Hartmut Johannes, *Industrial Property & Copyright in European Community Law* (A. W. Sijthoff-Leyden, 1976), pp. 28–30.

7.27   The application of Article 36 to specific factual situations will be discussed in following chapters.[13] For the present, it is sufficient to note that the first and second sentences of Article 36, taken together, provide a qualified but vital exception to the general prohibition against quantitative restrictions and measures having equivalent effect on trade between Member States.

IV. PROCEDURAL DIFFERENCES BETWEEN ARTICLES 30 TO 36 AND ARTICLES 85 AND 86

7.28   As is the case with Articles 85 and 86, Articles 30 to 36 are "directly applicable."[14] Here, however, the procedural similarity between the two ends.

7.29   From the point of view of a potential complainant, Articles 30 to 36 are procedurally "second best," and are therefore usually only resorted to when Articles 85 or 86 are for some reason not available. Articles 30 to 36 are not as flexible as the competition Articles largely because there is no implementing Regulation like Regulation 17/62. In consequence, there is no clearcut procedure whereby the Commission may initiate proceedings against an undertaking to bring to an end an infringement of the "free movement of goods" provisions of the Treaty, in the same way as it can Articles 85 and 86, either on its own motion or on the application of a third party under Article 3 of Regulation 17/62.

7.30   This said, the Commission is charged generally with ensuring that the provisions of the Treaty are complied with,[15] and may take decisions to that end.[16] The Commission will therefore rely upon its general powers to enforce the provisions concerning free movement of goods against "undertakings," in appropriate cases. There may, of course, also be circumstances where an infringement of Articles 85 (1) or 86 is involved in addition to a contravention of Articles 30 to 36.

---

[13] See particularly Chaps. 8, 9, and 12.

[14] That this is so is apparent from the European Court's judgments in, *e.g. Procureur Du Roi* v. *Dassonville* [1974] E.C.R. 837; [1974] 2 C.M.L.R. 436; *Deutsche Grammophon Gesellschaft GmbH* v. *Metro-SB-Grossmärkte GmbH & Co. KG* [1971] E.C.R. 487; [1971] C.M.L.R. 631; *Centrafarm BV* v. *Sterling Drug Inc.* [1974] E.C.R. 1183; *Centrafarm BV* v. *Winthrop BV* [1974] 2 C.M.L.R. 489; *Hoffmann-La Roche & Co. AG* v. *Centrafarm* [1978] E.C.R. 1139; *Centrafarm BV* v. *American Home Products Corporation* [1978] E.C.R. 1823; [1979] 1 C.M.L.R. 326; *Van Zuylen Frères* v. *Hag AG* [1974] E.C.R. 731; [1974] 2 C.M.L.R. 127. Note also the opinion of Advocate General Karl Roemer in *Capolongo* v. *Azienda Agricola Maya* [1974] 1 C.M.L.R. 230 at p. 242. In reply to a question by the national court as to whether Art. 30 was directly applicable, Advocate General Roemer replied: "As regards Article 30, one can point to the judgment in *Salgoil*. It is probably the accepted view that this direct applicability has existed at least since the end of the transitional period...." The position with regard to Greece is governed by Articles 35 to 40 of the Act concerning the conditions of accession of the Hellenic Republic and the adjustments to the Treaties.

[15] Art. 155.

[16] Art. 189.

7.31   The Commission would then be in a position, in practice, to enforce both sets of provisions by following the procedure laid down for the implementation of Articles 85 and 86.[17]

7.32   Notwithstanding these possibilities for direct intervention by the Commission, a party wishing to rely on Articles 30 to 36 will generally invoke those Articles before a national court. The national court may, of course, in turn refer the relevant questions to the European Court for a preliminary ruling, pursuant to Article 177. Indeed, many of the most important developments in Community law relating to intellectual property rights have taken place as a result of such references.[18]

7.33   Despite their procedural limitations, Articles 30 to 36 are increasingly important provisions of the EEC Treaty. The mere fact that those Articles must, in the first instance, usually be raised before a national court is in no sense a bar to their effectiveness, as will be seen in the succeeding chapters. Indeed, it should not be forgotten that parties also frequently raise Articles 85 and 86 before the national courts as a matter of choice.

V. ADDITIONAL PROVISIONS RELATING TO PERFORMING RIGHTS AS AN ELEMENT OF COPYRIGHT: ARTICLES 59 AND 60

7.34   Articles 59 and 60 of the Treaty are concerned with free movement of services, and in the context of intellectual property have to date been held relevant only to performing rights as an element of copyright.[19]

Articles 59 and 60 are fully set out in Appendix 1 and they have been held to prohibit restrictions on the free movement of services in ways not dissimilar to the prohibition imposed by Articles 30 to 34 on the free movement of goods.[20]

7.35   The Treaty does not in terms contain any article analogous to Article 36 relating to services, as distinct from goods. In the *Coditel* case,[21] however, the European Court held that principles akin to those which it has developed in applying Article 36 to restrictions imposed on the free movement of goods apply also to restrictions imposed on the free movement of services. It follows that although performing rights, such as those involved in a television broadcast, will not be affected by the provisions of Articles 30 *et seq.* because the intellectual property does not subsist in "goods," but

---

[17] See *Tanabe Seiyaku Co.* v. *Bayer AG* [1979] 2 C.M.L.R. 80. Note also the Commission's Eighth Report on Competition Policy, at pp. 95 and 96.

[18] *e.g.* all the cases referred to in n. 14 above; *EMI Records Ltd.* v. *CBS United Kingdom Ltd.* [1976] E.C.R. 811, 871, 913; [1976] 2 C.M.L.R. 235; *Terrapin (Overseas) Ltd.* v. *Terranova Industrie C.A. Kapferer & Co.* [1976] E.C.R. 1039; [1976] 2 C.M.L.R. 482.

[19] Case 62/79 *Coditel SA and Others* v. *Ciné Vog Films SA* (not yet reported).

[20] *Ibid.* See also Case 52/79 *Procureur du Roi* v. *Debauve and Others* (not yet reported); more generally, see the annotations to Art. 59 and 60 in App. 1.

[21] *Coditel SA, supra,* n. 19.

rather in "services," the doctrines which the Court has developed when considering the application of Articles 30 to 36 to goods protected by intellectual property may be relevant by analogy to performing rights as an element of copyright, and indeed generally when the provision of services is affected by intellectual property.

7.36   The *Coditel* case will be discussed in detail in Chapter 12.[22]

---

[22] See, *infra*, paras. 12.58.2, *et seq.*

Part II

Reliance on Intellectual Property

CHAPTER 8

OWNERSHIP OF INTELLECTUAL PROPERTY BY ONE ENTERPRISE IN THE COMMUNITY

I. *INTRODUCTION*

8.01   This chapter is concerned with the extent to which the Treaty limits the owner of an intellectual property right in the traditional exercise of that right *vis-à-vis* third party "infringers" with whom no contractual relationship exists. By "owner," is meant one or more undertakings which, as a matter of Community law, would be viewed as a single enterprise.[1] By contrast, the next chapter deals with ownership by two or more "enterprises" within the Community of an identical or a similar intellectual property right, and with the extent to which the Treaty affects the traditional non-contractual relationship between the two owners.

8.02   The scope of the two chapters may perhaps best be illustrated by example. This chapter will cover questions such as whether Articles 30 to 36 affect the position of the owner of a Dutch patent who, but for those Articles, would under Dutch law be able to exercise his patent to prevent a third party from importing into Holland goods manufactured and marketed by him abroad.[2] By contrast, the next chapter will be concerned with questions such as whether a German trade mark owner may "exercise" his trade mark to prevent the importation into Germany of goods manufactured in England and bearing a trade mark registered in England but, under German trade mark law, considered to be confusingly similar with the German trade mark, in circumstances in which both trade mark owners had legitimately and independently of each other acquired their respective rights.[3]

8.03   As this chapter deals with the position of an owner of intellectual property *vis-à-vis* third parties *in the absence of any contractual relationship between them*, Article 85 will not be relevant. The Articles which are of primary concern are Articles 30 to 36 of the Treaty. In addition, as the owner of the intellectual property may be in a dominant position, Article

---

[1] See generally *supra*, Chap. 4 at paras. 4.30 *et seq.* It would appear that the doctrine of enterprise entity applies also in the context of Articles 30 to 36, although the point has not to date been tested. See, *e.g.* the European Court's treatment of ownership of intellectual property rights by a group of companies in *Centrafarm BV* v. *Winthrop BV* [1974] 2 C.M.L.R. 480.

[2] Case 15/74, *Centrafarm BV* v. *Sterling Drug Inc.* [1974] E.C.R. 1183; [1974] 2 C.M.L.R. 480.

[3] *Terrapin (Overseas) Ltd.* v. *Terranova Industrie* [1978] 3 C.M.L.R. 102.

86 must also be borne in mind. Finally, Articles 59 and 60 may be relevant, for example where the intellectual property concerned is a performing right as an element of copyright.

8.04   Articles 30 to 36 will first be considered, and then Article 86.

II. ARTICLES 30 TO 36—IMPACT ON A SINGLE OWNER OF INTELLECTUAL PROPERTY

A. GENERAL REMARKS

8.05   The decided cases affecting the relationship between the owner of an intellectual property right and a third party infringer may usefully be divided into the following categories:

Category 1

Goods covered by an intellectual property right in one EEC Member State ("A") are manufactured (but not marketed) in State "A" by the owner of the right ("O"). The goods are marketed in a second Member State ("B") by "O," or with his consent. A subsequent purchaser of the goods seeks to market them in Member State "A," where "O," under national law, is entitled to prevent such marketing. Under Community law, may "O" exercise his intellectual property right in State "A" to prevent such marketing?

Category 2

Goods covered by an intellectual property right in one EEC Member State ("A"), are manufactured *and* marketed in that State by the owner of the right "O" or with his consent. A subsequent purchaser seeks to market the goods in a second Member State ("B"), in which "O" also owns or enjoys the benefit of a parallel right. Under Community law, may "O" exercise his right in the second Member State ("B") to prevent such marketing?

Category 3

Goods not covered by an intellectual property right are manufactured and marketed in a Member State of the Community ("A"). A subsequent purchaser seeks to market those goods in a second Member State ("B") in which similar goods, which *are* covered by an intellectual property right, are manufactured and marketed by the owner of that right ("O"). Under Community law, may "O" exercise his right in the second state ("B"), to prevent importation of the goods from the first state ("A")?

Category 4

Goods are manufactured outside the EEC and imported into an EEC Member State in circumstances which would involve the infringement of an intellectual property right owned by an independent party in that Member State ("O"). Under Community law, may "O" exercise his right to prevent importation of the goods from outside the EEC?

8.06   It is proposed in this chapter to discuss the decided cases falling within each of these four categories. The degree to which a given right may be exercised without contravening the provisions of the Treaty dealing with free movement of goods may, of course, vary depending upon the nature of the right in question. Where such variations exist these will be mentioned, after the general position has been established.

B. Category 1

Goods covered by an intellectual property right in one EEC Member State ("A") are manufactured (but not marketed) in State "A" by the owner of the right ("O"). The goods are marketed in a second Member State ("B") by "O", or with his consent. A subsequent purchaser of the goods seeks to market them in Member State "A", where "O" under national law, is entitled to prevent such marketing. Under Community law, may "O" exercise his intellectual property right in State "A" to prevent such marketing?

(1) *The Deutsche Grammophon Case*

8.07   The starting point here must be the European Court's judgment in the *Deutsche Grammophon* case.[4] The facts, as so often, were relatively straightforward.

(a) The facts

8.08   Deutsche Grammophon GmbH is the well-known German record manufacturer. In Germany it supplied its records direct to retailers and to two book wholesalers which, in turn, supplied certain retail bookshops. At the time of the proceedings, 1970,[5] retail price maintenance was permitted by German law and records which Deutsche Grammophon sold under its "Polydor" mark were sold subject to a retail price maintenance system. Deutsche Grammophon required that retailers sign an appropriate undertaking in this regard. The undertaking was expressed to apply to Deutsche Grammophon records acquired from third parties as well as to those supplied by Deutsche Grammophon direct, and also provided that Deutsche Grammophon records could only be imported from abroad with the authorisation of Deutsche Grammophon. The authorisation was only

---

[4] Case 78/70 *Deutsche Grammophon Gesellschaft mbh.* v. *Metro-SB-Grossmärkte* [1971] E.C.R. 487; [1971] C.M.L.R. 631.

[5] The proceedings before the Hanseatische Oberlandesgericht took place in 1970, while the European Court gave its judgment in 1971.

given if the retailer undertook to observe the retail price maintenance system in respect of such imported products. Deutsche Grammophon marketed its "Polydor" label records in France through its French subsidiary, Polydor SA. On occasion, however, records manufactured in Germany were also supplied to Polydor SA.

8.09   Metro-S.B.Grossmärkte GmbH of Hamburg had purchased Polydor records from Deutsche Grammophon during the period from April to October 1969 but had failed to observe the retail price maintenance system, and business relations between it and Deutsche Grammophon were accordingly broken off. In early 1970, however, Metro succeeded in obtaining from a Hamburg wholesaler Polydor records which had been manufactured in Germany. The records had apparently been supplied by Deutsche Grammophon to its Paris subsidiary, and reached the Hamburg wholesaler via Switzerland. Metro then proceeded to sell the records at a price below that fixed by Deutsche Grammophon for the Federal Republic of Germany.

8.10   On learning of Metro's conduct, Deutsche Grammophon obtained an interim injunction from the Hamburg Landgericht, prohibiting Metro from selling or distributing the relevant Polydor records. The Landgericht's judgment was based on the relevant German statute relating to copyright and similar protection rights.[6]

8.11   Metro duly appealed the Landgericht's judgment to a higher German Court. It is noteworthy that although Metro adduced a variety of arguments based both on EEC law and on German national law, it did not in fact contend that Deutsche Grammophon might by its conduct be contravening Articles 30 to 36. So far as the EEC considerations were concerned, it contended instead that Articles 85 and 86 were infringed having regard to the contractual relationship existing between Deutsche Grammophon and its French subsidiary, considered in conjunction with Deutsche Grammophon's resale price maintenance system. The national court duly suspended its proceedings and referred two questions to the European Court pursuant to Article 177 the first dealing with the Article 85 allegations and the second with Article 86 allegations.

---

[6] Gesetz Uber Urheberrecht Und Verwandte Schutzrechte of September 9, 1965. The provisions of this statute relied upon were ss. 85 and 97. s. 85 states: "The manufacturer of a sound recording has the exclusive right to reproduce and to distribute the recording." s. 97 states: "Any person who unlawfully infringes the copyright or any other right protected by this statute may, at the suit of the person whose rights are infringed, be ordered to abate the infringement, or, if there is danger of repetition, be restrained by injunction, and if he is found to have acted with intent or negligence he may be ordered to pay damages." See the *Deutsche Grammophon Gesellschaft* case, *supra*, n. 4, at p. 635. In addition, and though it was not referred to by the European Court in its judgment, s. 17 of the same statute should be noted; see discussion *infra*, at para. 8.20. It was much referred to, both by the German national courts and by the Advocate General in his opinion. s. 17.2 states: "If the original or reproductions of the work have been brought into circulation with the consent of the person entitled to distribute them in the Territory to which this statute applies by means of alienation, their further distribution is permitted."

8.12   The question referred to the European Court concerning Article 85 was in the following terms:

1. Does an interpretation of Sections 97 and 85[7] of the Statute concerning Copyright and Similar Protection Rights ..., whereby a German manufacturer of sound recordings, by virtue of its distribution rights, can prohibit the marketing in the German Federal Republic of recordings which it has itself supplied to its subsidiary in France which is legally separate but economically completely dependent, conflict with Article 5 (2) or Article 85 (1) of the EEC Treaty?

(b) The Court's judgment

8.13   The Court rephrased the question in the following terms:

"... the question posed really seeks to ascertain whether Community Law is infringed if the exclusive right conferred on a manufacturer of recordings by national legislation to distribute protected products can be used to prohibit the domestic marketing of products that have been brought onto the market in the territory of another Member State by this manufacturer or with his consent."[8]

8.14   As the European Court was quick to point out, neither Article 5 (2) nor Article 85 (1) were relevant to the situation at hand. In particular, Article 5 (2) does no more than impose a general obligation on Member States not to take measures which will prejudice the attainment of the objectives of the Treaty, and one must then look to other provisions of the Treaty to find more concrete requirements.[9] Article 85 (1) was also of no assistance to Metro because there was no agreement between two independent undertakings.[10]

8.15   The Court then went on to consider the relevance of Articles 30 to 36, read in conjunction with Article 3 (*f*) of the Treaty, which provides for "the institution of a system ensuring that competition in the Common Market is not distorted."[11]

8.16   The Court assumed that a right equivalent to a copyright would come within the phrase "industrial and commercial property" as used in Article 36, but affirmed at the same time that while the Treaty does not affect the existence of national intellectual property rights the manner in which those rights are exercised may well be prohibited. It noted also that the first sentence of Article 36 permits restrictions on the free movement of goods justified for the protection of industrial and commercial property, but

---

[7] For the text of these provisions, see *supra*, n. 6.

[8] *Ibid. Deutsche Grammophon Gesellschaft mbH* v. *Metro-SB-Grossmärkte* [1971] E.C.R. 487; [1971] C.M.L.R. 631 at p. 656.

[9] See, however, Hartmut Johannes, *Industrial Property and Copyright in European Community Law*, p. 26. Dr. Johannes there expresses the view that in its judgment the European Court "did use ... wording which closely resembles that of Article 5 (2)."

[10] See Chap. 4 at para. 4.11 *et seq.* and Chap. 7 at para. 7.05.

[11] See discussion *supra*, Chap. 1 at para. 1.12.

construed this to mean that restrictions could only be justified within the meaning of that sentence to the extent that they were "... for the protection of the rights that form the specific object of this property," presumably as distinct from attributes of the right which do not form part of its "specific object."

8.17   Having thus drawn a distinction between rights which are and are not part of the specific object of intellectual property, the Court went on:

> "If a protection right analogous to copyright is used in order to prohibit in one Member State the marketing of goods that have been brought onto the market by the holder of the right or with his consent in the territory of another Member State solely because this marketing has not occurred in the domestic market, such a prohibition maintaining the isolation of national markets conflicts with the essential aim of the Treaty, the integration of the national market into one uniform market. This aim could not be achieved if by virtue of the various legal systems of the Member States private persons were able to divide the market and cause arbitrary discriminations or disguised restrictions in trade between the Member States.
>
> Accordingly, it would conflict with the provisions regarding the free movement of goods in the Common Market if a manufacturer of recordings exercised the exclusive right granted to him by the legislation of a Member State to market the protected articles in order to prohibit the marketing in that Member State of products that have been sold by him himself or with his consent in another Member State solely because this marketing had not occurred in the Territory of the first Member State."[12]

8.18   As will be apparent, the Court's reasoning is not entirely clear. In substance, however, it seems to have reasoned that where goods protected by an intellectual property right in one Member State are first marketed in another Member State, by the owner of the right or with his consent, for that same person then to prevent the subsequent importation of those goods into the first State solely because they were not originally marketed, there must amount to an "arbitrary discrimination or a disguised restriction" between Member States within the meaning of the second sentence of Article 36. Moreover, to maintain the isolation of national markets by such conduct conflicts with the essential aim of the Treaty.

8.19   By implication, the Court must also have been saying that any entitlement of an owner of a right analogous to a copyright to prevent goods covered by that right from circulating freely within the Community, once the goods have been placed on the market by the owner or with his consent, does not constitute in terms of EEC Law part of the "specific object" or essential being of that right and, in consequence, is not entitled to the

---

[12] *Deutsche Grammophon Gesellschaft* [1971] C.M.L.R. 631 at pp. 657 and 658.

protection afforded to intellectual property by Articles 222 and 36 (first sentence) of the Treaty.

(c) Possible explanation of the Court's judgment

8.20   The Court's reasoning remains, however, difficult to understand, at least without speculating on the degree to which it may have been influenced by the proceedings in the national court and by the opinion of the Advocate General. Briefly, one of the issues before both the German Court of first instance (*i.e.* the Landgericht) and the Appellate Court (*i.e.* the Oberlandesgericht) was how section 17 of the German copyright statute should be interpreted. The section essentially provided that once the protected goods have been placed in circulation with the consent of the person entitled to distribute them in the territory that person's rights are exhausted, so that the goods may thereafter be freely distributed by third parties.[13]

8.21   Both German Courts had to consider whether such "exhaustion" only occurred when the goods were placed in circulation within the Federal Republic of Germany, or whether the delivery of the goods by Deutsche Grammophon to its French subsidiary constituted placing the goods in circulation within the meaning of the statute, so that Deutsche Grammophon had "exhausted" its rights by doing so.

8.22   The German Court of first instance concluded that Deutsche Grammophon's delivery of the records to its French subsidiary had not "exhausted" its rights, within the meaning of section 17 of the copyright statute.[14]

8.23   The German Appeals Court was in principle of the same view, though with reservations. It stated:

"The wording of Section 17 (2) of the URG leaves it open as to whether a marketing abroad exhausts the dissemination rights. However, in the opinion of this Chamber, the principle of territoriality must also be applied to copyright, i.e., that the distribution rights only relate to the home territory. The owner of a copyright can prohibit only imports of reproductions from abroad into the Federal Republic by virtue of his exclusive distribution rights, but not acts of distribution abroad. The distribution rights cannot be exhausted therefore by a previous foreign marketing."[15]

8.24   The German Court was, however, clearly concerned as to whether this interpretation was compatible with the EEC Treaty.

8.25   In the same vein, the Advocate General said:

"... the present case mainly concerns the problem of so-called "exhaustion" of a national industrial property right similar to a copyright conferred by Section 17 of the German Copyright Statute.

---

[13] For the wording of s. 17, see *supra*, n. 6.
[14] *Deutsche Grammophon Gesellschaft, supra.*
[15] *Ibid.* at p. 643.

The Oberlandesgericht has declared that the *wording* of this provision leaves it open as to whether a marketing abroad with the
consent of the holder of the rights also exhausts its distribution rights
in Germany. Apparently, in view of the territoriality principle, as it is
widely understood in this field, the court is inclined to hold that the
rights are not thereby exhausted."[16]

8.26   Not surprisingly, however, the Advocate General came to a different
view. In his view, the territoriality principle was not part of the substance or
essence of the relevant intellectual property right. This being the case he
concluded that:

"... it should be decisive that the purpose of the industrial protection
rights was fulfilled when the goods were first marketed, since it was
possible to use the monopolistic opportunity for gain ... It would
undoubtedly go beyond the purpose of the protection rights conferred if the holder was permitted to control further marketing, in
particular to prohibit re-imports, and free trade in goods was prevented. Thus in view of the proviso in Article 36, the fundamental
aims of the Treaty and the principles of the Common Market, and in
spite of the guarantee of the subsistence of industrial property rights,
in a situation such as that in the present case it may be held that the
rights have been extinguished, i.e. the exercise of the distribution
rights is precluded."[17]

2. *The Position with regard to other Intellectual Property*

8.27   Deutsche Grammophon was, of course, concerned with a particular type of
German intellectual property, generally considered to be analogous to a
copyright.[18] There has been no similar case since Deutsche Grammophon
involving either copyright or other types of intellectual property, so that
some slight doubt must remain as to the general applicability of the case.
This said, and with the exception of performing rights as an element of
copyright, there is no obvious reason to distinguish between a right analogous to a copyright and other types of intellectual property in the context of
the issues raised, so that in the absence of any decision to the contrary it
would seem reasonable to assume that the European Court's judgment in
Deutsche Grammophon is equally applicable to other types of intellectual
property.

8.27.1   Special considerations apply to performing rights. In particular, the
European Court recognised in the *Coditel* case[18a] that there is an essential

---

[16] *Ibid.* at p. 646.
[17] *Ibid.* at pp. 648 and 649.
[18] As to its particular characteristics, however, see Dietz, *Copyright Law in the European
Community* (Sijthoff & Noordhoff, 1978) pp. 196–198.
[18a] Case 62/79 *Coditel SA and Other* v. *Ciné Vog Films SA* (unreported).

factual difference between performing rights, as an element of copyright, and copyright in literary and artistic works such as books and records. Thus, a film is made available to the public "by performances which are infinitely repeated,"[18b] whereas books and records are made available to the public by placing the requisite number of copies on the market, *i.e.* by selling individual copies to the public. The *Coditel* case is discussed fully in Chapter 12.[18c] For present purposes it is sufficient to note the European Court's holding that:

(i) the broadcasting of a film by television involves the provision of a "service" and is, therefore, covered by Articles 59 and 60 of the Treaty rather than by Articles 30 to 36, and

(ii) the exhaustion doctrine does not and cannot apply to such broadcasting, having regard to the particular way in which a film is made available to the public, namely by performance.

It would appear, therefore, that the doctrines established by the European Court in the *Deutsche Grammophon* case would not apply, at least without qualification, in the context of performing rights as an element of copyright.

C. CATEGORY 2

Goods covered by an intellectual property right in one EEC Member State ("A"), are manufactured *and* marketed in that State by the owner of the right "O" or with his consent. A subsequent purchaser seeks to market the goods in a second Member State ("B"), in which "O" also owns or enjoys the benefit of a parallel right. Under Community law, may "O" exercise his right in the second Member State ("B") to prevent such marketing?

8.28   This situation differs from that with which the *Deutsche Grammophon* case was concerned,[19] in that in this case the goods are manufactured in a different country from that in which the owner of the relevant intellectual property right is seeking to prevent their importation. As will be apparent, however, from the four cases discussed in this section, this distinction does not materially affect the principles involved.

8.29   The four cases in question are, *Centrafarm BV* v. *Sterling Drug Incorporated*,[20] *Centrafarm BV* v. *Winthrop*,[21] *Hoffmann-La Roche & Co. AG* v. *Centrafarm*[22] and *Centrafarm BV* v. *American Home Products Corporation*.[23] It will be noted that all these cases involved Centrafarm BV, a Dutch company which has proved adept at turning this area of EEC law

---

[18b] *Ibid.* at para. 12.
[18c] See discussion, *infra*, Chap. 12 at para. 12.58.2.
[19] See description of Category I, *supra*, at paras. 8.06 *et seq*.
[20] [1974] E.C.R. 1183; [1974] 2 C.M.L.R. 480.
[21] [1974] E.C.R. 1183; [1974] 2 C.M.L.R. 480.
[22] [1978] E.C.R. 1139; [1978] 3 C.M.L.R. 217.
[23] [1978] E.C.R. 1823; [1979] 1 C.M.L.R. 326.

to commercial advantage. The first two cases were "joined" cases, and will in so far as appropriate be considered together. The remaining two cases will then be considered in turn.

1. *Centrafarm BV* v. *Sterling Drug Incorporated ("Sterling Drug") and Centrafarm BV* v. *Winthrop BV ("Winthrop")*

(a) The facts

8.30   The facts in both these cases were similar, save that the *Sterling Drug* case was concerned with patents while the *Winthrop* case was concerned with trade marks.

8.31   Briefly, Sterling Drug Incorporated was a company incorporated in New York which owned patents in various countries including Holland and the United Kingdom, covering the method of preparation of a drug for use in the treatment of urinary tract infection. Sterling Drug Incorporated had an English subsidiary, Sterling-Winthrop Group Limited, and this company in turn owned, in Holland, a subsidiary named Winthrop BV.

8.32   The drug was marketed under the trade mark "Negram," and this trade mark was owned in the United Kingdom by Sterling-Winthrop Group Limited and in Holland by its subsidiary, Winthrop BV. Thus, while the relevant English and Dutch patents were directly owned by the ultimate United States parent company, the corresponding trade marks were owned by the English and Dutch subsidiaries. The drug was apparently not manufactured in Holland by any of the Sterling Group's companies, but it was distributed in Holland by Winthrop BV.

8.33   Centrafarm BV imported the drug into Holland (without the agreement of Sterling Drug Incorporated) from England and Germany, both countries where it had been properly put on the market by subsidiaries of Sterling Drug Incorporated. By importing from the United Kingdom Centrafarm benefited from the considerable price difference between England and Holland, due to action taken by the British authorities to control the prices of "Negram."

8.34   On June 16, 1971, Sterling Drug Incorporated and Winthrop BV both instituted proceedings in Rotterdam, requesting interim relief against the dealings of Centrafarm and its director, and injunctive relief against the infringement of Sterling Drug Incorporated's patent and against any directly or indirectly abusive use of Winthrop's "Negram" trade mark.

8.35   In the *Winthrop* (trade mark) case the President of the District Court of Rotterdam gave Winthrop BV the relief requested. The Court of Appeal in The Hague dismissed the subsequent appeal and, in consequence, Centrafarm and its director appealed against that dismissal to the Dutch Supreme Court.

8.36   By contrast, in the *Sterling Drug* (patent) case the President of the District Court refused the relief sought by Sterling Drug Incorporated, in reliance on his conclusion that under the Dutch Patent Act a product is to be regarded as properly placed in circulation by the Dutch patentee even when the Dutch patentee places the product in question on the market in another country.[24] The Dutch Court of Appeal, however, reversed the President and again Centrafarm and its director appealed to the Dutch Supreme Court. On March 1, 1974, the Dutch Supreme Court stayed proceedings in both cases and referred various questions to the European Court of Justice under Article 177.

8.37   It is worth setting out in full the first question referred by the Dutch Supreme Court to the European Court:

"As regards the rules concerning the free movement of goods
  (a) assuming that:
    1. a patentee has parallel patents in several of the countries belonging to the EEC,
    2. the products protected by those patents are lawfully marketed in one or more of those countries by undertakings to whom the patentee has granted licences to manufacture and/or sell,
    3. those products are subsequently exported by third parties and are marketed and further dealt with in one of those other countries,
    4. the patent legislation in the last mentioned countries gives the patentee the right to take legal action to prevent products thus protected by patents from being there marketed by others, even where these products were previously lawfully marketed in another country by the patentee or by the patentee's licensee;

Do the rules in the EEC Treaty concerning the free movement of goods, notwithstanding what is stated in Article 36, prevent the patentee from using the right under 4 above?"

8.38   Leaving aside for the moment the fact that the *Deutsche Grammophon* case was concerned with a right analogous to a copyright, whereas the *Sterling Drug* and *Winthrop* cases are concerned with a patent and a trade mark, these cases differ materially on their facts from *Deutsche Grammophon* in only two respects. First, the product in question was here manufactured in a Member State other than that in which the opposition to its importation arose, and secondly, its importation into that second State was in fact opposed by a subsidiary of the manufacturer rather than by the manufacturer itself, that is to say by a separate legal entity.[25]

In the light of this similarity, it is not surprising that the Court adopted similar reasoning to that followed in its *Deutsche Grammophon* judgment.

---

[24] Relief would in similar circumstances also not have been available under Enlgish law, even before the U.K. joined the EEC. See in this connection *Betts* v. *Willmot* [1871] L.R. 6 Ch. App. 239. Note also the discussion of this case in Terrell, *The Law of Patents* (12th ed.), at pp. 158 and 159.

[25] See the submissions of A. G. Trabucchi, at p. 494 of the *Sterling Drug* case.

(b) The Court's decision in the Sterling Drug (Patent) case

(i) *General*

8.39   In reply to the question referred to it the Court concluded that Sterling Drug was not entitled to invoke its Dutch patent rights in such a way as to prevent Centrafarm from importing the "infringing" drug into Holland. In so doing, however, it developed further both the nature of the distinction between the first and second sentences of Article 36 and the concept of the specific object of a patent.

(ii) *The Court's decision and Article 36*

8.40   Having reiterated that Article 30 prohibits measures having equivalent effect to quantitative restrictions on imports, and also that the first sentence of Article 36 derogates from this rule to the extent that the restrictive measure in question is justified for the protection of industrial and commercial property, it continued:

> "But it appears from that same Article, particularly from its second sentence, ... that while the Treaty does not affect the existence of the rights in industrial and commercial property recognised by the law of a member State, the exercise of such rights may nonetheless, according to circumstances, be affected by the prohibition in the Treaty ... Article 36 allows derogations to the free movement of goods only to the extent that such derogations are justified for the protection of the rights which constitute the specific object of such property."[26]

8.41   The interrelationship between the first and second sentences of Article 36 is by no means clear, notwithstanding this statement. It would appear from this statement, however, that when the European Court speaks of the existence of intellectual property, it equates the term "existence" with those characteristics of the intellectual property which it regards as constituting the "specific object" of that property. Further, those characteristics which constitute the specific object of the intellectual property can either by exercised "legitimately" or in such a way as to "constitute a means of arbitrary discrimination or a disguised restriction on trade between Member States", within the meaning of the second sentence of Article 36.

8.42   If this analysis is correct it follows that:

1. The first sentence of Article 36 only applies to those characteristics of intellectual property which are justified for the protection of the "specific object" of that property and, hence, which may be equated with its existence.

2. Even where one is concerned with a characteristic of intellectual property which can be justified for the protection of the "specific object" of that property, it may not be "exercised" in such a way as to "constitute a

---

[26] *Ibid.* at p. 503.

means of arbitrary discrimination or a disguised restriction on trade between Member States."

3. All those characteristics of intellectual property which cannot be equated with the "specific object" cannot be said to be "justified on grounds of ... the protection of industrial and commercial property," within the meaning of the first sentence of Article 36. Such attributes of intellectual property will, therefore, not enjoy any immunity from the basic prohibition of all measures having "equivalent effect" to quantitative restrictions, contained in Articles 30 to 34.

(iii) *The Court's decision and the specific object of a patent*

8.43 Having discussed the relationship between the first and second sentences of Article 36, the Court proceeded to define the specific object of a patent. In words reminiscent of *Deutsche Grammophon*, and to become in the future increasingly familiar, it stated:

"As regards patents, the specific object of industrial property is *inter alia* to ensure to the holder, so as to recompense the creative effort of the inventor, the exclusive right to utilise an invention with a view to the manufacture and first putting into circulation of industrial products, either directly or by the grant of licences to third parties, as well as the right to oppose any infringement."[27]

8.44 The Court thus identified the following characteristics as being part of the specific object of the patent:

1. The right of a patent owner to exploit an invention for the purpose of manufacturing and first marketing a product (whether directly or indirectly), and

2. The right of a patent owner to oppose an infringement. In this context, "infringement," must refer to action by a third party amounting either to the manufacture of the product without any licence to do so or original marketing of a product without any licence so to do.[28]

8.45 The Court's use of the phrase *"inter alia"* is noteworthy, for it suggests that there may well be other attributes of a patent which constitute a part of its specific object. Indeed, by implication the Court identifies two such possible characteristics, though without reaching a final conclusion. The two characteristics which are singled out in this way are, first, the right of a patent owner in one Member State to invoke his patent against a product

---

[27] *Ibid.*

[28] It is hard to see how a third party could first market a product covered by a patent without a licence so to do, unless that third party had also manufactured the product. Presumably, however, if the third party were to obtain possession of goods originally manufactured by the patent owner or with his consent without those goods having been first placed on the market and if that third party were subsequently to market those goods he would thereby be infringing the patent in a manner entitling the owner of the patent to oppose the infringement. The right to oppose the infringement in reliance on the patent in such circumstances would be justified for the protection of the patent.

imported from another Member State in which no patent protection for the invention is available, where the product in question was manufactured by a third party without the consent of the patentee and, secondly, the right of a patent owner in one Member State to invoke his patent against goods imported from another Member State where the manufacturer of those goods owns a corresponding patent and is legally and economically independent from the first mentioned patentee. Both of these situations will be discussed below.[29]

8.46   Still on the subject of the specific object of a patent, it is apparent from the answers given by the Court to various other questions referred to it in the *Sterling Drug* case that the following do *not* constitute part of the specific object of a patent and will, in consequence, not be entitled to the protection afforded by the first sentence of Article 36.

1. Any right under national law, for a patentee to prevent imports into a Member State of goods placed on the market by him or with his consent in another Member State, merely because such importation by a third party results in economic loss to him. This is so even if the economic loss is aggravated by price differences in the two Member States resulting from subsidies or other economic measures taken by the Government in the exporting State to control the prices of the goods in question in that State.[30]

2. Any right for a patentee, to control incidentally the distribution of pharmaceutical products in such a way as to protect the public against risks of defective products. Here the Court simply and, no doubt, correctly remarked that measures necessary for this purpose should be taken in the context of public health control, presumably by the Member State in question, "... and not by way of a misuse of the rules of industrial and commercial property. Besides the specific object of the protection of industrial and commercial property is distinct from the object of the protection of the public and any responsibilities that can imply."[31]

8.47   Having thus identified the specific object of a patent, the Court reasoned that any entitlement of a patentee under national patent legislation to oppose the import into his own State of a patented product marketed by him or with his consent in another State, may constitute an obstacle to the free movement of goods. Thus, a derogation from the principle of the free movement of goods would not be justified in circumstances in which goods have been placed on the market in the other Member States by the patentee or with his consent under a parallel patent. To conclude other-

---

[29] As to the first mentioned situation, see the discussion of the *Parke-Davis* case, *infra* at para. 8.81; and as to the second mentioned situation, see Chap. 9 and the discussion of the *Hag* case, *infra*, Chap. 12 at para. 12.32.

[30] [1974] E.C.R. 1183; [1974] 2 C.M.L.R. 480 at p. 505. Note also the remarks of A. G. Trabucchi on this subject, *ibid.* at pp. 497–498. (Presumably the price differences in question in this case resulted from the operation of the National Health Service in the U.K.)

[31] *Ibid.* at p. 505.

wise, the Court reasoned, would enable the patentee "... to partition the national markets and thus to maintain a restriction on the trade between the Member States without such a restriction being necessary for him to enjoy the substance of the exclusive rights derived from the parallel patents."[32]

8.48   By implication, therefore, the Court would appear to have concluded that the rights of a patentee are exhausted when goods are lawfully placed on the market in any Member State of the Community by that patentee or with his consent under a parallel patent. In so concluding, the Court did, however, expressly leave open for determination under national law the question of whether there is in fact an identity of the patented invention marketed in different Member States, in circumstances in which it is alleged that the patented invention is being marketed in two Member States by the owner of parallel patents or with his consent. This point has been further developed by the European Court in the context of trade marks, as will be seen from the discussion which follows.[33]

(c) The Court's decision in the Winthrop (Trade Mark) case

(i) *General*

8.49   Much of what the Court had said in the context of the *Sterling Drug* (Patent) case was expressly stated to apply in this case also and, therefore, by implication equally to trade marks. This said, it is again worth setting out in full the first question referred to the European Court in this case:

"1. In relation to the rules concerning free movement of goods:
>   (*a*) Assuming that:
>>   1. different undertakings in different countries belonging to the EEC forming part of the same concern are entitled to the use of the same trade mark for a certain product,
>>   2. products bearing that trade mark, after being lawfully marketed in one country by the trade mark owner, are exported by third parties and are marketed and further dealt with in one of the other countries,
>>   3. the trade mark legislation in one last mentioned country gives the trade mark owner the right to take legal action to prevent goods with the relevant trade mark from being marketed there by other persons even if such goods had previously been marketed lawfully in another country by an undertaking there entitled to that trade mark and belonging to the same concern,

---

[32] *Ibid.* at p. 504.
[33] See the discussion of *Hoffmann-La Roche & Co. AG* v. *Centrafarm* and *Centrafarm BV* v. *American Home Products Corp. infra*, at paras. 8.56 *et seq*. The extent to which those cases may be of relevance in the context of patents remains an open question.

Do the rules set out in the EEC Treaty concerning the free movement of goods, notwithstanding the provisions of Article 36, prevent the trade mark owner from making use of the right mentioned under "3" above?"[34]

8.50　So far as facts are concerned, the only noteworthy difference between the position here and the position in the *Sterling Drug* case is that here the relevant trade mark rights are owned in each country by the company trading in that country, rather than being owned by the American parent company and licensed to the operating subsidiary as had been done in the case of the patents.

8.51　Not surprisingly, the Court in this case followed very similar reasoning to that in the *Sterling Drug* case, and concluded that the owner of a trade mark in one Member State (B) may not exercise a right granted to him under that State's national trade mark law in such a way as to prohibit the importation of products bearing that trade mark and lawfully marketed in another EEC Member State (A), provided that the goods were placed on the market in that Member State (A) either by the trade mark owner or by a third party with the trade mark owner's consent. In the Court's view, exercise of trade mark rights to prevent imports in such circumstances would be incompatible with the free movement of goods Articles of the EEC Treaty.

(ii) The Court's decision and the specific object of a trade mark

8.52　In a noteworthy passage, however, the Court addressed itself to the specific object of a trade mark. In the Court's words, the specific object of a trade mark "... is inter alia to ensure to the holder the exclusive right to utilise the mark for the first putting into circulation of a product, and to protect him thus against competitors who would take advantage of the position and reputation of the mark by selling goods improperly bearing the mark."[35]

8.53　As the Court suggests, if this is the specific object of a trade mark, it follows that a right under national trade mark law to oppose the importation into a Member State of goods lawfully put on the market in another Member State, on the grounds that marketing abroad does not exhaust a trade mark owner's rights, "may constitute an obstacle to the free movement of goods."[36] In the Court's view, such an obstacle to the free movement of goods within the Community cannot be justified when the goods have been placed on the market in another Member State by the trade mark owner or with his consent, "... in such a way that there can be no question of abuse or infringement of the mark."[37] In the Court's view, this must be so because to hold otherwise would enable a trade mark owner to

---

[34] [1974] E.C.R. 1183; [1974] 2 C.M.L.R. 480 at pp. 486 and 487.
[35] *Ibid.* at p. 508.
[36] *Ibid.* at p. 509.
[37] *Ibid.*

impose restrictions on trade between Member States, without such restrictions being necessary in order for the trade mark to enjoy the substance, *i.e.* the specific object, of the trade mark.

8.54   Interestingly enough, and as it had done in the *Sterling Drug* case in the context of patents, the Court qualified its definition of the specific object of a trade mark, by the use of the phrase "*inter alia.*" This suggests that there may be other characteristics of the specific object of a trade mark, which the Court did not refer to in this case.

8.55   The principles established by the European Court in the *Sterling Drug* and *Winthrop* decisions were to be developed further in two later cases to come before the European Court, both of which again involved Centrafarm BV as the defendant. These cases, *Hoffmann-La Roche & Co. AG v. Centrafarm*[38] and *Centrafarm BV v. American Home Products Corporation*[39] were each to require the European Court to consider different facets of the question: In what circumstances may the owner of a trade mark in two different EEC Member States use its national trade mark rights in one State in order to prohibit the importation into that State of goods lawfully placed on the market in the other State?

2. *Hoffman-La Roche & Co. AG v. Centrafarm Vertriebsgesellschaft*

8.56   The issue at the heart of this case once again had its origins in the lower prices charged for drugs in the United Kingdom, as compared with certain other EEC countries, particularly The Netherlands and Germany. As will be apparent from the last two cases discussed, these lower prices create ideal conditions for a parallel exporter, such as Centrafarm, to turn to advantage.

(a) The facts

8.57   The case was concerned with the well-known tranquilliser "Valium." "Valium" was developed by the Roche-SAPAC Group in 1963, and the Swiss parent company of the group, Hoffmann-La Roche & Co. AG of Basel ("Roche-Basel") owns the relevant trade marks "Valium" and "Roche," both of which are protected by international registration. Licences to manufacture the drugs were granted by Roche-Basel, *inter alia*, to Roche's German subsidiary ("Roche-Germany") and Roche's English subsidiary ("Roche-Britain").

8.58   Both Roche-Germany and Roche-Britain enjoyed the right to use the "Valium" and "Roche" trade marks, in respect of Valium manufactured by them. Roche-Germany sold the Valium in packets of 20 or 50 tablets, in which form they were intended for use by individuals. These packets were,

---

[38] [1978] E.C.R. 1139; [1978] 3 C.M.L.R. 217.
[39] [1978] E.C.R. 1823; [1979] 1 C.M.L.R. 326.

in turn, further packaged (five small packets at a time) in quantities of 100 or 250 tablets for hospital use. Roche-Britain also manufactured Valium, which it sold in packages of 100 and 500 tablets and, as indicated, at prices considerably below those charged in Germany.

8.59   Centrafarm BV of The Netherlands took advantage of this price differential by purchasing quantities of the drug from Roche-Britain, of course in the original packages. It re-packaged the drug in The Netherlands, under the supervision of a pharmacist, into batches of 1,000 tablets. The re-packed drug was then sold by Centrafarm BV to its German subsidiary, for sale in Germany. Although the packaging was different in appearance, the names "Valium" and "Roche" still appeared, together with the number of the entry in the relevant official German register.[40] Centrafarm BV also added to the package its own name and the words "Marketed by Centrafarm GmbH," with its address and telephone number. The new packaging contained an information leaflet in German, almost identical to the information leaflet used by Roche-Germany, but again indicating that the drug was marketed by Centrafarm.

8.60   Roche-Germany considered this conduct an infringement of the "Valium" and "Roche" trade marks and proceedings were duly instituted in the name of Roche-Basel and Roche-Germany claiming an interim injunction to restrain Centrafarm's German subsidiary from using the trademarks in Germany in this manner. An interim injunction was granted by the Landgericht Freiburg.[41]

8.62   Thereafter, in the course of considering the merits of the action, the Landgericht referred two questions to the European Court for interpretation, the first of which related to Article 36.[42] By this question the European Court was asked whether a person (*i.e.* Hoffman-La Roche) owning trade mark rights in Member State A and in Member State B may, in reliance on Article 36, "... prevent a parallel importer from buying from the proprietor of the mark or with his consent in Member State A of the Community medicinal preparations which have been put on the market with his trade mark lawfully affixed thereto and packaged under this trade mark from providing them with new packaging, affixing to such packaging

---

[40] *i.e.* at the Bundesgesundheitsamt.

[41] Centrafarm appealed the Landgericht's interim injunction to the Oberlandergericht Karlsruhe. The Oberlandergericht itself referred three questions to the European Court under Art. 177. By the first of these questions, the European Court was asked whether the Oberlandergericht was bound, by virtue of Art. 177 (3), to make a reference where, even though no appeal was possible, the proceedings were of an interlocutory nature and the whole position would be reviewed again when the case was considered in full. In reply to this question, the European Court ruled that a reference was not compulsory in such circumstances, and refrained from dealing with the two substantive questions which had also been put to it by the Oberlandergericht. Case 107/76 [1977] E.C.R. 957; [1977] 2 C.M.L.R. 334.

[42] The second question referred to the European Court concerned Art. 86. See discussion *infra*, at para. 8.103.

the proprietor's trade mark and importing the preparations distinguished in this manner into Member State B?"[43]

8.63   The crucial difference between this case and its predecessors is, of course, that here Centrafarm actually *re-packaged* the goods which it had purchased and then affixed the proprietor's trademark (*i.e.* Valium) to the *new* packet.

(b) The Court's judgment

(i) *General*

8.64   The Court began its consideration of the question referred to it by reiterating the by then well established distinction between "existence" and "exercise," and by again affirming that Article 36 only permits derogations from the free movement of goods provisions to the extent that such derogations are justified for the protection of "rights which constitute the specific subject matter of the property."[44]

8.65   The Court confirmed also that the specific subject matter of a trade mark includes the trade mark owner's exclusive right to use the trade mark in order to place the product into circulation for the first time, together with the right to use the trade mark against competitors selling products illegally bearing that trade mark.[44]

8.66   Having thus identified the "rights which constitute the specific subject matter of the property," however, the Court was left with the question whether those rights include the right to prevent a trade mark being affixed to products by a third party, once those products have been placed on the market and after they have been re-packaged by that third party. Faced with this question the Court concluded that it must have regard to "the essential function of the trade mark," which it identified as being "to guarantee the identity of the origin of the trademarked product to the consumer or ultimate user, by enabling him without any possibility of confusion to distinguish that product from products which have another origin."[44] The Court then reasoned:

> "This guarantee of origin means that the consumer or ultimate user can be certain that a trademarked product which is sold to him has not been subject at a previous stage of marketing to interference by a third person, without the authorisation of the proprietor of the trade mark, such as to affect the original condition of the product. The right attributed to the proprietor of preventing any use of the trade mark which is likely to impair the guarantee of origin so understood is therefore part of the specific subject matter of the trade mark right.
>   It is accordingly justified under the first sentence of Article 36 to recognise that the proprietor of a trade mark is entitled to prevent an

---

[43] *Hoffman-La Roche, supra*, at p. 340.
[44] *Ibid.* at p. 341.

importer of a trademarked product, following re-packaging of that product, from affixing the trade mark to the new packaging without the authorisation of the proprietor."[44]

8.67 The specific subject matter of the trade mark is, therefore, now broadened to include not only the right to be the first to place a product on the market bearing a specific trade mark and the right to prevent a third party from affixing that trade mark to products without authorisation, but also the right to prevent any use of a trade mark by a third party which may undermine the guarantee of origin provided by a trade mark.

8.68 Had the Court felt able to stop here, Hoffman-La Roche and Co. would no doubt have been well satisfied. The Court had concluded, after all, that the proprietor of a trade mark is entitled to the benefit of the first sentence of Article 36 in circumstances in which he seeks to enforce his trade mark rights so as to prevent an importer of the trademarked product from first re-packaging the product and then affixing the trade mark to it without prior authorisation, on the grounds that in such circumstances while the action of the trade mark owner in enforcing the trade mark is a restriction within the meaning of the free movement of goods provisions, it is one "justified for the protection of industrial and commercial property."

(ii) *Disguised restriction on trade between Member States*

8.69 The Court felt it necessary, however, to consider whether the "exercise" of the trade mark owner's right in such circumstances nonetheless in fact amounted to a "disguised restriction on trade between Member States" within the meaning of the second sentence of Article 36, in which case the benefit of the first sentence of that Article would, of course, be lost. The Court speculated that such a disguised restriction might arise if the trade mark owner were to enforce his rights to prevent re-packaging by a third party even if the re-packaging by the third party were carried out in such a way it could neither affect the original condition of the product nor its identity of origin.

8.70 From this perspective the issue in this case could be reduced to whether the re-packaging undertaken by a third party of a trademarked product "is capable of affecting the original condition of the product?"[45]

8.71 More generally, if the re-packaging will affect either the identity of the origin of the product or its original condition then there is little doubt that the trade mark owner will be entitled to exercise his trade mark rights by virtue of the first sentence of Article 36. By contrast, the Court concluded that the exercise of trade mark rights to prevent such re-packaging may constitute a disguised restriction on trade between Member States where the original condition *and* guarantee of origin of the product are not impaired, and further that it *will* constitute a disguised restriction on trade

---

[45] *Ibid.* at p. 343.

between Member States within the meaning of the second sentence of Article 36 where:

>   (i) it is established that the use of the trade mark right by the proprietor, having regard to the marketing system which he has adopted, will contribute to the artificial partitioning of the markets between Member States;
>
>   (ii) it is shown that the re-packaging cannot adversely affect the original condition of the products;
>
>   (iii) the proprietor of the mark receives prior notice of the marketing of the re-packaged product; and
>
>   (iv) it is stated on the new packaging by whom the product has been re-packaged.[46]

8.72   It would appear from this conclusion that Hoffmann-La Roche might not, therefore, be entitled to enjoin the future activities of Centrafarm in the particular circumstances of this case.[47] By contrast, in the fourth case involving Centrafarm, *Centrafarm BV* v. *American Home Products Corporation*,[48] the facts were sufficiently different to clearly enable the trade mark owner to enforce his rights.

(3) *Centrafarm BV v. American Home Products Corporation*

(a) The facts

8.73   This case was factually not dissimilar from the *Hoffman-La Roche* case. The drug in question was also a tranquilliser, Oxazepamum, which was sold by American Home Products under the "Seresta" trade mark in Holland, France and Belgium, under the "Serenid D" trade mark in the United Kingdom. Both trade marks were owned by the American Home Products Corporation, which also owned patents in The Netherlands and the United Kingdom for the drug. American Home Products Corporation's subsidiaries in the United Kingdom and The Netherlands were "licensed" to use the trade marks registered in their respective countries. The therapeutic effects of the "Seresta" and "Serenid D" drugs were identical, but their composition differed slightly. From the consumer's point of view, the most noteworthy difference was one of taste. Centrafarm bought "Serenid D" in the United Kingdom, and sold the drug in The Netherlands under the "Seresta" mark. On the packaging it affixed, in addition to the mark, the words "Centrafarm BV Rotterdam, Telephone 010-151411." Thus, the only substantive factual differences between this case and the Hoffman-La Roche case were that here there was a pharmaceutical difference, however

---

[46] *Ibid.* at p. 343.
[47] The German Courts, however, appear to be having difficulties in applying the European Court's judgment on the *Hoffmann-La Roche* case. See in this connection Rottger and Brett [1979] European Intellectual Property Review 283, at p. 285.
[48] [1978] E.C.R. 1823; [1979] 1 C.M.L.R. 326.

slight, between the drugs "Serenid D" and "Seresta" and that in this case
the Dutch trade mark was substituted for the English trade mark.

8.74   Predictably, litigation was started in The Netherlands, against Centrafarm BV by American Home Products Corporation. American Home
Products applied to the Dutch Courts for interim relief, and on August 2,
1977, the President of the Aaerondissementsrechtbank, Rotterdam, made
an order prohibiting Centrafarm from infringing American Home Products' rights arising from the "Seresta" mark. Thereafter, in the "main
action" Centrafarm claimed that the Dutch Court should rule that it was
entitled to market Oxazepamum, which had previously been lawfully
distributed in other EEC countries, on the Dutch market under the
"Seresta" mark. American Home Products submitted that Centrafarm's
claim should be refused, and counter-claimed that the Dutch Court should
rule that Centrafarm's conduct infringed its "Seresta" trade mark. The
Dutch Court duly stayed proceedings on December 19, 1977, and under
Article 177 referred two questions to the European Court for interpretation.

By its principal question, it asked the European Court, in effect, whether
on the facts of this case Article 36 prevented the proprietor of a trade mark
from exercising the rights conferred upon him under national law.[49]

(b) The Court's judgment

8.75   Predictably the Court first repeated its now traditional analysis in Article
36 cases, including reference to the need to have regard to the guarantee

---

[49] The actual questions referred to the European Court of Justice were in the following
terms:
"I. Assuming that:
1. For a certain product in various Member States belonging to the EEC one undertaking
or various undertakings belonging to the same group is/are entitled to use trade marks
whereby in Member State A only trade mark X is registered and in Member State B trade
mark Y only is registered;
2. Goods bearing the mark X, after being put on the market in Member State A by the
undertaking entitled to the trade mark, are bought by third parties who subsequently import
into Member State B;
3. The party importing the goods into the last mentioned State removes from them the
mark X, affixes the mark Y and subsequently puts the goods into circulation in that State;
4. The legislation relating to trade marks in the last mentioned State gives the person
entitled to the trade mark the right to oppose by legal measures the marketing in that country
by others of goods bearing the mark Y;
do the rules contained in the EEC Treaty concerning the free movement of goods notwithstanding the provisions of Article 36, prevent the person entitled to the trade mark from
making use of the right referred to under 4 *supra*?
II. For the answer to be given to Question 1 is it relevant whether legislative or administrative provisions are in force in Member State B which accord with the directive of January 26,
1965 adopted by the Council of the European Communities in this respect (65/65/EEC)
whereby those provisions—possibly in derogation from this Directive—start from the principle that the import of a pharmaceutical product from another Member State into Member
State B is possible under a mark other than that under which it is registered in the other
Member State?"

function of a trade mark, which it had first advanced in the *Hoffmann-La Roche* case. Whereas, however, in the *Hoffmann-La Roche* case the Court concluded that the guarantee of origin meant that a consumer could be assured that a trademarked product had not been interfered with without the authorisation of the trade mark owner,[50] here the Court emphasised another aspect of the guarantee of origin, namely the proprietor's right actually to affix the mark. The Court's reasoning in full was:

"This guarantee of origin means that only the proprietor may confer an identity upon the product by affixing the mark. The guarantee of origin would in fact be jeopardised if it were permissible for a third party to affix the mark to the product, *even to an original product*.[51] It is thus in accordance with the essential function of the mark that national legislation, even where the manufacturer or distributor is the proprietor of two different marks for the same product, prevents an unauthorised third party from usurping the right to affix one or other marks to any part whatsoever of the production or to change the marks affixed by the proprietor to different parts of the production. The guarantee of origin of the product requires that the exclusive right of the proprietor should be protected in the same manner where the different parts of the production, bearing different marks, come from two different Member States. The right granted to the proprietor to prohibit an unauthorised affixing of his mark to his product accordingly comes within the specific subject-matter of the trade mark. The proprietor of a trade mark which is protected in one Member State is accordingly justified pursuant to the first sentence of Article 36 in preventing a product from being marketed by a third party in that Member State under the mark in question even if previously that product has been lawfully marketed in another Member State under another mark held in the latter State by the same proprietor."[52]

8.76 First impressions may be that the Court here developed, and possibly departed significantly from, its earlier case law. In a sense, however, the Court merely saw fit on the particular facts of this case, to return to first principles. The Court, it must be recalled, had always affirmed that the specific subject matter of a trade mark included the exclusive right of a trade mark owner to use that trade mark for the twin purposes of initially placing a product in circulation and preventing third parties from improperly taking advantage of the reputation of a trade mark. What Centrafarm was doing in this case, at least on one view, was to undermine the

---

[50] See discussion, *supra*, at paras. 8.66 *et seq*.
[51] Emphasis added.
[52] [1978] E.C.R. 1823; [1979] 1 C.M.L.R. 326.

very specific subject matter of a trade mark which the Court had always affirmed to be sacrosanct.

8.77   Even in such circumstances, however, the Court reasoned that there might be situations in which the benefit of the first sentence of Article 36 would be lost, because the trade mark owner was using his trade mark in such a way as to constitute a "disguised restriction on trade between Member States," within the meaning of the second sentence of Article 36. The Court continued:

> "... it may be lawful for the manufacturer of a product to use in different Member States different marks for the same product. Nevertheless it is possible for such a practice to be followed by the proprietor of the mark as part of a system of marketing *intended*[53] to partition the markets artificially. In such a case the prohibition by the proprietor of the unauthorised affixing of the mark by a third party constitutes a disguised restriction on intra-Community trade for the purposes of the above mentioned provision. It is for the national court to settle in each particular case whether the proprietor has followed the practice of using different marks for the same product for the purpose of partitioning the markets."[54]

8.78   In this case, then, the test introduced by the Court for deciding whether the second sentence of Article 36 applies is clearly subjective, *i.e.* one of intent. This is clearly a different test from that established in the *Hoffmann-La Roche* case, and its predecessors. At the same time, there is arguably no inconsistency between this case and the other cases discussed in this Section, because the issue in this case was materially different from those in the other cases. Here the issue concerned the freedom of action of a third party *vis-à-vis* another's trade mark. In the other cases, the issue concerned the freedom of action of a third party *vis-à-vis* another's trademarked products.

4. *The Position with Regard to Other Types of Intellectual Property*

8.79   The *Sterling Drug* and *Winthrop* cases concerned respectively patents and trade marks. To date, there has been one European Court decision dealing with a similar question in the context of intellectual property.[54a] From the perspective of EEC law, however, and with the exception of performing rights as an element of copyright there is no obvious reason why the position in the context of other types of intellectual property should be materially different. Performing rights enjoy a special position in that the

---

[53] Emphasis added.
[54] [1978] E.C.R. 1823; [1979] 1 C.M.L.R. 326.
[54a] Cases 55 and 57/80, judgment of January 20, 1981.

exhaustion doctrine would appear not to apply to them, at least in some circumstances.[54b]

By contrast with the *Sterling Drug* and *Winthrop* cases, the *Hoffmann-La Roche* and *American Home Products* cases could, in the main, only have arisen because of the particular attributes of a trade mark. It is therefore doubtful whether one can generalise from these two cases, at least without having a specific situation in mind.

D. CATEGORY 3

Goods not covered by an intellectual property right are manufactured and marketed in a Member State of the Community (A). A subsequent purchaser seeks to market those goods in a second Member State (B), in which similar goods which *are* covered by an intellectual property right are manufactured and marketed by the owner of that right (O). Under Community law may "O" exercise his right in the second Member State (B), to prevent importation of the goods from the first State (A)?

8.80   It is noteworthy that only one case involving this type of factual situation has been before the European Court to date, namely the *Parke-Davis* case,[55] although another is currently pending.[55a] Moreover, the *Parke-Davis* case came before the European Court in 1968, and therefore antedated the case law which was to evolve later concerning the free movement of goods, beginning with the *Deutsche Grammophon* case.[56] Be that as it may, the *Parke-Davis* case continues to be the only direct authority on this point, and if only for that reason worthy of detailed consideration.

1. *Parke-Davis & Co. v. Probel and Others*

(a) The facts
8.81   Parke-Davis is an American Company, and at the time of the case it

---

[54b] See discussion, *supra*, at para. 8.27.1 and *infra*, Chap. 12 at para. 12.58. The Court gave judgment on January 20, 1981, in the following terms:
"Articles 30 and 36 of the Treaty must be interpreted as precluding the application of national legislation which permits a copyright management society, empowered to exercise the copyrights of composers of musical works reproduced on gramophone records or other sound recording devices in another Member State, to invoke those rights if those sound recording devices are distributed on the national market when they have been put into free circulation in that other Member State by or with the consent of the owners of those copyrights in order to claim the payment of a fee equal to the royalties ordinarily paid for marketing on the national market less the lower royalties paid in the Member State of manufacture."
[55] *Parke-Davis & Co. v. Probel and Others* [1968] C.M.L.R. 47.
[55a] Case 187/80 *Merck & Co. Inc. v. Stephar BV and Petrus Stephanus Exter.*
[56] See *supra*, paras. 8.07 *et seq.*

owned two Dutch patents, the first relating to a microbiological preparation and the second a chemical antibiotic preparation process called
Chloramphenicol. At the time, patent protection was not available in Italy
for pharmaceuticals,[56a] and Chloramphenicol was manufactured by Probel
and sold freely in that country. Probel, our old friend Centrafarm and
another defendant company resold Chloramphenicol in Holland which had
originally been marketed in Italy, of course, without authorisation from
Parke-Davis & Co. The latter instituted proceedings for patent infringement in Rotterdam.

On appeal, Centrafarm for the first time pleaded that Parke-Davis & Co.
was acting in breach of Articles 85 and 86, in using its Dutch patent in order
to prevent the import into Holland of Chloramphenicol initially marketed
in Italy.

8.82   Centrafarm affirmed that it had purchased Chloramphenicol from an
Italian company, Carlo Erba, in Milan. The Dutch Court issued an injunction to prevent further infringement of Parke-Davis & Co.'s patents by the
three Defendants, "except for the products obtained from Italy." With
reference to these products, the Court reserved its judgment, and referred
two questions to the European Court for interpretation. Only the first of
these questions is relevant for present purposes. In effect, the European
Court was asked whether the concept of a prohibited practice under Article
85 (1) and Article 86 "considered if necessary in conjunction with Articles
36 and 222," includes an action by a patent holder in a Member State
when, by virtue of that patent, the patent owner seeks to prohibit commercial dealing in the territory of that state in a product imported from another
Member State where patent protection is unavailable?"[57]

(b) The Court's judgment

8.83   The Court replied to the first question referred to it, in effect, that
Articles 85 (1) and 86, even when considered in conjunction with Articles
36 and 222, do not apply so as to prevent a patent holder in one Member
State from enforcing his national patent rights so as to prevent the import of
a product manufactured in a different Member State by a different manu-

---

[56a] By virtue of Article 14 of Italian patent law, since declared unconstitutional by the Italian
Constitutional Court, European Law Letter, April 1978 at p. 8. See also European Law
Letter, May 1978 at p. 5.
[57] The actual questions referred to the European Court were in the following terms:
1. Do the prohibited and improper practices referred to in Articles 85 (1) and 86 of the
EEC Treaty, considered if necessary in conjunction with Arts. 36 and 222, apply to the holder
of a patent issued by the authorities of a Member State, when he by virtue of a patent requests
the judicial authorities to prohibit all circulation, sale, hire, delivery stocking or utilisation in
the territory of that State of any product which comes from another Member State if the latter
does not grant an exclusive right to manufacture and sell the product?
2. Is the answer to the Question 1 different if the price at which the licensee markets the
product in the territory of the first Member State is higher than that asked of the consumer in
the same territory for the product when it comes from the second Member State?

facturer, in circumstances in which no patent protection for the products in question is available in the Member State of manufacture. The reasoning which the Court followed in reaching this decision is less than clear, perhaps understandably bearing in mind that the decision antedates the *Deutsche Grammophon* case by some three years.

8.84   Essentially, however, the Court reasoned that given that the national laws concerning industrial property rights have not yet been harmonised within the EEC, it is inevitable that differing national provisions will result in obstacles both to free circulation of the patented products and to unrestricted competition within the EEC. The Court also suggested that it is for this very reason that Article 36 countenances prohibitions and restrictions justified for the protection of industrial and commercial property, subject of course to the qualifications specified in that Article. Turning then specifically to Articles 85 and 86, the Court was able to dismiss a suggestion that Parke-Davis's conduct involved an infringement of Article 85 (1), on the basis that the rights flowing from a patent do not in and of themselves infringe that Article and, more particularly, that in order for Article 85 (1) to apply there must be an agreement, decision or concerted practice in existence.

8.85   The Court also concluded without difficulty that there was no abuse of a dominant position by Parke-Davis, merely because it sought to enforce patent rights.[58]

8.86   Whatever may be the weaknesses of the Court's reasoning in this early decision, the proposition established by the judgment is very clear: The owner of a patent in one country within the EEC may enforce its national patent rights so as to prevent the import into that country of goods manufactured by a third party in another EEC country where patent protection is not available.

8.87   This proposition, while clear, is also narrow. One may speculate, for example, whether the Court's decision would have been the same if, say, Parke-Davis had been able to obtain patent protection in Italy, but had simply not troubled to do so.[59] Similarly, what would have been the position had Parke-Davis had an earlier patent which had expired in Italy?

(c) Implications of the Court's judgment

8.88   One can only speculate on the likely outcome of future references to the European Court involving either of these two situations, although the position may be clearer following the Court's judgment in a case currently before it.[59a] Turning first to the possibility of patent protection being

---

[58] For further details concerning the Court's holding in the context of Art. 86, see discussion at p. 50, of the case and *supra*, Chap. 5 at para. 5.03.

[59] See, *supra*, n. 56a.

[59a] *Merck & Co. Inc., supra,* n. 55a.

available but a patent not having been obtained (for whatever reason), it is submitted that guidance is to be found in the Court's judgment in the *Sterling Drug* case.[60] With obvious reference to its decision in the *Parke-Davis* case and in considering provisions in national patent law to the effect that the rights of a patentee are not exhausted merely because the patented product has been marketed in another Member State so that the patentee in the first Member State could, as a matter of national law, prevent importation of the "infringing" product, the Court said:

> "While such an obstacle to free movement may be justifiable for reasons of protection of industrial property when the protection is invoked against a product coming from a member State in which it is not patentable and has been manufactured by third parties without the consent of the patentee ...., the derogation to the principle of free movement of goods is not justified when the product has been lawfully put by the patentee himself or with his consent, on the market of the Member State from which it is being imported e.g. in the case of a holder of parallel patents.[61]

8.89   It is submitted, in the light of the above passage, that the crucial question would be whether the patent owner, seeking to prevent importation of the "infringing product," could be said to have "consented" to the product being manufactured in the other EEC Member State. If patent protection was available in that state, and it could be shown that the patent owner could have obtained such patent protection had he chosen to do so, then there would seem no reason in principle why the patent owner should be entitled as a matter of EEC law to prevent importation of the "infringing" product. Arguably, by "choosing" not to obtain patent protection in the country of manufacture, the patent owner "consented" to manufacture by a third party in that country!

8.90   Turning next to the question whether the patent owner should be entitled to enforce his national patent rights in a situation in which he had been the owner of a patent in the Member State of manufacture, but this latter patent had expired, one may speculate as to whether in such circumstances it would be said that the patent owner's rights had been "exhausted" as regards goods manufactured in "the other country," at the moment in time when patent protection in that country became unavailable.

8.91   As against such a proposition, one would have to weight the argument

---

[60] Discussed in detail *supra*, at paras. 8.31 *et seq*.
[61] *Centrafarm BV* v. *Sterling Drug Inc.*, [1974] E.C.R. 1183; [1974] 2 C.M.L.R. 480 at pp. 503 and 504.

which would doubtless be advanced to the effect that this would unfairly disadvantage the patent owner's position in his own country.[62]

2. The Position with Regard to Other Intellectual Property

8.92 From the perspective of EEC law, there would again seem no obvious reason, in principle, to differentiate between the European Court's holding in the *Parke-Davis* case in the context of patents and the likely position on similar facts in the context of other types of intellectual property,[63] with the exception of performing rights as an element of copyright. It is difficult to imagine an analogous situation involving such rights. If such a situation were to arise, however, the outcome might well be governed by the Court's view that the exhaustion doctrine does not apply in relation to performing rights.[63a] On this basis, the copyright owner in the "country of importation" might well be able to enforce his rights.

8.93 It is true, of course, that the European Court has on occasion seen fit to suggest that in certain circumstances trade marks might not be entitled to a similar degree of protection as other industrial property rights including, in particular, patents.[64] It is, however, by no means clear how much weight should be attached to these remarks, or what bearing they might have on a factual situation analogous to that presented to the European Court in the *Parke-Davis* case save only that it involves patents.

E. Category 4

Goods are manufactured outside the EEC and imported into an EEC Member State in circumstances which would involve the infringement of an

---

[62] This argument is advanced forcefully in the so-called "Dietz Report," in the context of the different periods of protection afforded a copyright owner in various EEC member countries. The report concludes, on this subject: "These circumstances ... that a work is not (or is no longer) protected in certain countries cannot be solved as simply from a European aspect, as both countries are EEC countries, by the unrestricted application of the principle of the free movement of goods, because ... this would mean unjustified local advantage to the disadvantage of publishers in countries with more favourable, longer copyright protection periods. In these cases, it must be assumed that, within the terms of Art. 36 of the EEC Treaty, there is a prohibition of imports which is justified on the basis of copyright without there being arbitrary discrimination or a disguised restriction on trade between Member States. On the contrary, what is concerned here is the very core of the essentially upheld-national copyright. De lege ferenda a contradiction with the free movement of goods can therefore in the end only be cured here if the protection periods and the preconditions for protectability are the same in all nine countries." Dietz, *Copyright Law in the European Community* (Sijthoff & Noordhoff, 1978), pp. 97 and 98.

[63] But, with reference specifically to copyright, see n. 62 *supra*.

[63a] See discussion, *supra*, at para. 8.28.1 and, *infra*, Chap. 12 at para. 12.58.

[64] See, *e.g.* Case 40/70 *Sirena S.R.L.* v. *EDA S.R.L. and Others* [1971] E.C.R. 69; [1971] C.M.L.R. 260 at p. 273.

intellectual property right owned by an independent party in that Member State (O). Under Community law may "O" exercise his right to prevent importation of the goods from outside the EEC?

8.94   To date there has only been one European Court judgment directly in point, namely its judgment in the *EMI* cases referred to in Chapter 3.[65]

1. *The EMI v CBS Cases*

(a) The facts

8.95   As indicated in Chapter 3, references were made to the European Court under Article 177 by the national courts of three Member States—the United Kingdom, Denmark and Germany—as parallel proceedings were in progress in all three countries, essentially involving the same question.

8.96   The facts were extremely involved but, for present purposes, it is only necessary to note that all three references were concerned with the trade mark "Columbia." Although in the past the various trade mark registrations had been owned by associated undertakings, at the time of the references the "Columbia" trade mark in the United States was owned by CBS Incorporated, while the "Columbia" trade marks in all of the nine EEC Member States were owned by members of the EMI group. EMI Records Limited manufactured records in the United Kingdom under the "Columbia" mark, and records marketed under the "Columbia" mark were also manufactured by other EMI subsidiaries in most of the EEC Member States. CBS manufactured records in the United States and elsewhere, under the "Columbia" mark. A proportion of records manu-

---

[65] Case 51/75 *EMI Records Ltd.* v. *CBS nited Kingdom Ltd.* [1976] E.C.R. 811; [1976] 2 C.M.L.R. 235. See Chap. 3. Note, however, that a related question was explored by the English Court of Appeal, namely: Where goods protected by copyright are lawfully placed on the market by the owner of the copyright or with his consent ("O") in a country which is not a member of the EEC but which has a free trade agreement with the EEC, in circumstances in which O owns the copyright in a Member State of the EEC, may O exercise his copyright under domestic law to prevent a third party from importing the goods in question into that Member State? The countries in question were respectively Portugal and the U.K., and the goods being imported into the U.K. were records. The relevant provision in the Free Trade Agreement between the EEC and Portugal was Art. 14 (2), which provides: "Quantitative restrictions on imports shall be abolished on 1 January, 1973, and any measures having an effect equivalent to quantitative restrictions on imports shall be abolished not later than 1 January, 1975." The Court of Appeal chose not to decide the question itself but, instead, to make a reference. (*Polydor Limited and RSO Records* v. *Harlequin Record Shops Limited* [1980] 2 C.M.L.R. 413; Case 270/80 (unreported).) Note also *The Who Group Ltd. and Polydor Limited* v. *Stage One (Records) Limited* [1980] 2 C.M.L.R. 429, in which the High Court was faced in interlocutory proceedings with similar facts, except that the records in question had been lawfully manufactured in the U.S. and lawfully imported into Holland. The defendants argued that once lawfully placed on the market in Holland the records were entitled to circulate freely within the Community. Without deciding the point, Mr. Justice Megarry declined to grant an interlocutory injunction and indicated that a reference to the European Court of Justice might be necessary at a later stage in the proceedings. Note also Case 225/78 *Procureur de la République, Besançon* v. *Claude Bouhelier and Others* [1980] 2 C.M.L.R. 541.

factured by CBS in the United States were sold within the EEC, and in such cases the "Columbia" mark was sometimes obliterated or concealed by a label stuck to the record and the sleeve. On occasion, however, such obliteration was not carried out.

8.97   EMI Records Limited duly instituted parallel proceedings against the English, German and Danish subsidiaries of CBS Incorporated. As indicated, references were eventually made by the national courts in all three countries to the European Court of Justice, by which the Court was asked whether provisions of the Treaty on the free movement of goods prevented EMI from exercising its trade mark rights under national law in the relevant Member States of the EEC so as to prevent CBS from selling in those Member States goods bearing the "Columbia" trade mark.[66]

---

[66] The questions referred to the European Court by the High Court of Justice, London, were in the following terms:
"Should the provisions of the Treaty establishing the European Economic Community and in particular the provisions laying down the principles of Community law and the rules relating to the free movement of goods and to competition be interpreted as disentitling A from exercising its rights in the trademark under the appropriate national law in every Member-State to prevent:
(i) the sale by B in each Member-State of goods bearing the mark X manufactured and marked with the mark X by B outside the Community in a territory where he is entitled to apply the mark X, or
(ii) the manufacture by B in any Member-State of goods bearing the mark X?"
By way of clarification, the High Court supplied the following further information:
"(1) an economic unit "A" (comprising a parent company and its subsidiary companies) is the owner of a particular trade mark ("X") in the United Kingdom and all the other Member-States of the Community;
(2) A manufactures and sells on a large scale within the Community goods bearing the mark X;
(3) an economic unit "B" having no connection with A, owns the same trade mark X in a country or countries not members of the Community and lawfully applies the mark X to similar goods in those countries;
(4) B comprises (*inter alia*) a parent company established outside the Community and one or more wholly-owned subsidiary companies established within the Community and manufactures and sells within the Community large quantities or similar goods under different trade marks from the trade mark X;
(5) B now sells and proposes to continue to sell in the Community similar goods but bearing mark X;
(6) for some years well prior to the Second World War the trade mark X currently owned by A and B in their respective territories was held by the same interrelated undertakings (A having acquired its rights to the trade mark X by virtue of arrangements made between its predecessors in title and the predecessors in title of B at a time when such predecessors in title were wholly-owned subsidiary and parent companies respectively), but ownership of the trade mark X now owned by B has changed hands on a number of occasions.
(7) there is not now and never has been any legal, financial, technical or economic link between A and B as now constituted; and
(8) under the appropriate national laws of the Member-States of the Community (excluding Community law) A has the right to take proceedings for infringement of trade mark so as to prevent the manufacture and/or sale in Member-States of B's goods bearing the trade mark X."
The terms of the questions referred to the European Court by, respectively, the Danish and German Courts were in all material respects identical [1976] E.C.R 811; [1976] 2 C.M.L.R. 235 at p. 242 *et seq.* As to the differences between the three questions referred, see the Opinion of Advocate General Jean-Pierre Warner, *ibid.* at pp. 252 *et seq.*

(b) The Court's judgment

8.98 The Court replied categorically that EMI could enforce its trade mark rights against the "foreign" imports. The Court reasoned that both Article 3 (*a*) and Articles 30 *et seq.* expressly prohibit only quantitative restrictions and measures having equivalent effect "between Member States." In the Court's view this was particularly noticeable in the context of the second sentence of Article 36, which withdraws the benefit of the immunity conferred by the first sentence of that Article where prohibitions or restrictions allegedly justified for the protection of industrial and commercial property "constitute a means of arbitrary discrimination or a disguised restriction on *trade between Member States.*" In the Court's own words:

"Consequently the exercise of a trade mark right in order to prevent the marketing of a product coming from a third country under an identical mark, even if this constitutes a measure having an effect equivalent to a quantitative restriction, does not affect the free movement of goods between member-States and thus does not come under the prohibitions set out in Articles 30 et seq of the Treaty.

In such circumstances the exercise of a trade mark right does not in fact jeopardise the unity of the Common Market which Articles 30 et seq are intended to ensure."[67]

8.99 On this reasoning, the Court concluded that the provisions of the Treaty on the free movement of goods do not prevent the owner of a trade mark in *all* the Member States of the Community from exercising its trade mark rights so as to prevent, either the importation of products under the same mark from outside the Community or the manufacture and marketing of products with the same mark in the Community by a proprietor of the mark outside the Community.

(c) Implication of the Court's judgment

8.100 The Court emphasised throughout its judgment the importance which it attached to EMI's ownership of the "Columbia" trade mark in all nine countries of the Community. One may speculate, therefore, on the extent to which the judgment would have been different if EMI had owned trade mark rights in, say, only eight EEC Member States and CBS had manufactured and marketed in the ninth Member State. If neither party had owned a trade mark in the ninth Member State, the position would presumably be governed by the *Parke-Davis* case.[68] In other words, if no trade mark could be obtained by EMI for technical reasons, one would assume that EMI would have been able to enforce its rights in the other eight Member States. By contrast, for the reasons suggested in the context of the *Parke-Davis* case, rather more doubt exists as to whether EMI could have

---

[67] *Ibid.* at p. 265.
[68] See discussion, *supra*, at paras. 8.81 *et seq.*

enforced its rights against CBS in circumstances in which either EMI could have obtained trade mark protection in the ninth Member State but chose not to do so or, alternatively, it had at one time owned trade mark rights in that ninth state but these had now lapsed.

8.101   Be that as it may, wherever a trade mark owner within the EEC attaches importance to his trade mark and has the option of doing so, in the light of the *EMI* case there can be little doubt that it is advisable to register a trade mark at the earliest possible opportunity throughout the Community as a whole.

2. *The Position with Regard to Other Intellectual Property Rights*

8.102   To the extent that the European Court's judgment in the *EMI* case turned on its interpretation of the wording of Article 3 (*a*) and Articles 30 to 36, rather than upon considerations relating to the particular characteristics of trade marks, it is unlikely that the Court's ruling would have been substantially different had intellectual property other than a trade mark been involved, provided this related to goods.

8.102.1   Moreover, even where the intellectual property relates to services so that the position is governed by Articles 59 and 60 of the Treaty, it is thought likely that the Court's ruling would be similar. Thus, having regard to the *Coditel* case,[68a] if the television broadcast which was received in Belgium had been transmitted by an independent party from a country outside the EEC, the Court's conclusion would presumably have been the same as it in fact was: the Belgian copyright owner's exercise of his copyright to prevent the foreign transmission being relayed by cable television companies in Belgium would not have contravened EEC law relating to the free movement of services.[68b]

III. *ARTICLE 86—IMPACT ON A SINGLE OWNER OF INTELLECTUAL PROPERTY*

A. INTELLECTUAL PROPERTY AND DOMINANCE

8.103   As was pointed out in Chapter 5, it has long been abundantly clear that mere ownership of intellectual property rights does not, of itself, give rise to a dominant position within the meaning of Article 86.[69] The Court has expressly so held in the context of patents,[70] and reached a similar conclusion with regard to rights analogous to a copyright in the *Deutsche*

[68a] See discussion, *supra*, at para. 8.25 and, *infra*, Chap. 12 at paras. 12.58.1 *et seq.*
[68b] *Ibid.*

[69] See, *supra*, Chap. 5, paras. 5.02 *et seq.* Note particularly the wording there quoted from the European Court's judgment in the *Parke-Davis* case.
[70] *Ibid.*

Grammophon case[71] and with regard to trade marks in the *Hoffman-La Roche* case[72] and, again, in the *EMI* cases.[73]

8.104 The ownership of intellectual property rights may, of course, enable a particular undertaking to establish and to maintain a dominant position, but the existence or otherwise of the dominant position would be established according to the criteria discussed in Chapter 5, and without particular regard to the existence of intellectual property. Thus, for example, in the course of its judgment in the *EMI* case the European Court stated:

> "Although the trade mark right confers upon its proprietor a special position within the protected territory this, however, does not imply the existence of a dominant position ... in particular where, as in the present case, several undertakings whose economic strength is comparable to that of the proprietor of the mark operate in the market for the products in question and are in a position to compete with the said proprietor."[74]

By contrast, as mentioned in Chapter 5,[75] in the *Hoffman-La Roche* case ownership of patents was held to have contributed to Roche's technological lead over its competitors, and this technological lead was in turn held to be a "further indication" that Roche enjoyed a dominant position. The Court considered it immaterial that the patents in question had expired.[76]

B. INTELLECTUAL PROPERTY AND ABUSE

8.105 It is also clear that the mere exercise of an intellectual property right will not, in and of itself, constitute an abuse of the right.[76] This said, if it were established that a party owning intellectual property was in a dominant position, the exercise of an intellectual property right in a particular situation might be deemed to constitute an abuse of that dominant position. This, it is submitted, must be the meaning of the Court's statement in the *Parke-Davis* case that "the utilisation of the patent could degenerate into an improper exploitation of the protection."[77]

---

[71] *Deutsche Grammophon GmbH, supra* [1971] E.C.R. 487; [1971] C.M.L.R. 631 at pp. 858 to 859.

[72] *Hoffman-La Roche & Co. AG, supra,* [1978] E.C.R. 113; [1978] 3 C.M.L.R. 217 at p. 243.

[73] Case 51/75 *EMI Records Ltd.* v. *CBS United Kingdom Ltd.* [1976] E.C.R. 811; [1976] 2 C.M.L.R. 235.

[74] *Ibid.* at p. 267. Note also the European Court's judgment on the same point in the *Deutsche Grammophon* case, *supra,* at p. 658.

[75] *Hoffmann-La Roche AG* v. *EC Commission* [1979] E.C.R. 461; [1979] 3 C.M.L.R. 211 at p. 278.

[76] *Ibid.* See also *Parke-Davis & Co., supra,* at p. 59; *Hoffmann-La Roche & Co. AG, supra* at pp. 243 and 244; and *Deutsche Grammophon GmbH, supra* at pp. 658 to 659.

[77] *Parke-Davis & Co.* [1968] C.M.L.R. 47 at p. 59.

8.106   While, however, the possibility must exist that in appropriate circumstances the owner of intellectual property in a dominant position would be held to be abusing that position by the exercise of his intellectual property right, it is noteworthy that, to date, exercise of an intellectual property right has never been held to constitute such an abuse.

CHAPTER 9

OWNERSHIP OF INTELLECTUAL PROPERTY WITHOUT A "COMMON ORIGIN" BY TWO OR MORE ENTERPRISES IN THE COMMUNITY

I. *INTRODUCTION*

9.01   The last chapter dealt with the extent to which the Treaty limits a single owner of an intellectual property right in the traditional exercise of that right *vis-à-vis* third party "infringers" having no title to the intellectual property, and with whom no contractual relationship exists. By contrast, this chapter deals with ownership by two or more "enterprises" within the Community of identical or similar intellectual property rights which do not have a "*common origin*," and with the extent to which the Treaty affects the traditional non-contractual relationship between the two owners.

9.02   The "common origin" concept will be discussed in detail in Part IV,[1] since "common origin," by definition, only arises when an owner of intellectual property has voluntarily assigned a partial interest in his original rights or when there is some form of forced divestiture of a part of such rights (*e.g.* expropriation). In other words, two or more intellectual property rights can only have a common origin if, at some time in the past, they had a common owner. It must be borne in mind, however, that if identical or similar intellectual property currently owned by two or more enterprises in the Community enjoyed a common origin *at any time in the past*, the position of the present owners must be considered in the light of the principles discussed in Part IV.

9.03   The concern here is with the more usual situation in which two enterprises in the Community own intellectual property which can in no sense be said to have a common origin.

II. *CONCURRENT USER OF INTELLECTUAL PROPERTY WITH NO COMMON ORIGIN*

9.04   To date, there has only been one European Court judgment concerned with this situation, namely the *Terrapin* case,[2] which involved similar trade marks owned respectively by English and German enterprises.

---

[1] *Infra*, Chap. 12 at paras. 12.30 *et seq*.
[2] Case 119/75 *Terrapin (Overseas) Ltd.* v. *Terranova Industrie* [1976] E.C.R. 1039; [1976] 2 C.M.L.R. 482.

A. The Position with Regard to Trade Marks—The Terrapin Case

(1) *The Facts*

9.05 The facts of the *Terrapin* case were relatively straightforward. Terranova Industrie C.A. Kapferer & Co. ("Terranova") is a German company which manufactured and marketed prepared plaster for facades. It owned registered trade marks in Germany for "Terra," "Terra" with device, "Terra Fabrikate," "Terranova" and device and "Terranova" with a particular arrangement of letters. In the company's registry the German company's objects were stated to be "manufacture of dry prepared plaster, construction work and trade in building materials."

9.06 Terrapin (Overseas) Limited ("Terrapin") is an English company which manufactured and sold prefabricated houses which it marketed under the trade mark "Terrapin."

9.07 In 1961 Terrapin applied for registration of the "Terrapin" trade mark in Germany, and this application was opposed by Terranova. Terrapin was successful before the German Patent Office, but the decision of that office was revoked by the Federal Patent Court[3] on appeal by Terranova. Perhaps surprisingly, the Federal Patent Court accepted Terranova's contention that the products marketed by the two companies were similar, and the trade marks "Terrapin" and "Terranova" would be likely to give rise to confusion.

9.08 Notwithstanding its failure to obtain registration of "Terrapin" as a trade mark, Terrapin nonetheless continued to market its products in Germany under that trade mark. This resulted in a proliferation of litigation between Terrapin and Terranova.

9.09 For present purposes it is enough to note that the reference to the European Court arose from a judgment of the Oberlandesgericht Munich, restraining Terrapin from using "Terrapin" in Germany either as a company name or as a trade mark, and ordering Terrapin to pay damages. Terrapin appealed that judgment to the Bundesgerichtshof. In October 1975 the Bundesgerichtshof stayed proceedings, and referred the following question to the European Court for a preliminary ruling under Article 177 of the Treaty:

"Is it compatible with the provisions relating to the free movement of goods (Articles 30 and 36 of the EEC Treaty) that an undertaking established in member State A, by using its commercial name and trade mark rights existing there, should prevent the import of similar goods of an undertaking established in member State B if these goods have been lawfully given a distinguishing name which may be confused with the commercial name and trade mark which are protected

---

[3] *i.e.* the Bundespatentgericht.

in State A for the undertaking established there, if there are no relations between the two undertakings, if their national trade mark rights arose autonomously and independently of one another (no common origin) and at the present time there exists no economic or legal relations of any kind other than those appertaining to trade marks between the undertakings?"[4]

9.10   The potential conflict between German law and EEC law was succinctly expressed by the Advocate General, when he advised the European Court that "under German law ... the judgment appealed against must be confirmed; Terranova could therefore by exercising its rights to the trade mark and the company name prohibit the importation into the Federal Republic of Germany of certain products which have lawfully been given the mark "Terrapin" in another State. A query however arises, with regard to Community law. ..."[5]

(2) The Court's Judgment

(a) General

9.11   The Court noted that Article 30 prohibits quantitative restrictions on imports and all measures having equivalent effect, and again repeated its analysis both of the scope of Article 36 and of the inter-relationship between the first and second sentences of that Article. Then, addressing itself to the question referred to it, the Court said:

"... In the present state of Community law an industrial or commercial property right legally acquired in a member State may legally be used to prevent under the first sentence of Article 36 of the Treaty the import of products marketed under a name giving rise to confusion where the rights in question have been acquired by different and independent proprietors under different national laws. If in such a case the principle of the free movement of goods were to prevail over the protection given by the respective national laws, the specific objective of industrial and commercial property rights would be undermined. In the particular situation the requirements of the free movement of goods and the safeguarding of industrial and commercial property rights must be so reconciled that protection is ensured for the legitimate use of the rights conferred by national laws, coming within the prohibitions on imports 'justified' within the meaning of Article 36 of the Treaty, but denied on the other hand in respect of any improper exercise of the same rights of such a nature as to maintain or effect artificial partitions within the Common Market."[6]

---

[4] *Terrapin (Overseas) Ltd.* v. *Terranova Industrie* [1976] 2 C.M.L.R. 482.
[5] *Ibid.*
[6] *Ibid.* at p. 506.

9.12   The Court then answered the question referred to it by the Bundesgerichtshof to the effect that an undertaking does not infringe the free movement of goods provisions of the Treaty, by relying on national intellectual property "... to prevent the importation of products of an undertaking established in another Member State and bearing by virtue of the legislation of that state a name giving rise to confusion with the trade mark and commercial name of the first undertaking, provided that there are no agreements restricting competition and no legal or economic ties between the undertakings and that their respective rights have arisen independently of one another."[6]

9.13   The Court, therefore, upheld that in the circumstances at issue enforcement of trade mark rights is "justified" within the meaning of the first sentence of Article 36. Furthermore, it reached this conclusion by reasoning that such enforcement is "justified" in order to safeguard the guarantee function of a trade mark which is a part of its specific subject matter, *i.e.* in order to preserve to consumers the guarantee provided by a trade mark that goods on which it is fixed have originated with a particular manufacturer. This is only true, however, if there are no restrictive agreements between the manufacturers, no legal or economic links between them and, finally, that their rights have arisen independently of each other.[7]

(b) The issues of discrimination and similarity

9.14   Before reaching its conclusion, however, the Court dealt at some length with the question of whether there could be circumstances in which the provisions of the Treaty on free movement of goods would be infringed by a trade mark owner in one Member State seeking to enforce national trade mark rights in order to prevent the importation of goods bearing an allegedly similar trade mark by a trade mark owner in another Member State. The relevant passage in the Court's judgment is of sufficient importance to justify quotation in full. Referring to the finding of similarity between the Terrapin and Terranova trade marks by the German Courts, the European Court said:

> "(4) Although this finding has been questioned during the oral procedure the Court does not have to rule on this point since no question has been put to it with regard to the matter. It is right however to stress that the answer given below does not prejudge the question of whether an allegation by one undertaking as to the similarity of products originating in different Member States and the risk of confusion of trade marks or commercial names legally pro-

---

[7] As to the position where restrictive agreements between the manufacturers are present, see generally Chaps. 4, 10 and 11; as to the position where legal or economic links exist between the manufacturers, see generally Chaps. 7, 8 and 12; and as to the position where the respective property rights have not arisen independently of each other, see generally Chap. 12.

tected in those States may perhaps involve the application of Community law with regard in particular to the second sentence of Article 36 of the Treaty. It is for the court of first instance, after considering the similarity of the products and the risk of confusion, to enquire further in the context of this last provision into whether the exercise in a particular case of industrial and commercial property rights may or may not constitute a means of arbitrary discrimination or a disguised restriction on trade between Member States. It is for the national court in this respect to ascertain in particular whether the rights in question are in fact exercised by the proprietor with the same strictness whatever the national origin of any possible infringer."[8]

9.15 Clearly, it follows from the last sentence of this passage that enforcement of trade mark rights in the circumstances mentioned can give rise to an arbitrary discrimination or a disguised restriction within the meaning of the second sentence of Article 36. This will be so, in particular, if the trade mark rights are exercised by their owner in a discriminatory way, based on nationality.

9.16 Rather more doubt exists as to whether the actual finding by a national court of "similarity" between two different trade marks could, in appropriate circumstances, be challenged before the European Court and be found to fall under the second sentence of Article 36. This possibility certainly seems implicit in the first two sentences quoted above.[9]

9.17 This said, and whatever the outcome of a reference to the European Court on the question might be, there can be little doubt that it would be difficult to persuade a national court actually to make such a reference. To do so would involve persuading the national court that the finding of similarity by a national tribunal could, in certain circumstances, properly be the subject of "judicial review" by the European Court.

(B) The Position with Regard to Other Intellectual Property

9.18 It is thought that the European Court would follow its *Terrapin* decision, should an analogous situation arise involving goods protected by intellectual property other than trade marks. This would seem clear, bearing in mind that the Court appears to regard trade marks as at best the equal of other intellectual property and, at worst, of considerably less importance than, say, patents.

---

[8] *Terrapin (Overseas) Ltd.* [1976] 2 C.M.L.R. 482.

[9] Such a course would, for example, be consistent with Johannes's view that the instrument which disrupts the free movement of goods within the Community is not so much the individual who institutes that action based on industrial property rights, but rather "the legislative instrument which confers such rights or the judicial act which upholds them"; (Johannes, *Industrial Property and Copyright in European Community Law* 1976), p. 24.

9.19   Further with specific reference to performing rights or an element of copyright, the outcome would probably be the same although the relevant provisions would be Articles 59 and 60 relating to services. Certainly, there is nothing in the *Coditel* case that suggests otherwise.[10]

---

[10] See discussion, *infra*, Chap. 12 at paras. 12.58.1 *et seq.*

Part III

Licensing of Intellectual Property

CHAPTER 10

INTRODUCTION

I. *GENERAL*

10.01 From the earliest days in the development of the Community's competition policy it has been clear that licensing agreements involving intellectual property may give rise to particular difficulties under Article 85 (1).[1] Implementation of the competition policy by the Commission dates, in practice, from Regulation 17 which came into force on March 13, 1962.[2] Before the end of that year, the Commission had made its first general statement on the relationship between Article 85 and patent licences in a Notice published in December 24, 1962, the so-called "Christmas Communiqué."

10.02 That Notice was, in fact, the first of several attempts by the Commission to give general guidance on this problem. With the development of its competition policy and with the development of the Community itself since 1962, the attitude of the Commission towards licensing agreements has changed. Thus, for example, the 1962 Notice suggested that a straightforward exclusive patent licence would not infringe Article 85 (1).[3] In a series of Decisions in the early and mid-seventies,[4] it became clear that, in many cases, an exclusive licence would amount to an infringement, although frequently one capable of exemption under Article 85 (3). This general shift in the Commission's view is confirmed by its proposed draft block exemption for exclusive patent licences[5] where the grant of exclusive rights is included among the clauses which will be covered by the exemption.[6]

10.03 The draft block exemption is the latest indication of the Commission's thinking in this area, and shows its increasingly strict view of the compata-

---

[1] See *supra*, Chap. 4 for a general discussion of Art. 85. Art. 85 (1) only applies to agreements "between undertakings." Thus, licensing agreements between members of the same group of companies will not normally be affected. See, *e.g.* Cases 15 & 16/74 *Centrafarm BV* and *de Peijper* v. Sterling Drug Inc. and Centrafarm BV and *de Peijper* v. *Winthrop BV* [1974] E.C.R. 1147, 1183; [1974] 2 C.M.L.R. 480.

[2] Reg. 17/62 (J.O. 1962, 204); (O.J. 1959–1962, 87).

[3] See para. 1.E.

[4] *e.g.* see App. 9; *Re Burroughs/Delplanque* [1972] C.M.L.R. D. 67; *Re Kabelmetal/ Luchaire Agreement* [1975] 2 C.M.L.R. D. 40. For a fuller discussion of exclusivity see *infra* Chap. 11, paras. 11.11–11.44.

[5] Proposal for a Commission Regulation on the application of Art. 85 (3) of the Treaty to certain categories of patent licensing agreements (O.J. 1979 C58/12). See App. 8.

[6] See Art. 1 (1) (3) and (4).

bility of licensing agreements with Article 85 (1). In broad terms, the Commission seems to have moved from considering licences of intellectual property generally to be eligible for a negative clearance (in other words, not infringing Article 85 (1) at all) to considering them as infringing Article 85 (1) but qualifying for an exemption under Article 85 (3).[7]

10.04   The distinction between the *existence* and the *exercise* of rights in intellectual property, which was first developed by the European Court in cases where licensing was not involved, is just as valid in the licensing context. The Commission's Fourth Report on Competition Policy contains in paragraphs 19 to 32 a section dealing with patent licence agreements in which the Commission says:

> "... any appraisal of particular patent licensing provisions requires prior differentiation between terms which are germane to the existence, and those which relate to the exercise, of patent rights, in order to establish upon which provisions the Commission may properly rule. While the differentiation remains to be more fully worked out by future decisions of the Court, it is clear that patent licensing agreements are not automatically within Article 85 (1) if the agreements simply confer rights to exploit patented inventions against payment of royalties, but that questions of applicability of Article 85 (1) arise if a grant is accompanied by terms which go beyond the need to ensure the existence of an industrial property right, or where the exercise of such right is found to be the object, means or consequence of a restrictive agreement."[8]

There is little doubt that the same distinction applies to other types of intellectual property.

10.05   As will be seen in Chapter 11, the distinction has been applied by the Commission in individual cases in such a way that, in practice, the majority of terms in a licensing agreement will "relate to the exercise" of the licensed right, and very few will be "germane to [its] existence."

10.06   In addition to the 1962 Notice and the draft block exemption, indications of the Commission's general thinking on the relationship between Article 85 and licensing agreements are to be found in later Notices,[9] in its Annual Reports on Competition Policy,[10] and in various Regulations and draft Regulations.

---

[7] For the distinction between a negative clearance and an exemption see *supra*, Chap. 4, para. 4–97.

[8] See Fourth Report on Competition Policy pt. 20.

[9] *e.g.* Commission Notice of December 18, 1978 covering its assessment of certain subcontracting agreements in relation to Art. 85 (1) of the EEC Treaty (O.J. 1979, C1/2). See App. 12.

[10] In particular, the Fourth Report published in April 1975.

II. *NOTICES*

A. GENERAL

10.07   Over the years since the original 1962 Notice, a number of other Notices[11] have been issued to give general guidance on the application of Article 85 (1) to particular situations. In effect, they amount to a series of "block negative clearances." Although Notices of this type are always issued "without prejudice to the view that may be taken . . . by the Court of Justice of the European Communities,[12] they may not be entirely devoid of legal effect. In publishing for comments the draft block exemption for patent licensing agreements the Commission said:

> "The Commission intends to withdraw the Notice on patent licensing agreements of 24th December 1962. Until the entry into force of the above mentioned Regulation, undertakings conducting their affairs on the basis of that Notice will not be fined by the Commission under Article 15 (2) of Regulation 17."[13]

10.08   If, however, a Notice is to be relied upon, it is vital to ensure that the agreement or conduct in question does not go beyond the specific terms of the Notice.[14]

B. THE 1962 NOTICE ON PATENT LICENCE AGREEMENTS

10.09   On December 24, 1962, the Commission issued a Notice on Patent Licence Agreements,[15] which set out five types of clauses frequently found in patent licence agreements which, at that time, the Commission considered did not infringe Article 85 (1). Although certain of the clauses specified in the Notice have subsequently been viewed in a different light by the Commission in specific Decisions, and the Notice has, for some time, been considered unreliable, it is clear, on a careful reading, that the scope of the Notice was always limited. The opening words state that it is issued "on the basis of the facts known at present," that is to say in 1962 before the

---

[11] Notices are issued to serve a variety of purposes, *e.g.* Notices under Art. 19 (3) of Reg. 17 of the Commission's intention to issue a negative clearance or grant an exemption for a notified agreement; Notice on Imports of Japanese Products of October 21, 1972 (J.O. 1972, C111/13).

[12] *e.g.* final paragraph of Commission Notice of December 18, 1978 concerning its assessment of certain sub-contracting agreements in relation to Art. 85 (1) of the EEC Treaty (O.J. 1979, C1/2).

[13] O.J. 1979, C58/11.

[14] See, *e.g. Putz* v. *Kawasaki Motors (U.K.) Ltd.* and the *Community* v. *Kawasaki Motoren GmbH* [1979] 1 C.M.L.R. 448 where Kawasaki Motors (U.K.) Ltd. sought to rely on the Commission's Notice on agreements of minor importance (J.O. 1970, C64/1; [1970] C.M.L.R. D. 15), but in calculating the relevant turnover limits overlooked the fact that the turnover of parent and subsidiary undertakings had to be consolidated under the terms of Pt. II of the Notice.

[15] On the same date it also issued a Notice on Exclusive Agency Contracts.

Commission had begun to study in detail notified agreements involving patents.

10.10   The Notice was limited, in its terms, to a single licence and did not apply to joint ownership of patents, reciprocal licences or parallel multiple licences. It also dealt only with "patent licence contracts," and probably did not apply where ancillary know-how was included in the licence. Certainly, it did not cover other types of intellectual property and it specifically envisaged that further notices would be issued dealing with "agreements relating to the exploitation of other industrial property rights or of creative activities not protected by law and constituting technical improvements."[16]

10.11   Where relevant the provisions of the Notice dealing with particular clauses in patent licences will be discussed in detail in the relevant sections of Chapter 11.

C. THE NOTICE ON SUB-CONTRACTING AGREEMENTS

10.12 The only other Notice concerned primarily with intellectual property[17] is the Notice issued on December 18, 1978 dealing with sub-contracting agreements.[18] Sub-contracting agreements are defined as "agreements under which one firm, called 'the contractor,' whether or not in consequence of a prior order from a third party, entrusts to another, called 'the sub-contractor,' the manufacture of goods, the supply of services or the performance of work under the contractor's instructions, to be provided to the contractor or performed on his behalf." The view of the Commission, as expressed in the Notice, is that agreements of this type will not normally infringe Article 85 (1), even where they involve restrictions on the sub-contractor's right to use intellectual property belonging to the contractor.

10.13   The thinking behind the Notice is similar to the thinking behind the Notice on exclusive agency contracts.[19] Thus, even though the contractor and the sub-contractor are legally separate undertakings and any agreements between them will, therefore, be "agreements between undertakings" in terms of Article 85 (1), the relationship between them, from an economic point of view, is one of dependence and not of independence. In the same way that a commercial agent is considered only to perform "an auxiliary function," so a sub-contractor is described in this Notice as "providing goods, services or work in respect of which he is not an independent supplier in the market."

---

[16] See 1962 Notice Pt. III.

[17] The Notice on co-operation agreements of July 29, 1968 does not refer in terms to intellectual property although it may be indirectly relevant to certain parts of the Notice if, *e.g.* the joint research and development referred to in Pt. I (3) results in a patent or other right.

[18] Commission Notice of December 18, 1978 concerning its assessment of certain sub-contracting agreements in relation to Art. 85 (1) of the EEC Treaty (O.J. 1979, C1/2).

[19] See, *supra*, n. 15.

10.14   Sub-contracting agreements are considered by the Commission as being "a form of work distribution," where the sub-contractor is operating entirely on instructions from the contractor. Against that background, it is clearly right that the use by the sub-contractor of technology or equipment belonging to the contractor should be restricted "to whatever is necessary for the purposes of the agreement," and that the results of the sub-contractor's work should be supplied exclusively to the contractor. Frequently, of course, the contractor's technology will be protected "in the form of patents, utility models, designs protected by copyright, registered designs or other rights," or will be in the form of secret know-how. The decisive test, however, is that "even though not covered by industrial property rights nor containing any element of secrecy" the contractor's technology or equipment should "permit the manufacture of goods which differ in form, function or composition from other goods manufactured or supplied on the market."

10.15   If, however, the contractor gives no more than general instructions, and any specialised technology and equipment required are obtained by the sub-contractor from some other source, restrictions on the sub-contractor may well infringe Article 85 (1), as they "could deprive the sub-contractor of the possibility of developing his own business in the fields covered by the agreement." In other words, the required element of dependence of the sub-contractor on the contractor would no longer be present.

10.16   The same relationship of dependence between contractor and sub-contractor underlies the section of the Notice dealing with improvements. If the improvements "are incapable of being used independently of the contractor's secret know-how or patent" the sub-contractor can be required to pass them on exclusively to the contractor. In other circumstances, the general rules developed by the Commission apply[20] and the sub-contractor can only be required to make the improvements available to the contractor on a non-exclusive basis.

D. REPORTS ON COMPETITION

10.17 For each year since 1971, the Commission has published a Report on Competition Policy as an annexe to the General Report for that year on the activities of the Communities. The Reports on Competition Policy for each year are normally published in April or May of the following year. The Reports deal with the general trend of developments in the area of competition, and contain a commentary on important decisions of the Court and the Commission during the year.

10.18   Of particular interest as far as patent licensing agreements are concerned is a section in the Fourth Report on Competition Policy published in April

---

[20] See, *infra*, Chap. 11, paras. 11.110–11.116.

1975.[21] The views expressed there on particular clauses in patent licensing agreements were the result of a conference held in December 1974 at which the Commission and Government experts of the Member States exchanged views on these questions. The detailed comments will be discussed in the sections of Chapter 11 dealing with these particular clauses.

III. *REGULATIONS*[22]

A. REGULATION 17

10.19 Licences of intellectual property are among the agreements specifically referred to in Article 4 (2) of Regulation 17, as agreements which may benefit from an exemption, even if they have not been notified under Article 4 (1) of the Regulation.[23] Specifically, the Regulation covers agreements where:

> "(2) Not more than two undertakings are party thereto and the agreements only:
>
> ...
>
> (b) impose restrictions on the exercise of the rights of the assignee or user of industrial property rights—in particular patents, utility models, designs or trade marks—or of the person entitled under a contract to the assignment, or grant, of the right to use a method of manufacture or knowledge relating to the use and to the application of industrial processes."

10.20 The precise effects of this provision are, however, unclear. Generally, it seems to be of limited benefit. Thus, for example, in the *Advocaat Zwarte Kip* Decision, the Commission held that the trade mark assignment at issue there was not exempt from notification by virtue of Article 4 (2) (*b*)[24] of Regulation 17 "given that its effect is to prevent the vendor and third parties from freely importing and exporting within the Community products bearing the same trade mark."[25]

B. REGULATION 19

10.21 Regulation 19[26] was issued by the Council on March 2, 1965, and gave power to the Commission to issue block exemptions under Article 85 (3)

---

[21] Paras. 19 to 32.

[22] For a general discussion on the status of Reg. see, *supra*, Chap. 2, paras. 2.26–2.35.

[23] For a general discussion on notification see, *supra*, Chap. 4, paras. 4.97–4.119.

[24] For a fuller discussion of Art. 4 (2) (b) of Reg. 17 see *supra*, Chap. 4, para. 4.110–112.

[25] *Re Advocaat Zwarte Kip* [1974] 2 C.M.L.R. D. 79 at D. 86 and see Chap. 12, para. 12.22–27 as to why the Commission took this view on the facts.

[26] J.O. 1965, 533; O.J. 1965/66, 35.

for certain categories of agreements and concerted practices. It envisaged block exemptions for two types of agreement, first exclusive dealing agreements,[27] and, secondly, agreements imposing restrictions in relation to the acquisition or use of industrial property rights. In each case, the block exemption can only apply to agreements to which only two undertakings are a party, and block exemptions will always only be granted for a specified period.

10.22 A block exemption may apply with retroactive effect, and may also give a period of grace for agreements to be amended by the parties so as to benefit from the exemption. The Commission is required to publish a draft for comments, and to consult the Advisory Committee on Restrictive Practices and Monopolies.[28]

10.23 Block exemptions issued under the Regulation are required to specify restrictions or clauses which must not be contained in agreements if they are to benefit from the exemption and conditions which must be satisfied. It is in pursuance of this provision that Article 3 of Regulation 67/67, giving a block exemption for certain types of exclusive dealing agreements, provides that the exemption shall not apply:

"Where:

. . .

(b) The contracting parties make it difficult for intermediaries or consumers to obtain the goods to which the contract relates from other dealers within the Common Market, in particular where the contracting parties:

(i) exercise industrial property rights to prevent dealers or consumers from obtaining from other parts of the Common Market or from selling in the territory covered by the contract goods to which the contract relates which are properly marked or otherwise properly placed on the market."

Thus, even had Regulation 67/67 been in force at the time of the *Grundig and Consten* case,[29] Consten's appointment as exclusive distributor of Grundig products in France would not have fallen within the terms of the block exemption because of the attempt to give absolute territorial protection by allowing Consten to use the GINT mark registered in its own name to prevent imports.

C. Proposed Draft Block Exemption

10.24 The Commission is proposing to issue a block exemption under Article 1 (1) (b) of Regulation 19/65, for certain categories of patent licensing

---

[27] Subsequently enacted as Reg. 67/67 (J.O. 1967, 849); (O.J. 1967, 10).
[28] The Advisory Committee was set up pursuant to Reg. 17, Art. 10.
[29] Cases 56 & 58/64 *Etablissements Consten SA and Grundig-Verkaufs GmbH* v. *EEC Commission* [1966] E.C.R. 299; [1966] C.M.L.R. 418. See *supra*, Chap. 4, paras. 4.41–4.45.

agreements. The draft was published for comments, as required by Article 5 of Regulation 19 on March 3, 1979,[30] and it is understood that, following discussions with interested parties, some changes will be made. The fundamental approach of the draft Regulation seems unlikely to be changed substantially.

10.25   The main Articles of the Regulation are Article 1 which lists various clauses in patent licensing agreements which can benefit from the exemption, provided, of course, that there are no more than two parties to the agreement, Article 2 which lists various further clauses which may be included without the benefit of the block exemption being lost, and Article 3 which lists clauses which, if included, will mean that the block exemption does not apply.

10.26   The provisions of the Regulation which will also cover know-how and trade marks ancillary to the licensed patent will be considered in detail, in relation to individual clauses in Chapter 11.

---

[30] O.J. 1979, C58/11.

SPECIFIC CLAUSES IN LICENCES

I. INTRODUCTION

A. GENERAL

11.01 The previous chapter dealt with the attempts by the Commission to provide solutions of general application to the problem of reconciling licences of intellectual property with the Community's Competition Rules, in particular Article 85. This chapter will be concerned with the way in which Article 85 has been applied to specific individual clauses in licence agreements.

11.02 The general principles governing Article 85 have already been discussed in Chapter 4, and those general principles must always be borne in mind. Thus, in order for Article 85 (1) to apply the licence agreement must be between economically independent undertakings and not between members of the same group of companies.[1] Further, the effects of the licence agreement both on competition and on trade between Member States must be appreciable. If the combined turnover and market shares of the parties to the agreement fall below the limits set out in the Notice on Agreements of Minor Importance[2] the effects may not be sufficiently appreciable.[3] Finally, the effects of the agreement must be felt within the Common Market.[4]

11.03 Assuming therefore that Article 85 could apply to the agreement, it is then necessary to consider how Article 85 has been applied to specific individual clauses. Most of the decisions discussed in this chapter are decisions of the Commission, as very few cases involving licences of intellectual property have yet found their way to the European Court.

11.04 Unless overruled by the European Court, a decision of the Commission is, of course, binding on the parties to whom it is addressed.[5] As a general

---

[1] See Chap. 4, paras. 4.27–4.34. See also Cases 15 & 16/74, *e.g. Centrafarm BV and de Peijper* v. *Sterling Drug Inc.; Centrafarm BV and de Peijper* v. *Winthrop BV*; [1974] 2 C.M.L.R. 480.

[2] Commission Notice of December 19, 1977 O.J. 1977, C313/3.

[3] On the other hand, particularly in the case of a patent and know-how licence it may be unwise to rely on the Notice. Even if the parties' market share is very small, or even nil, at the beginning of the Agreement, it may increase considerably during the course of the Agreement if the patent proves in practice to be valuable.

[4] See *Re the Agreement of A. Raymond* [1972] J.O. L143/39; [1972] C.M.L.R. D.45 where a negative clearance was granted for an Agreement between a German company and a Japanese company, where the licensed territory was Japan and certain other countries in the Far East.

[5] See Art. 189 (4) EEC and Chap. 2, paras. 2.41–2.47.

statement of the legal position, it carries as much weight as a decision of the Court until there is a decision of the Court on the point. This was accepted, albeit somewhat hesitantly, by Graham J. in one of the *British Leyland* cases[6] where he said:

">... it seems to me that a decision by the EEC Court of Justice that there had been at the relevant time an abuse of dominant position by the plaintiffs contrary to the Rome Treaty would give the defendants a good defence to the present action for infringement of copyright. If such an abuse were proved, the plaintiffs ought not to be allowed by an English court in those circumstances to rely upon rights of copyright as against the defendants. I think also, though it is not expressly stated in the Act [i.e. the European Communities Act 1972][7] that in the circumstances envisaged, a decision of the Commission which is not appealed ought to be treated by the courts here as having the same effect as one of the Court of Justice itself."[8]

B. "Existence v. Exercise"

11.05 In applying Article 85 to licence agreements, the Commission has tried to use the same approach as that adopted by the Court of Justice in the cases involving Articles 30 to 36.[9] Indeed, the Commission seems to consider that it is obliged to do so. In a section in its Fourth Report on Competition Policy entitled "Patent Licensing Agreements," the Commission said:

"On a legal plane, the Commission faces the problems of definition exposed by the Court of Justice in its distinction between the existence of nationally protected industrial property rights, which is not to be affected by Community law, and the exercise of these rights, which can be subject to the Treaty Rules. Accordingly, any appraisal of particular patent licensing provisions requires prior differentiation between terms which are germane to the existence, and those which relate to the exercise, of patent rights, in order to establish upon which provisions the Commission may properly rule. While the differentiation remains to be more fully worked out by future decisions of the Court, it is clear that patent licensing agreements are not automatically within Article 85 (1) if the agreements simply confer rights to exploit patented inventions against payment of royalties, but that questions of applicability of Article 85 (1) arise if a grant is accompanied by terms which go beyond the need to ensure the

[6] *British Leyland Motor Corporation Ltd. and Others* v. *Wyatt Interpart Co. Ltd.* [1979] 3 C.M.L.R. 79.
[7] It is strongly arguable that this point is, in fact, expressly stated in the European Communities Act bearing in mind the very wide terms in which s. 2 (1) is framed.
[8] *British Leyland* v. *Wyatt, supra,* n. 6 at p. 83.
[9] See Chaps. 8 and 9.

existence of an industrial property right, or where the exercise of such right is found to be the object, means or consequence of a restrictive agreement."[10]

11.06   In practice, this distinction between "existence" and "exercise" is often less clear cut in the context of licensing agreements, and it is one which has not always been applied by the Commission in a particularly logical way. A logical analysis would impose a two-stage approach: First, it would be necessary to see whether a particular provision was "germane to the existence" of the right or whether it merely related "to the exercise." If it was found to be the former, then Article 85 would not apply. If it was found to be the latter, it would then be necessary to decide whether the effects were restrictive. In practice, the Commission has tended in its decisions to confuse these two aspects.

11.07   For example, in its *Kabelmetal* decision[11] certain provisions of the agreement, including the licensee's undertaking to keep secret the know-how made available to it, were found not to be caught by Article 85 (1) "because they do not have as their object or effect a *substantial restriction of competition*[12] within the Common Market."[13] In other words, the effects were not restrictive. In explaining further its views on the secrecy obliga-tion, however, the Commission stated that "the *very essence of technical know-how*[12] which is a collection of industrial processes unprotected by the law on industrial property is *secrecy.*"[14] In other words, secrecy is "germane to the existence" of know-how, and is not merely a non-restrictive exercise of the rights in the know-how. If this is so, there should have been no need to consider whether the effects of the secrecy obligation were restrictive, given that Article 85 (1) did not in any event apply.

C. LICENCE AGREEMENTS AND EXEMPTIONS

11.08   Even if a particular provision of a licence agreement is found to infringe Article 85 (1) the Commission may be prepared to grant an exemption under Article 85 (3).[15] Indeed, it is noteworthy that while some clauses are extremely unlikely to be capable of benefiting from an exemption, the Commission has been at pains to point out that there is no such thing as a *per se* infringement. In the Fifth Report on Competition Policy, for instance, the Commission said:

"One comment has been that the Commission regards some clauses in patent licences as *per se* infringements of Article 85 (1) of the EEC

---

[10] Fourth Report on Competition Policy, Pt. 20.
[11] *Re Kabelmetal's Agreement* [1975] O.J. L222/34; [1975] 2 C.M.L.R. D.40.
[12] Emphasis added.
[13] *Re Kabelmetal, supra,* n. 11 at D.46.
[14] *Ibid.* at D. 47.
[15] For the distinction between negative clearance and exemption see Chap. 4, paras. 4.97–4.119.

Treaty. This is not so. The facts of each case have to be examined before it can be decided whether Article 85 (1) has been infringed. The terms of the Article must be satisfied in each case. These in turn require the consideration of such features as the economic power of the parties, the nature of the market or business in which they are engaged, their share of the market, the number of competitors and the significance of the licensed invention or know-how."[16]

D. The Draft Block Exemption for Patent Licences

11.09 Patent licences may, of course, benefit from the block exemption[17] once that comes into force. The position under the draft will be considered repeatedly in this chapter in relation to individual clauses in patent licences.

E. Other Types of Intellectual Property

11.10 It will be apparent from the statements of the Commission quoted already in this chapter and it will become even more apparent in the sections that follow, that the Commission's thinking on the relationship between licences of intellectual property and Article 85 has been developed primarily in relation to patent and know-how licences. The same or similar reasoning has then been applied to some other types of intellectual property. In the case of many of the specific clauses discussed in this chapter there have not yet been any decisions involving rights other than patents. This is particularly true of copyright licences where to date the Commission has issued no more than a few press releases on cases settled by agreement without a formal decision.[18]

II. *EXCLUSIVITY*

(a) Summary of the present position

11.11   At the risk of over-simplification, the present position with regard to exclusivity is that, assuming the general criteria for the application of Article 85 (1) are met,[19] then the grant of exclusive manufacturing and selling rights will infringe Article 85 (1), although the Commission may be prepared to use its powers under Article 85 (3) to grant an exemption.[20]

---

[16] Fifth Report on Competition Policy, Pt. 10.

[17] See Chap. 10, paras. 10.24–10.26.

[18] *e.g. Re Ernest Benn Ltd.* Press Release dated October 23, 1979; Ninth Report on Competition Policy, Pts. 118–119; *Re English League Football/London Weekend Television*; Ninth Report on Competition Policy, Pts. 116–117.

[19] See, *e.g.* para. 11.02 above.

[20] *e.g. Davidson Rubber Co.* [1972] J.O. L143/31; [1972] C.M.L.R. D. 52; *Re Kabelmetal* [1975] 2 C.M.L.R. D. 40; *Re Davide Campari Milano SpA* [1978] O.J. L70/69; [1978] 2 C.M.L.R. 397.

(b) Basis of the Commission's reasoning: "existence v. exercise"

11.12   The reasoning behind this view of exclusivity has been repeated by the Commission using similar wording in numerous decisions.[21] For example, in the earliest of those decisions in 1971, concerning an exclusive patent licence it said:

> "A patent confers on its holder the exclusive right to manufacture the products which are the subject of the invention. The holder may cede, by licences, for a given territory, the use of the rights derived from its patent. However, if it undertakes to limit the exploitation of its exclusive right to a single undertaking in a territory and thus confers on that single undertaking the right to exploit the invention and prevent other undertakings from using it, it thus loses the power to contract with other applicants for a licence."[22]

11.13   Although that particular case was concerned with an *exclusive* licence, the same reasoning applies to a sole licence.

11.14   It might be thought that by granting a licence, albeit exclusively, the owner of a patent or other right is increasing competition in that without the licence, the licensee will be unable to make use of the patent at all. Even if the licensor himself undertakes not to use the patent it could be argued that competition overall will not be affected, as the licensee merely replaces the licensor as far as the exploitation of the right is concerned.

11.15   Whilst the Commission acknowledges that benefits may be obtained by the grant of a licence, the view has been expressed[23] that those benefits can be obtained without exclusivity. The requirement of exclusivity is only imposed because one or other of the parties to the agreement is in a strong enough economic position to do so. The relative strengths and weaknesses of a licensor and licensee are clearly independent of the rights which are being licensed and are therefore susceptible to control by means of competition law.

11.16   Thus, whilst the right to grant a licence may form part of the existence of a patent or other intellectual property right, the grant of an *exclusive* licence will relate to exercise, and, as such, may well be restrictive of competition.

11.17   Exclusivity involves a contractual restriction on the licensor and such a restriction it seems cannot be part of the existence of the patent or other

---

[21] *e.g. Re Burroughs/Delplanque* [1972] J.O. L13/50; [1972] C.M.L.R. D. 67 at D. 70; *Re Burroughs-Geha* [1972] J.O. L13/53; [1972] C.M.L.R. D. 72 at D. 74; *Re Davidson Rubber Co., supra*, n. 20 at D. 59; *Re Kabelmetal, supra*, n. 20; at D. 45; *Re Eisele-INRA Agreement* [1978] O.J. L286/23; [1978] 3 C.M.L.R. 434 at p. 450.

[22] *Re Burroughs-Delplanque, supra*, n. 21 at D. 70.

[23] By Dr. Hartmut Johannes, the Head of the Special Service for Industrial Property Rights in the Directorate General for Competition in his book, *Industrial Property and Copyright in European Community Law*.

right.[24] This was stated in particularly clear terms in the Commission's decision in *AOIP* v. *Beyrard*,[25] where it said:

> "Contractual obligations upon the licensor such as that which results from the granting of an exclusive licence are not matters relating to the existence of the patent for a contractual obligation which restricts the holder of a right in his exercise thereof cannot call into question the very existence of that right."[26]

(c) Development of the Commission's reasoning

11.18   The Commission's view of exclusivity has clearly changed since its original 1962 Notice on Patent Licence Agreements.[27] In that Notice, the Commission stated that "on the basis of the facts known at present" it did not consider that the following clauses were covered by Article 85 (1):

> "E. Undertakings on the part of the licensor;
>   (i) Not to authorise anyone else to exploit the invention;
>   (ii) Not to exploit the invention himself."

11.19   The explanation given at the end of the Notice for this view was as follows:

> "By the undertaking mentioned at I (E)—not to authorise the use of the invention by any other person—the licensor forfeits the right to make agreements with other applicants for a licence. Leaving out of account the controversial question whether such exclusive undertakings have the object or effect of restricting competition, they are not likely to affect trade between Member States as things stand in the Community at present. The undertaking not to exploit the patented invention oneself is closely akin to an assignment of the right and accordingly does not seem to be open to objection."

11.20   The change in the Commission's perception of exclusivity came in 1971, with the first Decisions on patent licences in the two *Burroughs* cases and the *Davidson Rubber* case.[28] In those cases, the Commission first established that, assuming the general criteria for the application of Article 85 (1) are satisfied[29] the grant of exclusive manufacturing or selling rights will infringe Article 85 (1). Presumably, the Commission considered that by 1971 trade between Member States had developed to such an

---

[24] See Recital 17 in the "Proposal for a Commission Regulation on the application of Article 85 (3) of the Treaty to certain categories of patent licensing agreements" March 3, 1979 [1979] O.J. C58/12.

[25] *AOIP* v. *Beyrard* [1976] O.J. L6/8; [1976] 1 C.M.L.R. D. 14.

[26] *Ibid.* at D. 22.

[27] See, *supra*, Chap. 10, paras. 10.9–10.11.

[28] *Re Burroughs-Delplanque* and *Burroughs-Geha* [1972] C.M.L.R. D. 67 and D. 72 and *Re Davidson Rubber* [1972] C.M.L.R. D. 52.

[29] In the *Burroughs* cases the Commission granted negative clearances because the restrictions on competition involved in the exclusive manufacturing rights were not, on the particular facts, "noticeable."

extent that it could now be affected by a patentee granting an exclusive licence and thus forfeiting the right to license anyone else.

11.21 Since 1971, the Commission's view has broadly remained the same, and in recent years has been extended from patents to trade marks[30] and plant breeders rights.[31] In assessing whether or not an exclusive licence infringes Article 85 (1), the Commission appears to consider it irrelevant whether the licensed territory comprises the whole of the Common Market, or only one Member State.[32] This is, however, consistent with its general approach to the need to show an affect on trade *between* Member States to satisfy the requirements of Article 85 (1).[33]

(d) Possibility of an exemption

(i) *General*

11.22 Having established as a general principle that, for the reasons already referred to, the grant of exclusive rights will generally infringe Article 85 (1), the Commission has nevertheless recognised that exclusivity can frequently be of great benefit. It has therefore been prepared, on a number of occasions, to use its powers to grant an exemption under Article 85 (3).[34] In using its powers, the Commission has invariably drawn a distinction between exclusive manufacturing rights and exclusive sales rights, and has been more ready to grant an exemption for the former than for the latter.

11.23 Each case ultimately depends on its own facts, but some useful guidance can be obtained from the Commission's decisions to date. Further, once the block exemption for exclusive patent licences[35] comes into force, the position should become clearer, at least as far as licences of patents with ancillary know-how and trade marks are concerned. Although other types of intellectual property will not be covered by the block exemption,[36] it seems likely that where the analogy can properly be drawn, the Commission may well adopt the same approach as that in the block exemption when granting individual exemptions. This would, at any rate, be consistent with its policy to date in granting exemptions on an individual basis, where it has applied reasoning which was originally developed in the context of patent licences to both trade mark licences and licences of plant breeder's rights.

---

[30] *Re the Agreements of Davide Campari-Milano SpA* [1978] 2 C.M.L.R. 397.
[31] *Re the Eisele-INRA Agreement* [1978] 3 C.M.L.R. 434.
[32] See Recital 9 draft block exemption; also *Europirair-Duro-Dyne Agreement* [1975] O.J. L29/11; [1975] 1 C.M.L.R. D. 62.
[33] See Chap. 4, paras. 4.59–4.64.
[34] For a general discussion of exemption see Chap. 4, paras. 4.114–4.119. For examples of cases where an exemption has been granted see, *supra*, n. 20.
[35] *Supra*, n. 24.
[36] Know-how and trade marks will also not be covered unless licensed as ancillary to patents.

(ii) *Exemption and the relationship between exclusive manufacturing and exclusive selling rights*

11.24   In its first decisions on licence agreements in the two *Burroughs* cases[37] the question of an exemption did not arise as the Commission found on the facts of those cases that there was not a sufficient restriction on competition for Article 85 (1) to apply. Part of its reason for reaching that conclusion was undoubtedly that the exclusivity only applied to the manufacturing rights, as each individual licensee and the licensor itself were free to sell anywhere in the Common Market.

11.25   In its second decision on an exclusive patent licence in the *Davidson Rubber* case,[38] on the other hand, the Commission found that Article 85 (1) was infringed by the grant of an exclusive manufacturing licence. The exclusive sales rights which Davidson's licensees had originally enjoyed had been mitigated, following representations from the Commission, so that the licensees were free to sell outside the territories for which they were primarily responsible.

11.26   The Commission in its decision considered in turn each of the requirements of Article 85 (3),[39] and found them to be met. As far as the exclusive manufacturing rights were concerned, the Commission concluded:

> "The exclusivity granted . . . for given territories and which was stated above to fall under Article 85 (1) of the Treaty may, as regards the exploitation of the Davidson patents, and the know-how attached thereto, be considered as indispensable to the attainment of the favourable objectives set out in the preceding paragraphs. In fact, given the situation of the market in those products in 1959, the Davidson Rubber Company would not have succeeded in having its new process used in Europe by third parties if it had not agreed to limit its licensees in that part of the world to a smaller number of undertakings by giving them an assurance that in the territories assigned to them it would not cause them to have competition from new licensees. Indeed, in the present case, without exclusivity the licensees would not have agreed to make the investments necessary to develop the process and adapt it to the requirements of the European market."[40]

---

[37] *Re Burroughs-Delplanque* and *Burroughs-Geha* [1972] C.M.L.R. D. 67 and D. 72.

[38] *Re Davidson Rubber* [1972] C.M.L.R. D. 52.

[39] Article 85 (3) requires that four criteria be met:
   1. that the agreement "contributes to improving the production or distribution of goods or to promoting technical or economic progress";
   2. it allows "consumers a fair share of the resulting benefits";
   3. it does not "impose on the undertakings concerned restrictions which are not indispensable to the attainment of these objectives;
   4. it does not afford "the possibility of eliminating competition in respect of a substantial part of the products in question."

[40] *Re Davidson Rubber, supra,* at D. 61.

11.27 Similar reasoning was applied in the *Kabelmetal* case[41] where again the Commission required that the licensee be free to sell outside its allotted territory before it was prepared to grant an exemption. As far as the exclusive manufacturing rights were concerned, the Commission expressed the view that:

"Kabelmetal's undertaking to grant Luchaire exclusive rights contributes to promoting economic progress, since it made possible the licensing agreement in question by guaranteeing Luchaire a sufficient return on its investments by virtue of the territorial advantages it derives from the exclusion of any other firm which might be interested in manufacturing on the basis of the licensor's techniques within the territory for which the licence is valid. This provision has therefore enabled another manufacturer within the EEC to use improved techniques for machining steel parts—techniques which, compared with the traditional deep drawing processes, make possible considerable savings in raw materials and the production of high quality finished products."[42]

11.28 It is noteworthy that whereas in the *Davidson Rubber* case the Commission had found that without the exclusivity the licensees would not have been prepared to make the investments in the first place, in *Kabelmetal* the exclusivity was justified merely on the basis that without it the licensee would not have been able to make a sufficient return on its investment.

11.29 In the *Bronbemaling* case,[43] on the other hand, the Commission issued a preliminary decision under Article 15 (6) of Regulation 17,[44] in which it provisionally refused to grant an exemption for an agreement between a Dutch licensor and its four Dutch licensees by its terms restricting the grant of further licences. It reasoned that:

"by allowing the number of firms authorised to exploit the patented process to be restricted they [i.e. the licensor] hinder wider use of the process and prevent know-how from being enriched by a broader range of experience. This process is already well known and widely used in Holland; confining its exploitation to a limited number of licensees has no beneficial economic effect such as might be expected of an exclusive licence having the prime purpose of facilitating penetration of a new market."[45]

11.30 In the *Beyrard* case,[46] too, the Commission refused to grant an exemption for an exclusive manufacturing and sales licence. Its refusal was,

---

[41] [1975] 2 C.M.L.R. D. 40.
[42] *Ibid*. at D. 47.
[43] *Zuid-Nederlandsche Bronbemaling en Grondboringen BV* v. *Heidemaastchappij Beheer NV* [1975] O.J. L249/27; [1975] 2 C.M.L.R. D. 67.
[44] For a general discussion of Art. 15 (6) see, *supra*, Chap. 6, paras. 6.28–6.32.
[45] *Bronbemaling, supra,* n. 43 at D. 72.
[46] [1976] 1 C.M.L.R. D. 14.

however, based primarily on other grounds and it hinted that had those other grounds not existed, it might have been prepared to exempt the exclusivity. In fact, it seems relatively unlikely that the Commission would have been prepared to exempt the exclusive provisions as the agreement in that case had already been in existence since 1951.

11.31   In these cases, all of which involved primarily patents, either the sales rights were non-exclusive, or an exemption was refused.

11.32   In the *Campari* case,[47] on the other hand, the Commission granted an exemption for exclusive trade mark licences which gave the licensees not only exclusive manufacturing rights but also, to a limited extent, exclusive sales rights. On this occasion, the Commission's intervention did not result in the sales rights being converted to non-exclusive rights, but led instead to a situation which was analogous to that in Regulation 67/67.[48] Ultimately, whilst each licensee undertook not to carry out an active sales policy and not to set up branches or advertise outside its territory, it was allowed to meet unsolicited orders.

11.33   In the *Maize Seed* case,[49] which involved a licence of plant breeder's rights, the Commission again hinted that it might have been prepared to grant an exemption for the exclusive propagation rights, but felt unable to grant exemption for the exclusive selling rights which were accompanied by a specific ban on exports. It said:

"In relation to the exclusive character of the licence:

(a) In principle, just as in the case of a patent, where exclusive propagation rights are granted by the holder of breeder's rights to a licensee within the Common Market ... the exclusivity is capable of being considered to have satisfied all the tests for exemption under Article 85 (3). There are even circumstances in which exclusive selling rights linked with prohibitions against exporting could also be exempted, for example, when the exclusivity is needed to protect small or medium sized under-takings in their attempts to penetrate a new market or promote a new product, provided that parallel imports are not restricted at the same time.

(b) In the present case, however, the Commission leaves open the assessment under Article 85 (3) of the exclusive propagation rights ..., since the tests for exemption of the exclusive selling rights and their accompanying export prohibitions are in any event not satisfied. This is for the following reasons:

— there is no question of a new market being penetrated or a new product being launched;

---

[47] [1978] 2 C.M.L.R. 397.
[48] Reg. 67/67 "On the application of Article 85 (3) of the Treaty to certain categories of exclusive dealing agreements" J.O. 1967 849; as amended by Reg. 2591/72.
[49] *Re Eisele-INRA Agreement* [1978] 3 C.M.L.R. 434.

— in any event when the INRA varieties 200 and 258 were launched or when they were introduced in Germany, Mr. K. Eisele enjoyed absolute territorial protection in respect of the distribution in Germany of the seeds for which he had exclusive rights. The absolute nature of this protection has had the sole and direct consequence of totally preventing imports from other channels of the original products."[50]

11.34   That decision is currently the subject of an appeal to the Court of Justice,[51] the first such appeal primarily concerned with a licence of intellectual property.

(e) The draft block exemption for patent licences

11.35   The Commission's reasoning on exclusive sales in the *Maize Seed* case undoubtedly reflected the provisions of the draft block exemption for patent licences, the preparation of which was by then well under way. The block exemption itself, however, specifically will not apply to plant breeder's rights.[52] The distinction between exclusive manufacturing rights and exclusive sales rights has been maintained in the draft block exemption. Although both exclusive manufacturing rights and exclusive sales rights will be covered by the exemption contained in Article 1 of the Regulation, exclusive sales rights will only be exempted subject to certain conditions.

11.36   As far as exclusive manufacturing rights are concerned, Article 1 (1) of the Regulation, which grants the basic exemption, provides that it will apply to patent licensing agreements between not more than two undertakings which include:

"1. the obligation on the part of the licensor not to manufacture or use the patented product or not to use the patented process within the Common Market or a defined area of the Common Market (licensed territory) or not to permit others to do so;

2. the obligation on the part of the licensee to refrain from manufacturing or using the patented product or from using the patented process outside the licensed territory."

11.37   The exemption for such clauses is granted without conditions. The reasoning set out in the recitals reflects, to a certain extent, the reasoning in the specific decisions of the Commission which have already been discussed. In particular, Recital 6 states that provisions of this sort:

"contribute in general to the production of goods and to promoting technical progress, since they usually increase the number of production facilities and the quantity of goods in question produced in the

---

[50] *Ibid.* at p. 455.
[51] Case 258/78.
[52] See Art. 5 of the draft block exemption.

Common Market and make it possible for undertakings other than the patentee to manufacture goods using the latest techniques and to develop these techniques further; the availability of such licences makes patentees more willing to grant them and makes it easier for other undertakings to decide to run the risks involved in investing capital in the manufacture, use or distribution of a new product or the use of a new process."

11.38　　Exclusive sales rights in a patent licensing agreement[53] will also be covered by the block exemption which treats such clauses as being akin to export bans. Thus Article 1 (1) of the draft extends the block exemption to:

"3.　the obligation on the part of the licensor to refrain from selling the patented product or product manufactured by a patented process within the licensed territory, or to impose a corresponding prohibition on other licensees;

4.　the obligation on the part of the licensee to refrain from selling the patented product or product manufactured by a patented process within the defined territory of the Common Market reserved by the licensor for himself or in the licensed territories of other licensees."

11.39　　Those paragraphs are, however, subject to the conditions set out in Article 1 (2) as follows:

"Exclusivity of sales and analogous prohibitions on the sale of patented products outside the licensed territory shall be exempted pursuant to paragraph 1 (3) and (4) only:

(a)　where the total annual turnover of the licensor or licensee whose market is to be protected by an export ban imposed on the other party or on another licensee does not exceed 100 million units of account[54]; paragraph 1 (3) and (4) shall remain applicable notwithstanding that this turnover is exceeded by up to 10% in two consecutive financial years; in calculating total turnover, sales of all goods and services recorded in the last financial year by the undertaking concerned and all undertakings having economic connections with it shall be taken into account; and

(b)　if the exclusivity of sale and export bans have been agreed at most for the duration of the most recent patent existing at the time when the agreement was entered into; this period may not be extended in respect of such obligations by licensing agreements in respect of patents for new applications or improvements[55]; and

---

[53] Exclusive sales rights unrelated to manufacturing rights will not be covered by this block exemption, as they are already dealt with in Reg. 67/67. See Recital 11 in the draft patent licence block exemption.

[54] As at December 1980, one unit of account = approx. £155. See generally in connection with units of account Chap. 6, n. 67.

[55] See, *infra*, paras. 11.75–11.77 and 11.82–11.84.

(c) if the patented product or product manufactured by the patented process may be sold throughout the Community by commercial undertakings which have no economic connections with the licensor or licensee; and

(d) if the licensee either manufactures the licensed products himself, or has them manufactured by an undertaking that has economic connections with him."

11.40   It should be noted that all four conditions must be satisfied.

11.41   The turnover limits, according to Recital 10 in the Regulation, have been deliberately fixed at quite a high figure. The reason for exempting exclusive sales licences are explained in Recital 10 as follows:

"The territorial protection that arises from exclusive sales rights and related export bans can only be allowed if it is requisite for ensuring the expansion of technical progress. The Commission accepts that this protection is necessary for the majority of undertakings as a determining factor to facilitate decisions on investments relating to the development and marketing of new technologies. For undertakings with very high turnovers this protection would not, on the other hand, seem appropriate having regard to their extensive financial resources. The turnover limit set in the Regulation will ensure that most independent undertakings in the Community that grant or take licences will be able to qualify for the exemption."

(f) Other types of intellectual property

11.42   The principles developed by the Commission on exclusivity would seem to be applicable to all types of intellectual property. Even in the case of copyright and neighbouring rights, the Commission has adopted the same approach.

11.43   Thus, under pressure from the Commission, the English Football League and London Weekend Television withdrew from arrangements made between them which would have involved the independent television companies having the exclusive right in England to record and transmit football league matches. In commenting on that case in the Ninth Report on Competition Policy the Commission said:

"The effect would have been to exclude the BBC from recording and transmitting such football matches in the United Kingdom. This would have had the further consequence of ruling out any possibility of obtaining recordings for transmission in other Member States, except from the one source of the independent programme companies."[56]

11.44   The only distinction likely to be made is that made by the European Court with regard to performing rights in its decision in the *Coditel* case.[57]

---

[56] Ninth Report on Competition Policy, Pt. 116.
[57] Case 62/79 *Coditel SA and Others* v. *Ciné Vog Films SA* judgment of March 18, 1980.

In that case, the Court was prepared to apply different treatment to an exclusive copyright licence which gave the licensee the right to show a particular film in Germany. The reasoning of the Court appears to have been based on the fact that in all other cases the use of intellectual property, be it a patent, trade mark, plant breeder's rights, know-how or copyright, results in the production of a tangible object. Even in the *London Weekend Television* case the Commission's comment suggests that a tangible object was involved, namely recordings for transmission in other Member States. In the case of performing rights, there is no tangible product as a result of using the right, but merely a performance which is intangible. The exclusive right to show a film is part of the existence of the right, therefore, and is no longer related to its exercise, as is the position in the case of other intellectual property rights.

III. EXPORT BANS

(a) Summary of the present position

11.45   As will be clear from the preceding section on exclusivity, exclusive sales licences have been treated by the Commission as akin to export bans. Because the right to sell is granted for a particular territory, the implication is that there is no right to sell outside that territory. Thus, there is an export ban. This was certainly the Commission's view in the *Raymond-Nagoya* case[58] where the Commission referred to "the prohibition on Nagoya exporting to countries situated outside the sales territory (and therefore including the Common Market) the attachment components which it manufactures through exploiting the Raymond technique, *a prohibition which follows from the limitation of its sales rights to that territory.*"[59,60]

11.46   This section, however, deals with clauses in licences which impose a direct ban on exports by the licensee. In general, a direct export ban will infringe Article 85 (1), although it may in certain circumstances qualify for an exemption under Article 85 (3).[61]

(b) Basis of the Commission's reasoning: "existence v. exercise"

11.47   In reaching this conclusion the Commission has applied very similar reasoning to that used in relation to exclusivity, reasoning which was expressed in particularly uncompromising terms in the *Beyrard* case[62] where the Commission said:

"The existence of the patent right is not at issue when the licensor

---

[58] [1972] C.M.L.R. D. 45.
[59] Emphasis added.
[60] *Re Raymond, supra,* n. 4 at D. 49.
[61] *e.g. AOIP* v. *Beyrard* [1976] 1 C.M.L.R. D 14; "*The Old Man and the Sea*" *Press Release* January 31, 1977; [1977] 1 C.M.L.R. D. 121.
[62] *Supra,* n. 23.

prohibits the licensee from exporting to countries in which the licensor has granted a licence or assigned his patent. The protection of one licensee or assignee against the competition of another licensee or assignee constitutes a restriction of competition within the meaning of Article 85 (1), when such protection results from a contractual prohibition on exports or imports."[63]

11.48   That case was concerned with a patent, but the Commission has used similar reasoning in the case of a licence for plant breeder's rights[64] where it concluded that a system of licences, each containing absolute prohibitions on exports, amounted to market sharing:

"The fact that third parties may not import the same seed from other Community countries into Germany, or export from Germany to other Community countries, makes for market sharing and deprives German farmers of any real room for negotiation since seed is supplied by one supplier and one supplier only."[65]

11.49   In other words, a ban on exports is viewed by the Commission as a contractual provision imposed by a licensor when exercising the rights in intellectual property. As such, it will usually be a restrictive exercise of those rights, and can never be part of their existence.

(c) Development of the Commission's reasoning

(i) *General*

11.50   The Commission's thinking generally on export bans has been developed in relation to other types of agreements than licensing agreements, particularly distribution agreements.[66] As far as licences of intellectual property are concerned it has frequently been treated as a related aspect of exclusivity, because in most of the cases in which export bans have been considered, exclusivity has also been involved.[67]

11.51   Although the Commission now seems to have adopted a very firm view on export bans, at the time of the Fourth Report on Competition, it was less clear-cut in its condemnation. It recognised then, rather more than in its later decisions, the inherent problem. In the Report it said:

"The question whether a licensor should be able by contract to prohibit licensees from making direct imports into territories he wishes to reserve for himself can be approached from different premises which lead to

---

[63] *AOIP* v. *Beyrard, supra*, n. 25 at D. 22.

[64] *Re Eisele-INRA* [1978] 3 C.M.L.R. 434.

[65] *Ibid.* at p. 450.

[66] See, *e.g. Grundig-Consten* [1964] J.O. 25/45; [1964] C.M.L.R. 489; *Re Pioneer Hi-Fi Equipment* [1980] 1 C.M.L.R. 457.

[67] The 1962 Notice on Patent Licence Agreements did not refer specifically to export bans although in para. 1.A.(4) (*b*) it indicated that territorially limited licences would fall under the Notice. To the extent that such a licence operates as an export ban it is clear the Commission no longer considers it to be "covered by the patent."

conflicting conclusions. Views in favour of permitting export restrictions for the protection of a licensor's territory rest mainly on grounds of preserving the attribute of patent rights as an incentive to inventiveness and to licensing. If a patentee's rewards were reduced to unacceptable levels by exposing him to competition from his foreign licensees, he could be discouraged from granting licences altogether. In particular, small and medium-sized licensors should be protected against being 'swamped' by competition from their more economically powerful licensees. Moreover, any considerable discouragements to the granting of licences could induce large enterprises to retain their innovations and enter foreign markets themselves, rather than by licensing to disseminate innovations and to help the promotion of alternative production and marketing units. However, seen against the background that a licensor is in a position to choose whether to grant licences or not, that licences are subject to royalties in his favour and that a licensor normally enjoys advantages in time and in cost when competing with his licensees, it is open to doubt that an export restriction should in these circumstances be regarded as essential for the protection of a licensor's property rights. Special concessions to licensors in particular circumstances could in any appropriate cases rank for consideration for exemption under Article 85 (3). In principle, however, a reservation to a licensor of a defined area within the Community, possibly an area where price levels are highest, appears to create problems of conflict with the objectives of market unity.

    Views in support of permitting contractual restrictions to protect a licensee from direct imports into his territory from other licensees are generally based on the proposition that a licensee needs sole marketing rights in his territory in order to safeguard his investment in the initial promotion of production and sale. It is argued that, in the absence of such protection, there would be a disinclination to accept licences and that patentees would therefore be in danger of losing their rewards. Any such particular situations can be considered for exemption under Article 85 (3). However, in cases of some important inventions, it has been the practice for licensors to grant several concurrent non-exclusive licences without restrictions as to territory. Moreover, it is improbable that export prohibitions to protect licensees *inter se* can affect the existence of patent rights, since these are vested in patentees and are not the property rights of licensees."[68]

11.52   As has already been mentioned, the Commission has now taken the view that a contractual restriction on exports or imports will generally be a breach of Article 85 (1), although one which may qualify for exemption in appropriate circumstances.

(ii) *Export bans operating outside the Community*

11.53   This reasoning is obviously primarily concerned with export bans operat-

---

[68] Fourth Report on Competition Policy, Pts. 23–26.

ing between Member States of the Community. Although it is less likely that export bans affecting other parts of the world will infringe Article 85 (1), it is by no means inconceivable. In the *Campari* case,[69] for example, the Commission found that "in this case" the following was not an infringement of Article 85 (1):

"the obligation upon each licensee to refrain from exporting Bitter Campari directly or indirectly outside the Common Market. It is true that this obligation not only eliminates the freedom of the licensees and their trade customers to do business in the relevant product outside the EEC, but also prevents any distributor in a non-member country from buying the product from the licensees or from a previous purchaser for resale in the Common Market. However, any purchaser within the Community may obtain supplies of the products covered by the agreements not only directly from the licensee on his own territory but also, directly or indirectly, from other licensees or from Campari-Milano itself. Given these possibilities, reimportation into the Common Market of Bitter previously exported outside the Community by licensees or their trade customers would seem unlikely, in view of supplementary economic factors such as the accumulation of trade margins and of excise duties and taxes on alcohol levied by importing countries as well as the duties charged on crossing the European Economic Community borders. This assessment also applies to states with which the EEC has entered into free trade agreements, particularly as trade between the Community and these States in alcoholic beverages such as Bitter Campari is still subject to customs duties."[70]

11.54   This therefore suggests that where re-importation into the Common Market is a practical possibility or in the case of products which are not subject to customs duties when re-imported from EFTA countries, a ban on exports outside the Community may well infringe Article 85 (1).[71]

(d) Possibility of an exemption

11.55   Unlike other types of agreement where the Commission generally is unsympathetic to export bans, the Commission has indicated in some of its decisions the grounds on which it might be prepared to grant an exemption in a licensing context. Thus, in the *AOIP/Beyrard* case,[72] the Commission stated that:

"An exemption can also be granted in an appropriate case for a prohibition on exports applicable to the first sale only and of limited duration, the object of which is the mutual protection of the parties or of other licensees."[73]

---

[69] [1978] 2 C.M.L.R. 397.   [70] *Ibid.* at p. 408.
[71] See *Kabelmetal* [1975] 2 C.M.L.R. D. 40 where an exemption was granted despite the prohibition in the Agreement on exports by the Licensor to Spain and Portugal, and by the licensee to other non-EEC countries; see also *Junghans* [1977] O.J. L30/10; [1977] 1 C.M.L.R. D. 82.
[72] [1976] 1 C.M.L.R. D. 14.
[73] *Ibid.* at D.26.

11.56   Similarly in the *Maize Seed case*,[74] the Commission said:
"There are even circumstances in which exclusive selling rights linked with prohibitions against exporting could also be exempted, for example, when the exclusivity is needed to protect small or medium sized undertakings in their attempts to penetrate a new market or promote a new product, provided that parallel imports are not restricted at the same time."[75]

11.57   In both those cases an exemption was not granted on the particular facts.

(e) The draft block exemption for patent licence

11.58   As has already been mentioned above in relation to exclusive sales licences, a ban on exports in a patent licence will be capable of benefiting from the block exemption when that comes into force, provided certain conditions are met. Thus, in Article 1 (1) (4) of the draft, the following will benefit from the exemption:
"the obligation on the part of the licensee to refrain from selling the patented product or products manufactured by a patented process within the defined territory of the Common Market reserved by the licensor for himself or in the licensed territories of other licensees."

11.59   That clause is subject to the same conditions as those imposed on exclusive sales licences,[76] and the reasoning in Recital 10 specifically refers to "exclusive sales rights and related export bans."

(f) Other types of intellectual property

11.60   There seems no reason with regard to export bans to differentiate between different types of intellectual property. The Commission has issued decisions on export bans in licences of patents,[77] plant breeder's rights[78] and trade marks.[79] It has also applied the same reasoning to copyright licences in *Re Ernest Benn Limited*[80] which was settled without a formal decision. In its Press Release, the Commission stated:
"Export restrictions on books within the Common Market are contrary to the EEC competition rules in the same way as export restrictions on other goods. It is also the Commission's opinion that any partitioning of the Common Market by means of copyright licences must be justified under Article 85 (3) of the EEC Treaty."[81]

11.61   Again, the only distinction which seems likely to be made is that between licences of intellectual property which involve the creation of a tangible object, and licences of performing rights, where different criteria may apply.

---

[74] *Re Eisele-INRA* [1978] 3 C.M.L.R. 434.
[75] *Ibid.* at p. 455.
[76] *Supra*, para. 11.39.   [77] *AOIP* v. *Beyrard* [1976] 1 C.M.L.R. D. 14.
[78] *Eisele-INRA*, *supra*, n. 21.   [79] *Campari* [1978] 2 C.M.L.R. 397.
[80] Press Release issued on October 23, 1979; [1979] 3 C.M.L.R. 636.
[81] See also *"The Old Man and the Sea"* [1977] 1 C.M.L.R. D. 121.

IV. *FIELD OF USE RESTRICTIONS*

(a) Summary of the present position

11.62   Generally, field of use restrictions will not infringe Article 85 (1). This is, however, only so for genuine field of use restrictions where different technical fields and materially different products are involved.[82]

(b) Basis of the Commission's reasoning: "existence v. exercise"

11.63   Field of use restrictions are clearly of most relevance in the case of patents and know-how and in this area the Commission's approach has been reasonably consistent. Thus, where a patent or know-how can be used in two entirely separate technical applications, to grant a licence restricted to only one of those applications will be treated as part of the existence of the right and not as a restrictive exercise of the right.

(c) Development of the Commission's reasoning

11.64   Field of use restrictions were referred in the 1962 Notice on Patent Licence Agreements which stated in paragraph I.A (2) that Article 85 (1) would not apply to obligations imposed on the licensee which involved:
"the limitation:
(a) of the manufacture of the patented product;
(b) of the use of the patented process, to certain technical applications"
Such a clause was stated later in the Notice not to fall within Article 85 (1) because it is "covered by the patent."

11.65   In its Fourth Report on Competition Policy dealing with the year 1974, the Commission specifically dealt with field of use restrictions and said:
"When patented inventions are capable of use in different applications, a licensor may, in the Commission's view, normally limit a licence to a distinct field of use. In these circumstances, he may give several licences to different licensees for respectively different applications. It is, however, possible that Article 85 (1) could bear on such cases in which a segregation of different fields of use is shown to be the result or means of implementing an agreement to eliminate competition between licensees or between the parties."[83]

11.66   Although this suggests a subjective approach, in that it indicates that the Commission looks at the motive for imposing the field of use restriction, in practice it has not been applied in that way. There have been no published decisions yet dealing specifically with field of use restrictions, but in one case settled by agreement, the Commission drew attention to the type of restriction which is not acceptable. That case was reported in the Ninth

---

[82] Fourth Report on Competition Policy, Pt. 28; also draft block exemption Art. 2 (1) (1).
[83] Fourth Report on Competition Policy, Pt. 28.

Report on Competition Policy dealing with the year 1979 under the heading "French State/Suralmo." In that case the patents related to improved systems for diesel engines and engine assemblies incorporating the improvements. The engine systems and the engine assemblies could be used for civilian or military purposes. The French Governmental agency which owned the patents had granted a licence subject to a restriction that any sub-licences for military use were to require its prior written permission. In commenting on this in the Ninth Report the Commission said:

"The Commission informed the parties to the agreement that, in its opinion, the different terms for the exercise of Suralmo's right to grant sub-licences, depending on whether these related to applications for military or civilian use, constituted a field of use restriction and could therefore fall within the prohibition in Article 85 (1) of the EEC Treaty."[84]

It seems, in fact, open to doubt whether such a restriction is truly a field of use restriction. The restriction did not relate to a particular technical field covered by the patent, but to a particular use to which the same product could be put.

(d) The draft block exemption for patent licences

11.67   In the draft block exemption for patent licences, field of use restrictions appear in Article 2 which lists the obligations which may be imposed without affecting the validity of the block exemption granted by Article 1. Among those obligations is:

"1.   The obligation to restrict the manufacture of the patented product or the use of the patented process to one or more different technical fields of application of the invention within the patent claims. For the purposes of this sub-paragraph there are different technical fields of application where the relevant products in each of the fields from which the licensee is excluded differ in a material respect from the products for which the licence is granted."

(e) Other types of intellectual property

11.68   To the extent to which the concept of a field of use restriction is relevant to intellectual property other than patents and know-how, there seems no reason to expect that the Commission will apply different reasoning. For instance, where a trade mark is registered for a number of different products, and a licence is granted in respect of some only of the goods for which registration has been obtained, the grant of such a limited licence would probably be regarded as germane to the existence of the trade mark. Similarly, it would form part of the existence of a copyright to limit the licensee to a particular form of exploitation.

---

[84] Ninth Report on Competition Policy, Pt. 114.

V. *LIMITATIONS OF PERIOD OF USE*

(a) Summary of the present position

11.69   In general, a limitation on use which restricts the licensee to a period shorter than the life of the relevant intellectual property right will not infringe Article 85 (1), whereas a provision which attempts to restrict a licensee once the intellectual property right has ceased to exist will infringe Article 85 (1).[85] In the latter case, such a restriction will not be capable of benefiting from an exemption under Article 85 (3).

11.70   It is convenient to consider these two provisions separately and it should be noted that particular problems arise in the context of combined licences and improvement patents.

(b) Shorter period than the life of the right

(i) *Basis of the Commission's reasoning: "existence v. exercise"*

11.71   As far as a shorter period than the life of the right is concerned, this has never presented any difficulty. It has always been clear that such a limitation is part of the existence of the right and not part of its exercise.

(ii) *Development of the Commission's reasoning*

11.72   Thus, in the 1962 Patent Notice, the Commission listed among the obligations imposed on a licensee which were not caught by Article 85 (1):
"the limitation of exploitation:
(a) in time (a licence of shorter duration than the patent)."[86]
That limitation was described later in the Notice as being "covered by the patent."

11.73   Again, in its Fourth Report on Competition Policy, the Commission said:
"In the view of the Commission, Article 85 (1) does not in principle touch upon the contractually fixed duration of a patent licence agreement, if this is for the life of a single licensed patent or a shorter term."[87]
No specific cases have, however, been concerned with such a situation.

(iii) *The draft block exemption for patent licences*

11.74   Finally, in the draft block exemption for patent licences the Commission lists in Article 2 obligations which will not prevent the application of the block exemption granted by Article 1, including:
"2. the obligation not to exploit the patent after expiry of the agreement, where the patent is still in force."

---

[85] See, *e.g. AOIP* v. *Beyrard* [1976] 1 C.M.L.R. D. 14.
[86] para. I.A. (4) (*a*).
[87] Fourth Report on Competition Policy, Pt. 29.

(c) Longer period than the life of the right

(i) *Basis and development of the Commission's reasoning: "existence* v. *exercise"*

11.75   By contrast, a licence for a longer period than the life of the right concerned must amount to a restrictive exercise of the right. It certainly cannot relate to the existence of the right, when, by definition, the right has come to an end.[88]

11.76   Thus, Article 3 of the block exemption for patent licences, which lists the provisions which will prevent the application of the block exemption includes:

> "4.   the obligation on the part of the licensee to pay royalties,
>
>   . . .
>
>   (b)   despite the fact that the licensed patent has ceased to be in force;
>   (c)   after expiry of the last licensed patent;
>   (d)   after manufacturing processes or other know-how communicated under the licence have entered into the public domain, unless entry into the public domain is attributable to some default on the part of the licensee, or of an undertaking that has economic connections with him."

11.77   While the general principles are clearcut and uncontroversial, difficulties may arise where one licence includes several rights, some of which may not have expired, or, in the case of a patent licence, where future improvement patents are also licensed.

(d) Combined licences

11.78   The situation where a licence includes several different types of intellectual property has not been dealt with in any individual decisions of the Commission, but it will be covered by the draft block exemption for patent licences.

11.79   The solution adopted in the block exemption is that a reduced rate of royalty should be payable. This is proposed both for ancillary know-how and for ancillary trade marks which are licensed with patents. Thus, Article 3 (4), which provides that the block exemption does not apply if the licensee is required to pay royalties after the patent has ceased to exist, is expressed to be:

> "without prejudice to any right of the licensor to receive appropriately reduced royalties where the licensing agreement continues in respect of manufacturing processes or other know-how that have not entered into the public domain."[88a]

---

[88] *AOIP* v. *Beyrard* [1976] 1 C.M.L.R. D. 14; *Peugeot-Zimmern* December 7, 1976; [1977] 1 C.M.L.R. D. 22.   [88a] See *Cartoux* v. *Terrapin* [1981] 1 C.M.L.R. 182.

11.80   Similarly, in the case of an ancillary trade mark, Article 3 (5) of the draft block exemption provides that the benefit of the exemption will be lost if the licence agreement includes:

> "the obligation on the part of the licensee to continue after the patent has expired or ceased to be in force to pay the *full*[89] royalties stipulated by the licence for the use of a patent and a trade mark."

11.81   No guidance is given in the block exemption as to what an "appropriately reduced royalty" would be, and this must, in practice, depend on the economic value of the ancillary know-how and/or trade mark, as compared with the basic patent.

(e) Improvement patents

11.82   The other situation referred to above, where a licence includes future improvement patents was dealt with in the Commission's decision in *AOIP/Beyrard*.[90] In that case, the Commission condemned an agreement which was to remain in force "for the life of the most recent original or improvement patent, whether or not already held."[91] It reasoned:

> "Such a clause enables the licensor to extend unilaterally and indefinitely the duration of the licensing agreement; it has restrictive effects at least when, as in the present case, it is combined with other restrictions on competition (exclusivity, export prohibition, no challenge clause, non-competition clause, payment of royalties even where a patent is not exploited) that is to say, when it is provided against a licensee, along with other restrictive provisions, that a licensing agreement shall have a duration which is longer than the life of the last patent to have been granted at the date when the agreement was made. The parties are free to agree later, whether in a new contract or by means of a supplementary or modifying agreement, to extend the term of the original agreement ... But such an extension may not be effected by the unilateral act of one of the parties."[92]

11.83   In the Fourth Report on Competition Policy, the Commission indicated that it might be concerned, not only where the licence included future improvement patents, but also where:

> "an agreement which covers more than one patent can be fixed beyond the life of the *first*[93] to expire of licensed patents.... This is likely to involve consideration of the nature of the conditions of the agreement and the economic and technical importance of the different licensed patents concerned."[94]

11.84   This approach has not been followed in the draft block exemption, which provides a more practical solution. Article 3 of the draft which, as already

---

[89] Emphasis added.   [90] *Supra*, n. 25.   [91] *Ibid.* at D.23.
[92] See also *Peugeot-Zimmern, supra*, n. 88.
[93] Emphasis added.
[94] Fourth Report on Competition Policy, Pt. 29.

mentioned, sets out the clauses which, if included in a patent licence, will prevent it benefiting from the block exemption provides in para (2):

"without prejudice to the second sentence of sub-paragraph 10[95] of this Article, an agreement that the duration of the agreement should extend beyond the expiry of the most recent patent existing at the time when the agreement is entered into, *unless such party has at least the yearly right after such expiry to terminate the agreement.*"[95a]

(f) Other types of intellectual property

11.85   To the extent to which this problem can arise in relation to intellectual property other than patents, the same reasoning should apply.

VI. *LIMITATIONS AS TO QUANTITY*

(a) Summary of the present position

11.86   Any specific restriction on the quantity of products to be produced by the licensee, whether a minimum number or a maximum number, will usually fall under Article 85 (1). The difference is that a requirement for a specific minimum quantity may well be capable of benefiting from an exemption under Article 85 (3),[96] whereas the imposition of a specific maximum quantity normally will not.[97]

(b) Basis of the Commission's reasoning: "existence v. exercise"

11.87   A specific limitation on the licensee's production will always be a restriction imposed by the licence agreement, and it can presumably therefore never form part of the existence of intellectual property. In many cases, it will be a restrictive exercise of the right, and thus will infringe Article 85 (1).

(c) Development of the Commission's reasoning

11.88   This analysis of quantity restrictions differs from the Commission's original approach in the 1962 Patent Notice. In that Notice, it indicated in paragraph I.A. (3) that the following would not be covered by the prohibition laid down in Article 85 (1):

"the limitation of the quantity of products to be manufactured or of the number of acts constituting exploitation."

---

[95] Sub-para. 10 of Art. provides:
"a clause prohibiting the licensee from using after the expiry of the agreement secret manufacturing processes or other secret know-how communicated by the licensor; this is without prejudice to any right of the licensor to require payment for the use of such processes or know-how for an appropriate period, even after the expiry of the agreement, but subject to para. 4 (*d*) of this Article."
[95a] Emphasis added.
[96] See *Burroughs* cases [1972] C.M.L.R. D. 67 and D. 72.
[97] Fourth Report on Competition Policy, Pt. 31.

The Commission took the view that such a provision was "covered by the patent," although it must be assumed that even at that time the Commission only had in mind minimum quantities and not maximum quantities.

11.89   In the Fourth Report on Competition Policy, the Commission dealt specifically with maximum quantities and found that:

"In the Commission's view, Article 85 (1) applies to contractual obligations imposed on a licensee which restrict his production to specified quantities, since the normal result of such restrictions would be to prevent a licensee from increasing his output and to make him less effective as a competitor. It is also possible for such restrictions, if imposed on a number of licensees, to have similar effect as export bans."[98]

11.90   Even though the maximum quantity may be expressed in terms of market share rather than specific numbers, the same principle will apply. In the *Maize Seed* case,[99] for example, one of the obligations specifically condemned by the Commission was:

"The obligation imposed on the licensee ... to import at least two thirds of the German market's requirements from France, and *not to produce,* himself or by others, *more than one third.*"[1, 2]

(d) The draft block exemption for patent licences

11.91   In the draft block exemption for patent licences, a clear distinction is made between minimum quantities and maximum quantities. Minimum quantities are covered by Article 1 (1), which grants an exemption for:

"6. the obligation on the part of the licensee to pay a minimum royalty or to produce a minimum quantity of the patented products or products manufactured by a patented process or to carry out a minimum number of operations employing the patented invention."

11.92   On the other hand, Article 3 (6) of the block exemption provides that the following will prevent the application of the block exemption:

"restrictions on the maximum number of products to be manufactured or marketed by the licensee or on the maximum number of operations employing the patent."

(e) Other types of intellectual property

11.93   There is no reason to suppose the same reasoning would not be applied to other types of intellectual property as well as patents.

---

[98] Fourth Report on Competition Policy, Pt. 31.
[99] *Eisele-INRA* [1978] 3 C.M.L.R. 434.
[1] Emphasis added.
[2] *Eisele-INRA, supra,* n. 21 at p. 451.

VII. *ROYALTIES*

(a) Summary of the present position

11.94   A provision for royalties to be paid by a licensee will not, in and of itself, infringe Article 85 (1). This was stated by the Commission in the Fourth Report on Competition Policy where it said:

> "It is clear that patent licensing agreements are not automatically within Article 85 (1) if the agreement simply confers rights to exploit patented inventions against payment of royalties."[3]

11.95   Problems of compatability with Article 85 (1) may, however, arise where a minimum royalty is payable, or where a royalty is payable after the intellectual property right has come to an end. A minimum royalty is obviously linked to the obligation to produce minimum quantities and the same reasoning will apply as that set out in section VI above.[4] Similarly, payment of a royalty after the right has ceased to exist is linked to the question of the permitted length of a licence agreement and the same reasoning will apply as that set out in section V above.[5] It is arguable that an unreasonably high royalty rate might amount to an infringement of Article 85 (1), although it seems very unlikely that the Commission would consider intervening, unless the licensor was in a dominant position under Article 86, when action might be taken under that Article.

(b) The draft block exemption for patent licences

11.96   As far as patents are concerned, the payment of a minimum royalty will be covered by the block exemption. Article 1 (6) will provide an exemption for:

> "the obligation on the part of the licensee to pay a minimum royalty...."

11.97   The payment of royalties after the licensed patent is no longer in force is dealt with in Article 3. That Article provides that the benefit of the block exemption will be lost if the following is included:

> "4. the obligation on the part of the licensee to pay royalties:
>   (a) on products covered neither wholly nor partly by the patent, or manufactured neither wholly nor partly by the patented process or by means of manufacturing processes or other know-how communicated under the licence;
>   (b) despite the fact that the licensed patent has ceased to be in force;
>   (c) after expiry of the last licensed patent;

---

[3] Fourth Report on Competition Policy, Pt. 20.
[4] *Supra*, paras. 11.86–11.93.
[5] *Supra*, paras. 11.75–11.85; *AOIP* v. *Beyrard* [1976] 1 C.M.L.R. D. 14; *Peugeot-Zimmern* [1977] 1 C.M.L.R. D. 22.

(d) after manufacturing processes or other know-how communicated under the licence have entered into the public
domain, unless entry into the public domain is attributable
to some default on the part of the licensee, or of an undertaking that has economic connections with him."

11.98   As already mentioned,[6] a reduced royalty may be charged where ancillary know-how or a trade mark continues to be licensed, after the relevant
patents have expired or otherwise ceased to be in force.

(c) Other types of intellectual property

11.99   Although the statement on royalties have all been in the context of
patent licences, there seems no reason to suppose that the same principles
would not, where relevant, be applied to other types of intellectual
property.

VIII. *QUALITY CONTROLS AND TYING OBLIGATIONS*

(a) Summary of the present position

11.100   In general, obligations imposed on a licensee designed to control the
quality of the products produced will not infringe Article 85 (1) and,
equally, tying obligations allied to quality controls will not infringe Article
85 (1). Tying obligations will amount to an infringement if unrelated to
quality control, however, and such an infringement will not be capable of
benefiting from an exemption under Article 85 (3).[7]

(b) Basis of the Commission's reasoning: "existence v. exercise"

11.101   Genuine quality controls, whether accompanied by tying obligations or
not, will always form part of the existence of the right. Without such
controls, the right itself could be in jeopardy. Tying obligations unrelated to
quality, on the other hand, can never form part of the existence of the right
and will always amount to a restrictive exercise.

(c) Development of the Commission's reasoning

11.102   This approach to quality controls has been followed consistently from
the time of the 1962 Patent Notice onwards. Thus, in Paragraph I.C. of the
Notice, the following were stated not to infringe Article 85 (1):

"Quality standards or obligations to procure supplies of certain products imposed on the licensee—in so far as they are indispensable for
the technically perfect exploitation of the patent."

11.103   This approach was followed in the Commission's first decision on patent
licences where the Commission stated that the following did not constitute
restrictions on competition:

---

[6] See, *supra*, paras. 11.78–11.81.
[7] See, *e.g. H. Vaessen BV* v. *Moris* [1979] O.J. L19/32; [1979] 1 C.M.L.R. 511.

"the obligations on Delplanque to manufacture the product in sufficient quantities and to comply with the technical instructions of Burroughs, because they are obligations which have no other purpose than to permit the sufficient and technically adequate exploitation of the rights conferred by the patents on their holder."[8]

11.104   The same principle was adopted and expanded in relation to trade marks in the *Campari*[9] case where the Commission held that the following were not covered by Article 85 (1):

"restrictions of the licence to those plants which are capable of guaranteeing the quality of the product. The effect of this restriction on the licensees' freedom of choice does not go beyond a legitimate concern for quality control; further, this obligation upon the licensees does not constitute an absolute limitation of production to any particular place, since it only gives Campari-Milano the right to oppose a change in the place of manufacture in cases where the new establishment proposed might adversely affect the quality of the products; this type of agreement as to quality control is very important for the licensor, since the maintenance of quality is referable to the existence of a trade mark right."[10]

11.105   In the *Campari* decision, too, the Commission considered tying obligations allied to quality control and also found such obligations to be unobjectionable where:

"the licensees are obliged to follow the licensor's instructions relating to the manufacture of the product and the quality of the ingredients, and to buy certain secret raw materials from the licensor itself. Here again, control over the quality of the products manufactured under licence and over their similarity to the original Italian product is in the present case very important for the licensor, in the sense that it is again bound up with its interest in the maintenance of quality, which is referable to the existence of the trade mark right. According to information provided by the parties, the standards enforced do not oblige the licensees to obtain supplies of albumin or bitter orange essence from any particular source, but only to choose between different products on the basis of objective quality considerations. This does not, however, apply to the colouring matter and the herbal mixtures, where the licensor's legitimate concern to ensure that the product manufactured under licence has the same quality as the original product can be protected only if the licensees obtain all their supplies from it."[11]

---

[8] *Burroughs/Delplanque* [1972] C.M.L.R. at D.70.   [9] [1978] 2 C.M.L.R. 397.
[10] *Ibid.* at p. 409.
[11] *Ibid.* at p. 409. Although tying obligations are not referred to specifically in Art. 2 of the draft which sets out the obligations which will prevent the application of the block exemption, the implication must be that a tying obligation which is *not* indispensable will infringe and will not be capable of benefiting from the exemption.

11.106   In the *Vaessen-Moris* case[12] on the other hand, the Commission made clear that a tying clause unrelated to quality infringed Article 85 (1) and was incapable of benefiting from an exemption:

> "Clause 2 of the agreement, which requires Imperial to obtain supplies of casings exclusively from ALMO when it intends to use the patented process and device licensed to it by Moris, has the object and effect of restricting competition since it deprives the sub-licensee of its business freedom to obtain supplies from other undertakings, perhaps on more favourable terms as in the case of its purchases from Vaessen.
>
> This clause is likewise not a requirement imposed by the industrial property right, for its deletion would in no way jeopardise the patent holder's exclusive right to work his invention himself or through others, since the products supplied by ALMO to Imperial are not covered by the patent; the clause thus constitutes an unlawful extension by contractual means of the monopoly given by the patent."[13]

(d) Draft block exemption for patent licences

11.107   The same approach is adopted in the draft block exemption for patent licences. Thus, simple quality controls will fall under Article 2 which permits the inclusion in the licence agreement of:

> "7. the obligation to respect the licensor's specifications concerning the minimum quality of the patented product or of the product manufactured using a patented process and to allow the licensor to carry out appropriate checks."

11.108   Tying obligations related to quality controls will be covered by the basic exemption in Article 1 (1) which applies to:

> "5. the obligation on the part of the licensee to procure supplies of certain products or services from the licensor or from an undertaking designated by the licensor, so far and so long as this obligation is indispensable in the interests of a technically unobjectionable exploitation of the invention."

(e) Other types of intellectual property

11.109   These principles in relation to quality controls and tying obligations have been applied to patents[14] and trade marks,[15] and there is no reason to suppose that they would not apply to other types of intellectual property to the extent to which they are relevant.

---

[12] *Re H. Vaessen BV* v. *Moris* [1979] 1 C.M.L.R. 511.
[13] *Ibid.* at p. 516.
[14] *e.g. Vaessen-Moris, supra,* n. 107.
[15] *e.g. Campari, supra,* n. 20.

IX. GRANT BACK CLAUSES AND IMPROVEMENTS

(a) Summary of the present position

11.110   The question of improvements developed by the licensor, and the extent to which a licence agreement can be unilaterally extended by licensing improvement patents has already been discussed above.[16] This section is concerned with improvements developed by a licensee.

11.111   The general principle is that a clause providing that the licensee's improvements belong to the licensor will infringe Article 85 (1) and will be incapable of benefiting from an exemption. On the other hand, a clause requiring the licensee to disclose improvements to the licensor and to grant back to the licensor a licence, will not infringe Article 85 (1), provided the licensor is under a similar obligation with regard to improvements developed by it, and provided the licence which the licensee is obliged to grant back is non-exclusive.

(b) Basis of the Commission's reasoning: "existence v. exercise"

11.112   Improvements, whether patented or not, developed by a licensor can never form part of the existence of the *licensor's* intellectual property. Control over the use to be made by the licensee of those improvements, namely to disclose them to the licensor and to grant back a licence can only be imposed by contract. That control may be restrictive if it is not matched by a corresponding obligation on the licensor and also if it forces the licensee to grant back an exclusive licence.

(c) Development of the Commission's reasoning

11.113   Again, the Commission's thinking on this point has been consistent. The 1962 Patent Notice in paragraph I.D. stated that the following would not infringe Article 85 (1).

> "Undertakings concerning the disclosure of experience gained in exploiting the invention or the grant of licences for inventions in the field of perfection or application; this however applies to undertakings entered into by the licensee only if those undertakings are not exclusive and if the licensor has entered into similar undertakings."

11.114   In several cases[17] the Commission has persuaded parties to an agreement to delete provisions requiring a licensee to assign any improvements which it develops to the licensor. In the *Kabelmetal* case, the amended version of the grant back clause was held not to infringe Article 85 (1). It imposed an obligation on the licensee, Luchaire, "to grant Kabelmetal and through Kabelmetal other possible licensees, non-exclusive licences in respect of such improvements as Luchaire itself may have made to the techniques in question."

---

[16] See paras. 11.82–11.84.

[17] *e.g. Re Kabelmetal* [1975] 2 C.M.L.R. D. 40; *Re Raymond-Nagoya* [1972] C.M.L.R. D. 45.

The Commission, in its decision, recognised that:

"This restricts Luchaire's freedom to make contractual dispositions in respect of such improvements, for although Luchaire remains free in theory to grant licences for improvements to other firms, which would not normally have access to Kabelmetal's basic processes, it cannot now refuse to grant such licences to competing firms using the same processes, which are therefore directly interested in any improvement. Luchaire's obligation to permit the granting of licences to its competitors, thus losing any competitive advantage which might result from the said improvements, would tend to discourage any effort which the company might normally make to obtain such an advantage. Such an effect may restrict competition, particularly in an oligopolistic market structure. In the market in question, as Luchaire is at present the only licensee in the Common Market and as it is unlikely that further licensees who could effectively compete with Luchaire will be appointed before the contract expires, the obligation in question cannot be regarded as having an appreciable effect on conditions in the EEC market."[18]

Thus, although the grant back clause was restrictive, it was not appreciably restrictive in the particular factual context and thus did not infringe Article 85 (1).

(d) The draft block exemption for patent licences

11.115 In the draft block exemption the Commission has not applied its previous reasoning in a particularly logical way. The provisions dealing with grant back clauses appear in Article 2 which lists obligations which will not prevent the application of the exemption, and not in Article 1 which grants the basic exemption. Included in Article 2 are:

"8. the obligation to pass on to the licensor any experience gained in working the invention and to grant back licences in respect of inventions related to improvements and new applications of the original invention, provided that this obligation is non-exclusive and the licensor is bound by a like obligation."

(e) Other types of intellectual property

11.116 Grant back clauses are clearly primarily relevant in relation to patents and know-how. Where a grant back clause could be relevant to other types of intellectual property, the same principles would apply.

X. *MARKS OF ORIGIN*

(a) Summary of the present position

11.117 An obligation on the licensee to mark the product in a particular way will

---

[18] At D. 46.

not amount to an infringement of Article 85 (1).[19] On the other hand, a prohibition against the licensee affixing its own mark will normally amount to an infringement and will not be capable of benefiting from an exemption under Article 85 (3).

(b) Basis of the Commission's reasoning: "existence v. exercise"

11.118   An obligation on the licensee to mark the product in a particular way is generally considered to form part of the existence of the right as without such an obligation the right itself may be in jeopardy. An obligation imposed on a licensee not to use its own mark can presumably never form part of the existence of the right which is the subject of the licence and it will be treated as a restrictive exercise of the right.

(c) Development of the Commission's reasoning

11.119   Again, the Commission's thinking on this point has been consistent. In paragraph I.B. of the 1962 Patent Notice, it was specifically stated that Article 85 (1) did not apply to: "Obligations whereby the licensee has to mark the product with an indication of the patent."

11.120   In the *Burroughs-Delplanque* case,[20] where the licensee was under an obligation to affix certain trade marks to the product and to indicate that they were "manufactured under licence from Burroughs Corporation" the Commission found that those clauses did not fall under Article 85 (1) "especially since Delplanque is entitled to affix other marks on the products manufactured under licence from Burroughs." Similarly it found:

> "The obligation on Delplanque to permit the identification of those products by a distinctive sign has no other purpose in the present case than to facilitate supervision by Burroughs of the quality and quantity of the products covered by the agreement."[21]

(d) The draft block exemption for patent licences

11.121   The same approach is adopted in the draft block exemption for patent licences, which provides in Article 2 (1) (4) that the following obligations will not prevent the application of the block exemption:

> "4. the obligation to mark the patented product or product manufactured using a patented process with an indication of the patentee's name, the patent or the patent licensing agreement."

11.122   Equally, the draft block exemption includes in Article 3, which lists the provisions which will prevent the application of the block exemption:

> "9. a clause prohibiting the licensee from using his own trade mark or business name or a specified get up; this is without prejudice to

---

[19] *Burroughs* [1972] C.M.L.R. D. 67 and D. 72; *Persil Trade Mark* [1978] 1 C.M.L.R. 395 where an arrangement between two holders of the "Persil" mark under which distinctive colourings were to be used was stated not to infringe Art. 85 (1).

[20] [1972] C.M.L.R. D. 67.   [21] *Ibid.* at D. 70.

Article 2 (1) (4) and to any obligation on the part of the licensee to make such use of the licensor's trade mark as is necessary to preserve its validity."

(e) Other types of intellectual property
11.123   Although these principles on marks of origin have been developed in the context of patents and trade marks, the same principles would apply in relation to other types of intellectual property, particularly copyright.

XI. *NON-COMPETITION*

(a) Summary of the present position
11.124   A clause prohibiting the licensee from dealing in competing products will normally infringe Article 85 (1) and will only occasionally be capable of benefiting from an exemption under Article 85 (3).[22]

(b) Basis of the Commission's reasoning
11.125   A restriction on dealing in competing products cannot be part of the existence of an intellectual property right, and can only be imposed when exercising the right. As such, it will usually be a restrictive exercise of the right. This was particularly clearly stated in the *AOIP/Beyrard* case,[23] where the Commission condemned a non-competition clause in uncompromising terms:

> "Clause 9 (1) of the licensing agreement obliges the contracting parties to refrain from competing with each other in any way. Such a provision does not relate to the existence of a patent, but constitutes a restriction of competition within the meaning of Article 85 (1)."[24]

(c) Development of the Commission's reasoning
11.126   This approach to non-competition clauses is clearly set out in the Fourth Report on Competition Policy where the Commission said:

> "A non-competition restriction could prevent a licensee from extending his product range and closely bind his future to that of a licensed patent. Consequently, a licensee so tied might have to go out of business when the licensed technology becomes obsolete. Non-competition prohibitions can have the effect of not only strengthening a monopoly position of a patentee, but also of weakening competition between manufacturers of substitute products. A licensee might no longer have worthwhile prospects in carrying out independent development. Accordingly, the Commission regards non-competition provisions as covered by Article 85 (1). Possibilities

---

[22] See, *e.g. Eisele-INRA* [1978] 3 C.M.L.R. 434; *AOIP-Beyrard* [1976] 1 C.M.L.R. D. 14.
[23] *Supra*, n. 25.
[24] *Ibid.* at D. 24.

of exemption under Article 85 (3) could only arise in special situations, particularly cases relating to specialisation agreements."[25]

11.127 The same approach was adopted on a non-competition provision in a licence for plant breeder's rights[26] and it is clear that a provision can never form part of the existence of the licensed right.

(d) The draft block exemption for patent licences

11.128 A non-competition provision is included among the clauses in Article 3 of the draft block exemption for patent licences which will prevent the application of the block exemption, although the wording used there is fairly general:

"3. without prejudice to Article 1 (1) to (4), a restriction on the licensor or the licensee against competing with the other party, with undertakings that have economic connections with the other party or with other licensees in respect of research and development, manufacture, use or sales."

(e) Other types of intellectual property

11.129 There is no reason to suppose that the same approach would not be adopted with other types of intellectual property.

XII. *NO-CHALLENGE*

(a) Summary of the present position

11.130 A clause in a licence obliging the licensee not to challenge the validity of the licensed right will infringe Article 85 (1) and will not be capable of benefiting from an exemption under Article 85 (3).

(b) Basis of the Commission's reasoning: "existence v. exercise"

11.131 It has been clear since the Commission's earliest decisions[27] that a no-challenge clause is not part of the existence of the right, and can only ever be a restrictive exercise of it.

(c) Development of the Commission's reasoning

11.132 In several early cases, the parties amended their agreements so as to remove no challenge clauses.[28] In the *AOIP/Beyrard* case,[29] on the other hand, where the parties refused to remove the restriction, a specific finding was made that such a clause amounted to an infringement:

"Clause 5 (2) of the licensing agreement prohibits the licensee from

---

[25] Fourth Report on Competition Policy, Pt. 30.
[26] *Eisele-INRA Agreement* [1978] 3 C.M.L.R. at p. 456.
[27] *Raymond Nagoya* [1972] C.M.L.R. D. 45. Second Report on Competition Policy, Pt. 45.
[28] *e.g. Davidson Rubber* [1972] C.M.L.R. D. 52; *Re Kabelmetal* [1975] 2 C.M.L.R. D. 40.
[29] [1976] 1 C.M.L.R. D. 14.

challenging the validity of the patents directly or indirectly. Such a no-challenge clause is not a matter pertaining to the existence of the patent. Rather, it constitutes a contractual restriction of competition in that it deprives the licensee of the possibility, which is available to everyone else, of removing an obstacle to his freedom of action in the commercial field by means of an action for revocation of the patents. This is no less the case where the relevant authority examines an application for novelty and degree of inventiveness before granting a patent, since such an examination does not affect the right of firms who might profit from the non-existence of the patent to oppose it or to bring actions for its revocation. Even if it is the licensee who is best placed to attack the patent on the basis of the information given to him by the licensor, the public interest in the revocation of patents which ought not to have been granted requires that the licensee shall not be deprived of this possibility."[30]

(d) Draft block exemption for patent licences

11.133   A no-challenge clause is included in Article 3 of the draft block exemption for patent licences which prevents the application of the exemption if the licence agreement contains a clause imposing:

"1. the obligation on the part of the licensee to refrain from challenging the validity of the licensed patent or other exclusive rights of the licensor or any other undertaking that has economic connections with the licensor; impeding such a challenge shall be treated as equivalent to prohibiting it. This is without prejudice to any right of the licensor to terminate the licensing agreement in the event of such a challenge."

11.134   It is not entirely clear what is meant by the last few lines of that Article. If, as a result of the challenge, the licensed patent is revoked, then the licence agreement will anyway come to an end as the subject matter will have disappeared. If, on the other hand, it means that the licence agreement even if it includes ancillary know-how and trade marks or other patents, can be terminated by the licensor if one patent is challenged, that in itself would appear to be a considerable disincentive to a licensee challenging a patent. Presumably, the Commission would seek to apply the first of these alternatives.

(e) Other types of intellectual property

11.135   The same principles apply to other types of intellectual property as well as patents, to the extent to which they are relevant.

---

[30] *Ibid.* at D. 23.

XIII. *ASSIGNMENTS AND SUB-LICENCES*

(a) Summary of the present position

11.136   A restriction on the licensee assigning his licence or granting sub-licences will not infringe Article 85 (1). Such obligations have been recognised by the Commission as necessary to protect the existence of the right and are not related to exercise.

(b) Development of the Commission's reasoning

11.137   Thus, in the 1962 Patent Notice, in paragraph I.A. (4) it was stated that the following would not infringe Article 85 (1):

"the limitation of exploitation:

...

(c) with regard to the person (limitation of the licensee's power of disposal e.g. prohibiting him from assigning the licence or from granting sub-licences)."

11.138   The Commission's reasoning was expanded a little further in its decision in the *Davidson Rubber*[31] case where it referred to:

"... the obligation on the licensees to grant sub-licences only with the approval of the Davidson Rubber Company since both that obligation is covered by the exclusive right of the licensor and also it is justified by the latter's interest in its know-how not being divulged without its agreement to undertakings other than those which have been authorised to use it."[32]

11.139   On the other hand, if a licence imposes restrictions on the grant of certain sub-licences but not on others then it seems that such a discriminatory approach will not be permitted. In the *Suralmo* case, which was settled without a formal decision, sub-licences for military use required the licensor's consent, whereas sub-licences for civilian use did not. The Commission, without taking a formal decision, persuaded the parties to agree to allow Suralmo to grant sub-licences without consent.[33]

(c) Draft block exemption for patent licences

11.140   The question of assignment and sub-licensing is dealt with in Article 2 of the draft block exemption for patent licences which provides that block exemption will still apply where the agreement contains: "3. the obligation to refrain from granting sub-licences or assigning the licence to a third party."

(d) Other types of intellectual property

11.141   It is assumed that the same principles apply to restrictions on assigning or sub-licensing licences of other types of intellectual property, as well as patents.

---

[31] [1972] C.M.L.R. D. 52.   [32] *Ibid.* at D. 60.
[33] See Ninth Report on Competition Policy, Pt. 114.

XIV. *"MOST FAVOURED LICENSEE"*

(a) Summary of the present position

11.142 The Commission's approach to most favoured licensee clauses is somewhat inconsistent. In practice, it has tended to find that such clauses do not infringe Article 85 (1), although it sometimes enters a *caveat* that in appropriate circumstances they may.[34]

(b) Basis of the Commission's reasoning: "existence v. exercise"

11.143 It seems clear that such a clause could never form part of the existence of the right, but could only be at best a non-restrictive exercise of the right.

11.144 In the *Kabelmetal*[35] case, for instance, the Commission dealt with a "most favoured licensee" clause as follows:

"The other provisions of the agreement between Kabelmetal and Luchaire are not caught by Article 85 (1), because they do not have as their object or effect a substantial restriction of competition within the Common Market. This is true in particular of the following:

    (i) Kabelmetal's undertaking not to grant any licence in respect of its techniques to any firm in any part of the world on terms more favourable than those applying to Luchaire (most favoured licensee clause). The licensor's undertaking to extend to the original licensee any more favourable terms subsequently granted to other licensees would not in general dissuade the licensor from granting further licences to third parties. In specific cases, however, particularly where the market situation was such that the only way to find other licensees was to grant them more favourable terms than those granted to the first licensee, this obligation could be an obstacle to the granting of further licences and therefore constitute an appreciable restriction of competition. In this specific case, however, none of the facts point to such a restriction."[36]

(c) Draft block exemption for patent licences

11.145 In the draft block exemption for patent licences, most favoured licensee clauses appear in Article 2, which lists the obligations which will not prevent the application of the block exemption. This extends to:

"9. the obligation on the part of the licensor to grant the licensee any more favourable terms that may be granted to another licensee during the life of the agreement."

---

[34] See *Kabelmetal* [1975] 2 C.M.L.R. D. 40.
[35] *Supra*, n. 11.
[36] *Ibid.* at D. 46.

11.146 Despite its inclusion in Article 2, it is nevertheless clear from Recital 17 to the draft that the Commission does not consider that such a provision could ever form part of the existence of the patent right, but merely that it does not consider such a provision will normally be a restrictive exercise of the right. That Recital states that: "Obligations on the part of the licensor are not matters which relate to the existence of the patent. Apart from ... most favoured licensee clauses, they satisfy the tests of Article 85 (3) in special cases only."

(d) Other types of intellectual property

11.147 It is assumed that the same principle will apply to other types of intellectual property.

XV. *OTHER CLAUSES*

A. ARBITRATION

11.148 In an earlier draft of the block exemption for patent licences which was published unofficially,[37] before the draft published officially in the *Official Journal* of March 3, 1979, the Commission included arbitration clauses among the restrictive clauses to which would be covered by the exemption. In the present draft, it has not adopted that policy, but has included a separate article, Article 4, dealing specifically with arbitration clauses as follows:

> "Where disputes as to the interpretation or operation of one of the provisions or measures listed in Articles 1 and 3 are settled by arbitration, the contracting parties are required to communicate the terms of the award forthwith to the Commission, together with the licensing agreement."

11.149 The reason for this is, presumably, to ensure that the arbitrators have applied the provisions of the block exemption correctly to the agreement. If, however, this is included in the final version of the block exemption, it might undermine one of the main advantages of arbitration, namely the absence of publicity. Although the award could presumably be communicated in confidence, the parties might well be reluctant to draw the attention of the Commission to their Agreement.

11.150 In earlier specific decisions, the Commission have not found arbitration clauses to infringe Article 85.[38]

11.151 The existence of an arbitration clause in an agreement will not prevent the Commission considering the terms of the agreement. This point was specifically made by the Commission in its Eighth Report on Competition

---

[37] [1977] 1 C.M.L.R. D.25.
[38] See, *e.g. Re Burroughs/Delplanque* [1972] C.M.L.R. D. 67.

Policy dealing with 1978. In referring to the *Pentacon* case, it said:
> "A dispute having arisen concerning the application of the licensing agreement, the GDR [German Democratic Republic] firms resorted to a clause in the agreement which specified that disputes were to be referred to the arbitration court of the GDR Chamber of Foreign Trade. This did not, however, prevent the Commission from examining the applicability of the rules of competition—which are a cornerstone of the Community's 'ordre public'—to the effects of the agreement in question within the Common Market. When industrial property right licences exist in one or more member states such effects are indisputable."[39]

B. Joint Patents and Cross-Licences

11.152 The principles discussed above do not necessarily apply to other than the straightforward situation where an owner of a right grants a licence to one licensee. Thus, the 1962 Patent Notice was specifically stated not to apply to:
> "(1) joint ownership of patents,
> (2) reciprocal licences,
> (3) parallel multiple licences."

11.153 Equally, Article 5 of the draft block exemption provides that:
> "This Regulation shall not apply to:
> 1. patent pools;
> 2. patent licensing agreements between competing firms that hold interests in a joint venture or between one of them and the joint venture, if the licensing agreement relates to the activities of the joint venture;
> 3. without prejudice to Article 2 (1) (8), agreements under which the parties grant each other rights on a reciprocal basis in relation to patents, trade marks or the communication of secret manufacturing processes or other secret know-how, even where separate agreements are involved; this shall also apply where one party is granted distribution rights over unprotected products."

---

[39] Eight Report on Competition Policy, Pt. 119.

Part IV

Alienation of Intellectual Property

CHAPTER 12

ASSIGNMENT AND EXPROPRIATION
(Articles 30 to 36, 59 and 60, 85 and 86)

I. INTRODUCTION

12.01 This chapter is concerned with the extent to which Articles 30 to 36, 59 and 60, 85 and 86 of the Treaty affect ownership of intellectual property within the Community when, as a result of assignment or expropriation, the intellectual property has either been sub-divided or completely alienated.

12.02 Where the intellectual property has merely been sub-divided, this chapter is similar to Chapter 9, in that it deals with the way in which the Treaty affects two owners of identical intellectual property within the Community. While, however, Chapter 9 was concerned with ownership by two or more "enterprises" within the Community of identical intellectual property which at no time had a "common origin," this chapter is concerned in part with the effect of the Treaty on ownership by two or more undertakings of intellectual property which, at one time, belonged to a single enterprise. The subsequent division of ownership may have resulted from assignment, expropriation or some variant of these.

12.03 In the context of alienation in general, Article 85 may be relevant where the transfer of ownership occurs in consequence of an agreement, such as an assignment. Articles 30 to 36 may be relevant to all "common origin" situations other than those involving performing rights as an element of copyright, and have expressly been held to apply where the sub-division of the intellectual property is attributable to an earlier expropriation. Articles 59 and 60 may be relevant to "common origin" situations involving performing rights, for example, a televised broadcast of a film protected by copyright. Finally, Article 86 may be relevant where an assignment of rights takes place in favour of a party which is in a dominant position. In this chapter the possible application of Articles 30 to 36, 59, 60, 85 and 86 will each be considered separately.

II. *ASSIGNMENT AND ARTICLE 85*

A. GENERAL REMARKS

12.04 In the *Sirena* case the Advocate General drew a distinction between two types of trade mark assignments.[1]

---

[1] Case 40/70 *Sirena SRL* v. *Eda SRL and Others* [1971] E.C.R. 69; [1971] C.M.L.R. 260 at pp. 266 and 267.

12.05   In the first type of assignment the assignee does not receive any protection over and above the rights conferred by national trade mark law on any owner of a registered trade mark. As the Advocate General pointed out, in this type of assignment the position of the assignee is very similar to that of the original owner, and the assignment cannot be regarded as caught by Article 85 (1), unless other special factors are involved such as a concerted practice which itself infringes Article 85 (1).

12.06   By contrast, the second type of assignment confers upon the assignee rights and obligations additional to those which would be enjoyed simply as a result of the operation of relevant national law, or alternatively should properly be regarded as part and parcel of a pattern of similar assignments having cumulative effects which go beyond the consequences of mere assignments. Article 85 (1) is clearly more likely to apply to assignments of this type.

12.07   The distinction is useful as a generalisation, and there is no reason in principle to restrict it to assignments involving trade marks. It would appear equally relevant to assignments involving other types of intellectual property.

12.08   It remains, however, very difficult to be sure whether any particular assignment will be caught by Article 85 (1). This difficulty is, no doubt, at least in part attributable to the very limited amount of case law available to date.

12.09   The European Court has only on one occasion been concerned exclusively with an assignment, in the *Sirena* case. Its judgment in that case delivered in 1971, is probably no longer good law. This is because, were Sirena to come before the European Court today, it is likely that it would be decided on the basis of Articles 30 to 36, rather than on the basis of Article 85 (1).[2]

12.10   Nonetheless, until the European Court is again asked to decide similar questions to those before it in that case, Sirena remains a landmark decision and, inevitably, the natural starting point in considering the circumstances in which Article 85 (1) may apply to assignments.

B. THE RELEVANT CASES (SIRENA,[3] EMI[4] AND ZWARTE KIP)[5]

12.11   The facts in the *Sirena* case, insofar as relevant, were fairly straightforward. In 1933 an American Company, Mark Allen, registered the trade mark "Prep" in Italy, in respect of shaving cream. In 1937 Mark Allen assigned the "Prep" trade mark to an Italian company, Sirena SRL. The assignment

---

[2] See discussion in the next section of this chap., *infra* at 12.30 *et seq.*
[3] *Sirena* [1971] C.M.L.R. 260.
[4] Case 51/75 *EMI Records* v. *CBS U.K. Ltd.* [1976] E.C.R. 811; [1976] 2 C.M.L.R. 235.
[5] *Re Advocaat Zwarte Kip: Soenen-Bouckaert* v. *Cinoco SA and Van Olffen VB* (74/432/EEC), [1974] 2 C.M.L.R. D. 79.

was of "all rights, title and interests in the said mark" for Italy.[6] Mark Allen later similarly assigned its "Prep" trademark for Germany to a German company. Both Sirena and the German company manufactured shaving creams under the "Prep" mark.

12.12   Eventually, the German company began to export its products to Italy through an independent Italian company by the name of Novimpex SRL. The German company's products were sold in Italy by Novimpex at much lower prices than those of Sirena. This led Sirena to institute proceedings before an Italian court against both Novimpex and certain retailers, alleging trade mark infringement. The defendants sought to rely on Articles 85 and 86 as a defence, whereupon the Italian Court suspended proceedings and referred two questions to the European Court.

12.13   Effectively, the European Court was asked whether Articles 85 and 86 apply to the effects of a trade mark assignment entered into before the Treaty came into force, and whether Articles 85 and 86 must be interpreted in such a way as to "... prevent the owner of a trade mark validly registered in one Member State from exercising the corresponding absolute right to prohibit third parties from importing from other Member States of the Community products which originally legally bore the same mark?"[7]

12.14   The Court accepted the Article 85 defence, after affirming that trade mark rights do not in and of themselves infringe Article 85 (1). It reasoned that on the other hand the exercise of those rights:

"... may come within the prohibitions of the Treaty if it is the object, the means or the consequence, of an agreement. If this exercise occurs by virtue of assignments to enterprises in one or more Member States it must be ascertained in each case whether it gives rise to situations prohibited by Article 85 ... The simultaneous assignment to several concessionaries of national trade mark rights for the same product, if it has the effect of re-establishing rigid frontiers between Member States, may prejudice trade between States and distort competition in the Common Market ... Article 85 therefore applies where, by virtue of trade mark rights, imports of products originating in other Member States, bearing the same trade mark because their owners have acquired the trade mark itself or the right to use it through agreements with one another or with other parties, are prevented. The fact that the national legislation makes trade mark rights dependent on circumstances of law and fact other than the aforementioned agreement, such as the registration of the trade mark or its undisturbed use, does not prevent the application of Article 85. If the agreements have been concluded before the entry into force of

---

[6] *Sirena, supra,* n. 1 at p. 272.
[7] *Ibid.* at p. 262.

the Treaty it is necessary and sufficient that their effects continue after this date."[8]

12.15 If the *Sirena* case is considered good law, it would follow that virtually any simultaneous assignment to several different assignees of national trade mark rights would infringe Article 85 (1), because such assignments would invariably have "the effect of re-establishing rigid frontiers between Member States."

12.16 In its much more recent judgment in the *EMI* cases, however, the European Court would appear tacitly to have overruled its Sirena judgment.

12.17 As indicated in Chapters 3 and 8,[9] the *EMI* cases involved references to the European Court under Article 177 by the national courts of three Member States—the United Kingdom, Denmark and Germany—as parallel proceedings were in progress in all three countries, essentially involving the same facts. All three references were concerned with the trade mark "Columbia." While at one time all the trade mark registrations had been owned by associated undertakings, at the time of the references the "Columbia" trade mark was owned in the U.S.A. by CBS Inc., and in all the EEC Member States by member companies of the EMI group.

12.18 There had in the past been a series of agreements between both predecessors of EMI and CBS and those companies themselves. These agreements were not trade mark assignments, though some of them had similar effects. They were arrangements for the interchange of record matrices between companies and, in some cases, market sharing agreements. Some of these agreements would on any interpretation have infringed Article 85 (1) had that Article been in force at the time. It was also established, however, that the last significant agreement of this type was terminated in 1952, although certain of its effects "lingered" until 1956. Further, although between 1962 and 1971 a number of agreements were entered into which, in the Commission's view, suggested a resumption of the prohibited conduct between the two groups, it was common ground that the last of these agreements came to an end in 1974.

12.19 Although the *EMI* cases were not directly concerned with assignments, the Court's judgment is particularly relevant in this context because it is here that it gave its clearest guidance to date on the criteria to be applied in deciding whether Article 85 applies to a relationship previously regulated by agreements which infringed Article 85 (1), but which are no longer in force.

12.20 The Court reasoned that for Article 85 to apply in circumstances such as those present in the *EMI* cases, involving agreements which are no longer in force:

---

[8] *Ibid.* at p. 274.
[9] See *supra*, paras 3.31 *et seq.* and paras 8.95 *et seq.*

"... it is sufficient that such agreements continue to produce their effects after they have formally ceased to be in force. An agreement is only regarded as continuing to produce its effects if from the behaviour of the persons concerned there may be inferred the existence of elements of concerted practice and of co-ordination peculiar to the agreement and producing the same result as that envisaged by the agreement. This is not so when the said effects do not exceed those flowing from the mere exercise of the national trademark rights."[10]

12.21   In the light of this judgment it is likely that the assignments at issue in the *Sirena* case would not now be held to infringe Article 85 (1), because those assignments apparently did not give rise to consequences which exceeded in any way those naturally resulting from the exercise of the national trade mark rights. They did not, for instance, contain contractual restrictions on the exercise of those rights.

12.22   An example of the type of assignment which infringes Article 85 (1) is provided by the Commission's decision in the *Advocaat Zwart Kip* case.[11] The facts were that in 1920 VB Van Olffen of Hatteu, a Dutch company, registered various designs and trade marks embodying the words "Advocaat Zwarte Kip" for Belgium, Holland and Luxembourg. Subsequently beginning in 1938, the trade mark rights for Belgium and Luxembourg were assigned on a number of occasions, most recently in 1955 to a company named Cinoco SA of Brussels. Cinoco produced and distributed spirits in Belgium and Luxembourg. In 1971 Van Olffen re-registered its rights as existing owner of "Advocaat Zwarte Kip" under the Benelux arrangements, with the exception of the rights for that mark in Belgium and Luxembourg. Similarly, and also in 1971, Cinoco SA re-registered under the Benelux arrangements its rights as owner of "Advocaat Zwarte Kip" for Belgium and Luxembourg.[12]

12.23   Cinoco learned that a Belgian wine merchant had purchased a quantity of Advocaat bearing the "Advocaat Zwarte Kip" trade mark from a Dutch dealer, and that the Advocaat in question had been manufactured and placed on the market by Van Olffen in Holland. Cinoco thereupon instituted proceedings before the Belgian Courts, claiming trade mark and design infringement, and seeking injunctive relief. In the course of these

---

[10] EMI Records Ltd. [1976] 2 C.M.L.R. 235 at p. 267.

[11] Advocaat Zwarte Kip [1974] 2 C.M.L.R. D. 79.

[12] It is noteworthy that under the 1962 Benelux Convention on Trade marks the question of existing rights is dealt with in Arts. 32 and 33. According to the Commission's decision, "Article 33 provides that where pursuant to Article 32 a trade mark is owned in different Benelux countries by different persons, the owner of the trade mark in one of these countries cannot object to the importation from another of the Benelux countries of a product bearing this same trade mark or claim compensation on account of such importations where the trade mark was affixed by the owner thereof in such other country or with his permission and where there exists between the two owners an economic link as regards the exploitation of the product concerned." *Ibid.* at P.D. 82 and D. 83.

proceedings the Belgian wine merchant complained to the European Commission, under Article 3 of Regulation 17, and this in turn led to the suspension of the domestic proceedings pending the outcome of the Commission's decision.

12.24 The Commission found as a fact that the 1938 Agreement concerning the use of the trade mark in Holland, Belgium and Luxembourg involved the partitioning of markets, and that this was confirmed by various letters including a letter sent by Van Olffen on October 13, 1971, to Cinoco which was written in Dutch and stated "we assure you that we will do everything possible to prevent delivery of our Advocaat from Holland to Belgium." The Commission also found as a fact that Van Olffen marketed Advocaat of different qualities in Holland under the same trade mark and that since 1973 it had supplied Cinoco with some of its Advocaat, which the latter had sold on the Belgian and Luxembourg markets. This latter Advocaat differed in a number of ways from that sold by Van Olffen in Holland, (*i.e.* as to composition, alcoholic content and presentation). So far as presentation was concerned, Van Olffen indicated alcoholic content on its bottles whilst Cinoco did not. Cinoco, for its part, indicated its name and address, even when the Advocaat had been manufactured by Van Olffen.

12.25 The Commission touched on the possible application of Articles 30 to 36 EEC, which will be dealt with in the next section.[13] Its actual decision, however, relied fairly and squarely on Article 85. The Commission reasoned that agreements concluded before the EEC Treaty came into force but having effects continuing after that date can infringe Article 85 (1), and noted that the exchange of correspondence between the parties provided clear evidence that the 1938 assignment had continuing effects. It therefore concluded that in so far as the "Advocaat Zwarte Kip" trade mark registrations were being used to prevent imports and exports, the 1938 Agreement had the effect of restricting competition within the EEC. Furthermore, it affirmed that any danger of consumers being misled as to differences in quality and the like could be avoided by providing adequate information on bottle labels. Accordingly differences in quality and considerations of consumer protection in such circumstances cannot justify a partitioning of markets.[14]

12.26 In substance, therefore, the Commission held that where an Agreement is entered into before the EEC Treaty came into force which includes a trade mark assignment and which, by its wording, indicates an intention to partition the EEC market, and where there is evidence that the effects of that Agreement continue to be felt after the Treaty came into force, the Agreement will restrict competition within the meaning of Article 85 (1).

12.27 Thus, in the *Advocaat Zwarte Kip* case, the facts were such as to provide

---

[13] See discussion, *infra*, at para. 12.53.
[14] *Advocaat Zwarte Kip* [1974] 2 C.M.L.R. D. 79 and D. 85.

clear evidence that the original assignment had effects that exceeded those which would ordinarily result from a mere assignment of national trade mark rights.

12.28   On the test provided by the European Court in the EMI judgments, the Commission's reasoning the *Zwarte Kip* case would appear sound, while the *Sirena* case would presumably not have been decided on Article 85 (1) grounds at all, but instead on Articles 30 to 36 grounds in accordance with the principles discussed in the next section.

C. The Position with Regard to Other Intellectual Property

12.29 In principle, the Commission's reasoning in the *Zwarte Kip* case would appear equally applicable to all types of intellectual property. There is no obvious reason why it should be confined to trade marks.[14a]

III. *COMMON ORIGIN AND ARTICLES 30 TO 36, 59 and 60*

A. General Remarks

12.30 The concerned in this section is with the effect of Articles 30 to 36 on the relationship between two or more undertakings, each of which own intellectual property which, at some earlier date, belonged to a single enterprise. It is immaterial whether the subsequent division of ownership resulted from voluntary assignment or forced divestiture. The material consideration is that intellectual property presently owned by two or more undertakings was, at some earlier date, owned by a single undertaking and, therefore, may be traced back to a "common origin."

12.31   Arguably, no single concept relating to free movement of goods or competition has caused so much controversy as the European Court's development of the common origin doctrine. This notwithstanding, the Court has, in fact, only applied the doctrine to one case, the *Hag* case,[15] the facts of which were unusual to say the least. As discussed below,[15a] special considerations apply in any case to performing rights as an element of copyright, in so far as the position is governed by Articles 59 and 60 of the Treaty, relating to services.

B. The Hag Case

12.32 **The facts.** Hag A G was founded in Germany, and before the First World War it registered the word "Hag" as a trade mark in Germany, Belgium

---

[14a] In the context of performing rights as an element of copyright, however, note the Court's reasoning in the *Coditel* case, discussed, *infra*, at paras. 12.58.2 *et seq.*

[15] Case 192/73 *Van Zuylen Frères* v. *Hag A G* [1974] E.C.R. 731; [1974] 2 C.M.L.R. 127.

[15a] See discussion, *infra*, at paras. 12.58.1 *et seq.*

and Luxembourg, in respect of its de-caffeinated coffees. In 1925 it ensured the further protection of its marks by international registration under the so called "Madrid Arrangements."[15b] In 1927 Hag AG created a subsidiary in Belgium, Cafe Hag SA ("Hag Belgium"). With effect from 1935, it transferred its "Hag" trade mark registration in Belgium and Luxembourg to Hag Belgium. Following the liberation of Belgium in the Second World War the shares in Hag Belgium were sequestrated as enemy property, and the shares were eventually sold to the Van Oevelen family. Then, in 1971, Hag Belgium transferred its Hag trade mark registrations in Belgium and Luxembourg to another company by the name of Van Zuylen Frères. Van Zuylen did not itself produce decaffeinated coffee, but instead brought it from Hag Belgium. Hag Belgium, in turn, no longer sold its coffee direct to the public, but only to the trade. Meanwhile, in 1972, the original German company, Hag AG, began delivering its coffees to Luxembourg retailers for sale under its German mark, "Hag." It had, incidentally, shortly after the war registered the mark "Hag" in Belgium and Luxembourg.

12.33   When Hag AG began to deliver its coffees direct to Luxembourg retailers under its German "Hag" mark, Van Zuylen Frères reacted by instituting two actions before the Luxembourg Courts, for trade mark infringement and for cancellation of the Belgian and Luxembourg trade mark registrations made by Hag AG. This litigation was further complicated by an application to intervene, made by a German trader, seeking to defend his independent rights to import into Luxembourg Hag products bought by him in Germany from Hag AG under the trade mark "Hag."

12.34   The case raised, therefore, two distinct questions:

1. Was Hag AG entitled itself to market products in Belgium and Luxembourg under the trade mark "Hag"?

2. Was an independent party entitled to market in Belgium and Luxembourg Hag AG products which had previously lawfully been placed on the market in Germany?

12.35   The Luxembourg tribunal stayed proceedings, and referred two questions to the European Court for a preliminary ruling.

The first question asked whether either the competition or the free movement of goods provisions of the Treaty prohibit a trade mark owner relying on his trade mark in a Member State to oppose the import into that State of products which bear an identical mark lawfully applied in another Member State when, originally, the two marks belonged to the same holder. The question made clear that the separation of ownership had come about as a result of "sequestration," and also that at the time of the referral there was "no legal, financial, technical or economic link" between the two trade mark owners.

[15b] See, *supra*. Chap. 1, n. 10a.

12.36   By the second question the Court was asked to indicate, whether its reply would have been the same if the trade in question in the second Member State had been carried out by an independent third party who had properly acquired the product after it had been lawfully placed on the market in the first Member State.[16]

12.37   **The Court's reasoning.** The Court's starting point was its by now familiar analysis of the relationship between Articles 30 and 36 and, in particular, its conclusion that "Article 36 only allows derogations from the free circulation of goods in so far as such derogations are justified by the protection of the rights which constitute the specific object of such property."[17] It then went on to distinguish between trade marks and other intellectual property, on the grounds that trade marks contribute particularly to the division of markets because, unlike other intellectual property, their duration is not limited.[18] For this reason, if for no other, the Court concluded that a trade mark owner should not be entitled to rely upon his trade mark in order to prohibit trading in goods lawfully produced and marked in another Member State, notwithstanding that the trade marks are identical provided that they have the same origin.

12.38   The Court stated in terms:

"The exercise of the trade mark right is such as to contribute to the partitioning of the markets and thus to affect the free circulation of goods between Member States, all the more so in that, as opposed to other industrial and commercial property rights, it is not subject to temporal limits.

It could not therefore be accepted that the exclusiveness of the trade mark right, which can be the consequence of the territorial

---

[16] The actual questions referred to the European Court were in the following terms:
1. Should Art. 85 and/or the rules for the free circulation of goods within the EEC, in particular Arts. 5, 30 *et seq.*, and especially Art. 36 of the Treaty be interpreted as meaning: that the present holder of a trade mark within a Member State A of the Community is entitled to resist, on the grounds of its rights in that trade mark imports into the Member State A *by the original holder of the same trade mark in another Member State B of goods from that Member State B bearing the same trade mark as the goods of the first Member State A, when it is established that:* (Emphasis added)
the trade mark at issue was assigned by the original holder within a Member State B to its subsidiary, constituted within another Member State A, pursuant to agreements which took effect before the coming into force of the Treaty;
this subsidiary, which was sequestrated after the Second World War by the Government of the State A, was subsequently sold with the trademark by that Government to a third party;
the said third party in turn assigned the trademark to the present holder in that State A;
there exists no legal, financial, technical, or economic link between the present holder and the original holder of the trade marks in States A and B?
2. Would the answer to question 1 be the same if the sale of the goods in Member State A was made not by the original holder of the trade mark in Member State B, but by a third party, such as an importer, who had duly obtained the goods in Member State B from the original holder? *Ibid.* pp. 129–130.
[17] *Ibid.* at p. 143.
[18] *Ibid.*

limits of the national laws, should be relied on by the holder of a trade mark with a view to prohibiting trading, in one Member State, in goods lawfully produced in another Member State under an identical mark which has the same origin.

    ... Such a prohibition ... would come into conflict with one of the fundamental aims of the Treaty, the fusion of the national markets into one single market."[19]

12.39   The Court briefly considered the possible confusion which could result to the consumer from its decision, but concluded that consumers can be informed of the origin of a trade marked product by other means than a trade mark such as labelling, which will not adversely affect the free movement of goods within the Community.

12.40   In answer to the first question referred to it, therefore, the Court concluded that "to prohibit trading in one Member State in a product which lawfully bears a trade mark in another Member State, for the sole reason that an identical mark, sharing the same origin, exists in the first State is incompatible with the provisions laying down the free circulation of goods within the Common Market."[20]

12.41   Turning to the second question referred to it, the Court said that its conclusion would apply equally to goods lawfully acquired by a *third party* in the first Member State, after they have been properly placed on the market in that State, and exported by him to the second Member State.

C. The Implications of Hag

1. *The Court's Answer to The First Question: A Trade Mark Owner in One Member State may not Prevent Direct Sales in that State of Products Manufactured in Another Member State by the Owner of an Identical Trade Mark in that Other State, Provided Both Trade Marks Share a Common Origin.*

12.42   One is hard pressed to think of any objective justification for the Court's reasoning in the *Hag* case, at least as regards its answer to the first question referred to it. There can surely be no good reason why a trade mark owner in one Member State should be prevented from relying upon his trade mark to stop *direct imports* by an independent enterprise of goods produced by it in another Member State, bearing an identical trade mark of common origin which was lawfully affixed in that other Member State, given that the original separation of ownership was due to sequestration. In such circumstances there can, after all, be no suggestion that the original owner in some way "consented" to another party within the Community owning the trade mark and, by so consenting, had "exhausted" his rights in the trade mark.

---

[19] *Ibid.* at pp. 143 and 144.
[20] *Ibid.* at p. 144.

12.43   Further, while it is undeniably true that trade marks are not the only way of providing consumers with information concerning the origin of products and, in particular, that other information can be added to the labels on products, there must be a real risk that consumers will be misled as to the origin of two products bearing identical trade marks but manufactured by independent parties, for example in the case of telephoned orders.[21]

12.44   Whatever the merit of this criticism, in the context of forced divestiture, the position is less clear cut where the original separation of ownership was due to a voluntary act, such as a straightforward assignment. In this situation, it can be argued that the voluntary act of assignment involved the consent of the original owner to the subdivision of the trade mark, so that the original owner has thereby exhausted his rights. While such consent will be present in the majority of common origin situations, traceable to ordinary assignments, it is clear that the European Court does not consider it essential.

12.45   Thus, in its Terrapin judgment the Court volunteered that where intellectual property has been sub-divided the position of its owner is analogous to that of an owner of intellectual property who seeks to prevent the import of a trade marked product which has been placed on the market in another Member State either by that owner, or with his consent. The Court said, in that case:

> "... the proprietor of an industrial or commercial property right protected by the law of a Member State cannot rely on that law to prevent the importation of a product which has lawfully been marketed in another Member State by the proprietor himself or with his consent. It is the same when the right relied on is the result of the sub-division, *either by voluntary act or as a result of public constraint*, of a trade mark right which originally belonged to one and the same proprietor. *In these cases the basic function of the trade mark to guarantee to consumers that the product has the same origin is already undermined by the sub-division of the original right.*[22]

12.46   Although the Court's remarks in the *Terrapin* case might be described in English legal terminology as *obiter dicta*, they must be taken at face value. In these circumstances, and unless and until the European Court holds to the contrary, it must be recognised that the common origin doctrine applies equally to both forced divestiture and voluntary assignment.

12.47   It follows that once a trade mark owner, owning registered trade marks in two Member States, assigns his trade mark registration in one of those

---

[21] The parties can, however, reduce this risk by, for example, agreeing to use their trade marks with a distinctive get up and colouring. The Commission concluded that an agreement of this type did not infringe Art. 85 (1) in *Re Persil Trade Mark* [1978] 1 C.M.L.R. 395. See also *Re Penney's Trade Mark* (78/193/EEC) [1978] 2 C.M.L.R. 100.

[22] Case 119/75 *Terrapin (Overseas) Ltd.* v. *Terranova Industrie CA Kapferer & Co.* [1976] E.C.R. 1039; [1976] 2 C.M.L.R. 482 at pp. 505 and 506. Emphasis added.

States to another party, the assignee will be entitled to export products bearing that trade mark direct into the assignor's territory.

     2. *The Court's Answer to the Second Question: A Trade Mark Owner in one Member State may not Prevent Sales by a Third Party of Products Placed on the Market in Another Member State by the Owner of an Identical Trade Mark in that State.*

12.48   Similarly, in the light of the Court's judgment in the *Hag* case, it must be recognised that the common origin doctrine applies in circumstances in which a third party imports into one Member State goods which have previously been placed on the market in another Member State bearing an identical trade mark lawfully affixed by its owner in that Member State. In such circumstances, the owner of an identical trade mark in the second Member State will not be able to rely upon his trade mark to prevent the imports by the third party.

12.49   The criticism of the application of the common origin doctrine to forced divestiture situations applies, in large measure, here also. In such cases there is, quite simply, no consent by the original trade mark owner at the time of the subdivision of the trade mark. There can, therefore, be no exhaustion of rights. This said, however, the Court's ruling on this second question is more understandable, because the goods in question had already been lawfully placed on the market, so that it may be argued that thereafter they should be entitled to circulate freely within the Community.

12.50   Moreover, the distinguishing aspect of the *Hag* case, forced divestiture, is in any case an exception. In the more usual common origin situation, namely a straightforward assignment, the subdivision of the trade mark will have come about with the consent of the original assignor.

12.51   In summary, the Court's judgment in the *Hag* case may be difficult to justify on objective grounds, but it remains for the present the only authoritative ruling by the Court of Justice on the application of Articles 30 to 36 in "common origin" situations.

12.52   In these circumstances, one may speculate on the manner in which the European Court would today decide the *Sirena* case. It is likely that the Court would not seek to rely on Article 85 at all, but would instead decide the case in reliance on Articles 30 to 36. The existence of common origin between the "Prep" marks owned by the Italian company and by the German company was established. It is likely, therefore, that the Court would apply similar reasoning to that of its Hag judgment, with the result that Sirena would remain unable to rely upon its Italian trade mark to prevent the import into Italy of shaving cream marketed there by an independent party who had acquired the products once they had been lawfully placed on the market in Germany.

12.53   Certainly, the Commission would consider this the proper result. This much is clear from its decision in *Re Advocaat Zwarte Kip* in which it said:

     "The fact of prohibiting in a Member State trade in a product legally trade marked in another Member State on the sole ground that an identical trademark of the same origin has been registered in the first Member State is incompatible with the provisions of the free movement of goods within the Common Market—namely Articles 30 and 36 of the EEC Treaty."[23]

D. The Common Origin and Third Country Trade Marks

12.54   As has already been mentioned,[24] in its judgment in the EMI cases the Court held that Articles 30 to 36 only apply to trade "between Member States," as distinct from trade with third countries. This is because Articles 30 to 36 are concerned with the free movement of goods *within* the Community, *i.e.* "between Member States."

12.55   It follows that the common origin doctrine will not be relevant where common origin between two identical trade marks exists, but one of the two present trade mark owners is an undertaking established in a third country and its trade mark is only registered outside the Community.

12.56   As the Court said in this connection, with reference to the particular facts involved in the EMI cases:

> "... if the same proprietor holds the trade mark right in respect of the same product in all the Member States there are no grounds for examining whether those marks have a common origin with an identical mark recognised in a third country, since that question is relevant only in relation to considering whether within the Community there are opportunities for partitioning the market."[25]

E. The Position with Regard to Other Intellectual Property

(1) *General*

12.57   Both the *Hag* and the *Advocaat Zwarte Kip* cases were concerned with trade marks. Moreover, in the *Hag* case both the Advocate General and the Court indicated that in their view trade marks were distinguishable from other intellectual property and, at least by implication, in consequence entitled to less protection than other intellectual property. In these circumstances, it is quite possible that the common origin doctrine would be held not to apply to intellectual property other than trade marks.

12.58   It is submitted that in such circumstances the common origin doctrine should not be applied to other intellectual property in the same way as it has been applied to trade marks. The point is, however, undecided, except in relation to performing rights as an element of copyright, where services rather than goods are the subject of protection.

---

[23] *Advocaat Zwarte Kip* [1974] 2 C.M.L.R. D. 79 and D. 84.
[24] See discussion *supra*, at paras. 8.98 *et seq.*
[25] *EMI Records Ltd.* [1976] 2 C.M.L.R. 235 at p. 265.

(2) *The Position with regard to Performing Rights as an Element of Copyright*

12.58.1 It is perhaps ironic that the only other case decided by the European Court having a direct bearing on the common origin doctrine is the *Coditel* case.[25a] Unlike the *Hag* case the *Coditel* case was not concerned with intellectual property having a common origin in the context of goods but rather with intellectual property having a common origin in the context of services, namely performing rights as an element of copyright. Accordingly, the relevant provisions of the Treaty were Articles 59 and 60,[25b] rather than Articles 30 to 36.

F. THE CODITEL CASE

12.58.2 **The facts.** By a 1969 contract the producer of a film granted to a Belgian film distributor ("Ciné Vog") the exclusive right for a period of seven years to exhibit the film in Belgium in cinemas and by television broadcasts, on condition that the right to broadcast the film on television in Belgium could not be exercised for a period of 40 months from the date of the first exhibit of the film in a cinema. The film was first exhibited on May 15, 1970.

12.58.3 At a later date the film producer assigned the right to broadcast the film on television in Germany to a German broadcasting station. The film was so broadcast in Germany on January 5, 1971, and the Belgian Cable Television Company, Coditel, received the transmission at its reception sites in Belgium and distributed the film by cable to its Belgian subscribers.

12.58.4 Proceedings were instituted before the Belgian Courts by Ciné Vog and others against the Coditel companies on the grounds that by relaying the German broadcast to their Belgian subscribers they were infringing Ciné Vog's Belgian copyright. At first instance, the Coditel companies were held to have infringed Ciné Vog's copyright, and they appealed to the Brussels Cour d'Appel. Before the Cour d'Appel the Coditel companies argued, *inter alia*, that the exercise by Ciné Vog of the exclusive right granted to it contravened Articles 59 *et seq.* of the Treaty, relating to the free movement of services.

12.58.5 By judgment of March 30, 1979, the Cour d'Appel concluded that Ciné Vog's copyright was infringed by the action of the Coditel companies, but it nonetheless stayed the proceedings and referred two questions to the European Court, the material one of which was in the following terms:

"... is it in accordance with the provisions of the Treaty on freedom to

---

[25a] Case 62/79 *Coditel SA and Others* v. *Ciné Vog Films SA* (unreported). Note also, however, the related case: Case 52/79 *Procureur du Roi* v. *Debauve and Others,* Case 155/73 judgment of March 18, 1980. See also *The State* v. *Sacchi* [1974] E.C.R. 409; [1974] 2 C.M.L.R. 177.

[25b] See discussion, *supra*, Chap. 7 at paras. 7.34 *et seq.*

provide services for the assignee of the performing right in a cinematographic film in one Member State to rely upon his right in order to prevent the defendant from showing that film in that State by means of cable television where the film thus shown is picked up by the defendant in the said Member State after having been broadcast by a third party in another Member State with the consent of the original owner of the right?"[25c]

12.58.6   **The Court's reasoning.** The Court found it unnecessary to refer expressly to the common origin doctrine in its judgment, although the Coditel companies had argued that the doctrine should be applied by analogy. Its starting point was the proposition that the question put to it raised the issue "of whether Articles 59 and 60 of the Treaty prohibit an assignment, limited to the territory of a Member State, of the copyright in a film, in view of the fact that a series of such assignments might result in the partitioning of the Common Market as regards the undertaking of economic activity in the film industry."[25d]

12.58.7   The Court then noted that there is an essential difference between the manner in which a film is made available to the public and the manner in which other categories of literary and artistic works protected by copyright are made available to the public: while the former are made available to the public by "performance," the latter are distributed by selling the relevant tangible objects, *e.g.* books or records. Relying on this factual difference, the Court reasoned that the owner of copyright in a film has "a legitimate interest" in calculating fees due in relation to numbers of performances, and in ensuring that a televised broadcast of the film will only take place after it has been exhibited in cinemas. It therefore concluded that the

---

[25c] The basis of the Cour d'Appel's judgment so far as infringement of copyright was concerned is summarised by the European Court in the following terms:

"The Cour d'Appel based its decision upon the Berne Convention on the Protection of Literary and Artistic Works in the revised Brussels version of 26 June 1948 approved by the Belgian Law of 26 June 1951 and in particular upon the first paragraph of Article 11 bis, which is worded as follows:

'Authors of literary and artistic works shall have the exclusive right of authorizing:
  (i) The radio-diffusion of their works or the communication thereof to the public by any other means of wireless diffusion of signs, sounds or images;
  (ii) Any communication to the public, whether over wires or not, of the radio-diffusion of the work, when this communication is made by a body other than the original one;
  (iii) The communication to the public by loudspeaker or any other similar instrument transmitting, by signs, sounds or images the radio-diffusion of the work.'
The Cour d'Appel ruled that that provision was applicable in the case before it and declared that the cable television undertakings must be considered as a body 'separate' from the broadcaster of the film, namely the German broadcasting station, and that the communication of the film to Belgian viewers was a communication 'to the public' as understood in the said provision."

[25d] *Ibid.* at para. 11.

specific object[25e] of such a performing right includes the right of the copyright owner and his assignees to require fees for each performance of a film, precisely because the owner of the performing right receives royalties based on performances rather than royalties based on initial sales of tangible objects.

12.58.8 The Court's reasoning in this regard is of sufficient importance to warrant setting out in full:

> "A cinematographic film belongs to the category of literary and artistic works made available to the public by performances which may be infinitely repeated. In this respect the problems involved in the observance of copyright in relation to the requirements of the Treaty are not the same as those which arise in connection with literary and artistic works the placing of which at the disposal of the public is inseparable from the circulation of the *material form* of the works, as in the case of books and records.
>
> In these circumstances the owner of the copyright in a film and his assigns have a legitimate interest in calculating the fees due in respect of the authorisation to exhibit the film on the basis of the actual or probable number of performances and in authorising a television broadcast of the film only after it has been exhibited in cinemas for a certain period of time....
>
> These facts ... highlight the fact that the right of a copyright owner and his assigns to require fees for any showing of a film is part of the essential function of copyright in this type of literary and artistic work."[25f]

12.58.9 Having thus analysed the essential nature of such performing rights the Court returned to the question before it. Although there is no equivalent of Article 36 in the free movement of services provisions of the Treaty, the Court appears to have applied the doctrines which it has developed in the context of that article by analogy, in order to permit derogations from the prohibition on restraints against the free movement of services established by Articles 59 and 60 of the Treaty. Indeed, using wording strikingly similar to that which it had repeatedly used in the context of the free movement of goods provisions of the Treaty, the Court said:

> "Whilst Article 59 of the Treaty prohibits restrictions upon freedom to provide services, it does not thereby encompass limits upon the exercise of certain economic activities which have their origin in the application of national legislation for the protection of intellectual property, *save where such application constitutes a means of arbitrary discrimination or a disguised restriction on trade between Member*

[25e] The Court in fact refers in this judgment to "essential function." It is thought, however, that the terms "essential function" and "specific object" of intellectual property are used interchangeably.

[25f] *Ibid.* at para. 12.14.

States. Such would be the case if that application enabled parties to an assignment of copyright to create artificial barriers to trade between Member States."[25g]

2.58.10 Although the above passage and those which follow it are less than clear, the Court appears to have reasoned that because the right to require royalties on the performance of a film protected by copyright is inherent to it, *i.e.* is part of the essential function or specific object of this type of copyright, even where it operates as a restriction on the free movement of services the exercise of this right escapes the prohibition on such restrictions imposed by Articles 59 *et seq.* unless such exercise amounts to either:

   (i) A means of arbitrary discrimination or,

   (ii) A disguised restriction on trade between Member States.

This will not be the case merely because the geographical limit of a particular assignment of performing rights coincides with national frontiers.[25h]

2.58.11 Consequently, the Court concluded in favour of Ciné Vog, holding that "the exclusive assignee of the performing right in a film for the whole of a Member State may therefore rely upon his right against cable television diffusion companies which have transmitted that film on their diffusion network having received it from a television broadcasting station established in another Member State, without thereby infringing Community Law."[25i]

G. The Implications of the Coditel Case

2.58.12 It is too early to predict the extent to which the Court would be prepared to extend its reasoning in the Coditel case to other situations involving performing rights as an element of copyright. The Court established, however, that the specific object of a performing right as an element of copyright may well be different from the specific object of other categories of copyright attaching to goods. Also, assignments of such a performing right will be governed by Articles 59 *et seq.* of the Treaty relating to services, rather than by the provisions concerning the free movement of goods.[25j] In consequence of these factors, it is at least clear that:

   (i) The common origin doctrine is unlikely to apply to such assignments.

   (ii) In deciding whether the exercise of a performing right under domestic legislation to enforce a territorial assignment will infringe

---

[25g] *Ibid.* at para. 15. Emphasis added.

[25h] *Ibid.* at para. 16.

[25i] *Ibid.* at para. 17.

[25j] On this point note also the opinion of Advocate General J.P. Warner, and Case 52/79 *Procureur du Roi* v. *Debauve and Others* judgment of March 18, 1980; 155/73 *Sacchi* [1974] E.C.R. 409; [1974] 2 C.M.L.R. 177.

Article 59, regard will be had to doctrines akin to those developed in applying Article 36 to intellectual property relating to goods.

(iii) At least in the form in which the exhaustion doctrine has been applied in the context of Articles 30 to 36, this has no application to performing rights as an element of copyright. One can imagine, however, that the doctrine might re-surface in this context in a modified form.

IV. *ASSIGNMENT AND ARTICLE 86*

A. GENERAL REMARKS

12.59 Where an assignment is made in favour of a party which is in a dominant position, Article 86 may be relevant. In particular, any terms or conditions imposed by the assignee in connection with the assignment must not be such as to amount to an abuse of the assignee's dominant position, within the meaning of Article 86.

12.60 The *SABAM* case[26] provides an interesting example of abusive conduct in this context.

B. SABAM AND RELATED CASES

12.61 SABAM is a Elgian Copyright co-operative association, having as its object the exploitation, administration and management of copyright and kindred rights, on its own behalf, and on behalf of its members, associates, clients and affiliated undertakings. In general, these are authors, composers and publishers. SABAM concluded standard form contracts with a composer and a songwriter, under which they were required to assign and transfer to SABAM their copyright in all their present and future compositions, as well as their present and future rights as performers and producers of gramophone records. Complex litigation eventually ensued before the Belgian Courts, and among the issues raised was the enforceability of certain provisions in SABAM's standard form contracts. In consequence, the Belgian proceedings were stayed, and a number of questions were referred to the European Court. The first two of these were in the following terms:

"1. Can the fact that an undertaking which enjoys a de facto monopoly in a Member State for the management of copyrights requires the global assignment of all such rights without drawing any distinction between specific categories be regarded as an abuse of a dominant position within the meaning of Article 86 of the EEC Treaty?

---

[26] *Belgische Radio En Televisie* v. *Société Belge Des Auteurs, Compositeurs et Editeurs (SABAM) and NV Fonior*; Case 127/73 *SABAM* v. *NV Fonior* [1974] E.C.R. 313; [1974] 2 C.M.L.R. 238.

2. Can abuse of a dominant position also consist in the fact that such an undertaking stipulates that an author shall assign his present and future rights, and in particular in the fact that, without having to give an account of its action, that undertaking may continue to exercise the rights assigned for five ... years following the withdrawal of the member?"[27]

12.62   The Court found that the answer to both questions depended upon whether SABAM was either directly or indirectly imposing unfair trading conditions, within the meaning of Article 86 (2) (*a*).[27a] It recognised that a balance must be struck between the desirability of maximum freedom for authors, composers and publishers to dispose of their work as they see fit, and the requirements of effective management of their rights by an undertaking such as SABAM, bearing in mind that, in practice authors have no alternative but to join. In the same vein, it accepted that for SABAM to perform its functions effectively it "must enjoy a position based on the assignment in its favour, by the associated authors, of their rights *to the extent required* for the association to carry out its activity on the necessary scale."[28]

12.63   The Court went on to emphasise, however, that the terms and conditions imposed by SABAM must be considered, with a view to ascertaining whether they were in all respects absolutely necessary to the attainment of SABAM's objectives, having regard to the interests of individual authors and, in particular, their interest in the right to dispose of their own works as they see fit. It continued:

"... a compulsory assignment of all copyrights, both present and future, no distinction being drawn between the different generally accepted types of exploitation, may appear an unfair condition, especially if such assignment is required for an extended period after the member's withdrawal."[29]

12.64   The Court concluded that conduct of the type engaged in by SABAM and not essential to SABAM's objectives might well constitute an abuse of dominant position within the meaning of Article 86, but held that it is for the National Court to decide whether such an "abuse" has taken place having regard to the criteria set out in its judgment.

12.65   More recently, in the *Greenwich Film Production* case,[30] the Court had to consider whether Article 86 could have been infringed by similar compulsory assignments in favour of the French performing rights society SACEM, in circumstances in which the royalties at issue related exclusively

---

[27] *Ibid.* at p. 243.
[27a] See discussion in Chap. 5, *supra*, at paras. 5.37 *et seq.*
[28] *Ibid.* at p. 283 emphasis added.
[29] *Ibid.* at pp. 283 and 284.
[30] Case 22/79 *Greenwich Film Production, Paris* v. *Société des Auteurs, Compositeurs et Editeurs de Musique (SACEM) and Société des Editions Labrador, Paris* [1980] 1 C.M.L.R. 629.

to film exhibitions outside the EEC. The Court concluded that Article 86 could be infringed even in such circumstances. It stated:

"... in certain Member States the management of composers' copyrights is usually entrusted by composers to associations whose object is to supervise the exercise of such rights and to collect the corresponding royalties on behalf of any composer working within the territory of the Member State in question. It is possible in those circumstances that the activities of such associations may be conducted in such a way that their effect is to partition the Common Market and thereby restrict the freedom to provide services which constitutes one of the objectives of the Treaty. Such activities are thus capable of affecting trade between Member States within the meaning of Article 86 of the Treaty, even if the management of copyrights, in certain cases, relates only to the performance of musical works in non-Member Countries. In considering whether Article 86 is applicable the performance of certain contracts cannot be assessed in isolation but must be viewed in the light of the activities of the undertaking in question as a whole.

It is clear from the foregoing that where an association exploiting composers' copyrights is to be regarded as an undertaking abusing a dominant position within the Common Market or in a substantial part of it, the fact that such abuse, in certain cases, relates only to the performance in non-Member Countries of contracts entered into in the territory of a Member State by parties within the jurisdiction of that State does not preclude the application of Article 86 of the Treaty."[31]

12.66   The Court's judgments in the *SABAM* and *Greenwich Film Production* cases were very much in line with the Commission's earlier decision in *Re GEMA*.[32] The facts in *Re GEMA* were again very similar to those in the *SABAM* case, in that the Commission was concerned with the conduct of the German authors rights society, GEMA, which had similar objectives to those of SABAM and also enjoyed a dominant position. The Commission, having instituted proceedings against GEMA, concluded that various provisions of its constitution and standard form assignment infringed Article 86, including among others, provisions in its standard form assignment which:

(i) required the assignor to give notice to GEMA of a change in his or her nationality.

(ii) restricted the assignor's freedom to assign to GEMA or another authors' rights society all or part of its rights for countries in which GEMA is not directly active.

---

[31] *Ibid.* at pp. 644–645.
[32] *Re GEMA* [1971] C.M.L.R. D. 35.

(iii) restricted the assignor from dividing his rights by category and between several authors' rights societies in countries in which GEMA does carry on direct activity.

(iv) restricted the assignor from withdrawing from GEMA the administration of certain categories of the assignor's rights after giving due notice.

(v) resulted, in effect, in the extension of copyright by contractual means to musical works which are not covered by copyright.

12.67   The Court's judgment in the *SABAM* and *Greenwich Film Production* cases and the Commission's earlier decision in *Re GEMA* are no more than examples of the many situations in which the terms of an assignment may be effected by the fact that the assignee is in a dominant position. Where the assignee is in a dominant position, there is always the possibility that his very insistence on the inclusion of certain terms in an assignment will constitute an abuse of his dominant position.

C. The Position with Regard to Other Intellectual Property

12.68   The principles illustrated in the *SABAM*, *Greenwich Film Production* and *GEMA* cases are of general applicability, so that they would apply by analogy to other types of intellectual property, in the same way as they were applied in the context of copyright in those cases.[33]

---

[33] Similar principles were, for example, applied by the Commission in the *Eurofima* case which was concerned with patents. See discussion *supra*, at paras. 5.40 *et seq.*

Part V

The Patent Conventions and the Trade Mark Regulation

CHAPTER 13

INTRODUCTION

I. *GENERAL*

13.01 Part V is concerned with the extent to which Articles 30 to 36, 85 and 86 of the Treaty are likely to affect the following types of intellectual property:
  (i) European Patents granted pursuant to the European Patent Convention[1];
  (ii) Community Patents granted pursuant to the Community Patent Convention[2];
  (iii) Community Trade marks granted pursuant to the Draft Council Regulation on the Community Trade Mark.[3]

13.02 No attempt will be made here to consider in any detail the nature of the rights granted under these instruments, nor to analyse them comprehensively. Any such exercise would be outside the scope of this book.[4]

13.03 It may, nonetheless, be helpful to note the present status of each instrument, and to outline briefly the rights which may be obtained pursuant to it.

II. *THE EUROPEAN PATENT CONVENTION ("EPC")*

13.04 The EPC was signed in Munich by 16 European States in 1973, and came into force on October 7, 1977.[5] All EEC Member States were at the time signatories, and all except Denmark and Eire have ratified the Convention.[5a] Under the EPC a European Patent Office was established, in Munich, with a branch in The Hague.

13.05 Essentially the EPC makes it possible to apply to the European Patent

---

[1] Convention on the Grant of European Patents (European Patent Convention), reprinted in, *e.g.* European Patent Handbook (by the Chartered Institute of Patent Agents), Oyez Publishing, London, Mathew Bender, New York, 1978, Chap. 51.

[2] Convention for the European Patent for the Common Market (Community Patent Convention) O.J. 1976, L17.

[3] Proposal for a First Council Regulation on Community Trade Marks O.J. 1980, C351; [1981] 1 C.M.L.R. 365. Note that the Commission on the same date proposed a complimentary First Council Directive to Approximate the Laws of the Member States Relating to Trade Marks.

[4] A useful treatment of the two patent conventions may be found in the European Patents Handbook, *ibid.*

[5] Written Question No. 567/77, submitted by Mr. Couste, Member of the European Parliament, to the Commission of the European Communities O.J. 1977, C277, p. 24. It has been possible to file European patent applications since June 1, 1978: Written Question No. 246/78 submitted by Mr. Couste, Member of the European Parliament, to the Commission of the European Communities O.J. 1978, C210, p. 10.

[5a] As at December 31, 1980, Greece had signed but not ratified the Convention.

Office for the grant of a European Patent having effect in each of the Contracting States designated by the applicant in his application. If a European Patent is granted, it has the same effect as a national patent *in each of the designated states*.[6] Indeed, the effect of a European Patent in a Contracting State for which it is granted is concisely stated in Article 2 (2) of the EPC, as follows: "The European Patent shall, in each of the Contracting States for which it is granted, have the effect of and be subject to the same conditions as a national patent granted by that state, unless otherwise provided in this Convention." In essence, therefore, the EPC enables the applicant to obtain a basket of national patents.

13.06 There is an exception to this rule, however, in the case of the Member States of the EEC. Once the Community Patent Convention is in force, designation of any one EEC country by an applicant for a European Patent will be deemed to constitute designation of all the EEC Member States jointly for a Community Patent, *unless the application is made during a transitional period and specifically states that a Community Patent is not desired*.[7]

III. THE COMMUNITY PATENT CONVENTION ("CPC")

13.07 Unlike the EPC, the CPC is not yet in force. Indeed, it may well not come into force for a considerable period of time.[8]

13.08 By contrast with the EPC, the CPC provides for the grant of a unitary patent throughout all the EEC Member States.[9] Because of its unitary nature, a Community Patent will be a distinct part of a European Patent where a patent is requested for both EEC Member States and non-EEC Member States. Similarly, where only EEC Member States are involved, the Community Patent will be a particular type of European Patent.[10]

13.09 The relationship between European Patents and Community Patents is concisely set out in Article 2 of the Community Patent Convention, which states as follows:

"1. European Patents granted for the Contracting States shall be called Community Patents.

2. Community Patents shall have a unitary character. They shall have equal effect throughout the territories to which this conven-

---

[6] Arts. 2, 3 and 79. Author's italics.

[7] See Art. 142 EPC and Art. 86 (1) and (4) CPC. Author's italics. Note that the applicant will only be entitled to indicate that he does not wish a Community Patent during a transitional period, which may be terminated by a decision of the Council of the European Communities. See discussion, *infra*, at para. 13.11.

[8] This is principally because entry into force of the CPC is conditional upon the EPC first entering into force in respect of all EEC Member States, (see Art. 98 CPC). Thus, the refusal of Denmark and Eire to ratify the EPC automatically results in a *de facto* veto over entry into force of the CPC (see para. 13.04 above).

[9] See Art. 95, CPC.

[10] Convention for the European Patent for the Common Market, *supra*, n. 2.

tion applies and may only be granted, transferred, revoked, or allowed to lapse in respect of the whole of such territories. The same shall apply mutatis mutandis to applications for European Patents in which the Contracting States are designated.

3. Community Patents shall have an autonomous character. They shall be subject only to the provisions of this Convention and those provisions of the European Patent Convention which are binding upon every European Patent and which shall consequently be deemed to be provisions of this Convention."[10]

13.10   Thus, the Community Patent will in effect be a European Patent which in the EEC Member States enjoys a unitary character and is governed by the provisions of the CPC.[11]

13.11   The CPC does, however, envisage that once it comes into effect there will be a transitional period, during which it will be possible to obtain a European Patent in respect of one or more Member States of the Community. During this transitional period, this may be accomplished by designating in an EPC application those Member States of the Community for which a European Patent is desired, and at the same time specifying that a Community Patent is not desired.[12] The transitional period, during which these special arrangements are permissible, "... may be terminated by decision of the Council of the European Communities, acting on a proposal from the Commission of the European Communities or from a Contracting Member State."[13]

13.12   As will be explained in Chapter 14,[14] however, certain provisions of the CPC will apply to a European Patent granted during the transitional period in respect of one or more designated countries, even when the applicant has specified that a Community Patent is not required.

IV. *THE DRAFT COUNCIL REGULATION ON THE COMMUNITY TRADE MARK*

13.13   The Draft Council Regulation on the Community Trade Mark is unlikely to be adopted by the Council of Ministers for some considerable time and,

---

[11] Such a variation of the European Patent is specifically envisaged by Art. 142 (1) of the European Patent Convention. The implementation of the CPC in the United Kingdom is provided for by s. 86, Patents Act 1977 (See also ss. 87 and 88 of that Act). In particular, s. 86 (1) of the Patents Act 1977 provides: "(1) All rights, powers, liabilities, obligations and restrictions from time to time created or arising by or under the Community Patent Convention and all remedies and procedures from time to time provided for by or under that Convention shall by virtue of this section have legal effect in the United Kingdom and shall be used there, be recognised and available in law and be enforced, allowed and followed accordingly."

[12] Art. 86 (1) and (4), Community Patent Convention. See also discussion, *supra*, at para. 13.06.

[13] Art. 86 (4) Community Patent Convention.

[14] See discussion in Chap. 14, at paras. 14.24 *et seq.*

quite possibly, without further amendments being made to the present draft in the meantime.

13.14   Very briefly, the present draft regulation[15] envisages a Community Trade Mark being available for goods and services[16] which could only be registered for the whole of the Community and which would have effect throughout the Community. Further, it provides that "... a Community trade mark shall not be transferred or surrendered or be the subject of a decision revoking the rights of the proprietor or declaring it invalid, nor shall its use be prohibited, save in respect of the entire area of the Community."[17] Thus, like the Community Patent, the Community Trade Mark would be unitary in character.

13.15   The proposed Community Trade Mark would be administered through a Community Trade Mark Office.[18, 19] It would be acquired by registration[20] and subsist "... subject to serious use in the Common Market ... in connection with the goods or services in respect of which it is registered, unless there exists legitimate reasons for not doing so."[21]

13.16   Most importantly for present purposes, Article 10 of the draft regulation specifies the rights which would be conferred by the Community Trade Mark in the following terms:

> "(1) A Community trade mark confers on the proprietor exclusive rights therein. The proprietor shall be entitled to prohibit any third party from using in the course of trade, save with his consent:
>
>   (a) any sign which is identical with or similar to the Community trade mark in relation to goods or services which are identical with or similar to those for which the Community trade mark is registered, where such use involves a serious likelihood of confusion on the part of the public;
>
>   (b) any sign which is identical with or similar to the Community trade mark in relation to goods or services which are not similar to those for which the Community trade mark is registered, where the Community trade mark is of wide repute and use of that sign is detrimental to that repute.

---

[15] Proposal for a First Council Regulation on Community Trade Marks App. 15. The present draft was preceded by Working Document No. 11, D.G. III/0. 753/78 of July/78 which was preceded by the Commission's Memorandum on the creation of an EEC trade mark and the Preliminary Draft of a Convention for a European Trade Mark, published in 1973.

[16] Art. 1 (1).

[17] Art. 1 (2).

[18, 19] Art. 2.

[20] Art. 5.

[21] Art. 13 (1).

(2) Use of the following kinds, *inter alia,* may be prohibited under paragraph (1):

    (a) affixing the sign to the goods or to the packaging thereof;

    (b) putting the goods on the market under that sign, or supplying services thereunder;

    (c) using the sign on business correspondence or invoices."

13.17 Furthermore, the above rights would only have effect as against third parties from the date of publication of the registration of the trade mark.[22]

13.18 Finally, except where the draft regulation otherwise provides, the Community Trade Mark would be dealt with as a national trade mark of that Member State of the European Community with which the applicant has the closest connection, determined in accordance with the specified criteria.[23]

---

[22] Art. 8 (3). Note, however, that certain limited rights to compensation would accrue to the proprietor of the trade mark, with effect from the date of publication of the application for the trade mark.

[23] Art. 16.

CHAPTER 14

THE TREATY AND THE EUROPEAN PATENT,
THE COMMUNITY PATENT AND THE
COMMUNITY TRADE MARK

I. *GENERAL*

14.01 This chapter is concerned with the effect of the provisions of the Treaty
concerned with Competition and the Free Movement of Goods on respectively the European Patent, the Community Patent, and the Community
Trade Mark. Thus, the effects on these three types of intellectual property
of Articles 85, 86 and 30 to 36 will be considered in turn.

14.02 It must be borne in mind, however, that to date only the European
Patent is a reality. Both the Community Patent and the Community Trade
Mark are, for the time being, moribund.[1] It is quite possible, therefore, that
the remarks which follow concerning the Community Patent and the
Community Trade Mark will require reappraisal in due course.

II. *ARTICLES 85 AND 86 AND THE EUROPEAN PATENT,
THE COMMUNITY PATENT AND THE COMMUNITY
TRADE MARK*

A. GENERAL

14.03 It will be recalled that Article 85 is concerned with agreements, decisions
and concerted practices which prevent, restrict or distort competition
within the Common Market and which affect trade between Member
States,[2] and that Article 86 is concerned with distortions of competition
resulting from abuse by one or more undertakings of a dominant position
within the Common Market.[3] The impact of these two Articles on national
intellectual property has been discussed above.[4]

14.04 The question to be considered in this section is whether Articles 85 and
86 will generally have the same effect on European Patents, Community
Patents and Community Trade Marks as they do on analogous national
intellectual property. To the extent that they will have the same effect, what

---

[1] See, *supra*, Chap. 13, at paras. 13.04, 13.07 and 13.13.
[2] See, generally, Chap. 4.
[3] See, generally, Chap. 5.
[4] For discussion concerning Art. 85, see generally Chaps. 4 and 11; for discussion concerning Art. 86, see generally Chaps. 5, 8 (at paras. 8.103 *et seq.*) and 12 (at paras. 12.59 *et seq.*).

has been said above concerning the application of Articles 85 and 86 on national intellectual property will be equally true in the context of European intellectual property.

B. ARTICLES 85 AND 86 AND THE EUROPEAN PATENT

14.05 The EPC is by no means solely concerned with the European Community and, as might in consequence be expected, it contains no express reference to the competition provisions of the Treaty. It is, however, clear from Article 64 of the EPC that a European Patent confers only the same rights as does a national patent. Article 64 is entitled "Rights Conferred by a European Patent," and it states:

(i) A European Patent shall, subject to the provisions of Paragraph 2, confer on its proprietor from the date of publication of the mention of its grant, in each Contracting State in respect of which it is granted, the same rights as would be conferred by a national patent granted in that State.

(ii) If the subject-matter of the European Patent is a process, the protection conferred by the Patent shall extend to the Products directly obtained by such process.

(iii) Any infringement of a European Patent shall be dealt with by national patent law.[5]

14.06 If a European Patent enjoys only "the same rights as would be conferred by a national patent," it follows that the competition provisions of the Treaty will affect the exercise of European Patent rights to the same extent as they affect the exercise of national patent rights. In particular, Article 85 will apply to licences and assignments of a European Patent in the same way as to licences and assignments of a national patent[6] and, similarly, Article 86 will apply to an owner or assignee of a European Patent who is in a dominant position within the Common Market in the same way as it does when the owner or assignee of a national patent is in a dominant position within the Common Market.[7]

14.07 It must be borne in mind, however, that once the CPC is in force, an application for a European Patent will automatically result in a Community Patent being granted if at least one EEC country has been designated in the application, except where the application for a European Patent is made during the transitional period and specifically states that a Community Patent is not desired.[8] It follows that when an application for a European Patent results in a Community Patent being granted the position with

---

[5] Convention on the Grant of European Patents (European Patent Convention) reprinted in, *e.g.* European Patent Handbook (by the Chartered Institute of Patent Agents).
[6] See, generally, Chaps. 11 and 12, paras. 12.04 *et seq.*
[7] See, generally, Chap. 8 at paras. 8.103 *et seq.* and Chap. 12 at paras. 12.59 *et seq.*
[8] See, *supra*, at paras. 13.06 and 13.11.

regard to the application of Articles 85 and 86 will be governed by the relevant provisions of the CPC, as explained below.

C. ARTICLES 85 AND 86 AND THE COMMUNITY PATENT

14.08 Two provisions of the CPC must be contrasted, namely Article 43 entitled "Contractual Licensing" and Article 93, entitled "Precedence of the Provisions of the Treaty establishing the European Economic Community."

14.09 The first two paragraphs of Article 43 state, respectively:

> "1. A Community Patent may be licensed in whole or in part for the whole or part of the Territory in which it is effective. A licence may be exclusive or non-exclusive.
>
> 2. The rights conferred by the Community Patent may be invoked against a licensee who contravenes any restriction in his licence which is covered by paragraph 1."[9]

14.10 On the face of it, Article 43 (1) provides that a licence of a Community Patent within the EEC may be geographically limited to specified territories and may be exclusive. Article 43 (2) would appear to go even further. For example, a licensor would appear to be entitled to rely upon his patent to prevent a licensee from exporting outside his licensed territory, when that licensed territory is less than the whole of the Common Market.

14.11 By contrast with these provisions, Article 93 states succinctly: "No provision of this convention may be invoked against the application of any provision of the Treaty establishing the European Economic Community."[10]

14.12 The apparent irreconcilability of these two provisions was discussed at length in the Commission's Fifth Report on Competition Policy. The Commission there stated:

> "11. The Convention for the European Patent for the Common Market, signed in Luxembourg on December 15, 1975, contains rules on patent licences. Article 43 (1) reads: 'A Community Patent may be licensed in whole or in part for the whole or part of the territories in which it is effective. A licence may be exclusive or non-exclusive.' Article 43 (2) continues: 'The rights conferred by the Community Patent may be invoked against a licensee who contravenes any restriction in his licence which is covered by paragraph 1.'
>
> In the course of the deliberations on the Convention, the Commission stated that the grant of an exclusive licence may fall within the scope of Article 85 of the Treaty, so that its legality would have to be assessed in the light of Article 85 (3). The Commission was not able to give its approval to Article 43 (2), since these provisions allow infringement proceedings to be

---

[9] Convention for the European Patent for the Common Market (Community Patent Convention) O.J. 1976, L17, at p. 12.

[10] *Ibid.* at p. 24. It is noteworthy that Art. 14 refers only to goods, as distinct from services.

brought against a licensee who supplies patented goods to customers outside his allotted territory but within the Common Market. The Commission's view is that the existence of the patent in no case gives the holder the right to shield one licensee against competition from another.

A clause in a contract prohibiting a licensee from supplying the territory of another licensee may be taken to be within the prohibition in Article 85 (1), and qualify for exemption only if the tests of Article 85 (3) are satisfied, and then only for a limited period.

The Commission has recently expressed its view in its decision of 2 December 1975, in AOIP v. Beyrard. It will be for the Court of Justice of the European Communities to resolve this difficulty in the final instance."[11]

14.13   For good measure, the Commission confirmed one year later that it "stands by the views which it has already expressed on Article 43 of the Convention for the European Patent for the Common Market."[12]

Only the passage of time and the adoption of the CPC will tell whether the European Court will adopt the views of the Commission or whether, instead, it will conclude that the competition provisions of the Treaty do not apply to a Community Patent in the same way as they do to a national patent. It is thought likely, however, that the Court will endorse the view expressed by the Commission. Certainly, such a course would be in line with the previous case law established by the Court in the context of national patents, and there would seem no obvious reason why a distinction should be made merely because a Community Patent is involved.

14.14   Admittedly, one can at this stage do no more than speculate. It is possible, however, that the European Court will seek to reconcile Articles 43 and 93 by, on the one hand, affirming that the competition rules are only infringed when the restrictive effects resulting from a licensor's actions are "appreciable" and, on the other hand, emphasising that provisions of the type envisaged by Article 43 may require notification and application for exemption pursuant to Article 85 (3) EEC.[13]

D. ARTICLES 85 AND 86 AND THE COMMUNITY TRADE MARK

14.15   The draft Council Regulation on the Community Trade Mark envisages that a Community Trade Mark could only be assigned in respect of the Common Market as a whole, though it would be possible to transfer the trade mark in respect of some only of the goods or services for which it is registered.[14]

---

[11] Fifth Report on Competition, pp. 22–23, at para. 11. Note also Johannes, *Industrial Property and Copyright in European Community Law*, Sijthoff, 1976, at pp. 75, 85.
[12] Sixth Report on Competition Policy, p. 18, at para. 4.
[13] See, *supra*, Chap. 4, at paras. 4.47 *et seq.*, 4.61 *et seq.* and 4.114 *et seq.*
[14] Proposal for a Council Regulation on Community Trade Marks, of November 27, 1980, O.J. 1980, C351; [1981] 1 C.M.L.R. 365.

14.16   By contrast, there is no obligation to grant Community wide licences. Article 21 of the Draft Regulation provides in relevant part:

"(1) Licences may be granted in respect of a Community trade mark for some or all of the goods or services for which it is registered.

(2) The rights conferred by a Community trade mark shall not be asserted *vis-à-vis* a licensee unless he operates his licence beyond the period of time for which it was granted or uses the trade mark in relation to goods or services for which it has not been registered or does not comply with the proprietor's instructions concerning the quality of the goods or services."

14.17   As the Commission points out in its commentary to Article 21, this wording is consistent with the granting of territorially limited licences and, equally, such licences may be granted either on an exclusive or a non-exclusive basis.[15]

14.18   There is no doubt, however, that the trade mark owner's right to grant licences in this way remains subject to the competition provisions of the Treaty. This will be the natural consequence of creating a Community Trade Mark by means of a Council regulation, under the authority of Article 235 of the Treaty. The regulation, if adopted, will be a secondary source of Community law deriving its validity solely from the provisions of the Treaty.[16]

14.19   It follows that while a proprietor may grant an exclusive and territorially limited trade mark licence, the licence will be subject to the normal operation of the competition provisions of the Treaty.

14.20   Similarly, it is interesting to note that the draft regulation contains no provisions which on their face appear to be irreconcilable with the competition provisions of the Treaty, such as Article 43 (2) of the CPC.

III. *ARTICLES 30 TO 36 AND THE EUROPEAN PATENT, THE COMMUNITY PATENT AND THE COMMUNITY TRADE MARK*

A. GENERAL

14.21   As discussed in Chapter 7, Articles 30 to 36 are concerned with the "free movement of goods" within the Community. Broadly, Articles 30 to 34 lay down a "basic rule," while Article 36 establishes a qualified exception to that rule. More specifically, Articles 30 to 34 prohibit quantitative restrictions on the import and export of goods between Member States and "all measures having equivalent effect." Article 36 then derogates from that rule in specified circumstances. Article 36 is particularly relevant to any consideration of the way in which the prohibition in Articles 30 to 34

---

[15] *Ibid.* at p. 43.
[16] See, generally, concerning the nature of regulations, *supra*, Chap. 3 at paras. 3.24 *et seq.*

applies to intellectual property, because in certain circumstances it exempts from that prohibition measures "justified on grounds of . . . the protection of commercial and industrial property."

14.22   The general terms of Articles 30 to 36 have already been discussed in Chapter 7, and in succeeding chapters the specific application of those Articles has been discussed with reference to ownership of intellectual property rights by one enterprise in the Community,[17] by two or more enterprises in the Community where no "common origin" is involved[18] and by two such enterprises where "common origin" is involved, *i.e.* in the context of assignments and expropriation.[19]

14.23   This part of Chapter 14 is concerned with the extent to which it may be assumed that Articles 30 to 36 will generally have the same effect on a European Patent, a Community Patent and a Community Trade Mark as they do on analogous national intellectual property.

B. Articles 30 to 36 and the European Patent Convention

14.24 The EPC contains no provisions expressly dealing with the circumstances in which the proprietor of a European Patent will be deemed to have "exhausted" his rights in that patent, so that he cannot rely upon it further against third parties. As has been pointed out, however, Article 64 (1) of the EPC provides that the proprietor of a European Patent enjoys only "the same rights as would be conferred by a national patent."[20]

14.25   Thus, until the CPC comes into force, it should broadly be the case that what has been said above concerning the application of Articles 30 to 36 to national patents will also be true in the context of a European Patent. Once the CPC is in force, however, two consequences for the European Patent must be borne in mind.

14.26   First, as had repeatedly been pointed out,[21] when the CPC comes into force, an application for a European Patent will automatically result in a Community Patent being granted if at least one EEC Member State has been designated in the application unless the application for a European Patent is made during the transitional period and expressly indicates that a Community Patent is not required. Clearly, when a Community Patent is granted the relevant provisions of the CPC will apply as discussed below.

14.27   Secondly, and also as discussed below, certain provisions of the CPC will affect national patents. Because the EPC confers upon a proprietor of a European Patent "the same rights as would be conferred by national patents," it follows that when the CPC comes into force owners of a

---

[17] See, generally, Chap. 8.
[18] See, generally, Chap. 9.
[19] See, generally, Chap. 12, at paras. 12.30 *et seq.*
[20] *Supra*, at para. 14.05.
[21] See, *supra*, at paras. 13.06, 13.11, and 14.07.

European Patent will be affected by those provisions in the same way as will owners of a national patent.

C. ARTICLES 30 TO 36 AND THE COMMUNITY PATENT CONVENTION

(1) *General*

14.28 By contrast with the EPC, the CPC contains express provisions specifying the circumstances in which the proprietor of a Community Patent will be deemed to have "exhausted" the rights conferred by that patent, so that he will not be able to invoke it *vis-à-vis* a third party. The CPC also contains similar provisions dealing with the circumstances in which the proprietor of a national or European Patent will be deemed to have "exhausted" his patent rights, so that he will not be able to rely upon them *vis-à-vis* third parties.

14.29   The provisions of the CPC relating to "exhaustion of rights" will be considered below first with reference to Community Patents and then with reference to national and European Patents.

(2) *Articles 30 to 36 and the Community Patent*

14.30 Article 32 of the CPC is entitled "Exhaustion of the Rights Conferred by the Community Patent," and is of sufficient importance to warrant setting out in full:

> "The rights conferred by a Community Patent shall not extend to acts concerning a product covered by that patent which are done within the territories of the Contracting States after that product has been put on the market in one of these States by the proprietor of the patent or with his express consent, unless there are grounds which, under Community law, would justify the extension to such acts of rights conferred by the patent."[22]

It is difficult to gauge the possible ramifications of this wording. At its simplest it does no more than restate the principle which is common to the *Deutsche Grammophon* and *Centrafarm* cases discussed in Chapter 8,[23] namely that the owner of intellectual property rights in one Member State will not be able to rely upon those rights to prevent the importation into that Member State of goods previously lawfully placed on the market by that same owner or with his consent in another Member State.

14.31   This said, it is noteworthy that, in all the cases in which this principle has been given effect to date, the proprietor of intellectual property rights has been seeking to rely upon them to prevent importation of goods from

---

[22] Convention for the European Patent for the Common Market (Community Patent Convention), at p. 9.
[23] See paras. 8.05–8.79.

another Member State.[24] Indeed, it will be recalled that in the *EMI* v. *CBS* cases the European Court expressly affirmed that Articles 30 to 36 are only relevant to "trade between Member States."[25]

14.32　　Arguably, then, Article 32 of the CPC goes further than does the existing case law of the European Court, because its application is not limited to circumstances in which the proprietor of a Community Patent is seeking in one Member State to prevent imports from another Member State of goods covered by that same patent and placed on the market in that other Member State with his consent. Article 32 might apply, for example, to limit the rights of the proprietor of a Community Patent who is seeking to rely on those rights to enforce a "field of use" restriction *in the country in which the protected goods have first been placed on the market.*[26] This is by no means certain, however, because the exhaustion doctrine established by Article 32 is in that same Article stated not to apply where ". . . there are grounds which, under Community law, would justify the extension to such acts (*i.e.* the acts complained of) of the rights conferred by the Patent." Much will obviously depend on how the European Court applies this wording.

14.33　　Finally, one may speculate on the gloss which the Courts, and in particular the European Court, may place on the reference to the goods being placed on the market with the "express consent" of the patent proprietor, as a condition to the application of the Exhaustion Doctrine. Taking again, as an example, a licence granted with a field of use restriction, if the licensee after disregarding the field of use restriction places the protected goods on the market, query whether such goods would be placed on the market with the "express consent" of the patent proprietor within the meaning of Article 32·CPC. The answer might well depend upon the enforceability of the field of use restriction!

14.34　　More generally, it is likely that the European Court will seek to interpret Article 32 consistently with its existing case law, established when considering the application of Articles 30 to 36 to national patents, to the extent that this is possible when the relevant intellectual property is a Community Patent.

(3) *Articles 30 to 36 and National and European Patents After Adoption of the CPC*

(a) General

14.35　　As has been noted, Article 32 of the CPC is concerned with the circumstances in which the rights conferred by a Community Patent are exhausted.[27] The counterpart to Article 32 in the context of national and European Patents is Article 81 of the CPC.

---

[24] Author's italics.
[25] See, *supra*, para. 8.98.
[26] Author's italics.
[27] See, *supra*, paras. 14.30–14.34.

14.36   Article 81 is entitled simply "Exhaustion of the Rights Conferred by a National Patent." It applies, however, equally to European Patents.[28] It is perhaps a measure of its potential importance that the definition of "infringement" contained in the Patents Act 1977 is expressed to be subject to "... any provisions in the Community Patent Convention relating to the exhaustion of the rights of the proprietor of the patent...."[29]

14.37   The wording of Article 81 (1) parallels in material respects the wording of Article 32. It states:

> "The rights conferred by a national patent in a Contracting State shall not extend to acts concerning a product covered by that patent which are done within the territory of that Contracting State after that product has been put on the market in any Contracting State by the proprietor of the patent or with his express consent, unless there are grounds which, under Community law, would justify the extension to such acts of the rights conferred by the patent."[30]

14.38   All that has been said above regarding the effect of Article 32 on a Community Patent would appear to apply by analogy also with regard to the effect of Article 81 (1) on a national or a European Patent. In particular, the following points are noteworthy.

14.39   First, the wording of Article 81 (1) is explicit to the effect that it will apply to limit the rights conferred by a national or a European Patent even when trade between Member States is not involved. This would appear to follow clearly from the fact that Article 81 (1) applies to limit the rights conferred by a national or European Patent once the protected goods have been placed on the market by the patent owner or with his consent "in *any* Contracting State."[31]

14.40   Secondly, the Exhaustion Doctrine established by Article 81 (1) with reference to a national and European Patent is stated in that same Article not to apply where there are grounds which, under Community Law, would justify the extension of the patent rights to the acts complained of. The wording once again parallels that found in Article 32.[32]

14.41   Thirdly, and like Article 32, Article 81 (1) only applies when the protected goods have been placed on the market "by the proprietor of the patent or with his *express* consent."[33] Again, therefore, one may speculate on exactly where the line will ultimately be drawn between "express consent" and a degree of consent falling short of this.[34]

---

[28] This is so by virtue of the operation of Art. 86 (3) CPC, which provides that references in Art. 81 CPC to a National Patent shall be construed as references to a European Patent.

[29] Patents Act 1977, s. 60 (4).

[30] Convention for the European Patent for the Common Market (Community Patent Convention) O.J. 1976, L17, at p. 21.

[31] Author's italics.

[32] See, *supra*, at para. 14.30.

[33] Author's italics.

[34] See discussion, *supra*, at para. 14.33.

14.42   In addition to the foregoing, it should be noted that where it is sought to rely upon national or European Patent rights to prevent the importation of goods previously placed on the market by the patent owner or with his consent in another Member State, it will be irrelevant that the goods do not enjoy patent protection in that other State, again unless such lack of protection would justify the enforcement of the patent rights "as a matter of Community law." This provision would seem to be in line with the present position under Community Law.[35]

(b) Special considerations where there are two or more national or European Patents

14.43   It has already been emphasised that Article 81 (1) parallels the one to be found in Article 32. It will be appreciated, however, that in the context of national and European Patents there is the possibility that two or more patents will be involved, at least until such time as application for a European Patent in respect of at least one EEC Member State results automatically and necessarily in grant of a Community Patent.[36]

14.44   Article 81 (2) of the CPC is relevant to such situations. It provides:
"Paragraph 1 shall also apply with regard to a product put on the market by the proprietor of a national patent, granted for the same invention in another Contracting State, who has economic connections with the proprietor of the patent referred to in paragraph 1. For the purpose of this paragraph, two persons shall be deemed to have economic connections where one of them is in a position to exert a decisive influence on the other, directly or indirectly, with regard to the exploitation of a patent, or where a third party is in a position to exercise such an influence on both persons."

14.45   The effect of paragraph 81 (2) is that the Exhaustion Doctrine as defined in Article 81 (1) will apply so as to prevent a patent owner in one Member State from exercising his patent rights to prevent imports of patented goods placed on the market in another Member State by another patent owner, provided only that there exist between the two patent proprietors "economic connections."

14.46   The loose definition of "economic connections" contained in the second sentence of Article 81 (2) suggests that the connections may, in fact, fall far short of a parent subsidiary relationship and, indeed, far short of what is normally required to establish "enterprise entity."[37]

14.47   It is noteworthy, however, that where the owner of national or European Patents in two or more Member States has assigned his patent rights in one of those States to a third party who is completely economically independent

---

[35] See, in particular, discussion of the *Deutsche Grammophon and Parke-Davis & Co.* cases, respectively, *supra*, at paras. 8.07 *et seq.* and, *supra*, at paras. 8.80 *et seq.*

[36] See discussion, *supra*, at paras. 13.06, 13.11 and 14.07.

[37] For a discussion of "enterprise entity" see, *supra*, Chap. 4, at paras. 4.30–4.34.

of the assignor, the second sentence of Article 81 (2) would not result in the assignor and the assignee being regarded as having "economic connections" with each other. It would appear that as a result the Exhaustion Doctrine would not apply so as to prevent the assignor from invoking patent rights which he has retained to prevent the import of goods placed on the market in another Member State by the assignee of the relevant patent rights for that State.[38] If this is so, it is in marked contrast to the present position under Community Law in the Trade Mark context as established by the European Court in the Hag case.[39]

C. Articles 30 to 36 and the Community Trade Mark

14.48 Like the CPC, the draft Council Regulation on the Community Trade Mark deals expressly with the circumstances in which the rights conferred by a Community Trade Mark will be exhausted. Article 11, entitled "Limits of the Rights Conferred by the Community Trade Mark," states:

"(1) A Community Trade Mark does not entitle the proprietor to prohibit its use in relation to goods which have been put on the market under that trade mark by the proprietor or with his consent.

(2) Paragraph (1) shall not apply:

(a) Where, the goods having been put on the market outside the Community, the proprietor is legally entitled to oppose their importation into the Community;

(b) Where the condition of the goods is changed or impaired after they have been put on the market;

(c) Where the goods are re-packaged by a third party; but this provision shall not apply where the third party proves that the use made of the trade mark by the proprietor, taking into consideration his system of marketing, tends to fragment the markets artificially and that the re-packaging could not affect the original condition of the goods, if the third party informs the proprietor beforehand that the re-packaged goods are to be put on the market and the new packaging indicates that the goods have been re-packaged by the third party."[40]

14.49 With one important difference, Article 11 (1) does no more than to restate the doctrine already well established by the European Court in

---

[38] Certainly, the European Commission considered such an interpretation a possibility. For this reason it suggested amendments which would make such an interpretation impossible. The Commission's suggested amendments were, however, not incorporated in the CPC as presently drafted. See Commission opinion of September 26, 1975, O.J. 1975, L261/26.

[39] See discussion, *supra*, at paras. 12.30 *et seq.*, and note particularly discussion of paras. 12.57 *et seq.*

[40] Art. 11, Proposal for a Council Regulation on Community Trade Marks, of November 27, 1980, Art. 11 (1), O.J. 1980, C351; [1981] 1 C.M.L.R. 372.

applying Articles 30 to 36 of the Treaty to a line of trade mark cases beginning with *Centrafarm BV* v. *Winthrop BV.*[41] The Court held in that case that the owner of a trade mark in one Member State may not exercise his national trade mark rights so as to prevent the importation of goods having that trade mark from another Member State where they have lawfully been placed on the market by that trade mark owner, or with his consent.[42] The difference is that in all those cases in which the European Court has applied Articles 30 to 36 to date so as to limit the traditional exercise of national trade mark rights, trade between Member States has been involved. By contrast, Article 14 of the proposed regulation does not require that there be trade between Member States at all, in order for the trade mark owner's rights to be limited. In this respect, the draft regulation is similar to the CPC.[43]

14.50   It is more difficult to be categorical about the likely interpretation which the European Court would give to Article 11 (2) (*a*), (*b*) and (*c*).

14.51   With regard to Article 11 (2) (*a*), one can only say at this stage that in principle the Exhaustion Doctrine will clearly apply even when goods are first placed on the market outside of the Community, unless such marketing takes place in circumstances in which "the proprietor is legally entitled to oppose their importation into the Community." The precise interpretation which will be given by the European Court to this phrase is, for the present, a matter of conjecture. In its commentary on Article 11 (2) (*a*), however, the Commission suggests by way of example that the proprietor of a Community trade mark would be able to invoke his trade mark against goods placed on the market in a country outside the Community by a duly appointed licensee, in circumstances in which that country had made it impossible for the licensor to control the quality of the goods produced by his licensee.[43a]

14.52   Turning finally to Article 11 (2) (*b*) and (*c*), the derogation from the basic Exhaustion Doctrine would appear consistent with the European Court's judgment in the *Hoffman-La Roche AG* v. *Centrafarm BV.*[44] At the risk of oversimplification, the Court there held that a trade mark owner may exercise his trade mark rights to prevent importation into one Member State of goods lawfully placed on the market by him or with his consent in another Member State, if the guarantee of origin provided by the mark or the original condition of the goods has been impaired.[45]

---

[41] [1974] E.C.R. 1183; [1974] 2 C.M.L.R. 480.

[42] See discussion, *supra*, at paras. 8.28 *et seq.*

[43] See discussion, *supra*, at paras. 14.28 *et seq.* and at paras. 14.38 *et seq.* Note also Art. 13 of the Proposal for a Council Regulation on Community Trade Marks, and the Commission's Commentary thereto.

[43a] Proposal for a Council Regulation on Community Trade Marks, *ibid.* at pp. 34 and 35.

[44] *Hoffman-La Roche & Co. A G* v. *Centrafarm* [1978] E.C.R. 1139; [1978] 3 C.M.L.R. 217.

[45] See discussion, *supra*, at paras. 8.56 *et seq.* Note also the discussion of *Centrafarm BV* v. *American Home Products Corporation*, *supra*, at paras. 8.73 *et seq.* and the Commission's Commentary of Art. 11 of the Draft Regulation, *ibid.* at pp. 34 and 35.

[The annotations in these Appendices are reproduced by kind permission of our publishers from the *Encyclopedia of European Community Law*]

Treaty Establishing the European Economic Community

ARTICLE 1

By this Treaty, the High Contracting Parties establish among themselves a EUROPEAN ECONOMIC COMMUNITY.

ARTICLE 2

The Community shall have as its task, by establishing a common market and progressively approximating the economic policies of Member States, to promote throughout the Community a harmonious development of economic activities, a continuous and balanced expansion, an increase in stability, an accelerated raising of the standard of living and closer relations between the States belonging to it.

ARTICLE 3

For the purposes set out in Article 2, the activities of the Community shall include, as provided in this Treaty and in accordance with the time-table set out therein:

(a) the elimination, as between Member States, of customs duties and of quantitative restrictions on the import and export of goods, and of all other measures having equivalent effect;

(b) the establishment of a common customs tariff and of a common commercial policy towards third countries;

(c) the abolition, as between Member States, of obstacles to freedom of movement for persons, services and capital;

(d) the adoption of a common policy in the sphere of agriculture;

(e) the adoption of a common policy in the sphere of transport;

(f) the institution of a system ensuring that competition in the common market is not distorted;

(g) the application of procedures by which the economic policies of Member States can be coordinated and disequilibria in their balances of payments remedied;

(h) the approximation of the laws of Member States to the extent required for the proper functioning of the common market;

(i) the creation of a European Social Fund in order to improve employment opportunities for workers and to contribute to the raising of their standard of living;

(j) the establishment of a European Investment Bank to facilitate the economic expansion of the Community by opening up fresh resources;

(k) the association of the overseas countries and territories in order to increase trade and to promote jointly economic and social development.

ARTICLE 5

Member States shall take all appropriate measures, whether general or particular, to ensure fulfilment of the obligations arising out of this Treaty or resulting from action taken by the institutions of the Community. They shall facilitate the achievement of the Community's tasks.

They shall abstain from any measure which could jeopardise the attainment of the objectives of this Treaty.

ELIMINATION OF QUANTITATIVE RESTRICTIONS BETWEEN MEMBER STATES

ARTICLE 30

Quantitative restrictions on imports and all measures having equivalent effect shall, without prejudice to the following provisions, be prohibited between Member States.

GENERAL NOTE

Quantitative restrictions (sometimes called "quotas") are measures designed to limit imports of particular classes of goods by reference to their number, weight, value or other quantitative criteria.

Measures having equivalent effect is a flexible phrase in this context. Some guidance as to its scope can be found in the answers to Written Question 118, J.O. 1967, 122 and 901.

In *State* v. *Cornet* [1965] C.M.L.R. 105, the Cour d'Appel de Lyon held that an obligation to obtain import licences does not constitute a quantitative restriction or a measure having equivalent effect within the meaning of Arts. 30 and 31 if the licences are granted automatically. Subsequently, the French Cour de Cassation held that the infliction of criminal penalties upon those who import without licence goods which are in free circulation in the common market does not constitute a measure equivalent to a quantitative restriction within the meaning of Arts. 30 and 31 (*State* v. *Cornet* [1967] C.M.L.R. 351). More recently the Court of Justice has held that an "all licences granted" system was compatible with this part of the Treaty (*International Fruit Company NV* v. *Produktschap voor groenten and fruit*, 51–54/71, Rec. XVII 1107). It would seem that, to be incompatible, measures must in fact be restrictive, or, at the very least, be seen to be capable of being restrictive in fact. See also *Capolongo* v. *Maya* [1974] 1 C.M.L.R. 230, at 242–243, *per* Adv.-Gen. Roemer.

The Court of Justice decided in 8/74 *Procureur du Roi* v. *Dassonville* [1974] E.C.R. 837, that all trading rules enacted by Member States which are capable of hindering, directly or indirectly, actually or potentially, intra-Community trade are to be considered as measures having an effect equivalent to quantitative restrictions. This would appear to give a wide interpretation to the prohibition. Thus, in the *Procureur du Roi* case, a requirement by a Member State of a certificate of authenticity which was less easily obtainable by importers of an authentic product (Scotch whisky) which had been put into free circulation in a regular manner in another Member State than by importers of the same product coming directly from the country of origin was held to constitute a "measure having equivalent effect." Similarly, in 12/74 *Re German Sparkling Wines and Brandies* [1975] 1 C.M.L.R. at 350, legislation which reserved certain familiar descriptive terms for national production and force the products of other Member States to use terms which were unknown to or less appreciated by the consumer was considered to favour the national producers at the expense of those in other Member States and thereby to constitute a measure equivalent to the quantitative restriction of imports. See also case 4/75, *Rewe-Zentralfinanz GmbH* v. *Landwirtschaftskammer* [1975] E.C.R. 843. Similarly, in case 65/75, *Riccardo Tasca* [1976] E.C.R. 291 it was held that although a maximum price applicable without distinction to domestic and imported products does not in itself constitute a "measure having equivalent effect"; it may nevertheless have such an effect when it is fixed at such a level that the sale of imported products becomes impossible or more difficult than that of domestic products. And in case 35/76, *Simmenthal* v. *Ministero Delle Finanze* [1976] E.C.R. 1871 compulsory veterinary and public health inspections carried out on livestock and meat at the frontier of a Member State were considered to be "of equivalent effect because, as a result of the delays inherent in the inspections and the additional transport costs which the importer may thereby incur, the inspections are likely to make importation more difficult or more costly."

The cases since *Procureur du Roi* v. *Dassonville, supra* have shown a consistent tendency to find even the most routine administrative requirements to be "measures having equivalent effect." In the recent case 68/76, *Re the Export of Potatoes: Commission* v. *France* [1977] 2 C.M.L.R. 161 the Court of Justice held that a statistical procedure whereby exports of potatoes from France were to be made conditional upon the submission of an export declaration endorsed by the French agricultural intervention body, even if such endorsement was "automatic," amounted to an obstacle to trade and was consequently a measure having an effect equivalent to a quantitative restriction on exports within the meaning of Art. 34 (*q.v.*). See also case 53/76, *Procureur de la République de Besançon* v. *Bouhelier* [1977] E.C.R. 197 (export licences and quality certificates held to be quantitative restrictions on exports or measures having equivalent effect within meaning of Art. 34).

In case 20/64, *Albatros* v. *Sopeco* [1965] E.C.R. 29 the Court of Justice held that although Arts. 30 *et seq.* prohibit the introduction of all new quantitative restrictions or discriminations and obliged Member States to abolish existing restrictions and discriminations by the end of the original transitional period, the existing restrictions and discriminations were not automatically abrogated on the date of the Treaty's entry into force; nor were the Member States obliged to abolish them immediately.

It appears that Art. 30 is to be regarded as directly applicable, at least since the end of the transitional period: *Capolongo* v. *Maya, supra*, at 242, *per* Adv.-Gen. Roemer.

For corresponding provisions relating to the new Member States, see Act of Accession, Arts. 42–43.

ARTICLE 31

Member States shall refrain from introducing between themselves any new quantitative restrictions or measures having equivalent effect.

This obligation shall, however, relate only to the degree of liberalisation attained in pursuance of the decisions of the Council of the Organisation for European Economic Cooperation of 14 January 1955. Member States shall supply the Commission, not later than six months after the entry into force of this Treaty, with lists of the products liberalised by them in pursuance of these decisions. These lists shall be consolidated between Member States.

GENERAL NOTE

This prohibition on the introduction of new quantitative restrictions or measures having equivalent effect relates only to the degree of liberalisation attained in pursuance of the decisions of the Council of the Organisation for European Economic Co-operation of January 14, 1955. Accordingly, Art. 31 includes a procedure for notification and consolidation of the products liberalised by the Member States in pursuance of the decisions. The measure of success of the OEEC liberalisation programme extended to 90 per cent. of goods imported by OEEC Member States from other OEEC Member States.

The clearest working illustration of Art. 31 is to be found in the decision of the Court of Justice in *Re Quantitative Restrictions on Imports of Pork Products into Italy: EEC Commission* v. *Italian Government* [1962] C.M.L.R. 39. By ministerial order in 1960 the Italian Government suspended the import from any source of certain pork products. Most of these products had already been listed as freed products in accordance with the OEEC decisions and the Italian Government, in pursuance of Art. 31, had previously notified the liberalisation to the EEC Commission. The Court of Justice held that by promulgating its ministerial order in 1960 the Italian Government had failed to fulfil its obligations under Art. 31.

In *Salgoil* v. *Foreign Trade Ministry of the Italian Republic* [1969] C.M.L.R. 181, the Court of Justice held that Art. 31 imposed a clear and unqualified obligation upon Member States and required no further action for its implementation. It is therefore directly applicable and can be relied upon by individuals before their national courts. See also *Società Biscotti Panettoni Colussi di Milano* v. *Ministero del Commercio con L'Estero* [1963] C.M.L.R. 133 (Italian Consiglio di Stato). For the meaning of "measures having equivalent effect," see annotation to Art. 30.

ARTICLE 32

In their trade with one another Member States shall refrain from making more restrictive the quotas and measures having equivalent effect existing at the date of the entry into force of this Treaty.

These quotas shall be abolished by the end of the transitional period at the latest. During that period, they shall be progressively abolished in accordance with the following provisions.

GENERAL NOTE

This provision was entirely transitional in design. In *Salgoil* v. *Foreign Trade Ministry of the Italian Republic* [1969] C.M.L.R. 181, the Court of Justice considered the first paragraph of Art. 32 to be directly applicable. Moreover, it would seem that a similar view would be taken of the second paragraph in view of the Court's approach to the analogous provisions of Art. 13 (2) in *S.p.a. SACE* v. *Italian Ministry of Finance* [1971] C.M.L.R. 123.

ARTICLE 33

1. One year after the entry into force of this Treaty, each Member State shall convert any bilateral quotas open to any other Member States into global quotas open without discrimination to all other Member States.

On the same date, Member States shall increase the aggregate of the global quotas so established in such a manner as to bring about an increase of not less than 20 per cent. in their total value as compared with the preceding year. The global quota for each product, however, shall be increased by not less than 10 per cent.

The quotas shall be increased annually in accordance with the same rules and in the same proportions in relation to the preceding year.

The fourth increase shall take place at the end of the fourth year after the entry into force of this Treaty; the fifth, one year after the beginning of the second stage.

2. Where, in the case of a product which has not been liberalised, the global quota does not amount to 3 per cent. of the national production of the State concerned, a quota equal to not less than 3 per cent. of such national production shall be introduced not later than one year after the entry into force of this Treaty. This quota shall be raised to 4 per cent. at the end of the second year, and to 5 per cent. at the end of the third. Thereafter, the Member State concerned shall increase the quota by not less than 15 per cent. annually.

Where there is no such national production, the Commission shall take a decision establishing an appropriate quota.

3. At the end of the tenth year, each quota shall be equal to not less than 20 per cent. of the national production.

4. If the Commission finds by means of a decision that during two successive years the imports of any products have been below the level of

257

the quota opened, this global quota shall not be taken into account in calculating the total value of the global quotas. In such case, the Member State shall abolish quota restrictions on the product concerned.

5. In the case of quotas representing more than 20 per cent. of the national production of the product concerned, the Council may, acting by a qualified majority on a proposal from the Commission, reduce the minimum percentage of 10 per cent. laid down in paragraph 1. This alteration shall not, however, affect the obligation to increase the total value of global quotas by 20 per cent. annually.

6. Member States which have exceeded their obligations as regards the degree of liberalisation attained in pursuance of the decisions of the Council of the Organisation for European Economic Cooperation of 14 January 1955 shall be entitled, when calculating the annual total increase of 20 per cent. provided for in paragraph 1, to take into account the amount of imports liberalised by autonomous action. Such calculation shall be submitted to the Commission for its prior approval.

7. The Commission shall issue directives establishing the procedure and timetable in accordance with which Member States shall abolish, as between themselves, any measures in existence when this Treaty enters into force which have an effect equivalent to quotas.

8. If the Commission finds that the application of the provisions of this Article, and in particular of the provisions concerning percentages, makes it impossible to ensure that the abolition of quotas provided for in the second paragraph of Article 32 is carried out progressively, the Council may, on a proposal from the Commission, acting unanimously during the first stage and by a qualified majority thereafter, amend the procedure laid down in this Article and may, in particular, increase the percentages fixed.

GENERAL NOTE
The purpose of Art. 33 was to provide a timetable for the abolition of quotas between Member States. In fact abolition was achieved in advance of the schedule. The last quotas on industrial goods were abolished on December 31, 1961, as a result of the first Acceleration Decision of May 12, 1960 (J.O. 1960, 1217). Quantitative restrictions on most agricultural products were eliminated in the process of establishing the market organisations pursuant to Art. 40 rather than under the Art. 33 timetable, but agricultural products not appropriated to market oragnisations were dealt with under Art. 33 as accelerated.

Art. 33 (7) empowered the Commission to issue directives requiring Member States to abolish measures (in existence when the Treaty entered into force) which had an effect equivalent to that of quotas. Five such directives were issued during the transitional period: 64/486, J.O. 1964, 2253; 66/682, J.O. 1966, 3745; 66/683, J.O. 1966, 3748; 70/32, J.O. 1970, L13/1; 70/50, J.O. 1970, L13/29.

ARTICLE 34

1. Quantitative restrictions on exports, and all measures having equivalent effect, shall be prohibited between Member States.

2. Member States shall, by the end of the first stage at the latest, abolish all quantitative restrictions on exports and any measures having equivalent effect which are in existence when this Treaty enters into force.

GENERAL NOTE
This provision is self-explanatory. For the meaning of "quantitative restrictions" and "measures having equivalent effect," see annotation to Art. 30, *supra*. For corresponding provisions relating to new Member States, see Act of Accession, Arts. 42–43.

ARTICLE 35

The Member States declare their readiness to abolish quantitative restrictions on imports from and exports to other Member States more rapidly than is provided for in the preceding Articles, if their general economic situation and the situation of the economic sector concerned so permit.

To this end, the Commission shall make recommendations to the States concerned.

GENERAL NOTE

Art. 35 authorised the acceleration of the above timetable and this was duly done by the so-called "Acceleration" Decisions of May 12, 1960 (J.O. 1960, 1217) and May 15, 1962 (J.O. 1962, 1284).

cf. Arts. 15 (2) and 24.

ARTICLE 36

The provisions of Articles 30 to 34 shall not preclude prohibitions or restrictions on imports, exports or goods in transit justified on grounds of public morality, public policy or public security; the protection of health and life of humans, animals or plants; the protection of national treasures possessing artistic, historic or archaeological value; or the protection of industrial and commercial property. Such prohibitions or restrictions shall not, however, constitute a means of arbitrary discrimination or a disguised restriction on trade between Member States.

GENERAL NOTE

This Article is in the nature of an escape clause designed to allow prohibitions or restrictions on imports, exports or goods in transit on certain grounds of public policy. It aims to balance the aim of liberalisation, as required under Arts. 30–34, against overriding public policy criteria.

The attractions of Art. 36 to Member States are obvious. However, experience of its working shows that it is an escape clause of limited potential. It is subjected to strict interpretation by the Court of Justice who made it clear in *Re Quantitative Restrictions on Imports of Pork Products into Italy* [1962] C.M.L.R. 39 (see annotation to Art. 31, *supra*), that it is for those who seek to invoke Art. 36 to prove its application and not for the Commission to make *a priori* assumptions as to its application. See also case 8/74 [1974] E.C.R. 837. A further illustration of the strict approach to Art. 36 can be seen in case 35/76, *Simmenthal* v. *Ministero delle Finanze* [1976] E.C.R. 1871 (as to which, see annotation to Art. 30, *supra*).

In *Marimex S.p.a.* v. *Ministro Delle Finanze* [1973] C.M.L.R. 486, a case concerning the levy of a sanitary tax on meat and live animal imports into Italy, the Court of Justice held that, even if Art. 36 does not place any obstacle in the way of sanitary controls, it could nonetheless not be interpreted as permitting the levying of customs duties, imposed on imported goods which have been subjected to these controls and intended to cover the costs of the controls. See also *Re Export Tax on Art Treasures* [1969] C.M.L.R. 1, which, like the *Marimex* case, concerns an unsuccessful attempt to invoke Art. 36 in circumstances unrelated to Arts. 30–34.

The protection of industrial property. Industrial property rights are at the present time granted and enforced by the individual Member States of the EEC and the exercise of these rights is controlled by Arts. 36, 85 and 86 of the EEC Treaty. "Industrial property" is not defined in the Treaty, but Reg. 17, Art. 4 (2) (*b*) states that the term "includes patents, utility models, designs and trade marks." In *Deutsche Grammophon Gesellschaft* v. *Metro-SB-Grossmärkte* [1971] C.M.L.R. 631, it was held that the term for material purposes also included copyright. A European Patent Convention was signed on October 5, 1973, and the Community Patent Convention on December 15, 1975, but neither of these measures has replaced the several national patent systems. There is also a proposal for a similar convention for a European trade mark.

The words "shall not constitute a means of arbitrary discrimination or a disguised restriction on trade between Member States" have been used as a guide to what is a proper exercise of industrial property rights in the context of Arts. 85 and 86 (the rules on competition applying to undertakings). See *Consten and Grundig* v. *Commission* [1966] C.M.L.R. 418; *Parke Davis* v. *Probel* [1968] C.M.L.R. 47; *Sirena* v. *Eda* [1971] C.M.L.R. 260.

In the *Deutsche Grammophon* case (*supra*) the Court of Justice considered restrictions imposed by exercise of a right analogous to copyright by an undertaking (not a government). Although neither of Arts. 85 and 86 was held to prohibit the acts in question, these acts were held to be prohibited on the basis of Art. 36 alone. And for a similar judgment regarding trade marks, see *Van Zuylen Frères* v. *Hag A.G.* [1974] 2 C.M.L.R. 127, where it was held that it was incompatible with the provisions of Art. 36 to prohibit trading in one Member State in a product which lawfully bore a trade mark in another Member State for the sole reason that an identical mark, sharing the same origin existed in the first state. This applies whether or not the person putting the trade-marked product on the market in the other Member State is the trade mark holder or a third party who has lawfully required the product in that other Member State. See also *Re Advocaat Zwarte Kip* [1974] 2 C.M.L.R. D79.

In case 119/75, *Terrapin (Overseas) Ltd.* v. *Terranova Industrie C.A. Kapferer & Co.* [1976] E.C.R. 1039 the Court of Justice held that an industrial property right (in that case, a trade mark) acquired in a Member State may lawfully be used to prevent under Art. 36 the import of products marketed under a name giving rise to confusion, where the rights in question have been acquired by different and independent proprietors under different national laws. However, the Court of Justice made it clear that a national court trying an action based on similarity of marks must ensure that the exercise of the rights in question does not constitute a means of arbitrary discrimination or disguised restriction on trade between Member States, particularly because the proprietor does not exercise his rights with the same strictness whatever the national origin of any possible infringer.

The Court of Justice has also applied these principles to a similar employment of patent rights in *Centrafarm BV* v. *Sterling Drug Inc.* [1974] 2 C.M.L.R. 480, where it indicated that in respect of each type of industrial property right Art. 36 only allows derogation from the free movement of goods to the extent that such derogation is justified for the protection of rights "which constitute the specific object of such property" (p. 503).

ARTICLE 37

1. Member States shall progressively adjust any State monopolies of a commercial character so as to ensure that when the transitional period has ended no discrimination regarding the conditions under which goods are procured are marketed exists between nationals and Member States.

The provisions of this Article shall apply to any body through which a Member State, in law or in fact, either directly or indirectly supervises, determines or appreciably influences imports or exports between Member States. These provisions shall likewise apply to monopolies delegated by the State to others.

2. Member States shall refrain from introducing any new measure which is contrary to the principles laid down in paragraph 1 or which restricts the scope of the Articles dealing with the abolition of customs duties and quantitative restrictions between Member States.

3. The timetable for the measures referred to in paragraph 1 shall be harmonised with the abolition of quantitative restrictions on the same products provided for in Articles 30 to 34.

If a product is subject to a State monopoly of a commercial character in only one or some Member States, the Commission may authorise the other Member States to apply protective measures until the adjustment provided for in paragraph 1 has been effected; the Commission shall determine the conditions and details of such measures.

4. If a State monopoly of a commercial character has rules which are designed to make it easier to dispose of agricultural products or obtain for them the best return, steps should be taken in applying the rules contained in this Article to ensure equivalent safeguards for the employment and standard of living of the producers concerned, account being taken of the adjustments that will be possible and the specialisation that will be needed with the passage of time.

5. The obligations on Member States shall be binding only in so far as they are compatible with existing international agreements.

6. With effect from the first stage the Commission shall make recommendations as to the manner in which and the timetable according to which the adjustment provided for in this Article shall be carried out.

SERVICES

ARTICLE 59

Within the framework of the provisions set out below, restrictions on freedom to provide services within the Community shall be progressively abolished during the transitional period in respect of nationals of Member States who are established in a State of the Community other than that of the person for whom the services are intended.

The Council may, acting unanimously on a proposal from the Commission, extend the provisions of this Chapter to nationals of a third country who provide services and who are established within the Community.

ARTICLE 60

Services shall be considered to be "services" within the meaning of this Treaty where they are normally provided for remuneration, in so far as they are not governed by the provisions relating to freedom of movement for goods, capital and persons.

"Services" shall in particular include:

(a) activities of an industrial character;

(b) activities of a commercial character;

(c) activities of craftsmen;

(d) activities of the professions.

Without prejudice to the provisions of the Chapter relating to the right of establishment, the person providing a service may, in order to do so, temporarily pursue his activity in the State where the service is provided, under the same conditions as are imposed by that State on its own nationals.

DEFINITIONS

"established," "establishment," see Art. 52.

"nationals of Member States," see Art. 7 and Art. 58, which is applicable by virtue of Art. 66. See also case 115/78, *Knoors* v. *Secretary of State for Economic Affairs* [1979] E.C.R 399.

"transitional period," see Art. 7.

REFERENCES
As to movement of capital, see Arts. 61 (2), 67 to 73 and 106.
As to movement of goods, see Arts. 9 to 37.
As to movement of persons, see Arts. 48 to 58.

GENERAL NOTE

It is best to take this Article and Art. 59 together. They are closely interconnected, if not obviously consistent with each other, and the notion of "services" is only capable of interpretation by reading the two with each other.

The descriptive definition of "services" is incomplete and is given mainly by exclusion. Art. 60 does not give a positive definition, but lists, in a four-fold classification, activities which the term "includes." These activities must also normally be performed in return for payment. An activity may be ancillary to some other main objective. In such cases Treaty provisions governing that main objective also govern freedom to offer the services (dealings in goods, movement of workers or self-employed persons and companies, transfers of capital—Art. 60, first para.; transport—Art. 61, para. (1)). Or the activity may be sufficiently linked to other objectives governed by the Treaty to require legislation for the one to be kept "in step" with that applying to the other (Art. 61, para. (2)). Again, the service activity itself may provide the principal and independent objective, as with craftsmen and the professions.

The instrumental definition, identifying the field of services the Chapter is meant to affect, is in two parts. The limitation in Art. 60, excluding from the application of the Chapter matters covered under the headings of free movement of goods, capital and persons, emphasises the residual, supplementary and complementary nature of the Chapter. However, the part in Art. 59 produces some confusion, by limiting the application of the Chapter, implicitly, by reference to:

(i) The nationality and State of establishment of the provider. *Both* must link him to EEC Member States. This would give a United Kingdom citizen established in Germany access to the whole Community, while if established in, say, Spain he would be excluded, except presumably from the United Kingdom itself (under national law). Similarly, unless and until the Council extends the Chapter under Art. 59, second para., non-EEC nationals, say Swedes, established in Member States do not share competitive access to the Community as a whole, nor can they rely on the enforceable rights conferred by Art. 65.

Establishment (but not necessarily nationality) must also link the provider to a different State from "that of" the proposed recipient. Thus a French freelance journalist or photographer established in France could work in Holland, selling his work to Dutch or German newspapers, but not to French ones.

(ii) The identity of the recipient's State. As seen above, this must be one in which the provider is not established, so that a United Kingdom travel agency would be entitled to offer its services throughout the Community to any EEC nationals apart from United Kingdom citizens as tourists. (*Quaere* as to the position of sub-contractors, and whether the "recipient" of their services is the agency or the individual tourist?)

Semble also the recipient's State—"that of the person for whom ..."—must also be an EEC State, such being the obvious reference of the word "that." If so, further irrational distinctions arise, permitting Member States to restrict the access of other EEC nationals to provide services within their territory for, say, *American* tourists, but not for EEC nationals (including the host State's own nationals).

Ignoring political implications, the clear legal implication is that the reader should not worry too much about what the Treaty *says*, but should rather examine what the Community *does*.

This brings us to the operational definition. It is indicated by the approach of the legislation (Regulation of the Council 1612/68 of October 15, 1968; J.O. 1968, L257/13). This does not concern itself with any of the complications referred to above. It provides for freedom of movement for any EEC national, whether as provider or as recipient of services, together with his *or her* spouse, children under twenty-one, and family dependants. The identity of the State of the other party to the contract for services is immaterial. Apart from the duration of the right to reside, entry to provide services is governed by conditions very similar to those applying to entry with a view to establishment, within the same directives. The only limits are those allowed under Arts. 55 and 56 (*q.v.*), relating to public order, public health, etc. (case 41/74, *Van Duyn* v. *Home Office* [1974] E.C.R. 1337; [1975] 1 C.M.L.R. 1).

With regard to "restrictions on the freedom to provide ..." again the wording is obscure, even contradictory. Art. 59, first para., clearly directs its attack against all *restrictions*, not just discriminatory ones, indicating that (at that moment at least) they were all perceived as restrictive practices to be swept away in the liberation of free market forces, first for EEC nationals, later for all EEC residents. Art. 60, third para., preserves the right of a Member State to retain existing *conditions* on the provision of services in its territory, these being perceived as part of the State's machinery for protecting consumers and the public, at least pending the evolving of acceptable EEC standards (*e.g.* the policing of motor-car insurance underwriters, or access to the professions, *cf.* case 2/74, *Reyners* v. *Belgium* [1974] E.C.R. 631, tests related to nationality infringe the Treaty, in relation to the legal profession, but ones related to a nationally based system of training and qualifications do not). Such restrictions are allowed if there is a genuine right of protection, but where the supplier of services is subject to an identical supervisory system in his State of establishment which governs his activities elsewhere there is *de facto* co-ordination and the freedom will be upheld (cases 110 & 111/78, *Ministère Public, etc.* v. *Van Wesemael, etc.* [1979] E.C.R. 35). *Quaere* whether this will apply if the supplier is aiming his activities at one State but is established in another? But, while from the date of the Treaty (or of accession) new *restrictions* may not be imposed, is this true of *conditions*? (*cf.* although strictly this comes rather within the provisions relating to transport, Opinion 77/137 addressed to the Government of Belgium on a draft Royal Decree relating to the introduction of a licence for transport brokers (O.J. 1977, L44/17).) Given another case of "V and G" magnitude, is it only Community action which is competent to tighten up the regulations in a Member State? It must depend on how the substantial effect of the new or modified rule is perceived by the Court, irrespective of its form. This should be a diminishing problem, as the Community achieves uniformity of standards by harmonisation and co-ordination (see Arts. 2 and 57). Note also the relation to restrictions on freedom to transfer funds in payment for services (see Art. 106).

The movements and persons affected are of three main types:

   (*a*) attracting customers across frontiers to come to the provider;

   (*b*) the provider crossing frontiers to take the service to recipients;

   (*c*) utilising methods of operation at a distance, neither provider nor recipient crossing frontiers personally.

On point (*b*), see case 39/75, *Coenen* v. *Sociaal-Economische Raad* [1975] E.C.R. 1547, where a Netherlands insurance broker moved to live in Belgium, although continuing to provide services in the Netherlands.

In many cases where neither party has to move across a frontier, the position may be governed by other parts of the Treaty. An example of this is the return of goods to a manufacturer for repair (*Re French Iron Casings* [1966] C.M.L.R. 332) or the distinction between a television broadcast (service) and any "hardware" such as a videotape recording (goods) (case 155/73, *Italy* v. *Sacchi* [1974] E.C.R. 409 at 427). The first two cases are provided for in the Community Secondary Legislation (particularly Reg. 1612/68, see above). Immigration control in the United Kingdom (apart from nationals of the Irish Republic, see British Nationality Act 1948, ss. 2 and 3, Ireland Act 1949, s. 2) has been brought into conformity by the Immigration Rules (House of Commons Papers 81 and 82, Session 1972–73, as amended by Cmnd. 5717 and 5718, 1974).

The activities listed in Art. 60, second para., have been the subject of directives and of proposals. In general, activities in industry, commerce, and the position of craftsmen have all come within the series of directives made in 1964–65, to which priority had to be given under Art. 63, para. (3). The professions have proved more difficult to integrate. (See, however, in respect of the freedom of lawyers to provide lawyers to provide services, Dir. 77/249 of March 22, 1977 (O.J. 1977, L78/17).) In part, this is the result of local variation in the organisation of the professions, and particularly in their constitutional position (*Reyners* v. *Belgium, supra*). While in some Member States, on a traditional pattern, more or less autonomous professional bodies such as the Inns of Court, Law Society, or the various Institutions of engineers, accountants and so on are involved, in others control is in the hands of central government ministries and, in Germany, the governmental bodies of the regions (*Länder*) have authority. Differences also exist in division of tasks and in methods, so that there has been controversy over whether, for instance, opticians are craftsmen or professional men. Proposals (the "de Crayencour proposals") were considered by the Council of the Six, on reference from the Commission, late in 1972. These were then sent back for further consideration and it appears that consultation and compromise in the enlarged Community must now begin virtually afresh. Details of legislation in force are to be found in Volume C. The result is that this has now fallen out of the timetable originally laid down; however, as a result of the judgments in the *Reyners* and *Van Binsbergen* cases, *supra*, the Commission has withdrawn, as being no longer necessary, a series of draft directives abolishing restrictions on the freedom of establishment and the freedom to provide services in respect of various activities. See also cases 110 & 111/78, *supra*.

RULES ON COMPETITION

RULES APPLYING TO UNDERTAKINGS

ARTICLE 85

1. The following shall be prohibited as incompatible with the common market: all agreements between undertakings, decisions by associations of undertakings and concerted practices which may affect trade between Member States and which have as their object or effect the prevention, restriction or distortion of competition within the common market, and in particular those which:

(*a*) directly or indirectly fix purchase or selling prices or any other trading conditions;

(*b*) limit or control production, markets, technical development, or investment;

(*c*) share markets or sources of supply;

(*d*) apply dissimilar conditions to equivalent transactions with other trading parties, thereby placing them at a competitive disadvantage;

(*e*) make the conclusion of contracts subject to acceptance by the other parties of supplementary obligations which, by their nature or according to commercial usage, have no connection with the subject of such contracts.

2. Any agreements or decisions prohibited pursuant to this Article shall be automatically void.

3. The provisions of paragraph 1 may, however, be declared inapplicable in the case of:

—any agreement or category of agreements between undertakings;

—any decision or category of decisions by associations of undertakings;

—any concerted practice or category of concerted practices;

which contributes to improving the production or distribution of goods or to promoting technical or economic progress, while allowing consumers a fair share of the resulting benefit, and which does not:

(*a*) impose on the undertakings concerned restrictions which are not indispensable to the attainment of these objectives;

(*b*) afford such undertakings the possibility of eliminating competition in respect of a substantial part of the products in question.

GENERAL NOTE

In order to ensure that competition within the common market is not distorted (Art. 3 (*f*), see *ante*), Arts. 85 and 86 provide the basis for control of the market behaviour of private enterprise which might otherwise hinder the establishment of a single market within the European Community and distort the operation of the principles of a free market economy, both of which underlie the objectives of the Treaty (Art. 2, *ante*. See cases 56 & 58/64, *Consten & Grundig* v. *Commission* [1966] E.C.R. 299 and Art. 86, *post*). The competition policy is designed to prohibit practices which are incompatible with these objectives and also to encourage activities which facilitate their attainment. The Commission also views the policy as an instrument which can assist in controlling inflation and provide ancillary support for other policies which are used to further the economic, social and political development of the Community in a changing economic climate (see Commission's *Annual Reports on Competition Policy*).

Art. 85 (1) prohibits (and gives examples of) certain forms of co-operation between undertakings which could adversely affect both the flow of trade between Member States and the conditions of competition within the common market. However, the prohibition is tempered by the possibility of individual or generic declarations of inapplicability being made in respect of agreements with certain beneficial effects as long as they involve no indispensable restrictions on the parties concerned and do not present the opportunity for the elimination of competition in a substantial part of the relevant product market. Those practices which fall within the prohibition of Art. 85 (1) and not exempted under para. (3) are stated to be automatically void under para. (2).

Prior to the entry into force of Reg. 17 (see Vol. C of this Encyclopedia, Part C4) the application of Arts. 85 and 86 was the responsibility of appropriate national authorities and the Commission (Arts. 88, 89, *post*) albeit with limited effect (case 13/61, *Bosch* v. *De Geus* [1962] E.C.R. 45). Reg. 17 provides that the prohibitions operate without any requirement of a decision to that effect (Art. 1 and see case 127/73, *SABAM* [1974] E.C.R. 51, confirming the direct effect of the prohibitions), but also gives extensive powers to the Commission to implement Art. 85 enabling it to decide, *inter alia*, that a practice does not fall within Art. 85 at all (grant a negative clearance, Art. 2); how and whether exemptions can be granted under para. (3) (Arts. 4–9); on the enforcement of the prohibition by requiring the termination of infringements (Art. 3) and/or the imposition of fines and periodic payments (Arts. 15, 16). (For investigative powers in Reg. 17 and procedural Regulations, *e.g.* Regs. 27, 99/63 (as amended) and Reg. 2988/74 (limitation periods) in Vol. C, Part C4.) Appeals against Commission decisions can be made to the Court of Justice (Art. 173, *post*, and Reg. 17, Art. 9) which can also review the imposition of pecuniary sanctions (Art. 172, *post*, Reg. 17, Art. 17) and moreover give rulings on competition issues in exercise of its preliminary ruling jurisdiction (Art. 177, *post*).

Para. (1)

The prohibition is directed at a variety of forms of co-operation between undertakings operating at the same or different levels of the economy (cases 56–58/64, *Consten-Grundig*, *supra*; case 32/65, *Italy* v. *Council and Commission* [1966] E.C.R. 389). The term "undertaking" encompasses both legal and natural persons engaging in economic or commercial activity as independent market actors and includes individuals (*e.g. AOIP/Beyrard*, O.J. 1976, L6/8; [1976] 1 C.M.L.R. D14; *Reuter/BASF* [1976] C.M.L.R. D44; *Re Unitel*, O.J. 1978, L157/39; [1978] 3 C.M.L.R. 306; *Vaessen B.V./Moris*, O.J. 1979, L19/32 [1979] 1 C.M.L.R. 511) and certain public bodies (see also Art. 90, *post*, *e.g.* case 155/73, *Sacchi* [1974] E.C.R. 409). Associations of undertakings include trade associations whether possessing legal personality or not (*e.g. German Ceramic Tiles*, J.O. 1971, L10/15, [1971] C.M.L.R. D6; *Pabst & Richarz/BNIA*, O.J. 1976, L231/24, [1976] 2 C.M.L.R. D63; *CEMATEX*, J.O. 1971, L227/26, [1973] C.M.L.R. D135). The agreements involved need not be legally enforceable (*Quinine*, J.O. 1969, L 192/5, [1969] C.M.L.R. D41, on appeal cases 41, 44 & 45/69, *ACF Chemiefarma et al.* v. *Commission* [1970] E.C.R. 661; *Franco-Japanese Ballbearings*, O.J. 1974, L343/19, [1975] 1 C.M.L.R. D8) as long as there is an expression of the joint intention of the parties concerned (*Quinine*, *supra*; *WEA/Filipacchi*, J.O. 1972, L303/52, [1973] C.M.L.R. D43). Agreements between associations of undertakings (*Belgian Central Heating*, J.O. 1972, L264/22; [1972] C.M.L.R. D130; *Frubo*, O.J. 1974, L237/16, [1974] 2 C.M.L.R. D89) and compliance with international fair trading rules (*Glass Containers*, O.J. 1974, L160/1, [1974] 2 C.M.L.R. D50; *Virgin Aluminium*, O.J. 1975, L228/3, [1975] 2 C.M.L.R. D50) have been treated as agreements. Formal co-operation may be evidenced by the constitution or rules of an association (*e.g. ASPA*, J.O. 1970, L6/8, [1970] C.M.L.R. D2; *Donck* v. *Central Bureau voor Rijwielhandel*, O.J. 1978, L20/18, [1978] 2 C.M.L.R. 194), policy decisions taken at meetings (*German Ceramic Tiles*, *supra*; case 8/72, *VCH* v. *Commission* [1972] E.C.R. 977) and exhibition rules compiled by such associations (*CEMATEX*, *supra*). Where informal co-operation takes place, this may amount to a concerted practice if the undertakings involved no longer pursue independently determined commercial strategies but "knowingly eliminate the risk of competition by co-operating to ensure that normal market conditions no longer obtain" (cases 48/69, etc., *I.C.I. et al.* v. *Commission* [1972] E.C.R. 619;

cases 40/73, etc., *Suiker Unie et al.* v. *Commission* [1975] E.C.R. 1663). Where highly concentrated or oligopolistic markets are involved, detailed market analysis is required in order to determine what normal market conditions are, or might otherwise be (cases 48/69, etc., *I.C.I. supra*; cases 40/73 etc., *Sugar, supra.* See also Commission Reports on the Oil and Naphtha Industries, *Fourth and Seventh Competition Policy Reports* and Annual Reports on Concentration within the Common Market). Concentrations of market power may also fall within Art. 86, *post*, and note Commission investigation of the acquisition by Deutsche BP of a holding in Ruhrgas A.G. (Bull. E.C. 3/79, point 2.1.29). Agreements between legally independent, but economically linked undertakings do not fall within Art. 85 if they merely amount to a division of tasks within a single economic unit (*e.g.* case 22/71, *Béguélin* [1971] E.C.R. 949; case 15/74, *Centrafarm B.V.* v. *Sterling Drug Inc.* [1974] E.C.R. 114); *Christiani and Nielsen*, J.O. 1969, L165/12, [1969] C.M.L.R. D36). True agency contracts are also excluded (Commission Announcement on Exclusive Agency Contract made with Commercial Agents (1962) (see Vol. C, Part C4) but see also *Pittsburgh Corning*, J.O. 1972, L272/35, [1973] C.M.L.R. D2; cases 40/73, etc., *Suiker Unie, supra*, and Commission's decision, O.J. 1973, L140/17, [1973] C.M.L.R. D65).

The compatability of practices prohibited by Art. 85 (1) is tested by reference both to their actual or potential impact on the pattern of trade between Member States and to the actual potential or intended effect of the structure of the competition within the common market. In order to determine whether such practices should be prohibited, the economic and market conditions in which they operate are fully examined. The Court and the Commission have adopted a *de minimis* approach and excluded those agreements etc. involving undertakings where, by virtue of their size and market share, no appreciable impact on trade or market conditions can be anticipated (case 56/65, *Société Technique Minière* v. *Maschinenbau Ulm* [1966] E.C.R. 235; case 5/69, *Völk* v. *Vervaecke* [1969] E.C.R. 295; see also Commission Notice on Agreements of Minor Importance, O.J. 1977, C313/3 although market share is not decisive, *e.g.* 26/76, *Metro* v. *Commission* [1977] E.C.R. 1875). The fact that the overall volume of trade might increase will not prevent the operation of the prohibition if the normal flow of trade within the Community's single market would be different (cases 56 & 58/64, *Consten & Grundig, supra*). National agreements will be prohibited in so far as they result in, or tend to consolidate, the partitioning of the relevant market along national boundaries (case 8/72, *VCH* v. *Commission* [1972] E.C.R. 977, case 73/74, *Groupement des Fabricants de Papiers Peints de Belgique* v. *Commission* [1975] E.C.R. 1491). Agreements, etc., concerning imports into or exports from the common market can also affect the flow of trade within the Community (see *e.g.* Commission Notice on Imports of Japanese Products, O.J. 1972, C111/13, and Vol. C, Part C4, *Franco-Japanese Ballbearings, supra; Preserved Mushrooms,* O.J. 1975, L29/26, [1975] 1 C.M.L.R. D83; *Omega*, J.O. 1970, L242/22, [1970] C.M.L.R. D49; *Junghans*, O.J. 1977, L30/10, [1977] 1 exports or parallel imports (*e.g.* cases 56 & 58/64, *Consten & Grundig, supra; WEA/Filipacchi, supra;* case 19/77, *Miller, supra; Arthur Bell,* O.J. 1978, L235/15, [1978] 3 C.M.L.R. 298; *Putz* v. *Kawasaki Motors (U.K.) Ltd.,* O.J. 1979, L16/9, [1979] 1 C.M.L.R. 448) or stipulating conditions for subsequent dealings (*Deutsche Phillips*, O.J. 1973, L293/40, [1973] C.M.L.R. D241; *Du Pont de Nemours*, O.J. 1973, L194/27, [1973] C.M.L.R. D226; *Donck, supra*), or indirectly, *e.g.* by operating different pricing policies on exported goods (*e.g. Pittsburgh Corning, supra; Kodak, supra; Distillers,* O.J. 1978, L50/16, [1978] 1 C.M.L.R. 400); *BMW*, O.J. 1978, L46/33, [1978] 2 C.M.L.R. 126); or through the use of industrial property rights, particularly trademarks, *e.g.* cases 56 & 58/64, *Consten & Grundig, supra;* case 28/77, *Tepea* [1978] E.C.R. 1391 or requirements on guarantee services (*Zanussi*, O.J. 1978, L322/26, [1979] 1 C.M.L.R. 81). Such agreements have repercussions on the competitive position of the parties to them and their competitors, as do restrictions on dealings with competing products, *e.g.* through "requirements" and/or exclusivity clauses (case 23/67, *Brasserie de Haecht (No.* 1), *supra; BMW*, O.J. 1975, L29/1, [1975] 1 C.M.L.R. D44; *Brooke Bond Liebig*, O.J. 1978, L53/20, [1978] 2 C.M.L.R. 116). Although the existence of industrial property rights is not prohibited by the Treaty, their exercise may fall within Art. 85 (1) if such is the "object, means or consequence of an agreement" (Art. 222, case 24/67, *Parke Davis* [1968] E.C.R. 55; cases 15 & 16/74, *Centrafarm* [1974] E.C.R. 1147, 1183; note also restrictions on the exercise of rights which would be contrary to free movement of goods provisions (Arts. 30–36, *ante*), or would amount to an abuse of a dominant position Art. 86, *post*), *e.g.* assignments alone or as reinforcements to other agreements (*e.g.* case 40/70, *Sirena* v. *Eda* [1971] E.C.R. 69; cases 56 & 58/64, *Consten*

& *Grundig, supra*); restrictions on their exercise (*Sirdar/Phildar*, O.J. 1975, L125/27, [1975] 1 C.M.L.R. D93; *Persil* [1978] 1 C.M.L.R. 395; *cf. Penneys*, O.J. 1977, C76/2, [1978] 2 C.M.L.R. 116; *Campari*, O.J. 1978, L70/69 [1978] 2 C.M.L.R. 397); or licensing of use, particularly of patents and know-how. In these latter cases, a balance is sought between those clauses which are essential to the existence of the right and those which restrict competition, *e.g.* export bans, limitations on field of use, no challenge clauses (see Commission Notice on Patent Licensing Agreements of December 24, 1962, in Part C4 of this Encyclopedia, subject to views expressed in *Fourth Report on Competition Policy* and decisions, *e.g. AOIP/Beyrard;* see also *Kabelmetal/Luchaire*, O.J. 1975, L222/34, [1975] 2 C.M.L.R. D40; *Bronbemaling/ Heidemaatscappij*, O.J. 1975, L249/27, [1975] 2 C.M.L.R. D67; Draft Regulation on patent licensing agreements, O.J. 1979, C58/12; [1979] 1 C.M.L.R. 478). Similar principles are applied to the licensing of other rights (copyright *"The Old Man and the Sea"* Sixth Report on Competition Policy; trademarks case 28/77, *Tepea* [1978] E.C.R. 1391; plant and seed varieties *INRA*, O.J. 1978, L286/23, [1978] 3 C.M.L.R. 434.

Para. (2)

If an agreement falls within the prohibition of para. (1) and does not receive the benefit of a declaration of inapplicability under para. (3), then it is declared to be automatically void. This consequence is in addition to any sanction imposed by the Commission, but can result without the requirement that a decision is made (Reg. 17, Art. 1, see also case 13/61, *Bosch, supra*; case 127/73, *SABAM, supra*; case 48/72, *Brasserie de Haecht (No. 2)* [1973] E.C.R. 77). The civil consequences of the nullity as between the parties are decided according to national law, and may involve the severability of the offending clauses (case 56/65, *Société Technique Minière* v. *Maschinenbau Ulm, supra; Chemidus Wavin* v. *TERI* [1976] 2 C.M.L.R. 387, High Court; [1978] 3 C.M.L.R. 514, C.A.). Whether third parties have any redress for damage suffered in consequence of the prohibited agreement is also a question for national law, subject to possible guidance through the use of the preliminary ruling procedure (Art. 177, *post*). (For suggestions as to English law, *Application des Gaz S.A.* v. *Falks Veritas Ltd.* [1974] 2 C.M.L.R. 75; *Valor International* v. *Application de Gaz S.A.* [1978] 3 C.M.L.R. 87).

Limited relief from automatic nullity can arise through the doctrine of "provisional validity." In the case of "old" agreements (those already in existence on March 13, 1962, or January 1, 1973, for agreements falling within the Treaty provisions as a result of accession) which have been duly notified (or are exempt from notification under Reg. 17, Art. 4 (2)) they may be enforced pending a decision of the Commission on Art. 85 (1) (case 13/61, *Bosch, supra*; case 10/69, *Portelange* v. *Smith Corona* [1969] E.C.R. 309), but see case 59/77, *De Bloos* v. C.M.L.R. 82 (and position as to EFTA countries), whether the undertakings are established in the common market or not (*ibid.*, see also on extraterritorial jurisdiction cases 48/69, etc., *I.C.I., supra*; case 22/71, *I.C.I. et al.* v. *Commission, supra*; case 22/71, *Béguelin, supra; Genuine Vegetable Parchment Association*, O.J. 1978, L70/54, [1978] 1 C.M.L.R. 534).

By prohibiting agreements, etc., which prevent, restrict or distort competition, Art. 85 (1) aims to ensure that market participants, whether manufacturers, suppliers, dealers or consumers, are free to take advantage of the most favourable market conditions and that artificial arrangements do not restrict their freedom to do so. The resulting competitive environment is then seen to be a stimulant and incentive to efficient and rational economic development (see Commission Notice on Co-operation Agreements (1968) and J.O. 1968, C75/3 and Vol. C, Part C4 and Notice on Subcontracting Agreements (1978), O.J. 1979, C1/2, Art. 85 (3), *post*); competition must be examined both as regards the undertakings parties to the agreement, etc., and also other market participants. Such examination calls for careful analysis of the economic context of the agreement (*e.g.* where it is one of a number of similar agreements: case 23/67, *Brasserie de Haecht (No. 1)* [1967] E.C.R. 407) and of the relevant market (cases 56 & 58/64, *Consten and Grundig, supra; WEA/Filipacchi, supra;* cases 19 & 20/74, *Kali und Salz and Kali Chemie* v. *Commission* [1975] E.C.R. 499; case 19/77, *Miller International Schallplatten* v. *Commission* [1978] E.C.R. 131, see also Art. 86, *post*).

The particular examples of practices which prima facie have undesirable effects on the common market can result from either vertical or horizontal dealings, *supra*. Although each case must be decided upon its own facts (see Art. 85 (3), *post*, on permitted forms of co-operation) certain types of agreements, etc., have repeatedly called for consideration. As between undertakings which co-operate at the same level of the economy, whether through arrangements such as contracts or agreements (*e.g. Glass Containers, supra*; case 41/69, *A.C.F. Chemiefarma, supra*) trade associations (*e.g. Glass Containers, supra*; *Groupement des Fabricants de Papiers Peints de Belgique, supra*), joint sales or purchasing agencies (*Kali und Salz*, O.J. 1973, L217/3, [1973] C.M.L.R. D219; *Cobelaz (No. 1)*, J.O. 1968, L276/13, [1968] C.M.L.R. D45; *Centraal Stikstof Verkoopkantor*, O.J. 1978, L242/15, [1979] 1 C.M.L.R. 11) or informally through concerted practices (case 41/69, *ACF Chemiefarma* v. *Commission, supra*; case 48/69, *supra*) any joint fixing of prices or trading conditions removes the opportunity for competition between them on these matters. Such practices are particularly serious in the case of oligopolistic markets. Similar disincentives can result from information agreements which require notification of commercial strategies and encourage "open pricing" systems, *e.g. Glass containers, supra; Genuine Vegetable Parchment Association*, O.J. 1978, L70/54, [1978] 1 C.M.L.R. 534; *White Lead Manufactures*, O.J. 1979, L21/16, [1979] 1 C.M.L.R. 464; see also Commission's *Seventh Report on Competition Policy*). Agreement on prices, etc., may be accompanied by market sharing and quota arrangements which can also tend to reinforce traditional market positions by discouraging the participants from exploiting potential competitive advantages over each other and removing the need to rationalise their operations (*Van Katwijk*, J.O. 1970, L242/18, [1970] C.M.L.R. D42; *NCH*, J.O. 1972, L22/16, [1973] C.M.L.R. D257).

Not only do such arrangements affect the competitive positions of the participants, *inter se*, but they also have repercussions on other undertakings, *e.g.* by making it more difficult for them to penetrate an artificially reinforced market (*e.g.* case 8/72, *VCH, supra*), or by limiting the freedom of choice of other undertakings (and consumers) (cases 40/73, etc., *Suiker Unie, supra*, and note use of rebates and discounts, *German Ceramic Tiles Discount Agreement*, J.O. 1971, L10/15, [1971] C.M.L.R. D6).

Adverse effects on competition and the flow of trade between Member States can result from "vertical" agreements including collective reciprocal agreements (*e.g. Belgian Central Heating Agreement*, J.O. 1972, L264/22, [1972] C.M.L.R. D130) standard conditions of sale (*e.g. Kodak*, J.O. 1970, L147/24, [1970] C.M.L.R. D19) and supply and/or distribution agreements (cases 56 & 58/64, *Consten & Grundig, supra,* note also networks of agreements, case 23/67, *Brasserie de Haecht (No. 1), supra*); these latter have been the subject of extensive consideration by the Community authorities (see also Art. 85 (3), *post*, on exemptions under Reg. 67/67). The fixing of prices and trading conditions may lead to an artificial division of markets along national boundaries: either directly, *e.g.* by banning *Bouyer* [1977] E.C.R. 2359). In the case of "new" agreements (those made after March 13, 1962, or after January 1, 1973, in the case of "accession" agreements), the doctrine of "provisional validity" does not apply whether the agreement is notifiable and notified, or non-notifiable (case 48/72, *Brasserie de Haecht (No. 2), supra*; but see *Grundig AG* v. *Metro-SB-Grossmärkte* [1979] 2 C.M.L.R. 564 (Landgericht Nuremberg-Fürth). (For the effects of granting or refusing a declaration under Art. 85 (3), see Reg. 17, Part C4 of this Encyclopedia; for discussion of the potential conflicts between decisions by the Commission and those of national courts "Conflicts of Resolution in European Competition Law," J. M. H. Faull, J. H. H. Weiler (1978) 3 E.L.Rev. 116.)

Para. (3)

The prohibition of para. (1) and its effects can be declared inapplicable to certain forms of co-operation where beneficial effects can be shown which will not be outweighed by adverse effects on the competitive positions of the parties (*e.g.* through indispensable restrictions) or on other competitors, actual or potential, in the same market; the implication being that such benefits could not be achieved under normal market conditions. The power to grant such exemptions, lies with the Commission (Reg. 17, Art. 9, see Part C4 of this Encyclopedia and note procedure for obtaining exemption, and imposition of conditions on granting thereof). The Commission has exercised powers granted to it by the Council for the purpose of exempting categories of agreements (Reg. 67/67, certain exclusive dealing agreements, under Reg. 19/65, note also draft amendment to Reg. 67/67 [1978] 1 C.M.L.R. D12 resulting from case 63/75, *Roubaix* v. *Roux* [1976] E.C.R. 11 and case 67/76, *Concordia* [1977] E.C.R. 65; and draft regulation on patent licensing agreements, O.J. 1979, C58/12; [1979] 1 C.M.L.R. 478; Reg. 2779/72 as amended by Reg. 2903/77 on specialisation agreements, under Reg. 2821/74), but where a practice falls outside these provisions, individual decisions are made taking account of the scope and likely outcome of the agreement and the resulting impact on market conditions.

Specialisation agreements which achieve rationalisation of production and an increase in efficiency and productivity (*JAZ/Peter*, J.O. 1969, L195/5, [1970] C.M.L.R. 129; *Lightweight Paper*, J.O. 1972, L182/24, [1972] C.M.L.R. D94), agreements on joint research and development (*MAN/Saviem*, J.O. 1972, L31/29, [1974] 2 C.M.L.R. D123; *Rank/Sopelem*, O.J. 1975, L29/20; [1975] 1 C.M.L.R. D72; *Bayer/Gist*, O.J. 1976, L30/13, [1976] 1 C.M.L.R. D98; *Beecham/Parke Davis*, O.J. 1979, L70/11; [1979] 2 C.M.L.R. 157), together with arrangements which improve the quality of goods and their distribution, have been granted exemptions despite the restrictions on the parties to them. (For the position concerning large undertakings, see *Henkel/Colgate*, J.O. 1972, L14/4.) These objectives may be attained through the use of joint ventures (*e.g. Henkel/Colgate, supra; Bayer/Gist, supra; United Processors*, O.J. 1976, L51/7, [1976] 2 C.M.L.R. D1; *Vacuum Interrupters*, O.J. 1977, L48/32, [1977] 1 C.M.L.R. D67; *De Laval/Stork*, O.J. 1977, L215/11, [1977] 2 C.M.L.R. D6; *GEC/Weir*, O.J. 1977, L327/26, [1978] 1 C.M.L.R. D42. Note also Commission's view on concentration expressed in Memorandum on concentration of enterprises in the common market (1966), proposed merger Regulation, O.J. 1973, C92/1 and see *Seventh Report on Competition Policy*.)

Technical and economic progress may also be facilitated by patent and know-how licensing, and restrictions on the parties may be exempted to enable exploitation of such rights and provide the incentive for the necessary investment and production effort (*Davidson Rubber*, J.O. 1972, L143/31, [1972] C.M.L.R. D52; *Kabelmetal*/Luchaire, supra; cf. AOIP/*Beyrard*, supra; *Peugeot/Zimmern* [1977] 1 C.M.L.R. D22).

Improvements in distribution may result from agreements involving joint selling or purchasing, joint advertising, and even limited market sharing (*e.g. Transocean Marine Paint Association*, J.O. 1967, 163/10, [1967] C.M.L.R. D9). See generally *First Report on Competition Policy*). Selective distribution systems may be exempted despite restrictions on the dealers concerned where "objectively necessary criteria" are applied, or, but more exceptionally, where technically sophisticated consumer goods are involved (*Omega*, J.O. 1970, L242/22, [1970] C.M.L.R. D49; *BMW*, O.J. 1975, L29/1, [1975] 1 C.M.L.R. D44; *SABA*, O.J. 1976, L28/19, [1976] 1 C.M.L.R. D61; case 26/76, *Metro/SABA* [1977] E.C.R. 1875.

In exempting agreements, the Commission must also ensure that the benefits, *e.g.* improved production and supply, lower costs, research results, do not fall only on the parties themselves, but that other market participants and consumers can expect to gain advantages from them, and further that the parties to the agreement will still be faced with competition in the relevant geographical or product market (cases 19 & 20/74, *Kali und Salz, supra*).

ARTICLE 86

Any abuse by one or more undertakings of a dominant position within the common market or in a substantial part of it shall be prohibited as incompatible with the common market in so far as it may affect trade between Member States. Such abuse may, in particular, consist in:

(*a*) directly or indirectly imposing unfair purchase or selling prices or other unfair trading conditions;

(*b*) limiting production, markets or technical development to the prejudice of consumers;

(*c*) applying dissimilar conditions to equivalent transactions with other trading parties, thereby placing them at a competitive disadvantage;

(*d*) making the conclusion of contracts subject to acceptance by the other parties of supplementary obligations which, by their nature or according to commercial usage, have no connection with the subject of such contracts.

GENERAL NOTE

Art. 86 provides a complementary means of control of market behaviour to Art. 85, *ante*, by prohibiting the activities of undertakings in particularly powerful positions where such behaviour would not be possible if those undertakings were open to the effects of competitive market forces. As in the case of Art. 85 the prohibition operates in the context of the objectives of the common market by seeking to ensure that competition is not distorted (Art. 3 (f), *ante*) and that other market participants (whether dealing directly with the dominant undertaking or being affected indirectly as ultimate consumers) are not otherwise prejudiced by unreasonable exploitation of market power. Thus the Court has explicitly rejected a narrow interpretation of Art. 86 and placed the prohibition in its wider setting (see Arts. 2 and 3 (f), *ante*; case 78/70, *DGG* v. *Metro* [1971] E.C.R. 487 and in particular, case 6/72, *Europemballage and Continental Can* v. *Commission* [1973] E.C.R. 215 and cases 6 & 7/73, *Commercial Solvents* v. *Commission* [1974] E.C.R. 223). The enforcement of the prohibition rests largely with the Commission through its powers to order termination of infringements (Reg. 17, Art 3, *e.g.* by ordering resumption of supplies, cases 6 & 7/73, *Commercial Solvents*; case 27/76, *United Brands* v. *Commission* [1978] E.C.R. 207; cease and desist orders; *sed quaere* orders of divestiture, *Continental Can*, J.O. 1972, L7/25, [1972] C.M.L.R. D11, on appeal case 6/72, *supra*), and to impose fines (Reg. 17, Art. 15 (2)) and periodic penalty payments (Reg. 17, Art. 10), subject to review by the European Court (Arts. 172 and 173, Reg. 17, Art. 17). A decision prohibiting conduct contrary to Art. 86 is not necessary before the prohibition can take effect (Reg. 17, Art. 1) and national courts are thus competent to apply the prohibition (case 127/73, *SABAM* [1974] E.C.R 51; case 155/73, *Sacchi* [1974] E.C.R. 409) and determine its effects according to national law (see Art. 85 (2), *ante*, *cf.* Art. 88, *post*). Art. 86 has no equivalent to Art. 85 (3) permitting exemption from the prohibition in certain cases (Art. 85).

Although Art. 86 is largely concerned with the conduct of private enterprise, the prohibition can, subject to Art. 90, *post*, extend to the behaviour of public bodies (case 155/73, *Sacchi*, *supra*, and also undertakings granted powers by public authorities (case 78/70, *DGG* v. *Metro*, *supra*; case 127/73, *SABAM*, *supra*; case 26/75, *General Motors* v. *Commission* [1975] E.C.R. 1367; case 90/76, *Van Ameyde* v. *U.C.I.* [1977] E.C.R. 1091; case 13/77, *INNO* v. *ATAB* [1977] E.C.R. 2115). (For meaning of "undertaking," see Art. 85, general note.)

In order to establish a violation, it must be shown that the undertaking (or undertakings) is in a dominant position, that there has been an improper exploitation of that position and that trade between Member States may be affected (case 24/67, *Parke Davis* [1968] E.C.R. 55). See generally Art. 85, general note on the latter concept and case 22/78, *Hugin Cash Registers* (not yet reported). The notion of a dominant position relates to "a position of economic strength enjoyed by an undertaking (or undertakings) which enables it (them) to prevent effective competition being maintained on the relevant market by giving it (them) the power to behave to an appreciable extent independently of its (their) competitors, customers and ultimately its consumers" (case 27/76, *United Brands*, *supra*; see also case 6/72, *Continental Can*, *supra*; *Hoffman-La Roche*, O.J. 1976, L223/27, [1976] 2 C.M.L.R. D25, on appeal, case 85/76 (not yet reported)). An undertaking's economic strength is determined not only by its market share, but also with reference to the degree of economic, technical and financial advantage, it has over other market participants (*ibid.*, see also decisions of Commission in *United Brands*, O.J. 1976, L95/1, [1976] 1 C.M.L.R. D28; *Continental Can*, J.O. 1972, L7/25, [1972] C.M.L.R. D11, and case 85/76, *Hoffman-La Roche*, *supra*). The notion of abuse as regards other market participants is closely connected with the determination of the existence of a dominant position in the relevant market, for only by reference to a particular market can the existence and exercise of economic strength be examined. Both the product and geographical market must be established. The existence of a particular product market is determined by reference to the possibilities of interchange or substitution with other products, both from the point of view of demand and supply, and also to any special features of the product which distinguish it from others (note problem of inadequate market analysis by Commission found by Court in case 6/72, *Continental Can*, *supra*). Separate markets have been found to exist for raw materials distinct from that of the finished product (cases 6 & 773, *Commercial Solvents*, *supra*); for different groups of vitamins (case 85/76, *Hoffman-La Roche*, *supra*); for bananas as distinct from fresh fruit (case 27/76, *United Brands*, *supra*) and for spare parts as opposed to the finished product (*Liptons/Hugin*, O.J. 1978, L22/23, [1978] 1 C.M.L.R. D19, on appeal case 22/78 (not yet reported). Where a monopoly exists in the relevant market, Art. 86 may apply (case 26/75, *General Motors*, *supra*; case 155/73, *Sacchi*, *supra*, and this includes the holding of industrial property rights case 78/70, *DGG* v. *Metro*, *supra*; case 24/67, *Parke Davis*, *supra*). Art. 86 prohibits abuses by one or more undertakings which may involve consideration of certain situations which could also fall within Art. 85 (1). (See Report of

Commission on Behaviour of Oil Companies, *Fifth Report on Competition Policy*; cases 40/73, etc., *Suiker Unie* v. *Commission* [1975] E.C.R. 1663) or examination of parent/subsidiary relationships (*e.g.* case 6/72, *Continental Can, supra*; cases 6 & 7/73, *Commercial Solvents, supra; Hoffman-La Roche, supra; Liptons/Hugin, supra*). Note also exercise of extra-territorial jurisdiction, see Art. 85, *ante*). See relationship between the application of Arts. 85 and 86 to joint ventures, *Fourth and Seventh Reports on Competition Policy, IMI/Heilmann*, Bull.E.C. 6/78.

As the prohibition of Art. 86 is intended to prevent the distortion of competition to the extent that such would be incompatible with the objectives of the common market, the geographical market is examined in order to determine whether the dominant position exists in the common market or a substantial part thereof. The area of operation is not decisive so much as the proportion of business carried on by the undertaking within the common market in relation to the total product market (cases 40/73, etc., *Suiker Unie et al., supra;* case 26/75, *General Motors, supra; Felixstowe Dock and Railway Co.* v. *British Transport Dock Board* [1976] 2 C.M.L.R. 405) or the actual or potential effect on the normal conditions of trade between Member States (cases 6 & 7/73, *Commercial Solvents, supra;* case 27/76, *United Brands, supra;* case 22/78, *supra*).

The examples of abuse given in paras. (*a*) to (*d*) are not exhaustive and relate mainly to the use of a dominant position to impose requirements on other undertakings which could not be maintained in conditions of competition, and are seen to be unfair or unreasonable and destructive of those undertakings' ability to maintain independently determined competitive strategies. The prohibition of unfair conditions as to prices requires that a dominant firm should not charge prices which are excessive in relation to the economic value of the goods or services provided, or result in objectively unjustifiable differential pricing policies (case 26/75, *General Motors, supra;* case 27/76, *United Brands, supra*, although see difficulties expressed by Commission in determining whether prices are abusive, *Fifth, Sixth and Seventh Reports on Competition Policy*), but should be such as to allow a reasonable margin of profit and possibilities for competitive action by other undertakings dealing with a dominant firm. Other trading conditions or supplementary obligations will be prohibited where they restrict the freedom of action of the undertakings subject to them (case 127/73, *SABAM, supra; Eurofima* [1973] C.M.L.R. D217; case 27/76, *United Brands, supra*), or where they lead to a strengthening of a dominant position, by dissuading transactions with other competitors, *e.g.* through the use of loyalty discounts or aggregated rebates (cases 40/73, etc., *Suiker Unie, supra;* case 85/76, *Hoffman-La Roche, supra*) Art. 86 prohibits a refusal to supply where no objective justification can be given (cases 6 & 73, *Commercial Solvents, supra;* 27/76, *United Brands, supra; Liptons/Hugin, supra;* case 77/77, *B.P.* v. *Commission* [1978] E.C.R. 1513).

On a wider objective interpretation, Art. 86 is used to prohibit activities which could eliminate or discourage competition (*e.g.* through mergers with competitors, case 6/72, *Continental Can, supra;* through refusal to supply, cases 6 & 7/73, *Commercial Solvents* and *Liptons/Hugin, supra;* through the strengthening of a dominant position on a weak competitive market, case 85/76, *Hoffman-La Roche, supra*), even if no causal connection can be shown between the dominant position and the abuse (see case 6/72). Thus Art. 86 is available not only to prohibit abusive market conduct, but also to protect the structure of the market and the consumer within it (*ibid.* note Commission's proposed merger Regulation and see also case 27/76, *United Brands, supra, First Report on Competition Policy*).

ARTICLE 87

1. Within three years of the entry into force of this Treaty the Council shall, acting unanimously on a proposal from the Commission and after consulting the Assembly, adopt any appropriate regulations or directives to give effect to the principles set out in Articles 85 and 86.

If such provisions have not been adopted within the period mentioned, they shall be laid down by the Council, acting by a qualified majority on a proposal from the Commission and after consulting the Assembly.

2. The regulations or directives referred to in paragraph 1 shall be designed, in particular:

(a) to ensure compliance with the prohibitions laid down in Article 85 (1) and in Article 86 by making provision for fines and periodic penalty payments;

(b) to lay down detailed rules for the application of Article 85 (3), taking into account the need to ensure effective supervision on the one hand, and to simplify administration to the greatest possible extent on the other;

(c) to define, if need be, in the various branches of the economy, the scope of the provisions of Articles 85 and 86;

(d) to define the respective functions of the Commission and of the Court of Justice in applying the provisions laid down in this paragraph;

(e) to determine the relationship between national laws and the provisions contained in this Section or adopted pursuant to this Article.

ARTICLE 88

Until the entry into force of the provisions adopted in pursuance of Article 87, the authorities in Member States shall rule on the admissibility of agreements, decisions and concerted practices and on abuse of a dominant position in the common market in accordance with the law of their country and with the provisions of Article 85, in particular paragraph 3, and of Article 86.

ARTICLE 89

1. Without prejudice to Article 88, the Commission shall, as soon as it takes up its duties, ensure the application of the principles laid down in Articles 85 and 86. On application by a Member State or on its own initiative, and in cooperation with the competent authorities in the Member States, who shall give it their assistance, the Commission shall investigate cases of suspected infringement of these principles. If it finds that there has been an infringement, it shall propose appropriate measures to bring it to an end.

2. If the infringement is not brought to an end, the Commission shall record such infringement of the principles in a reasoned decision. The Commission may publish its decision and authorise Member States to take the measures, the conditions and details of which it shall determine, needed to remedy the situation.

ARTICLE 90

1. In the case of public undertakings and undertakings to which Member States grant special or exclusive rights, Member States shall neither enact nor maintain in force any measure contrary to the rules contained in this Treaty, in particular to those rules provided for in Article 7 and Articles 85 to 94.

2. Undertakings entrusted with the operation of services of general economic interest or having the character of a revenue-producing monopoly shall be subject to the rules contained in this Treaty, in particular to the rules on competition, in so far as the application of such rules does not obstruct the performance, in law or in fact, of the particular tasks assigned

to them. The development of trade must not be affected to such an extent as would be contrary to the interests of the Community.

3. The Commission shall ensure the application of the provisions of this Article and shall, where necessary, address appropriate directives or decisions to Member States.

THE COURT OF JUSTICE

ARTICLE 173

The Court of Justice shall review the legality of acts of the Council and the Commission other than recommendations or opinions. It shall for this purpose have jurisdiction in actions brought by a Member State, the Council or the Commission on grounds of lack of competence, infringement of an essential procedural requirement, infringement of this Treaty or of any rule of law relating to its application, or misuse of powers.

Any natural or legal person may, under the same conditions, institute proceedings against a decision addressed to that person or against a decision which, although in the form of a regulation or a decision addressed to another person, is of direct and individual concern to the former.

The proceedings provided for in this Article shall be instituted within two months of the publication of the measure, or of its notification to the plaintiff, or, in the absence thereof, of the day on which it came to the knowledge of the latter, as the case may be.

GENERAL NOTE

The purpose of this article is to provide the means of annulling an "act." Annulment under this article, which has effect *erga omnes*, must be distinguished from the declaration of invalidity which can result from proceedings under Art. 177. While, as far as an individual who is successful under either article is concerned, the practical effects may be very similar, the general consequences differ greatly. This factor must be borne in mind if the relationship between the two articles is to be understood. It explains the contrast between the rigidity, as far as individuals are concerned, under this article and the liberality under Art. 177. (Compare case 48/65, *Lütticke* v. *Commission* [1966] E.C.R. 19 and cases 73 and 74/63, *N.V. International Crediet en Handelsvereniging* v. *Dutch Ministry of Agriculture and Fisheries* [1964] E.C.R. 1.)

This article covers several situations.

(a) The Member States, the Council or the Commission may challenge the "acts" of either of the latter bodies (who may also challenge the "acts" of each other). "Act" is not confined to those defined in Art. 189 (case 22/70, *Commission* v. *Council* [1971] E.C.R. 263) but stretches to all "acts" having legal consequences. A distinction must be drawn between those "decisions" of the Council which are purely political in their nature, or purely internal in their consequences, *e.g.* the laying down of general programmes, or of guidelines and those which bind in a more precise sense. The distinction is not always clear and the second category is probably broader in its scope than would be the case in the United Kingdom. The contrast is made in case 81/72 *Commission* v. *Council* [1973] E.C.R. 575 (the first staff salaries case). The Council had adopted a system for an experimental period, and had departed from it. The Council resolution was held to be one in which "the Council had gone beyond the stage of preparatory consideration and had entered the phase of decision-making." The frontier is not yet clearly defined. It would seem that a Member State is not debarred from using this possibility of challenge against a Council regulation, even though the regulation appears to have been adopted unanimously (case 151/73 *Ireland* v. *Council* [1974] E.C.R. 285).

273

(b) Any natural or legal person can challenge decisions addressed to him.
(c) Such persons may challenge decisions addressed to another person which are of direct and individual concern to the former. Under this head, an individual may challenge a decision even though addressed to a Member State if the other conditions are present (case 25/62, *Plaumann* [1963] E.C.R. 95, such a State being "another person"). It is important to note from case 132/77, *Société pour l'exportation des sucres* v. *Commission* [1978] E.C.R. 1061, that where a Regulation gives discretionary power to Member States, subject to control by the Commission, a specific act by the Commission must be found, otherwise challenge must be in national courts. In the context of competition law see case 26/76, *Metro SB Grossmärkte KG* v. *Commission* [1977] E.C.R. 1875 for the scope of admissibility to challenge a decision addressed to another, and note in the same case that a challenge of a refusal to re-open a decision may be regarded simply as a challenge to the original decision.
(d) Such persons may also challenge "concealed" decisions which have the form but not the nature of a regulation and are of like concern. For these concealed decisions, see cases 16 & 17/62, *Confédération nationale des producteurs de fruits et légumes* v. *Council* [1962] E.C.R. 471. More recently see case 100/74, *Société CAM S.A.* v. *Commission* [1975] E.C.R. 1393. The former case had indicated that a Regulation could be severable, in the sense that a provision in a genuine Regulation might be capable of being classified as a Decision and thus attackable by an individual under this article, if the conditions of direct and individual effect were present. The Commission Regulation in question (which dealt with monetary compensation amounts) provided a particular treatment for a group of traders. The Court held that "by adopting distinguishing criteria the contested measure affects a fixed number of traders identified by reason of the individual course of action which they pursued or are regarded as having pursued during a particular period" (p. 1403). Hence, even if the measure were part of a legislative act, it, in all the circumstances, was capable of being regarded as having the true nature of a decision and of being thus open to challenge. The clearest illustration of such a concealed decision is to be found in the group of anti-dumping cases related to ballbearings (case 113/77, *NTN Toyo Bearings Co.* v. *Council* and cases 118–121/77, [1979] 2 C.M.L.R. 257). The Regulation in question referred in the preamble to undertakings given by the four major Japanese producers and it was found that the Regulation "although drafted in general terms ... concerns only ... those major producers." Hence this amounted to a concealed decision or of individual concern. Moreover, since, although national implementing measures were involved, those measures were automatice there was also directness. On the latter point these cases should be compared with cases 103–109/78, *Soc. des Usines de Beauport* v. *Council* [1979] E.C.R. 17 in which the national authorities have a discretion as to the implementing measures and hence there could be no directness. (The same case indicates that an amendment, which is challenged, to an earlier measure will have the same nature as that earlier measure.) On the former point of "individuality" as affecting the character of a measure as a regulation the ballbearing cases should be compared with case 101/76, *Koninklijke Scholten Honig N.V.* v. *Council* [1977] E.C.R. 797 in which although it was possible to identify the firms who would be affected by a Regulation, the act was treated as a true Regulation since it "applied by virtue of an objective legal or factual situation defined by the measure in relation to the objective of the latter." In periods of currency fluctuation with consequential rapid changes in Regulations, it becomes more probable that, with a tightening of the system of advance fixing, a regulation may, in regard to accepted applicants have the nature of a decision, see case 112/77, *Töpfer and Co. GmbH* v. *Commission* [1978] E.C.R. 1019. It involved such a situation and admissibility was not challenged by the Commission, see §§ 9–12. On the same point of identification and on the point of direct and individual concern see too case 123/77, *UNICME* v. *Council* [1978] E.C.R. 845 where the refusal of an import licence under a Community Regulation would have been by national authorities and the Court rejected the application on the grounds of a lack of directness and individuality alone, without examining whether the act were, or not, a direct Regulation. It should also be noted that even if the party is able to surmount these obstacles, he must nevertheless show a legal 88/76, *Société pour l'exportation*

des sucres v. *Commission* [1977] E.C.R. 709 (involving the delayed publication of the *Official Journal*) in which case, although the action was declared inadmissible the claimant was allowed his costs.

The substance, not the form, of an act will be determining, see *e.g.* case 81/72, *supra*. Thus there may be a bundle of individual decisions wrapped up in a regulation, see *e.g.* cases 41–44/70, *International Fruit Company* [1971] E.C.R. 411. On the other hand, even though a finite number of persons might be affected by a regulation, it will retain its character as such if it governs a particular situation in a normative and abstract way. (See cases 63/69 and 64/69, *Cie française commerciale,* and 65/69, *Cie d'Approvisionement* [1970] E.C.R. 205, 221 and 229.) Nor, provided that this normative character is present, does the fact that a regulation has different impact on different persons affect its character (see, too, cases 6/68, *Zuckerfabrik Watenstedt* [1968] E.C.R. 409 and 101/76 above). The distinction may be grasped by comparing this group of cases with *International Fruit Co. (supra)*. That case related to a Regulation which was found to be in substance a "bundle" of individual decisions. A closer contrast to cases 65/69 and 6/68, *supra*, is the case 100/75, *CAM* referred to above where the normative character was lacking. On reaching that conclusion the element of individual effect upon known or identifiable members of a group had its effect. To some extent the importance of challenging by this route has been diminished once the autonomous character of Art. 215 has been recognised, so that annulment is not a necessary preliminary to raising an action based on the non-contractual liability of the Community. Validity, it must be remembered, may be challenged more easily by way of Art. 177.

"Individually" and "directly" are words which have created difficulty. To be individually concerned the individual must be in such a relationship to the decision that he is in effect in the position of a destinatory (see *e.g.* case 63/70, *Bock* [1971] E.C.R. 897, and if the decision is *e.g.* issued to a State, provided that State has no discretion as to its implementation: *Bock, supra,* and cases 106 & 107/63, *Toepfer* [1965] E.C.R. 405).

In looking at "individually" the Court will have regard to the whole market (case 1/64, *Glucoseries réunies* [1964] E.C.R. 413; 10 & 18/68, *Eridania* [1969] E.C.R. 459). A decision which confers a discretion on a Member State will not create a direct concern. (Case 69/69, *Alcan* [1970] E.C.R. 385.)

The word "directly" implies an immediate nexus between the Commission issuing the decision and the individual. Thus in *Toepfer* the effect of the decision had this effect by reason of Art. 22 of Reg. 19 under which it took immediate effect. The possibility that a Member State will refuse to obey a decision which is of that type and await proceedings under Art. 169 will not, it seems, prevent this direct effect. One which merely confers a faculty on a Member State will not create this effect. The issue of direct and individual concern can merge with that of whether the measure in question is or is not a true regulation. See case 88/76, *Société pour l'exportation des Sucres* v. *Commission* [1977] E.C.R. 709 where, by implication, a "Regulation" was held to be a concealed decision but in the particular cistumstances of the case the complaint was nevertheless held inadmissible since the company lacked a legal interest. The interest of this article for individuals has been greatly reduced, once it was admitted that proceedings under Art. 215 (*q.v.*) for compensation were possible even when an act had not been annulled. In most cases the real object was to secure compensation. Nevertheless, the rules evolved in the early cases may still be important. Compare case 72/74 *Union Syndicale etc.* v. *Council* [1975] E.C.R. 401 in which a number of unions representing Community officials were held to not to be directly and individually concerned by measures affecting the general interests of a category of persons even though formed to protect those collective interests. In practice this decision causes little difficulty since the Unions have a right to intervene in cases brought under Art. 179 (*q.v.*), and on the other hand there are practical advantages in having matters determined in concrete cases.

The Grounds

The grounds of challenge are limited to the four specified in para. (1). This is not an appeal to the full jurisdiction.

Lack of competence, apart from the obvious meaning of *ultra vires*, will include a challenge based on an excessive delegation of power (case 9/56, *Meroni* [1957 and 1958] E.C.R. 133) and even out of time the Court will look at fundamental incompetence (6 & 11/69 *France* [1969] E.C.R. 523). If such were found it seems that the act would not be annulled but be declared void *ab initio*. As to territorial limits, see cases 48, 49, 51–57/69, *I.C.I. and Others* v. *Commission* [1972] E.C.R. 619. The principle, of course, applies not only to the Commission, but also to the Council and in view of the economic evolution cases 80 & 81/77, *Ramel* v. *Receveur des Douanes* [1978] E.C.R. 927, an Art. 177 case, should be noted.

Infringement of an essential procedural requirement. There would fall under this head, the failure of an institution to consult another as required by the Treaty, or, case 230/78, *Eridania* (not yet reported), the inadequacy of the reasoning of a decision (see as to the limits of this, case 38/64, *Getreide-Import* [1965] E.C.R. 203). The reasoning must show the legal grounds and what considerations have moved the Commission. An inadequacy of reasoning which might prejudice the rights of the defence will amount to a defect under this head.

Breach of this Treaty. In examining this the court will enter into the economic justification for a decision but only in broad terms. (See *Bock* and *Toepfer, supra*.) As with other articles in this group, the head also comprises breaches of Community secondary legislation or the general principles of Community law. This last head will include breaches of fundamental rights (as defined by the Court), see *e.g.* case 4/73 *Nold* v. *Commission* [1974] E.C.R. 491 which is an ECSC case, but the principles are of general application. Another head of general principles which is assuming increased importance is that of legitimate confidence linked with the idea of legal certainty, see *e.g.* case 81/72 *Commission* v. *Council, supra*, and case 70/74 *Commission* v. *Council* [1975] E.C.R. 795, the first and second staff salaries cases. The concept has appeared in cases under Art. 215, *infra*, case 74/74, *CNTA* v. *Commission* [1975] E.C.R. 533, in which it was held that, in the absence of an overwhelming public interest, the failure to provide in a Regulation adequate transitional measures, was a sufficient breach of a superior rul of law, as to give rise to liability. It is not clear whether that fault would also suffice to establish invalidity. On the other hand those grounds of invalidity which are established in cases arising under Art. 177 are clearly applicable in cases under this article *e.g.* excessive delegation as in case 23/75, *Rey Soda* v. *Cassa Conquaglio Zucchero* [1975] E.C.R. 1279. Thus the ground of a "discriminatory distribution of costs between the various agricultural sectors" which was held to be sufficient to establish invalidity in case 116/76, *Granaria B.V.* v. *Hoofdproduktschap voor Akkerbouwproducten and Produktschap voor Margarine, vetten en Oliën* [1977] E.C.R. 1247 could, where the other conditions exist, be applicable to cases under this article. On equality before the law see cases 113/77, etc., the *Ballbearing* cases, above, where the argument was rejected that the Council, having made a Regulation under EEC, Art. 113 could nevertheless, in disregard of the procedure contained in that basic Regulation, make a further Regulation based directly on Art. 113. The rejection of that argument was also based on the assertion that such action would amount to an interference with the legislative system of the Community. There is little authority in cases under this Treaty on the point of how far the Court will go in reviewing the economic judgment which underlies a Regulation. This matter is discussed by the Advocate-General in his opinion in case 116/76, above, and the other joined cases. He there accepts that where the ground alleged invalidity is lack of proportionality, then the Court will consider economic issues. See also in the context of Art. 177 on this point cases 103 & 145/77, *Royal Scholten Honig* v. *Intervention Board* [1978] E.C.R. 2037 and case 56/77, *Agence européenne d'interims SA* v. *Commission* [1978] E.C.R. 2215, a challenge to the acceptance of tenders, which raises a similar point.

Misuse of powers covers the use of a legitimate power for an improper purpose, *i.e.* one for which the power was not provided. The concept should not be regarded as one involving anything necessarily sinister. It has never yet been used as a ground of annulment.

Provided that the pleadings indicate with adequate clarity what are the grounds on which challenge is based the pleadings need not, it seems, specify the precise head. This may be important, since, granted the terms of Art. 190 there can well be an overlap between the second and third heads.

Time Limits

The time limits in the fourth paragraph must be strictly observed. They apply even against States (case 2/71, *Germany* [1971] E.C.R. 669), except where a fundamental breach is in question (cases 6 & 11/69, *France* [1969] E.C.R. 523) and would no doubt also apply as between the Institutions, *cf.* case 22/70, *Commission* v. *Council* [1971] E.C.R. 263. Difficulties can arise, where the challenge is to a decision which has been issued to another, of fixing the starting point from which time runs. See *Alcan* and *Eridania, supra*. It should be noted that the initiation of proceedings has no suspensory effect (see Art. 185 and case 31/77, *Commission* v. *United Kingdom* [1977] 2 C.M.L.R. 359), but an application can be made to secure that result, see Protocol on the Statute of the Court of Justice Art. 36 and Rules Art. 83 *et seq.*

ARTICLE 175

Should the Council or the Commission, in infringement of this Treaty, fail to act, the Member States and the other institutions of the Community may bring an action before the Court of Justice to have the infringement established.

The action shall be admissible only if the institution concerned has first been called upon to act. If, within two months of being so called upon, the institution concerned has not defined its position, the action may be brought within a further period of two months.

Any natural or legal person may, under the conditions laid down in the preceding paragraphs, complain to the Court of Justice that an institution of the Community has failed to address to that person any act other than a recommendation or an opinion.

ARTICLE 177

The Court of Justice shall have jurisdiction to give preliminary rulings concerning:

(*a*) the interpretation of this Treaty;

(*b*) the validity and interpretation of acts of the institutions of the Community;

(*c*) the interpretation of the statutes of bodies established by an act of the Council, where those statutes so provide.

Where such a question is raised before any court or tribunal of a Member State, that court or tribunal may, if it considers that a decision on the question is necessary to enable it to give judgment, request the Court of Justice to give a ruling thereon.

Where any such question is raised in a case pending before a court or tribunal of a Member State, against whose decisions there is no judicial remedy under national law, that court or tribunal shall bring the matter before the Court of Justice.

GENERAL NOTE

Introduction

This is one of the most important articles. Its operation in the United Kingdom is reinforced by s. 3 (1) of the European Communities Act 1972, requiring that any question of the type here referred to which arises in any legal proceedings shall either be referred to the European Court or determined according to the principles laid down in any relevant decision of that Court. It is important to note that the use of this procedure is helped by the fact that proceedings under this article are covered by a Legal Aid Certificate *R.* v. *Marlborough Street Stipendiary, ex p. Bouchereau* [1977] 1 W.L.R. 419. Its general importance may be judged by the fact that even Regulations in the field of agriculture have, under this procedure, been held to be invalid on the ground that they imposed an unjustifiable discriminatory distribution of burdens between different agricultural sectors, case 114/76, *Bela Mühle* v. *Grows Farm* [1977] E.C.R. 1211. The Act has itself been implemented in Rules of Court, *e.g.* the new Ord. 114 in the Rules of the Supreme Court or the new Chapter VA in the Rules of Court of the Court of Session. As to the former, see *Bulmer Ltd.* v. *Bollinger S.A.* [1974] Ch. 401, although the rules refer to an appeal against an order for reference, but were silent on a refusal, the Court of Appeal held that appeal was available with leave against such an order. The whole case is discussed below against the general background of experience with this article. Whether or not rules have been made for any court or tribunal, the obligation or the discretion to refer contained in this article arises directly under it, and hence should be implemented under s. 2 (1) of the European Communities Act 1972. That it is within the power of any court (and even in *ex parte* proceedings) has recently been re-emphasised in case 70/77, *Simmenthal SPA* v. *Administrazione delle Finanze dello Stato* [1978] E.C.R. 1453. See too case 106/77, between the same parties [1978] E.C.R. 629 on the validity of references. The sort of body which can refer under this article is ultimately to be determined by the Court of Justice itself and by no one else. (See case 61/65, *Vaassen-Göbbels* below.)

General

The essence of this article (which is also applicable to the Accession Treaty and related texts as well as to Conventions such as those of Yaoundé or Lomé, see case 87/75, *Bresciani* v. *Italian Finance Department* [1976] E.C.R. 129) is to be found in (*a*) and (*b*). An example of (*c*) is to be found in the Statutes of the Administrative Commission for the Social Security of Migrant Workers (J.O. 1959, 1213). In addition, two protocols of June 3, 1971 (*q.v.*), have given an interpretative jurisdiction to the Court in respect of the Conventions on the mutual recognition of Companies and on the execution of judgments. The first three cases under those Conventions were dealt with by the Court in September 1976 and the jurisdiction under the latter convention (not yet ratified by the United Kingdom) is of growing importance. The two primary heads of jurisdiction under this particular article are interpretation and validity.

Validity is meant in the fullest sense. It is not merely formal validity (cases 73 & 74/63 *N.V. Rotterdam et G. A. Puttershoek* v. *Ministre de l'agriculture et de la pêche* [1964] E.C.R. 1) and it extends to validity under international law (cases 21–24/72, *International Fruit Co.* v. *Productschap voor Groenten en Fruit* [1972] E.C.R. 1219), as well as to questions under "Community" constitutional law such as case 25/70, *Einfuhr-und Vorratsstelle für Getreide und Futtermittel* v. *Köster* [1970] E.C.R. 1161 or case 23/75, *Rey Soda* v. *Cassa Conquaglio Zucchero* [1975] E.C.R. 1229 or case 35/78, *N. G. Schouten BV* v. *Hoofdproduktschap voor Akkerbouwprodukten* [1978] E.C.R. 2543 or under the general principles of Community law, *e.g.* case 114/76, *Bela Mühle KG* v. *Grows Farm* [1977] E.C.R. 1211—the discriminatory distribution of burdens between different sectors. The Court has also held a Regulation invalid on grounds of fact, case 131/77, *Milac* v. *HZA Saarbrücken* [1978] E.C.R. 1041, but it is doubtful how far in cases not involving a Community act, the Court would enter upon facts since the essential points are of law only. Since validity has this broad meaning Art. 177 is important as a means of overcoming the narrowness of the conditions of admissibility under Art. 173; compare case 101/76, *Koninklijk Scholten Honig NV* v. *Council* [1977] E.C.R. 797 with case 125/77, *The Same* v. *Hoofdproduktschap voor Akkerbouwprodukten* [1978] E.C.R. 1991. It is not yet certain whether this procedure can be used to challenge a Community act when that could have been challenged by the party under Art. 173, but no timeous challenge has been made, case 59/77, *Ets de Bloos* v. *Bouyer* [1977] E.C.R. 2359. It must be noted that a declaration of invalidity by this route does not result in annulment, but the Community act in question becomes inapplicable in the case in question. It should be noted that the procedure is available to ascertain the legal consequences of an earlier decision of the Court of Justice where that issue is relevant in proceedings before a national court (see the opinion of the Advocate-General in case 24/66, *bis Gesellschaft für Getreidehandel m.b.H.* v. *Commission* [1973] E.C.R. 1599). This can be important granted the limitations to the interpretation procedure under Art. 40 of the Statute of the Court.

The interpretative role was essential to maintain uniformity. The clearest example of the utility of the article may be found in the three cases 51/75, 86/75 and 96/75 all involving the same two companies (or their subsidiaries) but the actions originating in three different Member States, and the use of this article ensured uniformity of decision. The Court has defined its role as being limited to interpretation to the exclusion of application, which remains the task of national courts (case 26/62, *Van Gend en Loos* [1963] E.C.R. 1). It follows that it cannot in these cases pass upon the validity of national measures. Nor is it for the Court to deal with pure questions of national law (case 93/75, *Adlerblum* v. *Caisse nationale de veiellesse* [1975] E.C.R. 2147). It may, however, have to be concerned with the interpretation or classification of national law, when national and community law are intermeshed, as in social security legislation (case 17/76, *Brack* v. *Insurance Officer* [1976] E.C.R. 1429); or see case 51/76, *Verbond van Nederlandse Ondernemingen* v. *Inspecteur der Invoerrechten* [1977]

E.C.R. 113. It is for the national court to draw the conclusions from the interpretation (case 6/64, *Costa* v. *ENEL* [1964] E.C.R. 585). Nevertheless it can give clear indications to the national court of considerations to be taken into account in application (case 119/75, *Terrapin* v. *Terranova* [1976] E.C.R. 1039). The operation of Art. 177 is thus built upon a distinction in function between the national court and the European Court, and upon a loyal co-operation between the two. Hence the European Court will not question the pertinence of the question asked to the litigation (*Van Gend en Loos, supra* and case 117/77, *Besteuer van het Algemeneen Ziekerfonds* v. *Pierik* [1978] E.C.R. 825), and it is for the national court alone, to the exclusion of the parties, to determine the questions to be asked (case 13/67, *Becher* [1968] E.C.R. 187). Nevertheless in practice in the United Kingdom counsel are consulted and at times draft the questions; they cannot, however, decide finally on the questions and the decision to submit a point or not must remain that of the court in question. See too case 70/77, *Simmenthal* [1978] E.C.R. 1453, paras. 7–9. A private contract, containing an arbitration clause, cannot, whatever the terms of that clause, compel a reference, case 93/78, *Mattheus* v. *DOEGO* [1978] E.C.R. 2203. The European Court has emphasised the simplicity of the procedure and will itself abstract a question which it can properly answer from one inelegantly put (*Costa* v. *ENEL, supra*). It has also emphasised speed and directness (case 16/65, *Schwarze* [1965] E.C.R. 877). Nevertheless there are limits to informality. Mere incidental or imprecise references in the mode of posing the question to matters specifically asked are not sufficient to open up all these matters for an interpretation. See *e.g.* case 94/74, *IGAV* v. *ENCC* [1975] E.C.R. 699. As the Advocate-General in that case indicated, this limitation is required since otherwise the parties, who are entitled to submit observations under Art. 20 of the Statute of the Court, are deprived of a proper opportunity to express observation. Liberalism has therefore to have some limits.

It must be noted that the requirement of uniformity means that the Court may be called on to interpret acts which may not be directly applicable, *e.g.* directives (case 32/74, *Haaga* [1974] E.C.R. 1201 and case 111/75, *Mazzalai* [1976] E.C.R. 657 and case 51/76 above).

It is evident that the Court is master of the interpretation of Art. 177 itself. Thus the definition of what is a "court or tribunal" for the purposes of Community law can only be decided by the Court, and it does not necessarily correspond with the meaning in a national system (case 61/65, *Vaassen-Göbbels* [1966] E.C.R. 261, and the Advocate-General in case 17/76, *Brack* v. *Insurance Officer* [1976] E.C.R. 1429 on the status of the National Insurance Commissioner). The same is true of the phrase "court or tribunal ... against whose decisions there is no judicial remedy." It is evident that such a court is not limited to a court like the House of Lords (*Costa* v. *ENEL, supra*). It is uncertain what will be the position where leave to appeal is required, or where redress is by discretionary remedies, *e.g.* a declaration, or where appeal is on limited ground only. All such matters can only be determined by a reference since they are matters of interpretation of Art. 177 itself. Some light is thrown on this problem by case 107/76, *Hoffmann-La Roche AG* v. *Centrafarm Vertriebsgesellschaft pharmazeutischer Erzeugnisse mbH* [1977] E.C.R. 957. The question was whether a court making an interim order was so bound when no appeal was available against such an order. It was held that if a "177" point raised in the interim proceedings must in all circumstances be raised in the main action, or must be so raised if the unsuccessful party so wished, then the obligation under para. (3) did not exist (though the right to refer did). The test is whether each of the parties is entitled to raise further proceedings or to require proceedings to be instituted. If either condition be present, then the obligation to refer was lacking. The implication is therefore that where leave is required from the court giving a decision, or from the appellate court, or where the further proceedings might be so limited as to exclude debate on the point of Community law, then the court issuing the decision is under the obligation to refer.

The determination of what is a "final court" is important since such courts come under an obligation to refer (third para.). Other courts have the power to refer (second para.). Any attempt in national law to limit either the obligation or the discretion would be contrary to Community law. In many cases, as the reports already show, it is important to the saving of costs that reference should be made at the lowest level, since frequently the interpretation of Community law will effectively determine the case (*cf.* the course of *R.* v. *Henn and Darby* [1979] 2 C.M.L.R. 495). This has recently been re-emphasised in case 106/77, *Amministrazione delle Finanze dello Stato* v. *Simmenthal SPA* [1978] E.C.R. 629. The issue was one of a conflict between a Community Regulation and a subsequent national law. Earlier the Italian Constitutional Court had held that questions of the validity of Italian laws which conflicted with Community law had to be determined by that court alone and could not be determined by the court seized of the case. The European Court of Justice held firmly that "every national court must in a case within its jurisdiction apply Community law in its entirety ... and must accordingly set aside any provision of national law which may conflict with it, whether prior or subsequent to the Community rule." This duty is incumbent on every national court irrespective of its level. As was pointed out in that case this solution is essential for the effective operation of the concept of "direct effect." It is equally clear, in practical terms that, in litigation such as the *EMI* case referred to above, an early reference is essential to efficient administration of justice. This is particularly so when the question is whether a provision has direct effect. The early reference can avoid circuitous proceedings. This is underlined by case 166/73, *Rheinmühlen* [1974] E.C.R 33. It was there held that an inferior court although bound on points of law by a superior court, nevertheless retains the right to refer to the European Court, if for example it believes that the ruling of the superior court could lead to a breach of Community law. In many instances the utility of an appeal against an order of reference is very doubtful since that appeal can simply increase delays.

The obligation in the third para. is not, however, absolute. Where the Court has already interpreted a particular provision the obligation may be emptied of content (cases 28–30/62, *Da Costa en Schaake* [1963] E.C.R. 31). There is no "question." This is reflected in s. 3 (1) of the European Communities Act. There are risks of the emergence of a concept of *acte clair* injurious to the uniformity and thus to the efficiency of Community law, and changing circumstances may modify an intepretation. Thus the bias should be towards reference, particularly since phrases such as "migrant worker" may not in the Community setting have the meaning which would at first sight attach to them in national law. Mr. Advocate-General Warner has urged that national courts should be slow to hold that on a question of Community law the answer admits of no doubt (case 9/75, *Meyer-Burckhardt* v. *Commission* [1975] E.C.R. 1171 at p. 1186). In the same case he underlined that a failure to comply with the obligation in Art. 177, third para., could result in the commencement of proceedings under Art. 169, *infra*. While the national court from which the reference comes is bound by the interpretation, it may, if it is not adequately informed by it, seek clarification (case 29/68, *Milch- Fett-und Eierkonter* [1969] E.C.R. 165). It follows that the other courts are not absolutely bound and the faculty to refer remains. See further the observations of Advocate-General Warner in case 8/78, *Milac* v. *HZA Freiburg* [1978] E.C.R. 1721, at 1740. The word "necessary" in para. (2) should it seems be broadly interpreted, since often the importance of an interpretation cannot be adequately judged until an interpretation has been given.

It will be noted that much that was said in *Bulmer Ltd.* v. *Bollinger S.A.* [1974] Ch. 401 cannot easily be reconciled with the principles enunciated by the European Court. In particular, as has been said above, both the obligation and the discretion of the courts under this article are derived directly from Community law. See case 146/73 *Rheinmühlen* [1974] E.C.R. 139 and 147 and above all the terms of the opinion in case 106/77, *Simmenthal* cited above. Ss. 2 and 3 of the European Communities Act, and in particular s. 2 (1), merely reinforce this. It must also be noted that, in so far as there is reliance in *Bulmer's* case on decisions of other national courts on the correct use of Art. 177, these decisions lack authority. It follows from general principles and from the decisions of the European Court that ultimately no national jurisdiction can deprive any tribunal inferior to it of its powers in this respect. This is again reinforced by case 106/77, *Simmenthal* (above) and so any theory or practice that a reference should only be made by a superior, *e.g.* appellate court is not sustainable. Apart from the circumstances that appeals may lead to circuitous litigation as was pointed out by the Advocate-General in case 190/73 *Van Haaster* [1974] E.C.R. 1123 there are advantages in early reference in securing legal clarity. This is reinforced by considerations of the circumstances of case 67/74 *Bonsignore* v. *Oberstadtdirektor der Stadt Köln* [1975] E.C.R. 297 that an early reference can remove existing confusions which are creating difficulty. It seems therefore that the attitude adopted in *Van Duyn* v. *Home Office* [1974] 1 W.L.R. 1107 and in *EMI Records Ltd.* v. *CBS (UK) Ltd.* [1975] 1 C.M.L.R. 285 should normally be preferred. It is also clear that the suggestions that the House of Lords alone is bound to refer is, at least, doubtful. A certain shift of view is observable, even in the Court of Appeal, see *Macarthys Ltd.* v. *Wendy Smith* [1979] 3 C.M.L.R. 33, though difficulties remain, even with that decision. Generally, however, a satisfactory practice has grown up with references from, *e.g.* the National Insurance Commissioner and the utility of early reference (by a Resident Magistrate in *Pigs Marketing Board N.I.* v. *Redmond*, despite the potential constitutional implications of the case). For the proceedings in the European Court, see case 83/78, [1978] E.C.R. 2347 and for the subsequent proceedings see (1979) 4 E.L. Rev. 314. There has yet been no interpretation of the words "no judicial remedy" in the context of the English system; in Scotland it is clear that the High Court of Justiciary is bound and so may be the Court of Session. The position of a number of inferior tribunals remains for the moment undecided and the decision of the Commissioner in *Re A Holiday in Italy* (Decision R (S) 4/74 [1975] 1 C.M.L.R. 184) should be regarded as unsound in the light of the reasoning of case 107/76 above. The issue is only mentioned by the Advocate General in case 17/76, *Brack, supra*, but not discussed. These considerations affect also what is said in *Bulmer* of the *acte clair* doctrine and of the meaning of the word "necessary." The meaning of that word as it is used in Art. 177 can only be determined by the European Court and in view both of the new setting and of the multi-lingual background "clarity" derived from one familiar system should often not be assumed (*cf.* case 61/65, *supra*).

It is under this article that many of the fundamental doctrines of Community law, such as that of direct effect (in *Van Gend en Loos*) have emerged. To that fundamental case reference to case 106/77, *Simmenthal* (above) should now also be added since it defines for general purposes the consequences in time of this doctrine. (For an exceptional case, see case 43/75, *Defrenne* v. *Subena* [1975] E.C.R. 455.) Hence it is in many of the Art. 177 cases and their consequences in national courts that some of the most serious constitutional problems have emerged. The declaration that a provision has direct effect means, however, that it creates "rights for individuals which national jurisdictions are bound to protect." Thus frequently the use of Art. 177 is in proceedings against a Member State under national law. In actions between individuals, the validity of the acts of national authorities may also be in issue and hence the consistency of those acts (of whatever nature) with Community law may be the central issue in a reference under this article; see *e.g.* case 77/72 *Capolongo* v. *Maya* [1973] E.C.R. 611 on the direct effect of Art. 92 (1). The direct effect of Art. 93 (3) has been elaborated in cases such as 122/73 *Firma Nordsee* v. *Germany* [1973] E.C.R. 1511. By this road important issues of fundamental rights may be raised and a reconciliation achieved between national conceptions of *ordre public* and the obligation of Community law (case 36/75, *Rutilli* v. *Minister of the Interior* [1975] E.C.R. 1219). *Van Duyn* v. *Home Office, supra*, which was concerned with the problem of the direct effect of a directive illustrates these points and demonstrates the general importance of a ruling by the European Court. The obligation of national courts in the United Kingdom to give effect to such rulings is carried into s. 2 (1) of the European Communities Act. That that burden should fall upon them is a consequence of the distinction drawn between interpretation and application and of the decentralised system of administration of Community law.

Finally, it is important to note that the interpretation given may not only clarify the meaning and nature of a provision—whether it has direct effect or not—but it may also deal with the effect in time of that decision. In case 43/75, *Defrenne* v. *Sabena* [1976] E.C.R. 455 the Court held that Art. 119, on equal pay had direct effect, and should have had such effect since January 1, 1962, for the original Member States and since January 1, 1973, for the New Members, but because of ambiguities created by Member States and the Commission it held that, except as to proceedings already started, the decision only took effect *in futuro*. The case also illustrates by its treatment of the Resolution of the Member States of December 31, 1961, how this article can be used to control fundamental constitutional rules of the Communities. (For the further clarification of that case, see case 149/77, *Defrenne* v. *Sabena* [1978] 3 C.M.L.R. 312.) The decision thus has some resemblance to Art. 174, *supra*. Such constitutional issues touch the question of validity, see, *e.g.* cases 80 & 81/77, *Soc. des Commissaires Réunis Sarl and others* v. *Receveur des Douanes* [1978] E.C.R. 927 on the effect of the end of the transitional period even on the institutions. See also for the same effect in relation to the Treaty of Accession and on the interpretation of that in consonance with the basic Treaties case 118/78, *C. J. Meijer BV* v. *Department of Trade* [1979] 2 C.M.L.R. 398 (and the related case 231/78, *Commission* v. *United Kingdom* [1979] 2 C.M.L.R. 427). For the use of this procedure in regard to state aids and Art. 92 (which is not directly applicable), see case 78/76, *Steinike und Weinlig* v. *Germany* [1977] E.C.R. 595.

Procedure

As has been indicated, the procedure is simple. Its speed is likely to be increased by the implementation of the new Art. 165 (3), *supra*, in Rule 95 of the Rules of Procedure and the subsequent authorisation of three Chambers. References may be remitted by the full Court to a chamber where they concern matters which are essentially technical (*e.g.* customs classification as an example see case 120/75, *Riemer* v. *HZA Lubeck-West* [1976] E.C.R. 423) or in relation to which there is an established jurisprudence. This course is not possible when a Member State has filed observations under Art. 20 of the Statute, unless the State indicates readiness for the matter to be so dealt with. Nor can it be used if one of the Institutions in its observation asks that the matter be dealt with by the full Court. For comment on the use of a chamber or of the full court, see the Advocate-General in case 78/77, *Lührs* v. *HZA Hamburg-Jonas* [1978] E.C.R. 169. The Court has recently suggested the enlargement of this possibility and on the other hand the U.K. Government has drawn attention to certain difficulties which it sees in the preparation of observations by Member States, see *Agence Europe* October 12, 1978. The national court formulates and transmits the questions. Normally the debate is only on points of law. Facts are taken as put in the reference. It has been said by an Advocate-General that cases may arise where credence could be required, case 51/75, *EMI* [1976] E.C.R. 811 at 854. Such cases will be extremely rare except where the factual basis is relevant to the validity of a Community act, see case 131/77, *Milac* v. *HZA Saarbrücken* [1978] E.C.R. 1041. Under Art. 20 of the Statute of the Court these are transmitted to the parties, to the Member States and to the Commission and to the Council if the act originates from the latter; they have the right to present written observations. The Commission always does. No other person may intervene (*Costa* v. *ENEL*). They may also present oral argument. For the details of procedure, see Rule 103 of the rules of procedure. The costs of the parties are costs in the cause; those of a Member State or the Commission are borne by themselves.

Lodging an appeal against a reference in a national system does not debar the Court from proceeding with the reference (case 13/61, *Bosch* [1962] E.C.R. 45), though it may itself defer the hearing (case 31/68, *Chanel* [1970] E.C.R. 403). For the general principle, see case 106/77, *Simmenthal* (above) at § 10 of the opinion of the Court. It remains to be seen whether provisions like those contained in the Rules of Court, already referred to, which require that pending an appeal the reference should not be transmitted, are valid in Community law. In a situation where, *e.g.* a majority on appeal are against the proposed reference it may be that the numbers for and against reference are even. In such a case there clearly is in logic a "question" but a reference is prevented by a national rule, which may thus be invalid.

The ruling given by the Court as a result of proceedings under this article is binding on the national court making the references, case 52/76, *Benedetti* v. *Munari Fratelli S.A.S.* [1977] E.C.R. 163, subject to that Court making a further reference: case 29/68, *Milch- Fett-und Eierkontor GmbH* v. *HZA Saarbrücken* [1969] E.C.R. 165. The matter is further explored by Mr. Advocate-General Warner in his conclusion in case 112/76, *Renato Manzeni* v. *Fonds national de retraite des ouvriers mineurs* [1977] E.C.R. 1647 in which he expresses the view that all courts are bound by the *ratio decidendi* of an interpretation unless a further reference be made. For an application of this view in Germany, see *Re the Deportation of Aliens* [1977] 2 C.M.L.R. 255. This is reinforced in the United Kingdom by the wording of s. 3 (1) of the European Communities Act 1972. Hence a situation like that in C.E. December 22, 1978 *Cohn-Bendit* 1979 D(J) 155 could not properly arise.

The consequences

As has been said, this article is one of the most important. Nevertheless those clients who are interested in the advancement of legal theory (if not supported by legal aid) are valuable but rare. It should then be added that this article is also one of the most useful. Its utility in a number of commercial transactions is indicated by several of the cases cited above, as also is its utility in recovering taxes or other sums which are, in fact, though not by intent, unlawfully (under Community law) exacted by national authorities. A note of warming should be given; though (case 106/77, *Simmenthal* (above)) substantive obstacles to recovery are overcome by the doctrine of direct effect, procedural obstacles are not necessarily overcome, *e.g.* limitation periods: see *e.g.* case 45/76, *Comet* [1976] E.C.R. 2043. A third situation exists when a Community act is declared invalid. The long road of non-contractual liability may not be inviting. Hence decisions like cases 124/76 & 20/77 *SA Moulin et Huileries de Point-à-Mousson* v. *ONIC* [1977] E.C.R. 1795 should be noted in which (§ 28) the Court enjoins Community authorities to take appropriate steps to redress the consequences of the invalid acts, on which see Reg. 1125/78, O.J. 1978, L142/21.

PROVISIONS COMMON TO SEVERAL INSTITUTIONS

ARTICLE 189

In order to carry out their task the Council and the Commission shall, in accordance with the provisions of this Treaty, make regulations, issue directives, take decisions, make recommendations or deliver opinions.

A regulation shall have general application. It shall be binding in its entirety and directly applicable in all Member States.

A directive shall be binding, as to the result to be achieved, upon each Member State to which it is addressed, but shall leave to the national authorities the choice of form and methods.

A decision shall be binding in its entirety upon those to whom it is addressed.

Recommendations and opinions shall have no binding force.

GENERAL NOTE

The expression "in accordance with this Treaty" not only means that the Institutions must conform to the procedures provided for by the Treaty (*e.g.* consult the Assembly when so required) lest their acts might be annulled by the Court of Justice for "infringement of an essential procedural requirement" (see Art. 173, EEC). It refers in the first place to the fact that the Communities only enjoy those powers which have explicitly (or implicitly, see *infra*) been transferred to them by the European Treaties or other acts; in other words, the Institutions were not invested with general legislative powers. This is one of the reasons why each binding act of the Council and of the Commission explicitly refers to the Treaty provision on which it is based (see Art. 190, EEC).

Art. 235, EEC, is no exception to this principle: although it provides the possibility of creating additional powers in case of need, it does not open unlimited opportunity to increase the powers of the Communities. Art. 235 applies only when action is necessary to attain "one of the objectives of the Community" and furthermore it requires a unanimous vote of the Council. (See Art. 235, *post*.)

Neither does the theory of "implied powers" invalidate the principle of "conferred powers." In case 8/55 *Fédération Charbonnière de Belgique* v. *High Authority*, Rec. II 393 the Court of Justice held that "rules established by international agreement or by law are considered to imply those rules without which the first either would have no sense or could not be reasonably or successfully applied" (see also case 22/70, *Commission* v. *Council* [1971] E.C.R. 263). This does not allow extensive interpretation in regard to Community powers.

The first paragraph of Art, 189 provides for five kinds of Community acts. The distinctions are important primarily for the legality control by the Court of Justice, since natural or legal persons may institute proceedings only against a decision addressed to that person, not therefore against a directive or a regulation unless the latter is in reality a decision and of direct and individual concern to him; the same applies to decisions addressed to another person (see Arts. 173 and 175, EEC).

It is not the name given to an act which classifies it in one of the categories of Art. 189, but rather the content and objectives of its provisions (see case 20/58 *Phoenix-Rheinrohr* v. *High Authority*, Rec. V 181). Consequently, the same act can contain provisions pertaining to different categories (see cases 16 & 17/62 *Fruits et Légumes and others* v. *Council* [1962] E.C.R. 471).

The acts mentioned in Art. 189, EEC, are not the only forms of secondary Community legislation conferring rights and imposing obligations upon Community Institutions, Member States and natural and legal persons and consequently submitted to the juridical control of the Court of Justice (see Art. 173, EEC which refers to "acts ... other than recommendations or opinions") and, in so far as Commission acts are concerned, the political supervision of the Assembly.

Agreements with third countries or international organisations, for instance, are also an important source of Community law. Still other acts are decisions to amend the Treaty (*e.g.* Art. 33 (8), EEC) or complement it (Art. 88 (2), EEC).

283

Community law can also be created by agreements concluded by the Member States among themselves, regarding matters connected with the Treaties, either in pursuance of the latter (*e.g.* EEC, Arts. 50 and 220) or on their own initiative (see note to Art. 220, *infra*).

Another source of Community law is constituted by the "decisions of the Representatives of the Governments of the Member States meeting in Council" (*e.g.* J.O. 1960, 1217 and J.O. 1962, 1284).

Mention must also be made here of the "Resolutions" of the Council of the Representatives of the Governments of the Member States meeting in Council (*e.g.* First Resolution on regional aids, O.J. 1974 (2nd), IX, 57) or of both acting jointly, although these acts have no legal (as opposed to political) value. The same applies to "Programmes" (*e.g.* EEC, Arts. 54 (1)), "Declarations" and "Guidelines" of the Council or of the Member States.

Finally, the same is true from the "Communiques" issued by the Heads of State or of Government at their "summit meetings" (until Paris 1974) and for the decisions of the "European Council" (as from 1975, replacing the former).

Not all the provisions of an act have direct effect, *i.e.* create rights for individuals which national jurisdiction are bound to protect. For this it is "necessary and sufficient that the very nature of the provision of the Treaty in question should make it ideally adapted to produce direct effects on the legal relationship between Member States and those subject to their jurisdiction (*Molkerei-Zentrale* [1968] E.C.R. at 152). From this and other judgments it follows that in order to have direct effect a Community provision must (1) impose an obligation upon a Member State, (2) be clear, (3) be unconditional, and (4) be final, *i.e.* not require further implementing provisions to be effective (see also case 26/62, *Van Gend & Loos* [1963] E.C.R. 1; case 6/64, *ENEL* [1964] E.C.R. 585; case 9/70 *Grad* [1970] E.C.R. 825).

"Having direct effect" is not to be confused with "being directly applicable" (see under "Regulations"). It should be noted, however, that this distinction between "applicability" and "effects" is becoming less strict in the Court's case law. See *e.g.* case 43/75, *Defrenne* v. *Sabena* [1976] E.C.R. 455 where the Court answered the question whether or not EEC, Art. 119, had direct effect by stating that this provision can be directly applicable.

See case 111/75, *Impresa Costruzioni Comm. Quirino Mazzalai* v. *Ferrovia del Renon* [1976] E.C.R. 657 at 665, where "under Article 177, the Court of Justice has jurisdiction to give preliminary rulings concerning the interpretation of acts of the institutions ... regardless of whether they are directly applicable ... and leaves to the national courts the task of deciding whether ... a reference for a preliminary ruling is helpful for the purposes of the decision."

Regulations are those acts which have general application, *i.e.* "apply to situations which are objectively defined and have legal effect for categories of individuals which are defined in a general and abstract way" (case 6/68 *Zuckerfabrik Watenstedt* [1968] E.C.R. 595); in other words regulation provisions have "normative effect *erga omnes*" (case 8/55 *Fédération Charbonnière*, Rec. II 199). That a regulation shall be binding in its entirety means that, contrary to a directive for instance, all those to whom it applies are bound by all its provisions in exactly the same way as they would be by a national law.

"Directly applicable" indicates that regulations do not depend upon implementing legislation of the Member States to become effective and also that national authorities have no power to interfere with their application. (See the European Communities Act, s. 2: "are without further enactment to be given legal effect or used in the United Kingdom.")

Finally, a regulation is effective in like manner throughout the whole Community without exception; uniform interpretation is maintained by the Court of Justice through the procedure of preliminary ruling (see Art. 177, EEC).

Directives are binding acts for the Member States just as Regulations and Decisions are. Although Art. 189 leaves the Member States free as to the choice of forms and method of implementation of directives this freedom does not affect their obligation to choose the most appropriate forms and methods to ensure the effectiveness of the directives. See case 48/75, *Royer* v. *Procureur du Roi* [1976] E.C.R. at 519 (75). See also case 10/76, *Commission* v. *Italy* [1976] E.C.R. 1365 (11).

Binding Community acts—and other provisions of Community law—have precedence over conflicting national legislation. This was once more stated by the Court of Justice in its judgment of March 9, 1978, in case 106/77, *Administrazione delle Finanze dello Stato* v. *Simmenthal* [1978] E.C.R. 629 at 645: "A national court which is called upon, within the limits of its jurisdiction, to apply provisions of Community law is under a duty to give full effect to those provisions, if necessary refusing of its own motion to apply any conflicting provision of national legislation, even if adopted subsequently, and it is not necessary for the court to request or await the prior setting aside of such provisions by legislative or other constitutional means."

A directive by which a time-limit is fixed for a Member State to fulfil an obligation under the Treaty can have legal consequences which natural or legal persons can invoke when the provisions containing this obligation have, by their very nature, direct effect (case 33/70, *SACE* v. *Italian Ministry of Finance* [1970] E.C.R. 1213). See also case 51/76, *Nederlandse Ondernemingen* v. *Inspecteur der Invoerrechten* [1977] E.C.R. 113, concerning the direct effect of a directive imposing on a Member State the obligation to pursue a particular course of conduct.

An act must be considered to be a *decision* when it concerns a well defined party and has binding effect only for that party (case 25/62, *Plauman* v. *Commission* [1963] E.C.R. 95 and case 100/74, *C.A.M.* v. *Commission* [1975] E.C.R. at 1403 (19)).

Generally speaking *recommendations* aim at obtaining a certain action or behaviour from the addressee while *opinions* express a point of view at the request of a third party. The distinction, however, is legally irrelevant: neither can be submitted to the legality control of the Court of Justice (see Art. 173, EEC).

APPENDIX 2

Council Regulation 17 of February 6, 1962
First Regulation Implementing Articles 85 and 86 of the Treaty

(J.O. 1962, 204; O.J. 1959–1962, 87)

BIBLIOGRAPHY
Bellamy and Child, *Common Market Law of Competition* (2nd ed., 1978), Chaps. 5 and 12.
Mégret (ed.), *Le droit de la Communauté économique européenne*, Vol. 4.
EEC Commission, "First Report on Competition Policy" (1972), Pt. 1, Chap. II.

INTRODUCTION
Reg. 17 provides the machinery necessary for the implementation and enforcement of the principles set out in Arts. 85 and 86, EEC. Made by the Council under Art. 87, it came into force on March 13, 1962. It has since been amended by Council Regs. 59, 118/63 and 2822/71 and by the Act annexed to the Treaty of Accession.

The principal provisions of the Regulation may conveniently be divided into two broad parts, (*i*) those relating to applications by undertakings to the Commission, either for exemption under Art. 85 (3), EEC or for a declaration known as "negative clearance"; and (*ii*) those relating to the Commission's general powers of enforcing the provisions of Arts. 85 and 86.

Briefly, Reg. 17 provides two procedures for undertakings whose agreements, decisions or concerted practices fall, or may fall, within Art. 85 (1). First, the agreement may be notified to the Commission for the purpose of obtaining an individual exemption under Art. 85 (3), EEC (see Reg. 17, Arts. 4–8 and 25). Secondly, the parties may apply for a declaration that the agreement falls outside the Treaty altogether ("negative clearance" under Art. 2). Unlike an application for negative clearance, a notification for exemption under Art. 85 (3) gives the parties interim protection from fines (Reg. 17, Art. 15 (5)). In practice, an application for negative clearance should always be combined with a notification for Art. 85 (3) purposes, a course which can be conveniently followed by filling up both parts of Form A/B prescribed under Reg. 27 (*q.v.*).

The remainder of Reg. 17 provides a comprehensive code for the enforcement of Arts. 85 and 86. Under Art. 15 (2) of the Regulation the Commission has wide powers to impose fines for infringements of the Treaty or breaches of the provisions of Reg. 17. Under Reg. 17, Art. 3 the Commission may require the termination of infringement. Under Art. 16 the Commission may enforce its decisions through periodic penalty payments. Reg. 17, Arts. 11–14 give the Commission authority to require information, to make inquiries into sectors of the economy, and to carry out investigations into undertakings. Other provisions relate to liaison with the authorities of Member States (Arts. 10 and 13), review by the Court of Justice (Art. 17), hearings (Art. 19), professional secrecy (Art. 20), and other ancillary matters. Transitional provisions relating to accession are set out in Art. 25.

THE COUNCIL OF THE EUROPEAN ECONOMIC COMMUNITY

Having regard to the Treaty establishing the European Economic Community, and in particular Article 87 thereof;

Having regard to the proposal from the Commission;

Having regard to the Opinion of the Economic and Social Committee;

Having regard to the Opinion of the European Parliament;

Whereas in order to establish a system ensuring that competition shall not be distorted in the common market, it is necessary to provide for balanced application of Articles 85 and 86 in a uniform manner in the Member States;

Whereas in establishing the rules for applying Article 85 (3) account must be taken of the need to ensure effective supervision and to simplify administration to the greatest possible extent;

Whereas it is accordingly necessary to make it obligatory, as a general principle, for undertakings which seek application of Article 85 (3) to notify to the Commission their agreements, decisions and concerted practices;

Whereas, on the one hand, such agreements, decisions and concerted practices are probably very numerous and cannot therefore all be examined at the same time and, on the other hand, some of them have special features which may make them less prejudicial to the development of the common market;

Whereas there is consequently a need to make more flexible arrangements for the time being in respect of certain categories of agreements, decisions and concerted practices without prejudging their validity under Article 85;

Whereas it may be in the interest of undertakings to know whether any agreements, decisions or practices to which they are party, or propose to become party, may lead to action on the part of the Commission pursuant to Article 85 (1) or Article 86;

Whereas, in order to secure uniform application of Articles 85 and 86 in the common market, rules must be made under which the Commission, acting in close and constant liaison with the competent authorities of the Member States, may take the requisite measures for applying those Articles;

Whereas for this purpose the Commission must have the co-operation of the competent authorities of the Member States and be empowered, throughout the common market, to require such information to be supplied and to undertake such investigations as are necessary to bring to light any agreement, decision or concerted practice prohibited by Article 85 (1) or any abuse of a dominant position prohibited by Article 86;

Whereas in order to carry out its duty of ensuring that the provisions of the Treaty are applied the Commission must be empowered to address to undertakings or associations of undertakings recommendations and decisions for the purpose of bringing to an end infringements of Articles 85 and 86;

Whereas compliance with Articles 85 and 86 and the fulfilment of obligations imposed on undertakings and associations of undertakings under this regulation must be enforceable by means of fines and periodic penalty payments;

Whereas undertakings concerned must be accorded the right to be heard by the Commission, third parties whose interests may be affected by a decision must be given the opportunity of submitting their comments beforehand, and it must be ensured that wide publicity is given to decisions taken;

Whereas all decisions taken by the Commission under this regulation are subject to review by the Court of Justice under the conditions specified in the Treaty; whereas it is moreover desirable to confer upon the Court of Justice, pursuant to Article 172, unlimited jurisdiction in respect of decisions under which the Commission imposes fines or periodic penalty payments;

Whereas this regulation may enter into force without prejudice to any other provisions that may hereafter be adopted pursuant to Article 87;

HAS ADOPTED THIS REGULATION:

ARTICLE 1

Basic Provision

Without prejudice to Articles 6, 7 and 23 of this regulation, agreements, decisions and concerted practices of the kind described in Article 85 (1) of the Treaty and the abuse of a dominant position in the market, within the meaning of Article 86 of the Treaty, shall be prohibited, no prior decision to that effect being required.

GENERAL NOTE

Art. 1 provides, generally speaking, that the prohibitions of Arts. 85 and 86, EEC take direct effect without any prior decision to that effect being necessary. Prior to the introduction of Reg. 17 there was a controversy as to whether Arts. 85 and 86 were directly applicable; Art. 1 now resolves this controversy. Art. 1 does not affect the power of the Commission to give certain favourable decisions with retroactive effect (see Reg. 17, Arts. 6 and 7); nor does it affect minor transitional decisions under Reg. 17, Art. 23. Art. 1 does not, however, modify the application of Art. 85 (2), EEC: case 48/72, *Brasserie de Haecht* v. *Wilkin (No. 2)* [1973] E.C.R. 77.

ARTICLE 2

Negative Clearance

Upon application by the undertakings or associations of undertakings concerned, the Commission may certify that, on the basis of the facts in its possession, there are no grounds under Article 85 (1) or Article 86 of the Treaty for action on its part in respect of an agreement, decision or practice.

GENERAL NOTE

Art. 2 enables undertakings to obtain a decision from the Commission that their agreement falls outside Art. 85, EEC, or that they are not guilty of abusing a dominant position under Art. 86, EEC. The declaration made by the Commission pursuant to Art. 2 is made on the basis of the facts then in the Commission's possession.

Negative clearance must be distinguished from the declaration the Commission makes when granting exemption under Art. 85 (3), EEC, pursuant to a notification under Reg. 17, Art. 4 or 5. In the case of negative clearance, the agreement is found not to infringe Art. 85 (1) at all. In the case of an exemption under Art. 85 (3), the agreement is found to infringe Art. 85 (1), yet it satisfies the conditions of Art. 85 (3).

Unlike a notification for exemption under Art. 85 (3), application for negative clearance gives no protection from fines (see Reg. 17, Art. 15); nor can it give rise to provisional validity (see Reg. 17, Arts. 4–7). It may be revised upon the discovery of fresh facts or even a change in the law (see J.O. 1962 76/2136). To obtain protection against fines an application for negative clearance should be combined with a notification for exemption under Art. 85 (3) on Form

A/B, the form prescribed by Reg. 27 (which governs the procedure for making an application). For the post application procedure, see Reg. 17, Art. 19, and Reg. 99/63. For the publication of decisions, see Art. 21.

For examples of negative clearance, see *e.g. Re Christiani & Nielsen* [1969] C.M.L.R. D 36 (no agreement between undertakings: parent and subsidiary); *Rules of the Dutch Engineers & Contractors Association* [1965] C.M.L.R. 50 (only effective outside EEC); *Re SOCEMAS* [1968] C.M.L.R. D 28; *Re Safco* [1972] C.M.L.R. D 83; the *Burroughs* decisions [1972] C.M.L.R. D 67 and D 72 (no significant effect on competition); *Inter Group Trading* [1975] 2 C.M.L.R. D 14.

The Commission has also issued guidance as to certain agreements falling outside the Treaty in respect of which application for negative clearance or notification is usually unnecessary (see Announcement on Exclusive Agency Contracts with Commercial Agents; Announcement on Patent Licence Agreements; Notice on Co-operation Agreements; Notice Concerning Minor Agreements and Notice on Japanese Imports; Notice on Sub-contracting Agreements, *post*).

ARTICLE 3

Termination of Infringements

1. Where the Commission, upon application or upon its own initiative, finds that there is infringement of Article 85 or Article 86 of the Treaty, it may by decision require the undertakings or associations of undertakings concerned to bring such infringement to an end.

2. Those entitled to make application are:

   (*a*) Member States;

   (*b*) natural or legal persons who claim a legitimate interest.

3. Without prejudice to the other provisions of this regulation, the Commission may, before taking a decision under paragraph (1), address to the undertakings or associations of undertakings concerned recommendations for termination of the infringement.

GENERAL NOTE

Art. 3 enables the Commission to require undertakings to bring infringements to an end. The Commission may enforce its decision by imposing periodic penalty payments under Art. 16 (*e.g.* as in *Zoja* v. *Commercial Solvents Corporation* [1973] C.M.L.R. D 50; but see also cases 6 and 7/73, *Istituto Chemioterapico Italiano SpA and Commercial Solvents Corporation* v. *Commission* [1974] E.C.R. 223). The question whether the infringement was intentional or negligent is not relevant in deciding whether to impose a requirement under Art. 3; *Re GEMA* (*No.* 1) [1971] C.M.L.R. D 35 at D 55.

In most cases the Commission has ordered infringements to be terminated forthwith (*e.g. Re van Katwijk N.V.'s Agreement* [1970] C.M.L.R. D 43; *Re Bomée Stichting* [1976] 1 C.M.L.R. D 9; *Liptons Cash Registers* v. *Hugin Kassa* [1978] 1 C.M.L.R. D 19; *Distillers* [1978] 1 C.M.L.R. 400); sometimes parties are permitted time to make alternative arrangements (*e.g. Re Continental Can Company Inc.* [1972] C.M.L.R. D 11). A decision under Art. 3 brings to an end any provisional validity enjoyed by a duly notified agreement (see Art. 5, *post*). The Commission may have power to order interim measures: case 109/75R, *National Carbonising Co.* v. *Commission* [1975] E.C.R. 1193.

The Commission may act either on its own initiative (Art. 3 (1)) or as a result of a complaint from a Member State or other person (Art. 3 (2)). Investigating complaints forms an important part of the Commission's work. For the Commission's procedure in proceedings under Art. 3, see Reg. 17, Art. 19, *post*, and Reg. 99/63. For the publication of its decisions, see Art. 21.

Under Art. 3 (3), the Commission may recommend the termination of an infringement. A recommendation does not require to be published and is of no binding force. If the parties comply with a recommendation then the Commission has no need to take or publish a formal decision.

ARTICLE 4

Notification of New Agreements, Decisions and Practices

1. Agreements, decisions and concerted practices of the kind described in Article 85 (1) of the Treaty which come into existence after the entry into force of this regulation and in respect of which the parties seek application of Article 85 (3) must be notified to the Commission. Until they have been notified, no decision in application of Article 85 (3) may be taken.

2. Paragraph (1) shall not apply to agreements, decisions or concerted practices where:

(i) the only parties thereto are undertakings from one Member State and the agreements, decisions or practices do not relate either to imports or to exports between Member States;

(ii) not more than two undertakings are party thereto, and the agreements only:

(*a*) restrict the freedom of one party to the contract in determining the prices for or conditions of business on which the goods which he has obtained from the other party to the contract may be resold; or

(*b*) impose restrictions on the exercise of the rights of the assignee or user of industrial property rights—in particular patents, utility models, designs or trade marks—or of the person entitled under a contract to the assignment, or grant, of the right to use a method of manufacture or knowledge relating to the use and to the application of industrial processes;

(iii) they have as their sole object:

(*a*) the development or uniform application of standards or types;

[(*b*) joint research and development;

(*c*) specialisation in the manufacture of products, including agreements necessary for the achievement thereof;

—where the products which are the object of specialisation do not, in a substantial part of the common market, represent more than 15 per cent. of the volume of business done in identical products or those considered by the consumers to be similar by reason of their characteristics, price and use, and

—where the total annual turnover of the participating undertakings does not exceed 200 million units of accounts.

These agreements, decisions and concerted practices may be notified to the Commission].

AMENDMENTS
The words in square brackets are as amended by Reg. 2822/71 (J.O. 1971, L285/49; O.J. 1971, 1035).

GENERAL NOTE
Art. 4 governs the notification of new agreements for the purposes of an exemption under Art. 85 (3). New agreements comprise agreements that were or are made after March 13,

1962, restricting competition within the common market and affecting trade between the Six; or agreements made after January 1, 1973, restricting competition within the enlarged common market and affecting trade between any of the nine Member States (see Art. 25 (1)).

Notification is an essential step towards gaining an exemption under Art. 85 (3). Notification also results in interim protection from fines (Art. 15 (5), *post*). While notification of a new agreement does not automatically secure the enforceability of that agreement pending the Commission's decision (case 48/72, *Brasserie de Haecht* v. *Wilkin (No.* 2) [1973] E.C.R. 77), the fact that an agreement has been notified may assist the enforcement of the agreement pending that decision (see Bellamy and Child, 2nd ed., pp. 115 *et seq.*).

However, there is an important distinction between agreements which fall within Art. 4 (1) and agreements which fall within Art. 4 (2). Agreements falling within Art. 4 (1) must be notified to the Commission if an exemption under Art. 85 (3) is needed. No decision granting such an exemption can be taken prior to notification, nor can exemption take effect from a date earlier than the date of notification (see Art. 6 (1)). These requirements have been relaxed in respect of agreements within Art. 4 (2) "which are less prejudicial to the development of the common market" (see the Preamble). While such agreements may be notified, it appears that the Commission may grant an exemption under Art. 85 (3) even in the absence of notification; and a decision granting exemption to such an agreement may be retroactive to a date earlier than the date of notification (Art. 6 (1)).

However, a new agreement falling within Art. 4 (2) which is not notified is not expressly protected from fines under Art. 15 (5), *post* (although fines may be less likely in respect of an Art. 4 (2) agreement, *e.g. H. Vaessen BV* v. *Alex Moris* [1979] 1 C.M.L.R. 511). Also a new Art. 4 (2) agreement is affected by nullity under Art. 85 (2), EEC, whether notified or not, just like any other agreement within Art. 85 (1) (see case 48/72, *Brasserie de Haecht* v. *Wilkin (No.* 2) [1973] E.C.R. 77) (although the fact that the agreement falls within Art. 4 (2) might be material in the exercise of the Court's discretion to stay proceedings, referred to in *Brasserie de Haecht (No.* 2), *supra*).

There is no duty, as such, to notify an agreement which falls within Art. 85 (1) (*cf.* the Restrictive Trade Practices Act 1976, s. 24). However, if an agreement is notified, fines may not be imposed in respect of acts taking place after notification, but prior to the Commission's decision under Art. 85 (3), EEC (Reg. 17, Art. 15 (5); see also Art. 15 (6); and, in respect of agreements falling within Art. 4 (1), any exemption granted may not have retroactive effect to a date earlier than notification. For the notification procedure, see Reg. 27. For post notification procedure, see Reg. 17, Art. 19 and Reg. 99/63. As to penalties for supplying false information, etc., see Art. 15 (1) (*a*).

Para. (1)

Reg. 17 entered into force on March 13, 1962. In respect of agreements falling within the Treaty by virtue of accession, the date of accession is the relevant date (Art. 25 (1)).

Para (2)

In Art. 4 (2) (i), as to the meaning of agreements "which do not relate either to imports or exports between Member States," see case 43/69, *Bilger* v. *Jehle* [1970] E.C.R. 127. See also case 63/75, *S. A. Fonderies Roubaix Wattrelos* v. *Société Nouvelle des Fonderies A. Roux* [1976] E.C.R. 111. In *Re Stoves and Heaters* [1975] 2 C.M.L.R. D 1, an agreement was held to relate to imports and exports, where the parties included importers.

In Art. 4 (2) (ii), for the meaning of agreements "where not more than two undertakings are party," see case 1/70, *Parfums Marcel Rochas Vertriebs GmbH* v. *Bitsch* [1971] E.C.R. 515. Both Art. 4 (2) (ii) (*a*) and Art. 4 (2) (ii) (*b*) contemplate agreements where only very limited unilateral restrictions are placed on one party.

Art. 4 (2) (iii) was amended by Reg. 2822/71. Again an agreement only falls within one of the sub-paras. of Art. 4 (2) (iii) where the *sole* object of the agreement falls within one of the permitted categories. As to agreements relating to joint research, see *Re Eurogypsum* [1968] C.M.L.R. D 1, and the Commission's Notice on Co-operation Agreements, *post*; and *cf.* Reg. 2821/71 (which also refers to standardisation agreements). As to specialisation agreements, see Regs. 2821/71 and 2779/72 and the Commission decisions in *Jaz-Peter* [1970] C.M.L.R. 129; *Clima-Chappée-Buderus* [1970] C.M.L.R. D 7; *FN-CF*, J.O. 1971 L134/6; *Sopelem and Langen* [1972] C.M.L.R. D 77; *MAN-SAVIEM*, J.O. 1972, L31/29; *Lightweight Paper* [1972] C.M.L.R. D 94; *Bayer-Gist Brocades* [1976] 1 C.M.L.R. D 98.

APPENDIX 2

ARTICLE 5

Notification of Existing Agreements, Decisions and Practices

1. Agreements, decisions and concerted practices of the kind described in Article 85 (1) of the Treaty which are in existence at the date of entry into force of this regulation and in respect of which the parties seek application of Article 85 (3) shall be notified to the Commission [before November 1, 1962]. [However, notwithstanding the foregoing provisions, any agreements, decisions and concerted practices to which not more than two undertakings are party shall be notified before February 1, 1963].

2. Paragraph (1) shall not apply to agreements, decisions or concerted practices falling within Article 4 (2); these may be notified to the Commission.

AMENDMENTS

The words in the first set of square brackets in para. (1) were substituted by Reg. 59, Art. 1 (1).

The words in the second set of square brackets in para. (1) were added by Reg. 59, Art. 1 (2) (J.O. 1962, 1655; O.J. 1959–1962, 249).

GENERAL NOTE

Art. 5 governs the notification of agreements in existence at the date of entry into force of Reg. 17. Such agreements are either "old agreements" (*i.e.* agreements in existence on March 13, 1962, which affected trade between the six Member States and restricted competition in the then common market) or "accession agreements" (*i.e.* agreements existing on January 1, 1973, which fall within Art. 85 (1) by virtue of accession, see Reg. 17, Art. 25 (1)). In respect of accession agreements, Reg. 17, Art. 5 must be read together with Reg. 17, Art. 25 (see further, below). For notification procedure, see Reg. 27. As to penalties for supplying false information etc., see Art. 15 (1) (*a*).

Old agreements: Art. 5 (like Art. 4) draws a distinction between agreements of the kind described in Art. 4 (2) of Reg. 17 and other agreements (see Art. 5 (2) and the general note to Art. 4, *supra*).

Old agreements not of the kind described in Art. 4 (2): where exemption was sought under Art. 85 (3), these had to be notified by November 1, 1962, or if the agreement was bilateral, by February 1, 1963 (Reg. 17, Art. 5 (1) as amended by Reg. 59, Art. 1). If they were so notified, any exemption granted can be retroactive to March 13, 1962 (Art. 6 (2)). They also benefit from Art. 7 (1) (*q.v.*) (favourable decisions in respect of existing agreements duly amended by the parties to have retroactive effect).

Such agreements, if duly notified within the time limits, also enjoy "provisional validity" in civil law pending the Commission's decision, as to the meaning of which, see *Brasserie de Haecht (No. 2)*, *supra*; see also case 13/61, *De Geus* v. *Bosch* [1962] E.C.R. 45; case 10/69, *Portelange* v. *SCM International* [1969] E.C.R. 309; *Bilger* v. *Jehle*, *supra*; *Parfums Marcel Rochas* v. *Bitsch*, *supra*.

If such agreements were duly notified within the time limits, the parties enjoy immunity from fines in respect of acts taking place between March 13, 1962, and the date of the Commission's eventual decision (Art. 15 (5) (*a*) and Art. 15 (5) (*b*)).

Old agreements of the kind described in Art. 4 (2): these were not required to be notified within any time limit; exemptions under Art. 85 (3), EEC granted in respect of such agreements could be retroactive beyond the date of notification (Reg. 17, Art. 6 (2)) although Art. 7 (1) (*q.v.*) could only be applicable if such agreements were notified by January 1, 1967 (see Art. 7 (2)). An unnotified old agreement enjoys "provisional validity" (see above and also see in particular the *Bilger* case, *supra*; *Brasserie de Haecht* v. *Wilkin*, *supra*; *cf.* the *Bosch* case, *supra*, and note, case 59/77, *De Bloos* v. *Bouyer* [1977] E.C.R. 2359).

However, the parties to an unnotified old agreement falling within Art. 4 (2) are not expressly protected from fines. But if such an agreement *was* notified before January 1, 1967, the parties are protected from fines in respect of acts taking place between March 13, 1962, and the date of the Commission's eventual decision (Art. 15 (5) (a) and (5) (b) and Art. 7 (2)).

For Art. 4 (2) generally, see Art. 4, *supra*.

Accession agreements: an accession agreement is an agreement in existence on January 1, 1973, to which Art. 85 applies by virtue of accession (Reg. 17, Art. 25 (1)). Again it is necessary to draw a distinction between accession agreements of the kind described in Reg. 17, Art. 4 (2) and other accession agreements. As far as the Commission is concerned an agreement is not an accession agreement if it restricted competition within the EEC and affected trade between Member States even before January 1, 1973: *Sirdar/Phildar* [1975] 1 C.M.L.R. D 93; *Theal/Watts* [1977] 1 C.M.L.R. D 44, on appeal case 28/77, *Tepea* v. *Commission* [1978] E.C.R. 1391.

Accession agreements not of the kind described in Art. 4 (2): If exemption was sought for these under Art. 85 (3), EEC, they had to be notified by June 30, 1973 (Reg. 17, Art. 25 (2)). If they were so notified then: (i) no fines can be imposed for acts committed prior to notification (Art. 25 (3)); (ii) any exemption subsequently granted can be made effective retroactively from a date earlier than notification and back to January 1, 1973 (Reg. 17, Art. 25 and Art. 6 (2)); (iii) the parties may obtain the advantages of Reg. 17, Art. 7 (1) (*q.v.*) (favourable decisions in respect of accession agreements duly amended by the parties to have retroactive effect); (iv) the agreement almost certainly has provisional validity in accordance with the decisions cited above (there is no European Court decision, but see *Esso Petroleum Co. Ltd.* v. *Kingswood Motors (Addlestone) Ltd.* [1974] Q.B. 142).

Late notification of an accession agreement can be made, but the agreement will be void from January 1, 1973, onwards (see *Brasserie de Haecht* (*No. 2*), *supra*). If the agreement is subsequently exempted under Art. 85 (3), the exemption can only validate the agreement retroactively to the date of notification (Art. 6), see *e.g.* the Davidson-Maglum contract in *Re Davidson Rubber Co.* [1972] C.M.L.R. D 52 at D 62. The parties are also liable to fines in respect of acts committed before notification. Reg. 17, Art. 7 (1) does not apply to agreements notified out of time.

Accession agreements of the kind described in Art. 4 (2): these are not required to be notified within any time limit; exemptions under Art. 85 (3), EEC, granted in respect of such agreements can be retroactive beyond the date of notification (Art. 6 (2)). Accession agreements, which have not been notified, falling within Art. 4 (2) may enjoy provisional validity: see *Esso Petroleum Co. Ltd.* v. *Kingswood Motors (Addlestone) Ltd.*, *supra*, and the decisions of the European Court cited above.

However, the parties to an accession agreement, which has not been notified, falling within Art. 4 (2) are not expressly protected from fines. If such an agreement *was* notified before June 30, 1973, the parties are protected from fines in respect of Acts taking place between January 1, 1973, and the date of the Commission's eventual decision (Arts. 15 (5) (a) (b) and 25 (2)). Only agreements notified before June 30, 1973, may take advantage of Reg. 17, Art. 7 (1) and (2) (Art. 25 (2)).

As to Art. 4 (2) generally, see the note to Art. 4, *supra*.

ARTICLE 6

Decisions Pursuant to Article 85 (3)

1. Whenever the Commission takes a decision pursuant to Article 85 (3) of the Treaty, it shall specify therein the date from which the decision shall take effect. Such date shall not be earlier than the date of notification.

2. The second sentence of paragraph (1) shall not apply to agreements, decisions or concerted practices falling within Article 4 (2) and Article 5 (2), nor to those falling within Article 5 (1) which have been notified within the time limit specified in Article 5 (1).

GENERAL NOTE

Art. 6 governs the dates upon which the Commission's decisions granting exemption under Art. 85 (3), EEC, are effective. The general rule is that the decision may be retroactive, but not to a date earlier than the date of notification (Art. 6 (1)). But in certain cases the decision may take effect from a date earlier than notification (Art. 6 (2)). Such cases are first, those agreements within Art. 4 (2) and Art. 5 (2) (see the notes to Arts. 4 and 5, *supra*), and secondly, "old agreements" (in existence on March 13, 1962) or "Accession agreements" (in existence on January 1, 1973, and falling within the EEC Treaty as a result of accession) duly notified within the appropriate time limits (see the note to Art. 5, *supra*).

ARTICLE 7

Special Provisions for Existing Agreements, Decisions and Practices

1. Where agreements, decisions and concerted practices in existence at the date of entry into force of this regulation and notified [within the limits specified in Article 5 (1)] do not satisfy the requirements of Article 85 (3) of the Treaty and the undertakings or associations of undertakings concerned cease to give effect to them or modify them in such manner that they no longer fall within the prohibition contained in Article 85 (1) or that they satisfy the requirements of Article 85 (3), the prohibition contained in Article 85 (1) shall apply only for a period fixed by the Commission. A decision by the Commission pursuant to the foregoing sentence shall not apply as against undertakings and associations of undertakings which did not expressly consent to the notification.

2. Paragraph (1) shall apply to agreements, decisions and concerted practices falling within Article 4 (2) which are in existence at the date of entry into force of this regulation if they are notified [before January 1, 1967].

AMENDMENTS

The words in square brackets in para. (1) were added by Reg. 59, Art. 1 (3).

The words in square brackets in para. (2) were substituted by Reg. 118/63, Art. 1 (J.O. 1963, 2696; O.J. 1963–1964, 55).

GENERAL NOTE

Art. 7 is a transitional provision. Where the parties have notified an "old agreement" or an "Accession agreement" to the Commission (see note to Art. 5, *supra*), within the specified time limits, and the parties subsequently cease to give effect to the agreement, or they modify it so that if it either falls outside Art. 85 (1), or it may benefit from Art. 85 (3), the Commission may declare that Art. 85 (1) did not apply to the agreement prior to its determination or modification. The provision is designed to encourage parties to fall in with the wishes of the Commission. Hitherto, where parties have made appropriate amendments the Commission has consistently declared, under Art. 7 (1), that the prohibition of Art. 85 (1) did not apply as from the date of the entry into force of Reg. 17 (see *e.g. Re Lightweight Paper Application of BPICA* [1977] 2 C.M.L.R. D 43. For a refusal to apply Art. 7 (1), see *Re German Ceramic Tiles* [1971] C.M.L.R. D 6 at D 20).

The last sentence of Art. 7 (1) is intended to ensure that the legal position of parties who did not consent to notification cannot be adversely affected by a decision under Art. 7. If, for example, a party to an Art. 85 (1) agreement did not wish to be bound by it, and did not want to notify it, his position cannot be affected by the fact that the Commission subsequently validates the agreement retroactively under the provisions of Art. 7 (1).

Time limits: Accession agreements (whether falling within Art. 4 (2) or not) may only benefit from Art. 7 (1) if they were notified by June 30, 1973 (Reg. 17, Art. 25 (2)). Old agreements could only benefit if they were notified pursuant to the original time limits set out in Art. 5 (as amended by Reg. 59), unless such agreements fell within Art. 4 (2) in which case they had to be notified by January 1, 1967.

ARTICLE 8

Duration and Revocation of Decisions under Article 85 (3)

1. A decision in application of Article 85 (3) of the Treaty shall be issued for a specified period and conditions and obligations may be attached thereto.

2. A decision may on application be renewed if the requirements of Article 85 (3) of the Treaty continue to be satisfied.

3. The Commission may revoke or amend its decision or prohibit specified acts by the parties:

(a) where there has been a change in any of the facts which were fundamental in the making of the decision;

(b) where the parties commit a breach of any obligation attached to the decision;

(c) where the decision is based on incorrect information or was induced by deceit;

(d) where the parties abuse the exemption from the provisions of Article 85 (1) of the Treaty granted to them by the decision.

In cases to which sub-paragraphs (b), (c) or (d) apply, the decision may be revoked with retroactive effect.

GENERAL NOTE

Art. 8 lays down the Commission's powers in granting exemptions under Art. 85 (3), EEC, including the power to attach conditions (Art. 8 (1)) and to renew (Art. 8 (2)) or revoke (Art. 8 (3)) exemptions in certain circumstances. For an example of conditions imposed see *Re Henkel-Colgate*, J.O. 1972, L14/14. For the renewal of an exemption upon conditions see *Re Transocean Marine Paint Association* (*No.* 2) [1974] C.M.L.R. D 11 (annulled in part by the European Court of Justice [1974] 2 C.M.L.R. 459 and newly decided by the Commission [1975] 2 C.M.L.R. D 75). The period for which the Commission has granted exemption has usually been five or 10 years from the date of notification (for examples, and for the Commission's policy under Art. 85 (3), EEC, see the Commission's Annual Reports on Competition Policy (1972 onwards). If an agreement contains provisions which are not capable of exemption under Art. 85 (3) the Commission may nonetheless grant an exemption subject to the condition that such provisions should not be enforced: *De Laval/Stork*, O.J. 1977, L215/11.

ARTICLE 9

Powers

1. Subject to review of its decision by the Court of Justice, the Commission shall have sole power to declare Article 85 (1) inapplicable pursuant to Article 85 (3) of the Treaty.

2. The Commission shall have power to apply Article 85 (1) and Article 86 of the Treaty; this power may be exercised notwithstanding that the time limits specified in Article 5 (1) and in Article 7 (2) relating to notification have not expired.

3. As long as the Commission has not initiated any procedure under Articles 2, 3 or 6, the authorities of the Member States shall remain competent to apply Article 85 (1) and Article 86, in accordance with Article 88 of the Treaty; they shall remain competent in this respect notwithstanding that the time limits specified in Article 5 (1) and in Article 7 (2) relating to notification have not expired.

GENERAL NOTE

Para. (1)

Only the Commission has power to grant an exemption under Art. 85 (3), EEC, and national courts cannot apply Art. 85 (3). For review by the European Court of Justice, see Art. 173, EEC, and note case 26/76, *Metro/SABA* v. *Commission* [1977] E.C.R. 1875.

Para. (2)

This provision confirmed that the Commission has express power to apply Arts. 85 (1) and 86, EEC, although certain time limits for notification had not expired. All relevant time limits for notification have now expired.

Para. (3)

Art. 88, EEC, gave the authorities of Member States certain powers pending the introduction of the provisions contemplated by Art. 87. Art. 9 (3) of this Regulation apparently contemplates that such authorities may apply Arts. 85 (1) and 86, EEC as long as the Commission has not "initiated a procedure." The meaning of this latter phrase is not clear (but see *Brasserie de Haecht* [1973] E.C.R. 77).

There are no administrative authorities empowered under United Kingdom domestic law to apply Art. 85 (1) or Art. 86. Although the words "the authorities of Member States" have been held to include national courts (*Bilger* [1970] E.C.R. 127), nothing in Art. 9 (3) prevents national courts from applying the provisions of Art. 85 (1) or 86: case 127/73, *BRT* v. *SABAM* [1974] E.C.R. 51.

ARTICLE 10

Liaison with the Authorities of the Member States

1. The Commission shall forthwith transmit to the competent authorities of the Member States a copy of the applications and notifications together with copies of the most important documents lodged with the Commission for the purpose of establishing the existence of infringements of Articles 85 or 86 of the Treaty or of obtaining negative clearance or a decision in application of Article 85 (3).

2. The Commission shall carry out the procedure set out in paragraph (1) in close and constant liaison with the competent authorities of the Member States; such authorities shall have the right to express their views on that procedure.

3. An Advisory Committee on Restrictive Practices and Monopolies shall be consulted prior to the taking of any decision following upon a procedure under paragraph (1), and of any decision concerning the renewal, amendment or revocation of a decision pursuant to Article 85 (3) of the Treaty.

4. The Advisory Committee shall be composed of officials competent in the matter of restrictive practices and monopolies. Each Member State shall appoint an official to represent it who, if prevented from attending, may be replaced by another official.

5. The consultation shall take place at a joint meeting convened by the Commission; such meeting shall be held not earlier than fourteen days after dispatch of the notice convening it. The notice shall, in respect of each case to be examined, be accompanied by a summary of the case together with an indication of the most important documents, and a preliminary draft decision.

6. The Advisory Committee may deliver an opinion notwithstanding that some of its members or their alternates are not present. A report of the outcome of the consultative proceedings shall be annexed to the draft decision. It shall not be made public.

GENERAL NOTE

The United Kingdom authority to whom the Commission transmit a copy of notifications etc. is the Office of Fair Trading. An official from the Office of Fair Trading is represented on the Advisory Committee on Restrictive Practices and Monopolies. For other provisions relating to authorities of Member States, see Arts. 11, 13–14, *infra*.

ARTICLE 11

Requests for Information

1. In carrying out the duties assigned to it by Article 89 and by provisions adopted under Article 87 of the Treaty, the Commission may obtain all necessary information from the Governments and competent authorities of the Member States and from undertakings and associations of undertakings.

2. When sending a request for information to an undertaking or association of undertakings, the Commission shall at the same time forward a copy of the request to the competent authority of the Member State in whose territory the seat of the undertaking or association of undertakings is situated.

3. In its request the Commission shall state the legal basis and the purpose of the request and also the penalties provided for in Article 15 (1) (*b*) for supplying incorrect information.

4. The owners of the undertakings or their representatives and, in the case of legal persons, companies or firms, or of associations having no legal personality, the persons authorised to represent them by law or by their constitution, shall supply the information requested.

5. Where an undertaking or association of undertakings does not supply the information requested within the time limit fixed by the Commission, or supplies incomplete information, the Commission shall by decision require the information to be supplied. The decision shall specify what information is required, fix an appropriate time limit within which it is to be supplied and indicate the penalties provided for by Article 15 (1) (*b*) and Article 16 (1) (*c*) and the right to have the decision reviewed by the Court of Justice.

6. The Commission shall at the same time forward a copy of its decision to the competent authority of the Member State in whose territory the seat of the undertaking or association of undertakings is situated.

GENERAL NOTE

Art. 11 gives the Commission wide powers to require information from Member States and undertakings. As far as undertakings are concerned, the Commission may first request information (Art. 11 (2) and (3)) and if this is not supplied, it may take a decision requiring the information within a fixed time limit, imposing periodic penalty payments in default (Art. 11 (5); see also Art. 16 (1) (*c*)). For examples, see *CIGG—ZVE/ZPU* [1971] C.M.L.R. D23; SIAE [1972] C.M.L.R. D112; *SCV*, O.J. 1976, L192/27; *Unitel* [1978] 3 C.M.L.R. 306.

Although Art. 11 (4) requires undertakings to supply information in answer to a request, there is no sanction to compel them to do so until a formal decision (which can be appealed to the European Court of Justice) has been taken. For penalties for supplying false information, see Art. 15 (1) (b).

As far as Member States are concerned, the Commission may obtain necessary information from "the Governments and competent authorities." Although only the Secretary of State has been expressly designated as "a competent authority" in the United Kingdom (S.I. 1973 No. 1889), see the Fair Trading Act 1973, s. 133, and the Restrictive Trade Practices Act 1976, s. 41, relating to the disclosure, pursuant to a Community obligation, of information obtained under those Acts. For the power to make domestic legislation to give effect to EEC competition rules, see Vol. A, Parts A1 and A3.

For other relevant powers of the Commission, see Arts. 12–14 and 16. For the secrecy of information obtained under Art. 11, see Art. 20.

ARTICLE 12

Inquiry into Sectors of the Economy

1. If in any sector of the economy the trend of trade between Member States, price movements, inflexibility of prices or other circumstances suggest that in the economic sector concerned competition is being restricted or distorted within the common market, the Commission may decide to conduct a general inquiry into that economic sector and in the course thereof may request undertakings in the sector concerned to supply the information necessary for giving effect to the principles formulated in Articles 85 and 86 of the Treaty and for carrying out the duties entrusted to the Commission.

2. The Commission may in particular request every undertaking or association of undertakings in the economic sector concerned to communicate to it all agreements, decisions and concerted practices which are exempt from notification by virtue of Article 4 (2) and Article 5 (2).

3. When making inquiries pursuant to paragraph (2), the Commission shall also request undertakings or groups of undertakings whose size suggests that they occupy a dominant position within the common market or a substantial part thereof to supply to the Commission such particulars of the structure of the undertakings and of their behaviour as are requisite to an appraisal of their position in the light of Article 86 of the Treaty.

4. Article 10 (3) to (6) and Articles 11, 13 and 14 shall apply correspondingly.

GENERAL NOTE

Art. 12 (1) gives the Commission power to carry out general inquiries into economic sectors, in the course of which it may exercise not only the specific powers to require information, set out in Art. 12 (2) and (3), but, under Art. 12 (4), it also has the power to require information under Art. 11 or make investigations under Art. 14. It may request assistance from Member States' authorities under Art. 13, and must consult the Advisory Committee on Restrictive Practices and Monopolies (Art. 10 (3)–(6)).

Under Art. 12 the Commission has investigated the margarine industry and, currently, the tied house system (for decisions requiring information in that inquiry, see J.O. 1971, L161/2–10). For the secrecy of information obtained under Art. 12, see Art. 20. For penalties for supplying false information, see Art. 15 (1) (b).

ARTICLE 13

Investigations by the Authorities of the Member States

1. At the request of the Commission, the competent authorities of the Member States shall undertake the investigations which the Commission considers to be necessary under Article 14 (1), or which it has ordered by decision pursuant to Article 14 (3). The officials of the competent authorities of the Member States responsible for conducting these investigations shall exercise their powers upon production of an authorisation in writing issued by the competent authority of the Member State in whose territory the investigation is to be made. Such authorisation shall specify the subject-matter and purpose of the investigation.

2. If so requested by the Commission or by the competent authority of the Member State in whose territory the investigation is to be made, the officials of the Commission may assist the officials of such authority in carrying out their duties.

GENERAL NOTE

As to "competent authorities," see S.I. 1973 No. 1889 and note to Art. 12 above. For the secrecy of information obtained under Art. 13, see Art. 20. The competent authorities of Member States may, as well as carrying out investigations under Art. 14 (general powers of investigation), also carry out investigations under Art. 12 (general economic sector inquiries).

ARTICLE 14

Investigating Powers of the Commission

1. In carrying out the duties assigned to it by Article 89 and by provisions adopted under Article 87 of the Treaty, the Commission may undertake all necessary investigations into undertakings and associations of undertakings. To this end the officials authorised by the Commission are empowered:
   (a) to examine the books and other business records;
   (b) to take copies of or extracts from the books and business records;
   (c) to ask for oral explanations on the spot;
   (d) to enter any premises, land and means of transport of undertakings.

2. The officials of the Commission authorised for the purpose of these investigations shall exercise their powers upon production of an authorisation in writing specifying the subject-matter and purpose of the investigation and the penalties provided for in Article 15 (1) (c) in cases where production of the required books or other business records is incomplete. In good time before the investigation, the Commission shall inform the competent authority of the Member State in whose territory the same is to be made, of the investigation and of the identity of the authorised officials.

3. Undertakings and associations of undertakings shall submit to investigations ordered by decision of the Commission. The decision shall specify the subject-matter and purpose of the investigation, appoint the date on which it is to begin and indicate the penalties provided for in Article

15 (1) (c) and Article 16 (1) (d) and the right to have the decision reviewed by the Court of Justice.

4. The Commission shall take the decisions referred to in paragraph 3 after consultation with the competent authority of the Member State in whose territory the investigation is to be made.

5. Officials of the competent authority of the Member State in whose territory the investigation is to be made may, at the request of such authority or of the Commission, assist the officials of the Commission in carrying out their duties.

6. Where an undertaking opposes an investigation ordered pursuant to this Article, the Member State concerned shall afford the necessary assistance to the officials authorised by the Commission to enable them to make their investigation. Member States shall, after consultation with the Commission, take the necessary measures to this end before October 1, 1962.

GENERAL NOTE

Art. 14 empowers the Commission to carry out all necessary investigations into undertakings and associations of undertakings. The Commission has power to "look at the books" and ask for explanations "on the spot." However, if an undertaking refuses to submit voluntarily to an investigation, the Commission must take a decision requiring the undertaking to submit (Art. 14 (3)). Such a decision must be taken in consultation with the competent authority in the relevant Member State (Art. 11 (4)): *Business Records of Fides Unione Fiduciaria SpA* [1979] 1 C.M.L.R. 650. Once such a decision is taken, the Member State is obliged to carry out this obligation (Art. 14 (6)). Under Reg. 17, Art. 25 (4), the United Kingdom undertook to take the necessary measures to implement Art. 14 (6) by June 30, 1973, but have not done so so far.

Under Art. 13, at the Commission's request, the investigations contemplated under Art. 14 (1) and (3) may be carried out by the competent authorities of Member States (see note to Art. 12, *supra*).

For the secrecy of information obtained under Art. 14, see Art. 20. For penalties for producing incomplete books or refusing to supply information, see Art. 15 (1) (c). For periodic penalty payments to enforce decisions, see Art. 16. For Arts. 87 and 89, EEC, see Vol. B II of this Encyclopedia, Part B 10.

ARTICLE 15

Fines

1. The Commission may by decision impose on undertakings or associations of undertakings fines of from one hundred to five thousand units of account where, intentionally or negligently:

(a) they supply incorrect or misleading information in an application pursuant to Article 2 or in a notification pursuant to Articles 4 or 5; or

(b) they supply incorrect information in response to a request made pursuant to Article 11 (3) or (5) or to Article 12, or do not supply information within the time limit fixed by a decision taken under Article 11 (5); or

(c) they produce the required books or other business records in incomplete form during investigations under Article 13 or 14, or refuse to submit to an investigation ordered by decision issued in implementation of Article 14 (3).

2. The Commission may by decision impose on undertakings or associations of undertakings fines of from one thousand to one million units of account, or a sum in excess thereof but not exceeding 10 per cent. of the turnover in the preceding business year of each of the undertakings participating in the infringement where, either intentionally or negligently:

(*a*) they infringe Article 85 (1) or Article 86 of the Treaty; or

(*b*) they commit a breach of any obligation imposed pursuant to Article 8 (1).

In fixing the amount of the fine, regard shall be had both to the gravity and to the duration of the infringement.

3. Article 10 (3) to (6) shall apply.

4. Decisions taken pursuant to paragraphs (1) and (2) shall not be of a criminal law nature.

5. The fines provided for in paragraph (2) (*a*) shall not be imposed in respect of acts taking place:

(*a*) after notification to the Commission and before its decision in application of Article 85 (3) of the Treaty, provided they fall within the limits of the activity described in the notification;

(*b*) before notification and in the course of agreements, decisions or concerted practices in existence at the date of entry into force of this regulation, provided that notification was effected within the time limits specified in Article 5 (1) and Article 7 (2).

6. Paragraph (5) shall not have effect where the Commission has informed the undertakings concerned that after preliminary examination it is of opinion that Article 85 (1) of the Treaty applies and that application of Article 85 (3) is not justified.

GENERAL NOTE

Fines may be imposed both in respect of breaches of Reg. 17 (Art. 15 (1)) and in respect of breaches of the EEC Treaty (Art. 15 (2)). Under Art. 15 (1) fines up to 5,000 u.a. (1 u.a. = approx. £0.644) may be imposed for the supply of false information in a notification etc. (Art. 15 (1) (*a*)), or for the supply of incorrect information under Arts. 11 and 12, or for the failure to produce books etc. during investigations under Arts. 13 and 14. In the case of the non-supply of information, a decision to impose a fine may only be taken after an earlier decision requiring the information to be supplied has been disobeyed (*e.g. S.A. Raffinerie Tirlemontoise*, Bulletin No. 11 1971, Chap. 1, para. 5 and *Theal/Watts* on appeal, case 28/77, *Tepea* v. *Commission* [1978] E.C.R. 1391. See also Art. 16 for the power to enforce decisions by imposing periodic penalty payments. Community fines are payable in addition to fines payable under national law, *e.g.* German cartel law: case 14/68, *Wilhelm* v. *Bundeskartellamt* [1969] E.C.R. 1.

Fines in respect of infringements of the EEC Treaty, ranging up to 1 million u.a. or 10 per cent. of turnover in the preceding year, may be imposed on undertakings under Art. 15 (2), but not on individual directors or employees. For discussion of the meaning of "intentionally or negligently" see the Opinion of the Advocate-General in case 26/75, *General Motors Continental N.V.* v. *Commission* [1975] E.C.R. 1367; the intention itself to infringe Art. 85 was held a sufficient reason for imposing fines even where there was no significant effect on the market: see *French Taiwanese Mushroom Packers* [1975] 1 C.M.L.R. D 83; negligence was accepted in *Re the United Brands Co.* [1976] 1 C.M.L.R. D 28, on appeal, case 27/76, *United Brands* v. *Commission* [1978] E.C.R. 207, where the parties should have been aware of the anti-competitive effects of their conduct; see also case 19/77, *Miller International Schallplatten* v. *Commission* [1978] E.C.R. 131. Where more than one party is to be fined, the Commission's practice has been to have regard to the gravity of the infringement, and then to determine the individual liability of the parties in the light of their market share and individual conduct: see case 45/69, *Boehringer Mannheim* v. *Commission* [1970] E.C.R. 769; *BMW*

Belgium [1978] 2 C.M.L.R. 126. For determining the gravity of the infringement, account was taken of the importance of the goods to the consumer and to the high profits achieved as a result of the infringement: see *Re United Brands Co.* [1976] 1 C.M.L.R. D 28 (57), on appeal, case 27/76, *supra*; *Community* v. *Kawasaki Motors GmbH* [1979] 1 C.M.L.R. 448.

For other examples of fines being imposed, see *Aniline Dyes Cartel* [1969] C.M.L.R. D 23; on appeal cases 48–49/69, 51–56/69 [1972] E.C.R. 619; *Quinine Cartel* [1969] C.M.L.R. D 41; on appeal cases 41/69, 44/69, 45/69 [1970] E.C.R. 661; *Re Pittsburgh Corning Europe* [1973] C.M.L.R. D 2; *Re WEA-Filipachi Music S.A.* [1973] C.M.L.R. D 43; *Re Sugar Cartel* [1973] C.M.L.R. D 65 (on appeal cases 40 etc./73 [1975] E.C.R. 1663; *Re CSC-ZOJA* [1973] C.M.L.R. D 50; (on appeal [1974] E.C.R. 223; *Liptons Cash Registers* v. *Hugin Kassa* [1978] 1 C.M.L.R. D 19; *Distillers* [1978] 1 C.M.L.R. 400.

Duly notified agreements have certain immunity from fines under Art. 15 (5). See also Art. 25 (3) and the note to Arts. 4 and 5, *supra*. This immunity ceases when the Commission takes a decision under Art. 15 (6), but this procedure has hardly been used since the *Noordwijks Cement Accoord* decision by the European Court (cases 8–11/66 [1967] E.C.R. 75); but see *Zuid-Nederlandsche Brombemaling* [1975] 2 C.M.L.R. D 67; *Notification of SNPE & Leafields* [1978] 2 C.M.L.R. 758.

The fines imposed under Art. 15 (1) or (2) are expressed not to be criminal in nature (Art. 15 (4)). They may be enforced under Art. 192, EEC (see European Communities (Enforcement of Community Judgments) Order 1972 (S.I. 1972 No. 1590), *Westinghouse* (H.L.) [1978] 1 C.M.L.R. 100). The power of the Commission to impose fines is subject to a limitation period: see Reg. 2988/74.

ARTICLE 16

Periodic Penalty Payments

1. The Commission may by decision impose on undertakings or associations of undertakings periodic penalty payments of from fifty to one thousand units of account per day, calculated from the date appointed by the decision, in order to compel them:

   (a) to put an end to an infringement of Article 85 or 86 of the Treaty, in accordance with a decision taken pursuant to Article 3 of this regulation;

   (b) to refrain from any act prohibited under Article 8 (3);

   (c) to supply complete and correct information which it has requested by decision taken pursuant to Article 11 (5);

   (d) to submit to an investigation which it has ordered by decision taken pursuant to Article 14 (3).

2. Where the undertakings or associations of undertakings have satisfied the obligation which it was the purpose of the periodic penalty payment to enforce, the Commission may fix the total amount of the periodic penalty payment at a lower figure than that which would arise under the original decision.

3. Article 10 (3) to (6) shall apply.

GENERAL NOTE

The Commission may enforce decisions to end infringements of the EEC Treaty under Art. 3 by imposing default fines of up to 1,000 u.a. per day (see *e.g. Re CSC-Zoja* [1973] C.M.L.R. D 50 on appeal (cases 6–7/73 [1974] E.C.R. 223 and *Re the United Brands Co.* [1976] 1 C.M.L.R. D 28, on appeal, case 27/76 [1978] E.C.R. 207); *Liptons Cash Registers* v. *Hugin Kassa* [1978] 1 C.M.L.R. D 19; *Distillers* [1978] 1 C.M.L.R. 400 (Art. 16 (1) (*a*)). Such fines are additional to any fines for infringing the Treaty itself. (One u.a. = approx. one old U.S.$ (£0.644).) Similarly the Commission may impose such fines to enforce prohibitions connected with the revocation or amendment of exemptions (Arts. 8 (3) and 16 (1) (*b*)); or to enforce the supply of information (Arts. 15 (3) and 16 (1) (*c*)); or to enforce a requirement that undertakings submit to an investigation (Arts. 14 (3) and 16 (1) (*d*)).

The penalties may be mitigated if the undertaking complies with the Commission's requirements (Art. 16 (2)). Before imposing a fine under Art. 16 the Commission must consult the Advisory Committee on Restrictive practices and Monopolies (Art. 10 (3)–(6)). Such penalties may be enforced under Art. 192, EEC (see European Communities (Enforcement of Community Judgments) Order 1972 (S.I. 1972 No. 1590)).

ARTICLE 17

Review by the Court of Justice

The Court of Justice shall have unlimited jurisdiction within the meaning of Article 172 of the Treaty to review decisions whereby the Commission has fixed a fine or periodic penalty; it may cancel, reduce or increase the fine or periodic penalty payment imposed.

GENERAL NOTE

In respect of fines or periodical payments the European Court of Justice has "*une compétence de pleine jurisdiction*" under Art. 172, EEC. See *e.g.* cases 48, 49/69, 51–57/69, *I.C.I.* v. *Commission* [1972] E.C.R. 619; cases 40/73 etc., *Suiker Unie and others* v. *Commission* [1975] E.C.R. 1663; case 27/76, *United Brands* v. *Commission* [1978] E.C.R. 207; case 85/76, *Hoffmann-La Roche* v. *Commission* (not yet reported).

ARTICLE 18

Unit of Account

For the purposes of applying Articles 15 to 17 the unit of account shall be that adopted in drawing up the budget of the Community in accordance with Articles 207 and 209 of the Treaty.

GENERAL NOTE

See also Reg. 91/73 of April 25, 1973, Art. 10.

ARTICLE 19

Hearing of the Parties and of Third Persons

1. Before taking decisions as provided for in Articles 2, 3, 6, 7, 8, 15 and 16, the Commission shall give the undertakings or associations of undertakings concerned the opportunity of being heard on the matters to which the Commission has taken objection.

2. If the Commission or the competent authorities of the Member States consider it necessary, they may also hear other natural or legal persons. Applications to be heard on the part of such persons shall, where they show a sufficient interest, be granted.

3. Where the Commission intends to give negative clearance pursuant to Article 2 or take a decision in application of Article 85 (3) of the Treaty it shall publish a summary of the relevant application or notification and

invite all interested third parties to submit their observations within a time limit which it shall fix being not less than one month. Publication shall have regard to the legitimate interest of undertakings in the protection of their business secrets.

GENERAL NOTE
The procedure governing hearings of parties and third persons in proceedings prior to a decision is governed by Reg. 99/63, *post*, adopted under Art. 24. The notices referred to in Art. 19 (3) are published in the *Official Journal*.

ARTICLE 20

Professional Secrecy

1. Information acquired as a result of the application of Articles 11, 12, 13 and 14 shall be used only for the purpose of the relevant request or investigation.

2. Without prejudice to the provisions of Articles 19 and 21, the Commission and the competent authorities of the Member States, their officials and other servants shall not disclose information acquired by them as a result of the application of this regulation and of the kind covered by the obligation of professional secrecy.

3. The provisions of paragraphs (1) and (2) shall not prevent publication of general information or surveys which do not contain information relating to particular undertakings or associations of undertakings.

GENERAL NOTE
Art. 20 protects the confidentiality of information supplied to the Commission. Community officials who breach that provision risk disciplinary proceedings. The Commission may be liable in damages to the party concerned (Art. 215, EEC).

ARTICLE 21

Publication of Decisions

1. The Commission shall publish the decisions which it takes pursuant to Articles 2, 3, 6, 7 and 8.

2. The publication shall state the names of the parties and the main content of the decision; it shall have regard to the legitimate interest of undertakings in the protection of their business secrets.

GENERAL NOTE
Decisions granting negative clearance (Arts. 2 and 7), or exemption under Art. 85 (3), EEC (Arts. 6–8), or requiring an infringement to be ended (Art. 3) are published in the *Official Journal*. There is no obligation to publish decisions imposing fines and periodical payments, but the Commission will usually do so, and has been encouraged to do so by the European Court: case 41/69, *ACF Chemiefarma* v. *Commission* [1970] E.C.R. 661.

ARTICLE 22

Special Provisions

1. The Commission shall submit to the Council proposals for making certain categories of agreement, decision and concerted practice falling within Article 4 (2) or Article 5 (2) compulsorily notifiable under Article 4 or 5.

2. Within one year from the date of entry into force of this regulation, the Council shall examine, on a proposal from the Commission, what special provisions might be made for exempting from the provisions of this regulation agreements, decisions and concerted practices falling within Article 4 (2) or Article 5 (2).

GENERAL NOTE
As at December 1, 1974, no action had been taken under either Art. 22 (1) or Art. 22 (2).

ARTICLE 23

Transitional Provisions Applicable to Decisions of Authorities of the Member States

1. Agreements, decisions and concerted practices of the kind described in Article 85 (1) of the Treaty to which, before entry into force of this regulation, the competent authority of a Member State has declared Article 85 (1) to be inapplicable pursuant to Article 85 (3) shall not be subject to compulsory notification under Article 5. The decision of the competent authority of the Member State shall be deemed to be a decision within the meaning of Article 6; it shall cease to be valid upon expiration of the period fixed by such authority but in any event not more than three years after the entry into force of this regulation.
Article 8 (3) shall apply.

2. Applications for renewal of decisions of the kind described in paragraph (1) shall be decided upon by the Commission in accordance with Article 8 (2).

GENERAL NOTE
Art. 23 is a transitional provision relating only to the very few decisions taken under Art. 85, EEC, by authorities of Member States prior to March 13, 1962. It is no longer of practical significance.

ARTICLE 24

Implementing Provisions

The Commission shall have the power to adopt implementing provisions concerning the form, content and other details of applications pursuant to Articles 2 and 3, and of notifications pursuant to Articles 4 and 5, and concerning hearings pursuant to Article 19 (1) and (2).

Regulations made under this article are Reg. 27 (notification procedure), *post*, and Reg. 99/63 (hearings etc.), *post*.

[ARTICLE 25

1. As regards agreements, decisions and concerted practices to which Article 85 of the Treaty applies by virtue of accession, the date of accession shall be substituted for the date of entry into force of this regulation in every place where reference is made in this regulation to this latter date.

2. Agreements, decisions and concerted practices existing at the date of accession to which Article 85 of the Treaty applies by virtue of accession shall be notified pursuant to Article 5 (1) or Article 7 (1) and (2) within six months from the date of accession.

3. Fines under Article 15 (2) (*a*) shall not be imposed in respect of any act prior to notification of the agreements, decisions and practices to which paragraph (2) applies and which have been notified within the period therein specified.

4. New Member States shall take the measures referred to in Article 14 (6) within six months from the date of accession after consulting the Commission.]

[5. The provisions of paragraphs (1) to (4) above still apply in the same way in the case of the accession of the Hellenic Republic.]

AMENDMENTS
Art. 25 was added by the Act concerning the conditions of Accession and the Adjustments to the Treaty, Annex I.
Para. (5) was added by the Act concerning the conditions of Accession of the Hellenic Republic, Annex I.

GENERAL NOTE
Art. 25 was added by the Act concerning the conditions of Accession and the Adjustments to the Treaty, Annex I (Vol. BI, Part B9 of the Encyclopedia). It provides transitional arrangements for agreements in existence on January 1, 1973, which falls within Art. 85 by virtue of accession. For the purposes of accession agreements, Reg. 17 entered into force on January 1, 1973 (Art. 25 (1)).
For the notification of accession agreements, see the notes to Arts. 4–7, *supra*. Except for agreements within Art. 4 (2), agreements, in respect of which exemption under Art. 85 (3), EEC, was sought, had to be notified by June 30, 1973 (Art. 25 (3)). For the protection from fines referred to in Art. 25 (3), see also Art. 15 (5) and the notes to Arts. 4 and 5, *supra*. The United Kingdom had not as at May 1, 1979, taken the measures referred to in Art. 25 (4), for which see further Art. 14, *supra*.

This regulation shall be binding in its entirety and directly applicable in all Member States.

Done at Brussels, February 6, 1962.

Commission Regulation 27 of May 3, 1962
First Regulation Implementing Council Regulation 17

(J.O. 1962, 1118; O.J. 1959–1962, 132)

Form, Content and other Details concerning Applications
and Notifications

THE COMMISSION OF THE EUROPEAN ECONOMIC COMMUNITY

Having regard to the provisions of the Treaty establishing the European Economic Community, and in particular Articles 87 and 155 thereof;

Having regard to Article 24 of the Council Regulation 17 of February 6, 1962 (First Regulation implementing Articles 85 and 86 of the Treaty);

Whereas under Article 24 of Council Regulation 17 the Commission is authorised to adopt implementing provisions concerning the form, content and other details of applications under Articles 2 and 3 and of notifications under Articles 4 and 5 of that Regulation;

Whereas the submission of such applications and notifications may have important legal consequences for each of the undertakings which is party to an agreement, decision or concerted practice; whereas every undertaking should accordingly have the right to submit an application or a notification to the Commission; whereas, furthermore, an undertaking exercising this right must inform the other undertakings which are parties to the agreement, decision or concerted practice, in order to enable them to protect their interests;

Whereas it is for the undertakings and associations of undertakings to transmit to the Commission information as to facts and circumstances in support of applications under Article 2 and of notifications under Articles 4 and 5;

Whereas it is desirable to prescribe forms for use in applications for negative clearance relating to implementation of Article 85 (1) and for notifications relating to implementation of Article 85 (3) of the Treaty, in order to simplify and accelerate consideration by the competent departments, in the interests of all concerned;

HAS ADOPTED THIS REGULATION:

ARTICLE 1

Persons Entitled to Submit Applications and Notifications

1. Any undertaking which is party to agreements, decisions or practices of the kind described in Articles 85 and 86 of the Treaty may submit an

application under Article 2 or a notification under Articles 4 and 5 of Regulation 17. Where the application or notification is submitted by some, but not all, of the undertakings concerned, they shall give notice to the others.

2. Where applications and notifications under Articles 2, 3 (1), 3 (2) (*b*), 4 and 5 of Regulation 17 are signed by representatives of undertakings, or associations of undertakings, or natural or legal persons such representatives shall produce written proof that they are authorised to act.

3. Where a joint application or notification is submitted a joint representative should be appointed.

ARTICLE 2

Submission of Applications and Notifications

[1. [Eleven] copies of each application and notification and of the supporting documents shall be submitted to the Commission.]

2. The supporting documents shall be either originals or copies; copies must be certified as true copies of the original.

3. Applications and notifications shall be in one of the official languages of the Community. Supporting documents shall be submitted in their original language. Where the original language is not one of the official languages, a translation in one of the official languages shall be attached.

AMENDMENTS
Para. (1) was amended by Reg. 1699/75 (O.J. 1975, L172/11).
In para. (1) the word in square brackets was replaced by the Act concerning the conditions of Accession of the Hellenic Republic, Annex I.

ARTICLE 3

Effective Date of Submission of Applications and Registrations

The date of submission of an application or notification shall be the date on which it is received by the Commission. Where, however, the application or notification is sent by registered post, it shall be deemed to have been received on the date shown on the postmark of the place of posting.

ARTICLE 4

[*Content of Applications and Notifications*

1. Applications under Article 2 of Regulation 17 relating to the applicability of Article 85 (1) of the Treaty and notifications under Article 4 or Article 5 (2) of Regulation 17 shall be submitted on Form A–B as shown in the Annex to this regulation.

2. Applications and notifications shall contain the information asked for in Form A–B.

3. Several participating undertakings may submit an application or notification on a single form.

4. Applications under Article 2 of Regulation 17 relating to the applicability of Article 86 of the Treaty shall contain a full statement of the facts, specifying, in particular, the practice concerned and the position of the undertaking or undertakings within the common market or a substantial part thereof in regard to products or services to which the practice relates.]

AMENDMENTS
Art. 4 is printed as amended by Reg. 1133/68 (J.O. 1968, L189/1; O.J. 1968, 400).

ARTICLE 5

Transitional Provisions

1. Applications and notifications submitted prior to the date of entry into force of this regulation otherwise than on the prescribed forms shall be deemed to comply with Article 4 of this regulation.

2. The Commission may require a duly completed form to be submitted to it within such time as it shall appoint. In that event, applications and notifications shall be treated as properly made only if the forms are submitted within the prescribed period and in accordance with the provisions of this regulation.

ARTICLE 6

This regulation shall enter into force on the day following its publication in the *Official Journal of the European Communities*.

This regulation shall be binding in its entirety and directly applicable in all Member States.

Done at Brussels, May 3, 1962.

Form A/B
[This form and the supporting documents should be forwarded in seven copies together with proof in duplicate of the representative's authority to act.

If the space opposite each question is insufficient, please use extra pages, specifying to which item on the form they relate.

To the Commission of the European Communities
Directorate General for Competition
170, rue de la Loi, Brussels 4
(the present address is 200, rue de la Loi, 1040 Brussels)

A. Application for negative clearance pursuant to Article 2 of the Council Regulation 17 of February 6, 1962, relating to implementation of Article 85 (1) of the Treaty.

B. Notification of an agreement, decision or concerted practice under Articles 4 and 5 of Council Regulation 17 of February 6, 1962.

  I. Information regarding parties.

    1. Name, forenames and address of person submitting the application or notification. If such person is acting as representative, state also the name and address of the undertaking or association of undertakings represented and the name, forenames and address of the proprietors or partners or, in the case of legal persons, of their legal representatives.

    Proof of representative's authority to act must be supplied.

    If the application or notification is submitted by a number of persons or on behalf of a number of undertakings, the information must be given in respect of each person or undertaking.

2. Name and address of the undertakings which are parties to the agreement, decision or concerted practice and name, forenames and address of the proprietors or partners or, in the case of legal persons, of their legal representatives (unless this information has been given under I (1)).

   If the undertakings which are parties to the agreement are not all associated in submitting the application or notification, state what steps have been taken to inform the other undertakings.

   This information is not necessary in respect of standard contracts (see Section II 1 (b) below).
3. If a firm or joint agency has been formed in pursuance of the agreement, state the name and address of such firm or agency and the names, forenames and addresses of its legal or other representatives.
4. If a firm or joint agency is responsible for operating the agreement, state the name and address of such firm or agency and the names, forenames and addresses of its legal or other representatives.

   Attach a copy of the statutes.
5. In the case of a decision of an association of undertakings, state the name and address of the association and the names, forenames and addresses of its legal representatives.

   Attach a copy of the statutes.
6. If the undertakings are established or have their seat outside the territory of the common market (Article 227 (1) and (2) of the Treaty), state the name and address of a representative or branch established in the territory of the common market.

II. Information regarding contents of agreement, decision or concerted practice:
1. If the contents were reduced to writing, attach a copy of the full text unless (*a*), (*b*) or (*c*) below provides otherwise.
   (*a*) Is there only an outline agreement or outline decision?
        If so, attach also copy of the full text of the individual agreements and implementing provisions.
   (*b*) Is there a standard contract, *i.e.* a contract which the undertaking submitting the notification regularly concludes with particular persons or groups of persons (*e.g.* a contract restricting the freedom of action of one of the contracting parties in respect of resale prices or terms of business for goods supplied by the other contracting party)?
        If so, only the text of the standard contract need be attached.
   (*c*) If there is a licensing agreement of the type covered by Article 4 (2) (ii) (*b*) of Regulation 17, it is not necessary to submit those clauses of the contract which only describe a technical manufacturing process and have no connection with the restriction of competition; in such cases, however, an indication of the parts omitted from the text must be given.
2. If the contents were not, or were only partially, reduced to writing, state the contents in the space opposite.
3. In all cases give the following additional information:
   (*a*) Date of agreement, decision or concerted practice.
   (*b*) Date when it came into force and, where applicable, proposed period of validity.
   (*c*) Subject: exact description of the goods or services involved.
   (*d*) Aims of the agreement, decision or concerted practice.
   (*e*) Terms of adherence, termination or withdrawal.
   (*f*) Sanctions which may be taken against participating undertakings (penalty clause, expulsion, withholding of supplies, etc.).

III. Means of achieving the aims of the agreement, decision or concerted practice:
1. State whether and how far the agreement, decision or concerted practice relates to:
   —adherence to certain buying or selling prices, discounts or other trading conditions
   —restriction or control of production, technical development or investment
   —sharing of markets or sources of supply
   —restrictions on freedom to purchase from, or resell to, third parties (exclusive contracts)
   —application of different terms for supply of equivalent goods or services
2. Is the agreement, decision or concerted practice concerned with supply of goods or services:

(a) within one Member State only?
(b) between a Member State and third States?
(c) between Member States?

IV. If you consider Article 85 (1) to be inapplicable and are notifying the agreement, decision or concerted practice as a precaution only:

(a) Please attach a statement of the relevant facts and reasons as to why you consider Article 85 (1) to be inapplicable, e.g. that the agreement, decision or concerted practice:

1. does not have the object or effect of preventing, restricting or distorting competition; or

2. is not one which may affect trade between Member States.

(b) Are you asking for a negative clearance pursuant to Article 2 of Regulation 17?

V. Are you notifying the agreement, decision or concerted practice, even if only as a precaution, in order to obtain a declaration or inapplicability under Article 85 (3)?
If so, explain to what extent:

1. the agreement, decision or concerted practice contributes towards
   —improving production or distribution, or
   —promoting technical or economic progress;

2. a proper share of the benefits arising from such improvement or progress accrues to the consumers;

3. the agreement, decision or concerted practice is essential for realising the aims set out under 1 above; and

4. the agreement, decision or concerted practice does not eliminate competition in respect of a substantial part of the goods concerned.

VI. State whether you intend to produce further supporting arguments and, if so, on which points.

The undersigned declare that the information given above and in the annexes attached hereto is correct. They are aware of the provisions of Article 15 (1) (a) of Regulation 17.

[Date]

[Signatures]

European Communities Commission

Brussels, [date]
170, rue de la Loi
(present address is
200, rue de la Loi)

Directorate General
for Competition

To
Acknowledgment of receipt
(This form will be returned to the address inserted above if
completed in a single copy by the person lodging it.)

Your application for negative clearance dated_____
Your notification dated_____concerning:

(a) Parties:
1._____
2._____and others.
(There is no need to name the other undertakings party to the arrangement)

(b) Subject_____
(Brief description of the restriction on competition)
was received on_____and registered under No. IV.

_____

Please quote the above number in all correspondence].

_____

AMENDMENTS
This form was substituted by Reg. 1133/68.

Commission Regulation 99/63 of July 25, 1963
On the Hearings Provided for in Article 19 (1) and (2) of
Regulation 17

(J.O. 1963, 2268; O.J. 1963–1964, 47)

THE COMMISSION OF THE EUROPEAN ECONOMIC COMMUNITY

Having regard to the Treaty establishing the European Economic Community, and in particular Articles 87 and 155 thereof;

Having regard to Article 24 of Regulation 17 of February 6, 1962 (First Regulation implementing Articles 85 and 86 of the Treaty);

Whereas the Commission has power under Article 24 of Regulation 17 to lay down implementing provisions concerning the hearings provided for in Article 19 (1) and (2) of that Regulation;

Whereas in most cases the Commission will in the course of its inquiries already be in close touch with the undertakings or associations of undertakings which are the subject thereof and they will accordingly have the opportunity of making known their views regarding the objections raised against them;

Whereas, however, in accordance with Article 19 (1) of Regulation 17 and with the rights of defence, the undertakings and associations of undertakings concerned must have the right on conclusion of the inquiry to submit their comments on the whole of the objections raised against them which the Commission proposes to deal with in its decisions;

Whereas persons other than the undertakings or associations of undertakings which are the subject of the inquiry may have an interest in being heard; whereas, by the second sentence of Article 19 (2) of Regulation 17, such persons must have the opportunity of being heard if they apply and show that they have a sufficient interest;

Whereas it is desirable to enable persons who pursuant to Article 3 (2) of Regulation 17 have applied for an infringement to be terminated to submit their comments where the Commission considers that on the basis of the information in its possession there are insufficient grounds for granting the application;

Whereas the various persons entitled to submit comments must do so in writing, both in their own interest and in the interests of good administration, without prejudice to oral procedure where appropriate to supplement the written evidence;

Whereas it is necessary to define the rights of persons who are to be heard, and in particular the conditions upon which they may be represented or assisted and the setting and calculation of time limits;

Whereas the Advisory Committee on Restrictive Practices and Monopolies delivers its Opinion on the basis of a preliminary draft decision; whereas it must therefore be consulted concerning a case after the inquiry in respect thereof has been completed; whereas such consultation does not prevent the Commission from reopening an inquiry if need be;

HAS ADOPTED THIS REGULATION:

ARTICLE 1

Before consulting the Advisory Committee on Restrictive Practices and Monopolies, the Commission shall hold a hearing pursuant to Article 19 (1) of Regulation 17.

ARTICLE 2

1. The Commission shall inform undertakings and associations of undertakings in writing of the objections raised against them. The communication shall be addressed to each of them or to a joint agent appointed by them.

2. The Commission may inform the parties by giving notice in the *Official Journal of the European Communities*, if from the circumstances of the case this appears appropriate, in particular where notice is to be given to a number of undertakings but no joint agent has been appointed. The notice shall have regard to the legitimate interest of the undertakings in the protection of their business secrets.

3. A fine or a periodic penalty payment may be imposed on an undertaking or association of undertakings only if the objections were notified in the manner provided for in paragraph (1).

4. The Commission shall when giving notice of objections fix a time limit up to which the undertakings and associations of undertakings may inform the Commission of their views.

ARTICLE 3

1. Undertakings and associations of undertakings shall, within the appointed time limit, make known in writing their views concerning the objections raised against them.

2. They may in their written comments set out all matters relevant to their defence.

3. They may attach any relevant documents in proof of the facts set out. They may also propose that the Commission hear persons who may corroborate those facts.

ARTICLE 4

The Commission shall in its decisions deal only with those objections raised against undertakings and associations of undertakings in respect of which they have been afforded the opportunity of making known their views.

ARTICLE 5

If natural or legal persons showing a sufficient interest apply to be heard pursuant to Article 19 (2) of Regulation 17, the Commission shall afford them the opportunity of making known their views in writing within such time limit as it shall fix.

ARTICLE 6

Where the Commission, having received an application pursuant to Article 3 (2) of Regulation 17, considers that on the basis of the information in its possession there are insufficient grounds for granting the application, it shall inform the applicants of its reasons and fix a time limit for them to submit any further comments in writing.

ARTICLE 7

1. The Commission shall afford to persons who have so requested in their written comments the opportunity to put forward their arguments orally, if those persons show a sufficient interest or if the Commission proposes to impose on them a fine or periodic penalty payment.

2. The Commission may likewise afford to any other person the opportunity of orally expressing his views.

ARTICLE 8

1. The Commission shall summon the persons to be heard to attend on such date as it shall appoint.

2. It shall forthwith transmit a copy of the summons to the competent authorities of the Member States, who may appoint an official to take part in the hearing.

ARTICLE 9

1. Hearings shall be conducted by the persons appointed by the Commission for that purpose.

2. Persons summoned to attend shall appear either in person or be represented by legal representatives or by representatives authorised by their constitution. Undertakings and associations of undertakings may moreover be represented by a duly authorised agent appointed from among their permanent staff.

Persons heard by the Commission may be assisted by lawyers or university teachers who are entitled to plead before the Court of Justice of the European Communities in accordance with Article 17 of the Protocol on the Statute of the Court, or by other qualified persons.

3. Hearings shall not be public. Persons shall be heard separately or in the presence of other persons summoned to attend. In the latter case, regard shall be had to the legitimate interest of the undertakings in the protection of their business secrets.

4. The essential content of the statements made by each person heard shall be recorded in minutes which shall be read and approved by him.

ARTICLE 10

Without prejudice to Article 2 (2), information and summonses from the Commission shall be sent to the addressess by registered letter with acknowledgment of receipt, or shall be delivered by hand against receipt.

ARTICLE 11

1. In fixing the time limits provided for in Articles 2, 5 and 6, the Commission shall have regard both to the time required for preparation of comments and to the urgency of the case. The time limit shall be not less than two weeks; it may be extended.

2. Time limits shall run from the day following receipt of a communication or delivery thereof by hand.

3. Written comments must reach the Commission or be dispatched by registered letter before expiry of the time limit. Where the time limit would expire on a Sunday or public holiday, it shall be extended up to the end of the next following working day. For the purpose of calculating this extension, public holidays shall, in cases where the relevant date is the date of receipt of written comments, be those set out in the Annex to this regulation, and in cases where the relevant date is the date of dispatch, those appointed by law in the country of dispatch.

This regulation shall be binding in its entirety and directly applicable in all Member States.

Done at Brussels, July 25, 1963.

Annex

Referred to in the third sentence of Article 11 (3).

(List of public holidays)

New year	1 Jan.	Belgian National Day	21 July
Good Friday		Assumption	15 Aug.
Easter Saturday		All Saints	1 Nov.
Easter Monday		All Souls	2 Nov.
Labour Day	1 May	Christmas Eve	24 Dec.
Schuman Plan Day	9 May	Christmas Day	25 Dec.
Ascension Day		Boxing Day	26 Dec.
Whit Monday		New Year's Eve	31 Dec.

BIBLIOGRAPHY

Bellamy and Child, *Common Market Law of Competition*, Chap. 12, paras. 1213–1214, 1223–1224 and 1230.

Leigh, "Resurrection of the Provisional Decision" (1977) 2 E.L.Rev. 91.

Temple Lang, "The Procedure of the Commission in Competition Cases" (1977) 14 C.M.L.Rev. 155.

GENERAL NOTE

This Regulation lays down implementing provisions for the hearings provided for in Reg. 17, Art. 19 (1) and (2), and it is made pursuant to Reg. 17, Art. 24.

Reg. 17, Art. 19 (1) provides that any undertaking or association of undertakings concerned shall be given the opportunity of being heard on matters to which the Commission has taken objection before any decision is taken pursuant to Art. 2, 3, 6, 7, 8, 15 or 16 of the Regulation. (Reg. 17, Art. 2 is concerned with "negative clearance"; Art. 3 with the termination of infringements; Arts. 6, 7 and 8 with exemption under Art. 85 (3), EEC; and Arts. 15 and 16 with the imposition of fines and penalties for breaches of the Treaty and of Reg. 17.) The Commission appears to assume that a hearing under this Regulation is required before it may adopt a provisional decision under Art. 15 (6) of Reg. 17: see *Sirdar/Phildar*, O.J. 1975, L125/27; [1976] 1 C.M.L.R. D 93; *Bronbemaling/Heidemaatschappij*, O.J. 1975, L246/77; [1975] 2 C.M.L.R. D 67.

Reg. 17, Art. 19 (2), empowers the Commission to hear other interested parties, including Member States. The Commission must inform undertakings of the objections made against them (Art. 2). The Commission may only base any decision on objections which a party has been given an opportunity of dealing with (Art. 4; see also Art. 2 (3)). On the scope of disclosure required, see case 41/69, *ACF Chemiefarma* v. *Commission* [1970] E.C.R. 661 at 693 and case 85/76, *Hoffmann-La Roche* v. *Commission* (not yet reported). On the interaction between the defendant's right to be informed of the case against him and the Commission's duty of confidentiality under Art. 20 (2) of Reg. 17, see case 85/76 (*supra*). "Objections" in Arts. 2 and 4 of the Regulation consist of matters which would either bring the agreement within Art. 85 (1), EEC or prevent exemption from being granted under Art. 85 (3): conditions which the Commission may attach to a grant of exemption are not included. However, parties on whom the Commission intends to impose onerous conditions must, *as a matter of general principle*, be clearly informed, in good time, of the reasons for doing so, in order that they may be able to put their case (see case 17/74, *Transocean Marine Paint Association* v. *Commission* [1974] E.C.R. 1063. The undertakings are to make their views known in writing (Art. 3). Any other undertakings which show a "sufficient interest" to be heard under Reg. 17, Art. 19 (2), may also make written submissions (Art. 5). Complainants under Reg. 17, Art. 3, are also given an opportunity to be heard (Art. 6). Provision for oral hearings (which are not public) is made in Arts. 7–9. Oral hearings are not held unless the parties so request in their written submissions. The Commission may fix time limits for submitting observations (Arts. 2, 5, 6 and 11).

Only the *main* evidence need be known to a party: cases 56 & 58/64, *Consten & Grundig* v. *Commission* [1966] C.M.L.R. 418 at 469.

The statement of objections is not limited to matters which occurred before the Commission commenced proceedings: case 48/69, *I.C.I.* v. *Commission* [1972] C.M.L.R. 557 and 618.

A third party may be asked to submit views without prejudice to whether he has a "sufficient interest" to be heard: case 8/71, *Deutscher Komponistenverband* v. *Commission* [1973] C.M.L.R. 902.

As to Art. 9, see case 41/49, *ACF Chemiefarma* v. *Commission, supra*. At oral hearings under Art. 9 (2) undertakings may be represented by their staff or employees or by advocates: case 48/69, *I.C.I.* v. *Commission, supra*, at 631. The purpose of Art. 9 (4) is to enable the persons heard to check the accuracy of the record. Delay in sending the minutes to such persons could only affect the validity of an eventual decision if the record of statements contained therein were of doubtful accuracy: case 48/69, *I.C.I.* v. *Commission, supra*, at 620.

Council Regulation 19/65 of March 2, 1965
On Application of Article 85 (3) of the Treaty to Certain
Categories of Agreements and Concerted Practices

(J.O. 1965, 533; O.J. 1965–1966, 35)

THE COUNCIL OF THE EUROPEAN ECONOMIC COMMUNITY

Having regard to the Treaty establishing the European Economic Community, and in particular Article 87 thereof;

Having regard to the proposal from the Commission;

Having regard to the Opinion of the European Parliament;

Having regard to the Opinion of the Economic and Social Committee;

Whereas Article 85 (1) of the Treaty may in accordance with Article 85 (3) be declared inapplicable to certain categories of agreements, decisions and concerted practices which fulfil the conditions contained in Article 85 (3);

Whereas the provisions for implementation of Article 85 (3) must be adopted by way of regulation pursuant to Article 87;

Whereas in view of the large number of notifications submitted in pursuance of Regulation 17 it is desirable that in order to facilitate the task of the Commission it should be enabled to declare by way of regulation that the provisions of Article 85 (1) do not apply to certain categories of agreements and concerted practices;

Whereas it should be laid down under what conditions the Commission, in close and constant liaison with the competent authorities of the Member States, may exercise such powers after sufficient experience has been gained in the light of individual decisions and it becomes possible to define categories of agreements and concerted practices in respect of which the conditions of Article 85 (3) may be considered as being fulfilled;

Whereas the Commission has indicated by the action it has taken, in particular by Regulation 153, that there can be no easing of the procedures prescribed by Regulation 17 in respect of certain types of agreements and concerted practices that are particularly liable to distort competition in the common market;

Whereas under Article 6 of Regulation 17 the Commission may provide that a decision taken pursuant to Article 85 (3) of the Treaty shall apply with retroactive effect; whereas it is desirable that the Commission be also empowered to adopt, by regulation, provisions to the like effect;

Whereas under Article 7 of Regulation 17 agreements, decisions and concerted practices may, by decision of the Commission, be exempted from prohibition in particular if they are modified in such manner that they satisfy the requirements of Article 85 (3); whereas it is desirable that the Commission be enabled to grant like exemption by regulation to such agreements and concerted practices if they are modified in such manner as to fall within a category defined in an exempting regulation;

Whereas, since there can be no exemption if the conditions set out in Article 85 (3) are not satisfied, the Commission must have power to lay down by decision the conditions that must be satisfied by an agreement or concerted practice which owing to special circumstances has certain effects incompatible with Article 85 (3);

HAS ADOPTED THIS REGULATION:

ARTICLE 1

1. Without prejudice to the application of Regulation 17 and in accordance with Article 85 (3) of the Treaty the Commission may by regulation declare that Article 85 (1) shall not apply to categories of agreements to which only two undertakings are party and:

> (a)—whereby one party agrees with the other to supply only to that other certain goods for resale within a defined area of the common market; or
> —whereby one party agrees with the other to purchase only from that other certain goods for resale; or
> —whereby the two undertakings have entered into obligations, as in the two preceding sub-paragraphs, with each other in respect of exclusive supply and purchase for resale;
> (b) which include restrictions imposed in relation to the acquisition or use of industrial property rights—in particular of patents, utility models, designs or trade marks—or to the rights arising out of contracts for assignment of, or the right to use, a method of manufacture or knowledge relating to the use or to the application of industrial processes.

2. The regulation shall define the categories of agreements to which it applies and shall specify in particular:

> (a) the restrictions or clauses which must not be contained in the agreements;
> (b) the clauses which must be contained in the agreements, or the other conditions which must be satisfied.

3. Paragraphs (1) and (2) shall apply by analogy to categories of concerted practices to which only two undertakings are party.

ARTICLE 2

1. A regulation pursuant to Article 1 shall be made for a specified period.

2. It may be repealed or amended where circumstances have changed with respect to any factor which was basic to its being made; in such case, a period shall be fixed for modification of the agreements and concerted practices to which the earlier regulation applies.

ARTICLE 3

A regulation pursuant to Article 1 may stipulate that it shall apply with retroactive effect to agreements and concerted practices to which, at the date of entry into force of that regulation, a decision issued with retroactive effect in pursuance of Article 6 of Regulation 17 would have applied.

ARTICLE 4

1. A regulation pursuant to Article 1 may stipulate that the prohibition contained in Article 85 (1) of the Treaty shall not apply, for such period as shall be fixed by that regulation, to agreements and concerted practices already in existence on March 13, 1962, which do not satisfy the conditions of Article 85 (3), [; or]

[A regulation pursuant to Article 1 may stipulate that the prohibition contained in Article 85 (1) of the Treaty shall not apply, for such period as shall be fixed by that regulation, to agreements and concerted practices already in existence at the date of accession to which Article 85 applies by virtue of accession and which do not satisfy the conditions of Article 85 (3), where:]

—within three months from the entry into force of the regulation, they are so modified as to satisfy the said conditions in accordance with the provisions of the regulation; and

—the modifications are brought to the notice of the Commission within the time limit fixed by the regulation.

[The provisions of the preceding subparagraph shall apply in the same way in the case of the accession of the Hellenic Republic.]

2. Paragraph (1) shall apply to agreements and concerted practices which had to be notified before February 1, 1963, in accordance with Article 5 of Regulation 17, only where they have been so notified before that date.

[Paragraph (1) shall not apply to agreements and concerted practices to which Article 85 (1) of the Treaty applies by virtue of accession and which must be notified before July 1, 1973, in accordance with Articles 5 and 25 of Regulation 17, unless they have been so notified before that date.]

[Paragraph 1 shall not apply to agreements and concerted practices to which Article 85 (1) of the Treaty applies by virtue of the accession of the Hellenic Republic and which must be notified before July 1, 1981 in accordance with Articles 5 and 25 of Regulation 17, unless they have been so notified before that date.]

3. The benefit of the provisions laid down pursuant to paragraph (1) may not be claimed in actions pending at the date of entry into force of a regulation adopted pursuant to Article 1; neither may it be relied on as grounds for claims for damages against third parties.

AMENDMENTS

In para. (1) the words in the first and second sets of square brackets were added by the Act concerning the conditions of Accession, Annex I. In para. (2) the words in the first set of square brackets were added by *ibid.*

The words in the third set of square brackets were added by the Act concerning the conditions of Accession of the Hellenic Republic, Annex I. In para. (2) the words in the second set of square brackets were added by *ibid.*

ARTICLE 5

Before adopting a regulation, the Commission shall publish a draft thereof and invite all persons concerned to submit their comments within such time limit, being not less than one month, as the Commission shall fix.

ARTICLE 6

1. The Commission shall consult the Advisory Committee on Restrictive Practices and Monopolies:

(*a*) before publishing a draft regulation;
(*b*) before adopting a regulation.

2. Article 10 (5) and (6) of Regulation 17, relating to consultation with the Advisory Committee, shall apply by analogy, it being understood that joint meetings with the Commission shall take place not earlier than one month after dispatch of the notice convening them.

ARTICLE 7

Where the Commission, either on its own initiative or at the request of a Member State or of natural or legal persons claiming a legitimate interest, finds that in any particular case agreements or concerted practices to which a regulation adopted pursuant to Article 1 of this regulation applies have nevertheless certain effects which are incompatible with the conditions laid down in Article 85 (3) of the Treaty, it may withdraw the benefit of application of that regulation and issue a decision in accordance with Articles 6 and 8 of Regulation 17, without any notification under Article 4 (1) of Regulation 17 being required.

ARTICLE 8

The Commission shall, before January 1, 1970, submit to the Council a proposal for a regulation for such amendment of this regulation as may prove necessary in the light of experience.

This regulation shall be binding in its entirety and directly applicable in all Member States.

Done at Brussels, March 2, 1965.

Commission Regulation 67/67 of March 22, 1967
On the Application of Article 85 (3) of the Treaty to Certain Categories of Exclusive Dealing Agreements

(J.O. 1967, 849; O.J. 1967, 10)

THE COMMISSION OF THE EUROPEAN ECONOMIC COMMUNITY

Having regard to the Treaty establishing the European Economic Community, and in particular Articles 87 and 155 thereof;

Having regard to Article 24 of Regulation 17 of February 6, 1962;

Having regard to Regulation 19/65/EEC of March 2, 1965, on the application of Article 85 (3) of the Treaty to certain categories of agreements and concerted practices;

Having regard to the Opinions delivered by the Advisory Committee on Restrictive Practices and Monopolies in accordance with Article 6 of Regulation 19/65/EEC;

Whereas under Regulation 19/65/EEC the Commission has power to apply Article 85 (3) of the Treaty by regulation to certain categories of bilateral exclusive dealing agreements and concerted practices coming within Article 85;

Whereas the experience gained up to now, on the basis of individual decisions, makes it possible to define a first category of agreements and concerted practices which can be accepted as normally satisfying the conditions laid down in Article 85 (3);

Whereas since adoption of such a regulation would not conflict with the application of Regulation 17 the right of undertakings to request the Commission, on an individual basis, for a declaration under Article 85 (3) of the Treaty would not be affected;

Whereas exclusive dealing agreements of the category defined in Article 1 of this regulation may fall within the prohibition contained in Article 85 (1) of the Treaty; whereas since it is only in exceptional cases the exclusive dealing agreements concluded within a Member State affect trade between Member States, there is no need to include them in this regulation;

Whereas it is not necessary expressly to exclude from the category as defined those agreements which do not fulfil the conditions of Article 85 (1) of the Treaty;

Whereas in the present state of trade exclusive dealing agreements relating to international trade lead in general to an improvement in distributing because the entrepreneur is able to consolidate his sales activities; whereas he is not obliged to maintain numerous business contacts with a large number of dealers, and whereas the fact of maintaining contacts with only one dealer makes it easier to overcome sales difficulties resulting from linguistic, legal, and other differences; whereas exclusive dealing agreements facilitate the promotion of the sale of a product and make it possible to carry out more intensive marketing and to ensure continuity of supplies, while at the same time rationalising distribution; whereas, moreover, the appointment of an exclusive distributor or of an exclusive purchaser who will take over, in place of the manufacturer, sales promotion, after-sales service and carrying of stocks, is often the sole means whereby small and medium-size undertakings can compete in the market; whereas it should be left to the contracting parties to decide whether and to what extent they consider it desirable to incorporate in the agreements terms designed to promote sales; whereas there can only be an improvement in distribution if dealing is not entrusted to a competitor;

Whereas as a rule such exclusive dealing agreements also help to give consumers a proper share of the resulting benefit as they gain directly from the improvement in distribution, and their economic or supply position is thereby improved as they can obtain products manufactured in other countries more quickly and more easily;

Whereas this regulation must determine the obligations restricting competition which may be included in an exclusive dealing agreement; whereas it may be left to the contracting parties to decide which of those obligations they include in exclusive dealing agreements in order to draw the maximum advantages from exclusive dealing;

Whereas any exemption must be subject to certain conditions; whereas it is in particular advisable to ensure through the possibility of parallel imports that consumers obtain a proper share of the advantages resulting from exclusive dealing; whereas it is therefore not possible to allow industrial property rights and other rights to be exercised in an abusive manner in order to create absolute territorial protection; whereas these considerations do not prejudice the relationship between the law of competition and industrial property rights, since the sole object here is to determine the condition for exemption of certain categories of agreements under this regulation;

Whereas competition at the distribution stage is ensured by the possibility of parallel imports; whereas, therefore, the exclusive dealing agreements covered by this regulation will not normally afford any possibility of preventing competition in respect of a substantial part of the products in question;

Whereas it is desirable to allow contracting parties a limited period of time within which they may, in accordance with Article 4 of Regulation 19/65, modify their agreements and practices so as to satisfy the conditions laid down in this regulation, without it being possible, under Article 4 (3) of Regulation 19/65, to rely thereon in actions which are pending at the time of entry into force of this regulation, or as grounds for claims for damages against third parties;

Whereas agreements and concerted practices which satisfy the conditions set out in this regulation need no longer be notified; whereas Article 4 (2) (*a*) of Regulation 27, as amended by Regulation 153, can be repealed, since agreements which it was possible to notify on Form B1 would normally come within the scope of the exemption;

Whereas agreements notified on Form B1 and not amended so as to satisfy the conditions of this regulation should be made subject to the normal notification procedure in order that they may be examined individually;

HAS ADOPTED THIS REGULATION:

ARTICLE 1

1. Pursuant to Article 85 (3) of the Treaty and subject to the provisions of this regulation it is hereby declared that until [December 31, 1982] Article 85 (1) of the Treaty shall not apply to agreements to which only two undertakings are party and whereby

(a) one party agrees with the other to supply only to that other certain goods for resale within a defined area of the common market; or

(b) one party agrees with the other to purchase only from that other certain goods for resale; or

(c) the two undertakings have entered into obligations, as in (a) and (b) above, with each other in respect of exclusive supply and purchase for resale.

2. Paragraph (1) shall not apply to agreements to which undertakings from one Member State only are party and which concern the resale of goods within that Member State.

AMENDMENTS
The words "December 31, 1982" in para. (1) were substituted by Reg. 2591/72 (J.O. 1972, L276/15; O.J. 1972 (9–28 Dec.), 7).

ARTICLE 2

1. Apart from an obligation falling within Article 1, no restriction on competition shall be imposed on the exclusive dealer other than:

(a) the obligation not to manufacture or distribute, during the duration of the contract or until one year after its expiration, goods which compete with the goods to which the contract relates;

(b) the obligation to refrain, outside the territory covered by the contract, from seeking customers for the goods to which the contract relates, from establishing any branch, or from maintaining any distribution depot.

2. Article 1 (1) shall apply notwithstanding that the exclusive dealer undertakes all or any of the following obligations:

(a) to purchase complete ranges of goods or minimum quantities;

(b) to sell the goods to which the contract relates under trade marks or packed and presented as specified by the manufacturer;

(c) to take measures for promotion of sales, in particular:
—to advertise,
—to maintain a sales network or stock of goods,
—to provide after-sale and guarantee services,
—to employ staff having specialised or technical training.

ARTICLE 3

Article 1 (1) of this regulation shall not apply where:

(a) manufacturers of competing goods entrust each other with exclusive dealing in those goods;

(b) the contracting parties make it difficult for intermediaries or consumers to obtain the goods to which the contract relates from other dealers within the common market, in particular where the contracting parties:

(i) exercise industrial property rights to prevent dealers or consumers from obtaining from other parts of the common market or from selling in the territory covered by the contract goods to which the contract relates which are properly marked or otherwise properly placed on the market;

(ii) exercise other rights or take other measures to prevent dealers or consumers from obtaining from elsewhere goods to which the contract relates or from selling them in the territory covered by the contract.

ARTICLE 4

1. As regards agreements which were in existence on March 13, 1962, and were notified before February 1, 1963, the declaration contained in Article 1 (1) of inapplicability of Article 85 (1) of the Treaty shall have retroactive effect from the time when the conditions of application of this regulation were fulfilled.

2. As regards all other agreements notified before the entry into force of this regulation, the declaration contained in Article 1 (1) of inapplicability of Article 85 (1) of the Treaty shall have retroactive effect from the time when the conditions of application of this regulation were fulfilled, but not earlier than the date of notification.

ARTICLE 5

As regards agreements, which were in existence on March 13, 1962, notified before February 1, 1963, and amended before August 2, 1967, so as to fulfil the conditions of application of this regulation, the prohibition in Article 85 (1) of the Treaty shall not apply in respect of the period prior to the amendment, where such amendment is notified to the Commission before October 3, 1967. [As regards agreements, decisions or concerted practices for exclusive dealing already in existence at the date of accession to which Article 85 (1) applies by virtue of accession, the prohibition in Article 85 (1) of the Treaty shall not apply where they are modified within six months from the date of accession so as to fulfil the conditions contained in this regulation.] The notification shall take effect from the time of receipt thereof by the Commission. Where the notification is sent by registered post, it shall take effect from the date on the postmark of the place of dispatch.

[This provision shall apply in the same way in the case of the accession of the Hellenic Republic.]

AMENDMENTS

The words in the first set of square brackets were added by the Act concerning the conditions of Accession, Annex I.

The words in the second set of square brackets were added by the Act concerning the conditions of Accession of the Hellenic Republic, Annex I.

ARTICLE 6

The Commission shall examine whether Article 7 of Regulation 19/65 applies in individual cases, in particular when there are grounds for believing that:

(*a*) the goods to which the contract relates are not subject, in the territory covered by the contract, to competition from goods considered by the consumer as similar goods in view of their properties, price and intended use;

(*b*) it is not possible for other manufacturers to sell, in the territory covered by the contract, similar goods at the same stage of distribution as that of the exclusive dealer;

(*c*) the exclusive dealer has abused the exemption:

   (i) by refusing, without objectively valid reasons, to supply in the territory covered by the contract categories of purchasers who cannot obtain supplies elsewhere, on suitable terms, of the goods to which the contract relates;

   (ii) by selling the goods to which the contract relates at excessive prices.

ARTICLE 7

1. Article 4 (2) (*a*) of Regulation 27 of May 3, 1962, as amended by Regulation 153, is hereby repealed.

2. Notification, on Form B1, of an exclusive dealing agreement which does not fulfil the conditions contained in Articles 1 to 3 of this regulation shall, if such agreement is not amended so as to satisfy those conditions, be effected before October 3, 1967, by submission of Form B, with annexes, in accordance with the provisions of Regulation 27.

ARTICLE 8

Articles 1 to 7 of this regulation shall apply by analogy to the category of concerted practices defined in Article 1 (1).

ARTICLE 9

This regulation shall enter into force on May 1, 1967.

This regulation shall be binding in its entirety and directly applicable in all Member States.

Done at Brussels, March 22, 1967.

**Council Regulation 2988/74 of November 26, 1974
Concerning Limitation Periods in Proceedings and the Enforcement
of Sanctions under the Rules of the European Economic Community
relating to Transport and Competition**

(O.J. 1974, L319/1)

THE COUNCIL OF THE EUROPEAN COMMUNITIES

Having regard to the Treaty establishing the European Economic Community, and in particular Articles 75, 79 and 87 thereof;

Having regard to the proposal from the Commission;

Having regard to the Opinion of the European Parliament;

Having regard to the Opinion of the Economic and Social Committee;

Whereas under the rules of the European Economic Community relating to transport and competition the Commission has the power to impose fines, penalties and periodic penalty payments on undertakings or associations of undertakings which infringe Community law relating to information or investigation, or to the prohibition on discrimination, restrictive practices and abuse of dominant position; whereas those rules make no provision for any limitation period;

Whereas it is necessary in the interests of legal certainty that the principle of limitation be introduced and that implementing rules be laid down; whereas, for the matter to be covered fully, it is necessary that provision for limitation be made not only as regards the power to impose fines or penalties, but also as regards the power to enforce decisions, imposing fines, penalties or periodic penalty payments; whereas such provisions should specify the length of limitation periods, the date on which time starts to run and the events which have the effect of interrupting or suspending the limitation period; whereas in this respect the interests of undertakings and associations of undertakings on the one hand, and the requirements imposed by administrative practice, on the other hand, should be taken into account;

Whereas this Regulation must apply to the relevant provisions of Regulation 11 concerning the abolition of discrimination in transport rates and conditions, in implementation of Article 79 (3) of the Treaty establishing the European Economic Community, of Regulation 17: first Regulation implementing Articles 85 and 86 of the Treaty, and of Council Regulation 1017/68 of July 19, 1968, applying rules of competition to transport by rail, road and inland waterway; whereas it must also apply to the relevant provisions of future regulations in the fields of European Economic Community law relating to transport and competition.

HAS ADOPTED THIS REGULATION:

ARTICLE 1

Limitation Periods in Proceedings

1. The power of the Commission to impose fines or penalties for infringements of the rules of the European Economic Community relating to transport or competition shall be subject to the following limitation periods:
   (a) three years in the case of infringements of provisions concerning applications or notifications of undertakings or associations of undertakings, requests for information, or the carrying out of investigations;
   (b) five years in the case of all other infringements.
2. Time shall begin to run upon the day on which the infringement is committed. However, in the case of continuing or repeated infringements, time shall begin to run on the day on which the infringement ceases.

ARTICLE 2

Interruption of the Limitation Period in Proceedings

1. Any action taken by the Commission, or by any Member State, acting at the request of the Commission, for the purpose of the preliminary investigation or proceedings in respect of an infringement shall interrupt the limitation period in proceedings. The limitation period shall be interrupted with effect from the date on which the action is notified to at least one undertaking or association of undertakings which have participated in the infringement.
   Actions which interrupt the running of the period shall include in particular the following:
   (a) written requests for information by the Commission, or by the competent authority of a Member State acting at the request of the Commission; or a Commission decision requiring the requested information;
   (b) written authorisations issued to their officials by the Commission or by the competent authority of any Member State at the request of the Commission; or a Commission decision ordering an investigation;
   (c) the commencement of proceedings by the Commission;
   (d) notification of the Commission's statement of objections.
2. The interruption of the limitation period shall apply for all the undertakings or associations of undertakings which have participated in the infringement.
3. Each interruption shall start time running afresh. However, the limitation period shall expire at the latest on the day on which a period equal to twice the limitation period has elapsed without the Commission having imposed a fine or a penalty; that period shall be extended by the time during which limitation is suspended pursuant to Article 3.

327

ARTICLE 3

Suspension of the Limitation Period in Proceedings

The limitation period in proceedings shall be suspended for as long as the decision of the Commission is the subject of proceedings pending before the Court of Justice of the European Communities.

ARTICLE 4

Limitation Period for the Enforcement of Sanctions

1. The power of the Commission to enforce decisions imposing fines, penalties or periodic payments for infringements of the rules of the European Economic Community relating to transport or competition shall be subject to a limitation period of five years.
2. Time shall begin to run on the day on which the decision becomes final.

ARTICLE 5

Interruption of the Limitation Period for the Enforcement of Sanctions

1. The limitation period for the enforcement of sanctions shall be interrupted:
   (a) by notification of a decision varying the original amount of the fine, penalty or periodic penalty payments or refusing an application for variation;
   (b) by any action of the Commission, or of a Member State at the request of the Commission, for the purpose of enforcing payments of a fine, penalty or periodic penalty payment.
2. Each interruption shall start time running afresh.

ARTICLE 6

Suspension of the Limitation Period for the Enforcement of Sanctions

The limitation period for the enforcement of sanctions shall be suspended for so long as:
(a) time to pay is allowed; or
(b) enforcement of payment is suspended pursuant to a decision of the Court of Justice of the European Communities.

ARTICLE 7

Application to Transitional Cases

This Regulation shall also apply in respect of infringements committed before it enters into force.

ARTICLE 8

Entry into Force

This Regulation shall enter into force on January 1, 1975.

This Regulation shall be binding in its entirety and directly applicable in all Member States.

Done at Brussels, November 26, 1974.

**Proposal for a Commission Regulation on the Application of
Article 85 (3) of the Treaty to Certain Categories of Patent
Licensing Agreements**

(O.J. 1979, C58/12)

THE COMMISSION OF THE EUROPEAN COMMUNITIES

Having regard to the Treaty establishing the European Economic Community, and in particular Articles 87 and 155 thereof,

Having regard to Council Regulation 19/65 of March 2, 1965 (J.O. 1965, 533) on the application of Article 85 (3) of the Treaty to certain categories of agreements and concerted practices,

After consulting the Advisory Committee on Restrictive Practices and Dominant Positions in accordance with Article 6 of Regulation 19/65,

Whereas:

Under Regulation 19/65 the Commission has the power to apply Article 85 (3) of the Treaty by Regulation to certain categories of bilateral agreements and concerted practices falling within the scope of Article 85 (1) which include restrictions imposed in relation to the acquisition or use of industrial property rights, in particular patents, utility models, designs or trade marks, or to the rights arising out of contracts for assignment of, or the right to use, a method of manufacture or knowledge relating to the use or application of industrial processes.

From the experience so far gained on the basis of individual decisions, it is possible to define a category of agreements which can be accepted as generally satisfying the tests of Article 85 (3).

Since such a Regulation is without prejudice to the application of Council Regulation 17 (J.O. 1962, 204), undertakings will still have the right to apply in individual cases for negative clearance under Article 2 of Regulation 17 or a declaration under Article 85 (3) of the Treaty.

Patent licensing agreements of the category defined in Articles 1, 2 and 3 of this Regulation may fall within the scope of the prohibition in Article 85 (1). Patent licensing agreements to which undertakings in a single Member State only are party and which concern patents in that State only are also covered by this Regulation to the extent that they may affect trade between Member States.

It is not necessary expressly to exclude from the category as defined those agreements that do not fall within the circumstances envisaged in Article 85 (1) of the Treaty. Certainty as to the law for the parties concerned is better served if Articles 1 and 2 of the Regulation list all those obligations whose anti-competitive effect may be disputed. This is true in

330

particular for exclusivity and export prohibitions, definitive appraisal of which by the Court of Justice of the European Communities under Article 85 (1) is not prejudged by this Regulation. The Commission considers that since the end of the transitional period at the latest, export bans in intra-Community trade have been incompatible with the removal of barriers to trade, the free movement of goods and the unity of the common market.

Patent licensing agreements of the category defined in Articles 1 and 2 of this Regulation contribute in general to improving the production of goods and to promoting technical progress, since they usually increase the number of production facilities and the quantity of goods in question produced in the common market and make it possible for undertakings other than the patentee to manufacture goods using the latest techniques and to develop these techniques further; the availability of such licences makes patentees more willing to grant them and makes it easier for other undertakings to decide to run the risks involved in investing capital in the manufacture, use or distribution of a new product or the use of a new process.

This expansion of production at an improved level of technology represents a benefit in which consumers share as a rule, given the increase in the quantity and quality of goods available.

It must also be ensured that patent licensing agreements contain no restrictions that are not indispensable to the attainment of these objectives and do not afford the possibility of eliminating competition in respect of a substantial part of the products in question.

These conditions are satisfied as a rule even in the case of exclusive licences for the whole common market, since cases are rare in which a dominant position is founded on the legal monopoly arising from a patent, and in such cases it is exceptional for a patentee to grant exclusive licences, Where such a case arises, and it is found that the patent licensing agreement has led to the elimination of competition in respect of a substantial part of the products in question, the Commission will apply Article 7 of Regulation 19/65.

The territorial protection that arises from exclusive sales rights and related export bans can only be allowed if it is requisite for ensuring the expansion of technical progress. The Commission accepts that this protection is necessary for the majority of undertakings as a determining factor to facilitate decisions on investments relating to the development and marketing of new technologies. For undertakings with very high turnovers this protection would not, on the other hand, seem appropriate having regard to their extensive financial resources (Article 1 (2) (a)). The turnover limit set in the Regulation will ensure that most independent undertakings in the Community that grant or take licences will be able to qualify for the exemption. But the exemption will not be available for a number of firms which have particularly large financial resources and which, moreover, hold the bulk of the patents in force in the common market. Subject to this restriction, territorial protection may be allowed for the full duration of all patents extant at the time of the licensing agreement (Article 1 (2) (b)). Further, the protection can be conceded only for products in which intermediate trade is possible (Article 1 (2) (c)). Lastly, the Regulation assumes that the licensee himself undertakes investment for the manufacture of the licensed product (Article 1 (2) (d)).

It therefore does not apply to mere sales licences, which are subject to the provisions of Commission Regulation 67/67 (J.O. 1967, 849) on the application of Article 85 (3) of the Treaty to certain categories of exclusive dealing agreements.

The obligations listed in Article 2 are as a rule unobjectionable from the competition law aspect. So far as they fall within the scope of Article 85 (1), they should be exempted even where they are undertaken otherwise than in conjunction with one or more of the restrictions exempted by Article 1.

The Regulation must specify what obligations in restraint of competition may be contained in a patent licensing agreement. It may be left to the contracting parties to decide which of these obligations they specifically include in the patent licensing agreements so as best to achieve the desired advantages.

It is appropriate to extend this Regulation to patent licensing agreements containing ancillary provisions concerning the assignment or the right of use of secret manufacturing processes or know-how relating to the use or application of industrial technology, as in practice patent licensing agreements with such ancillary provisions are very frequent. Similarly, it is desirable to include ancillary provisions on trade marks in the scope of the Regulation. It should in this case be ensured that trade mark licences cannot be used to extend the effects of the patent licence beyond the life of the patent.

The Regulation must also determine the restrictions or clauses which may not be included in patent licensing agreements to which it applies. The restrictions, clauses or measures listed in Article 3 of this Regulation, to the extent that they apply to, or have effects within, the common market, do not, as a rule, lead to the benefits required by Article 85 (3) of the Treaty. They cannot therefore be exempted from the prohibition in Article 85 (1) by means of a Regulation. These clauses include firstly obligations which allow the patent to be formally upheld even when there is uncertainty as to whether the invention is patentable (Article 3 (1) and (4) (b)). The same applies to agreements to extend the effects of the patent either beyond its expiry (Article 3 (2), (4) (c) and (5)), if necessary by using trade marks or similar rights (Article 3 (9)), or to cover matters beyond its scope in the product field (Article 3 (4) (a), (7), (8) and (14)) or geographically (Article 3 (13)). An obligation on the part of the licensee to assign to the licensor all rights to or arising from his own inventions (Article 3 (12)) is also an injustified extension of the patent to matters beyond its scope. These clauses must also include obligations on the part of the licensee designed to give the licensor the same protection for secret know-how as for a patent, even though it is the objective of patent law only to grant such protection if the relevant invention has been made public in the patent application and the state of the art has thus been advanced (Article 3 (10) and (11)). The same applies to an obligation on the part of the licensee to pay licence fees for secret know-how even after it has entered into the public domain (Article 3 (4) (d)), since the licensee is thereby placed at a disadvantage in relation to competitors. The list of unjustified restrictions must also include the ban on competition (Article 3 (3)), since this makes research by either or both parties, particularly in fields parallel to the licensed patent, unlawful or economically unattractive and thus frustrates possible contributions to technical progress.

Since the Commission considers that control over the marketing of a licensed product within the common market is not a matter that relates to the existence of the patent, and since such control can be exercised indirectly by setting a maximum to the quantity of products the licensee may manufacture or market or to the number of operations for which he may employ the patent, the benefit of this Regulation is for this reason alone not available for such an obligation (Article 3 (6)).

Obligations on the part of the licensor are not matters which relate to the existence of the patent. Apart from exclusivity clauses, export bans and most-favoured-licensee clauses, they satisfy the tests of Article 85 (3) in special cases only; they cannot therefore be exempted from the prohibition in Article 85 (1) by means of a Regulation (Article 3 (3), (7) and (13)).

The obligation in Article 4 to inform the Commission forthwith of arbitration awards is advisable because Articles 85 and 86 form part of the Community's public policy, and there is an inherent risk in the case of arbitration that patent licensing agreements may be given an interpretation which goes beyond the limits imposed by this Regulation.

This Regulation applies to licences issued in respect of national patents of the Member States, Community patents (Convention for the European Patent for the common market (Community Patent Convention)) and European patents (Convention on the Grant of European Patents of October 5, 1973). It also applies to assignments of such patents to the extent that the risk associated with commercial exploitation continues to be with the assignor and that such assignments have as their object or effect restrictions of competition which correspond to those in Articles 1 and 3 of this Regulation (Article 12).

Since individual decisions issued so far have not yet provided adequate experience, this Regulation does not apply to patent pools, licensing agreements entered into in connection with joint ventures, reciprocal licensing or sales agreements or licensing agreements relating to plant breeding (Article 5).

Under Article 4 (1) of Regulation 19/65, contracting parties can be given a limited time within which to bring their agreements and practices into line with the requirements of this Regulation; under Article 4 (3) of that Regulation, however, the benefit of this provision may not be claimed in actions pending at the date of entry into force of this Regulation, nor may it be relied on as grounds for claims for damages against third parties.

Agreements which satisfy the tests of Articles 1 and 2 of this Regulation and which have neither the object nor the effect of restricting competition in any other way need no longer be notified.

HAS ADOPTED THIS REGULATION:

ARTICLE 1

1. Pursuant to Article 85 (3) of the Treaty and subject to the conditions of this Regulation, it is hereby declared that until [December 31, 1989]

Article 85 (1) of the Treaty shall not apply to patent licensing agreements to which only two undertakings are party and which include one or more of the following obligations imposed upon a party to the agreement or upon an undertaking having economic connections with such a party:

1. the obligation on the part of the licensor not to manufacture or use the patented product or not to use the patented process within the common market or a defined area of the common market (licensed territory) or not to permit others to do so;

2. the obligation on the part of the licensee to refrain from manufacturing or using the patented product or from using the patented process outside the licensed territory;

3. the obligation on the part of the licensor to refrain from selling the patented product or product manufactured by a patented process within the licensed territory, or to impose a corresponding prohibition on other licensees;

4. the obligation on the part of the licensee to refrain from selling the patented product or product manufactured by a patented process within the defined territory of the common market reserved by the licensor for himself or in the licensed territories of other licensees;

5. the obligation on the part of the licensee to procure supplies of certain products or services from the licensor or from an undertaking designated by the licensor, so far and so long as this obligation is indispensable in the interests of a technically unobjectionable exploitation of the invention;

6. the obligation on the part of the licensee to pay a minimum royalty or to produce a minimum quantity of the patented products or products manufactued by a patented process or to carry out a minimum number of operations employing the patented invention.

2. Exclusivity of sales and analogous prohibitions on the sale of patented products outside the licensed territory shall be exempted pursuant to paragraph 1 (3) and (4) only:

(a) where the total annual turnover of the licensor or licensee whose market is to be protected by an export ban imposed on the other party or on another licensee does not exceed 100 million units of account; paragraph 1 (3) and (4) shall remain applicable notwithstanding that this turnover is exceeded by up to 10 per cent. in two consecutive financial years; in calculating total turnover, sales of all goods and services recorded in the last financial year by the undertaking concerned and all undertakings having economic connections with it shall be taken into account; and

(b) if the exclusivity of sales and export bans have been agreed at most for the duration of the most recent patent existing at the time when the agreement was entered into; this period may not be extended in respect of such obligations by licensing agreements in respect of patents for new applications or improvements; and

(c) if the patented product or product manufactured by the patented process may be sold throughout the Community by commercial undertakings which have no economic connections with the licensor or licensees; and (*d*) if the licensee either manufactures the licensed products himself, or has them manufactured by an undertaking that has economic connections with him.

ARTICLE 2

1. Article 1 shall apply notwithstanding that one or more of the following obligations is imposed upon the licensor or the licensee or an undertaking that has economic connections with either of them:

1. the obligation to restrict the manufacture of the patented product or the use of the patented process to one or more different technical fields of application of the invention within the patent claims. For the purposes of this sub-paragraph there are different technical fields of application where the relevant products in each of the fields from which the licensee is excluded differ in a material respect from the products for which the licence is granted;
2. the obligation not to exploit the patent after expiry of the agreement, where the patent is still in force;
3. the obligation to refrain from granting sub-licences or assigning the licence to a third party;
4. the obligation to mark the patented product or product manufactured using a patented process with an indication of the patentee's name, the patent or the licensing agreement;
5. the obligation not to divulge secret manufacturing processes or secret know-how relating to the use or application of industrial technology; the licensee may also be bound by this obligation after the agreement has expired;
6. the obligation:
   (*a*) to inform the licensor of infringements of the patent;
   (*b*) to take legal action against an infringer;
   (*c*) to assist the licensor in any action against an infringer, provided that this obligation is without prejudice to the licensee's right to challenge the validity of the licensed patent;
7. the obligation to respect the licensor's specifications concerning the minimum quality of the patented product or of the product manufactured using a patented process and to allow the licensor to carry out appropriate checks;
8. the obligation to pass on to the licensor any experience gained in working the invention and to grant back licences in respect of inventions relating to improvements and new applications of the original invention, provided that this obligation is non-exclusive and the licensor is bound by a like obligation;
9. the obligation on the part of the licensor to grant the licensee any more favourable terms that may be granted to another licensee during the life of the agreement.

2. The exemption granted in Article 1 (1) shall apply also to the obligations listed in paragraph (1) of this Article, so far as they fall within the scope of Article 85 (1) of the Treaty, even if they are undertaken otherwise

335

than in conjunction with one or more of the restrictions of competition exempted by Article 1.

ARTICLE 3

Article 1 shall not apply if the agreement contains one or more of the following provisions or if one or both of the parties thereto take one or more of the following measures:

1. the obligation on the part of the licensee to refrain from challenging the validity of the licensed patent or other exclusive rights of the licensor or of any undertaking that has economic connections with the licensor; impeding such a challenge shall be treated as equivalent to prohibiting it. This is without prejudice to any right of the licensor to terminate the licensing agreement in the event of such a challenge;

2. without prejudice to the second sentence of sub-paragraph 10 of this Article, an agreement that the duration of the licensing agreement should extend beyond the expiry of the most recent patent existing at the time when the agreement is entered into, unless each party has at least the yearly right after such expiry to terminate the agreement;

3. without prejudice to Article 1 (1) to (4), a restriction on the licensor or the licensee against competing with the other party, with undertakings that have economic connections with the other party or with other licensees in respect of research and development, manufacture, use or sales;

4. the obligation on the part of the licensee to pay royalties:

   (a) on products covered neither wholly nor partly by the patent, or manufactured neither wholly nor partly by the patented process or by means of manufacturing processes or other know-how communicated under the licence;

   (b) despite the fact that the licensed patent has ceased to be in force;

   (c) after expiry of the last licensed patent;

   (d) after manufacturing processes or other know-how communicated under the licence have entered into the public domain, unless entry into the public domain is attributable to some default on the part of the licensee, or of an undertaking that has economic connections with him,

   without prejudice to any right of the licensor to receive appropriately reduced royalties where the licensing agreement continues in respect of patents or parts of patents that remain in force or of manufacturing processes or other know-how that have not entered into the public domain;

5. the obligation on the part of the licensee to continue after the patent has expired or ceased to be in force to pay the full royalties stipulated by the licence for the use of a patent and a trade mark;

6. restrictions on the maximum quantity of products to be manufactured or marketed by the licensee or on the maximum number of operations employing the patent;

7. restrictions on one or both parties concerning prices, price components or rebates, or recommendations from one party to the other concerning any of such matters;

8. without prejudice to Article 1 (1) to (4), restrictions on one or both parties as to uses of the licensed products going beyond the patent claims, particularly as regards the way in which and the customers to whom the products are to be sold;

9. a clause prohibiting the licensee from using his own trade mark or business name or a specified get-up; this is without prejudice to Article 2 (1) (4) and to any obligation on the part of the licensee to make such use of the licensor's trade mark as is necessary to preserve its validity;

10. a clause prohibiting the licensee from using after the expiry of the agreement secret manufacturing processes or other secret know-how communicated by the licensor; this is without prejudice to any right of the licensor to require payments for the use of such processes or know-how for an appropriate period, even after the expiry of the agreement, but subject to paragraph (4) (d) of this Article;

11. a restriction on the licensee against using secret manufacturing processes or other secret know-how communicated by the licensor except for specified purposes; without prejudice to any right of the licensor to require payments at an appropriately higher rate for any use by the licensee not covered by the agreement and not protected by patents of the licensor;

12. the obligation on the part of the licensee to assign to the licensor rights in or rights to patents for improvements or new applications of the licensed patent;

13. any impediment in the way of manufacture, use or sale of the licensed products in areas of the common market where neither the licensor nor an undertaking having economic connections with him holds a corresponding patent;

14. the licensor makes the granting of a licence for one or more patents dependent on the licensee's acceptance of other licences unwanted by the latter.

ARTICLE 4

Where disputes as to the interpretation or operation of one of the provisions or measures listed in Articles 1 and 3 are settled by arbitration, the contracting parties are required to communicate the terms of the award forthwith to the Commission, together with the licensing agreement.

ARTICLE 5

This Regulation shall not apply to:

1. patent pools;

2. patent licensing agreements between competing firms that hold interests in a joint venture or between one of them and the joint

venture, if the licensing agreement relates to the activities of the joint venture;

3. without prejudice to Article 2 (1) (8), agreements under which the parties grant each other rights on a reciprocal basis in relation to patents, trade marks or the communication of secret manufacturing processes or other secret know-how, even where separate agreements are involved; this shall also apply where one party is granted distribution rights over unprotected products;

4. licensing agreements relating to plant breeding.

ARTICLE 6

1. As regards agreements existing on March 13, 1962 and notified before February 1, 1963, the declaration of inapplicability of Article 85 (1) of the Treaty contained in this Regulation shall apply retrospectively from the time at which the conditions for application of this Regulation were fulfilled.

2. As regards all other agreements notified before this Regulation entered into force, the declaration of inapplicability of Article 85 (1) of the Treaty contained in this Regulation shall apply retrospectively from the time at which the conditions for application of this Regulation were fulfilled, or from the date of notification, whichever is the later.

ARTICLE 7

As regards agreements which were in existence on March 13, 1962, notified before February 1, 1963 and amended before [April 1, 1980] so as to fulfil the conditions for application of this Regulation, the prohibition in Article 85 (1) of the Treaty shall not apply in respect of the period prior to the amendment where such amendment is communicated to the Commission before [May 1, 1980]. The communication shall take effect from the time of its receipt by the Commission. Where the communication is sent by registered post, it shall take effect from the date on the postmark of the place of dispatch.

ARTICLE 8

As regards agreements to which Article 85 of the Treaty applies as a result of the accession of the United Kingdom, Ireland and Denmark, Articles 6 and 7 shall apply subject to the proviso that the relevant dates shall be January 1, 1973 instead of March 13, 1962 and July 1, 1973 instead of February 1, 1963.

ARTICLE 9

The Commission shall examine whether Article 7 of Regulation 19/65 is applicable in any individual case, in particular where:

1. it appears likely that the patented products or products manufactured by the patented process have no competition within the licensed territory from products considered by consumers to be similar by reason of their characteristics, use and price;

2. the licensor does not have the right to terminate exclusivity of manufacture or use (Article 1 (1) (1)) within five years from the date when the agreement was entered into and at least yearly thereafter, should the licensee have failed to exploit a patent or have done so inadequately;

3. the licensee does not have the right to terminate his obligation to pay a minimum royalty, or to produce a minimum quantity of products or to carry out a minimum number of operations (Article 1 (1) (6)) within five years from the date when the agreement was entered into and at least yearly thereafter, subject to his giving up any exclusivity he may have;

4. without prejudice to Article 1 (1) (5)), either the licensor or the licensee is hindered from procuring supplies of certain products or services for the exploitation of the invention from anywhere in the common market;

5. Article 4 is infringed or an arbitration award communicated under that Article does not state the reasons on which it is based.

ARTICLE 10

1. This Regulation shall apply to:
(*a*) patent applications;
(*b*) utility models;
(*c*) applications for registration of utility models;
(*d*) "certificats d'utilité and certificats d'addition" under French law; and
(*e*) applications for "certificats d'utilité and certificats d'addition" under French law;
in the same way as it applies to patents.

2. This Regulation shall also apply to patent licensing agreements where the licensor is not the patentee but is authorised by the patentee to grant licences.

ARTICLE 11

For the purposes of this Regulation, two undertakings shall be deemed to have economic connections where one of them is in a position to exert a decisive influence on the other, directly or indirectly, with regard to the exploitation of a patent, or where a third undertaking is in a position to exercise such an influence on both of them.

ARTICLE 12

This regulation shall apply to assignments of a patent or of a right to a patent where the sum payable in consideration of the assignment is dependent upon the turnover attained by the assignee in respect of the patented products or on the quantity of such products manufactured or on the number of operations carried out employing the patented invention.

ARTICLE 13

This Regulation shall enter into force on [January 1, 1980].

This Regulation shall be binding in its entirety and directly applicable in all Member States.

APPENDIX 9

Announcement of December 24, 1962, on Patent Licence Agreements

(J.O. 1962, 2922)

I. On the basis of the facts known at present, the Commission considers that the following clauses in patent licence contracts are not covered by the prohibition laid down in Article 85, paragraph (1), of the Treaty:

    A. Obligations imposed on the licensee which have as their object:
        1. the limitation to certain of the forms of exploitation of the invention which are provided for by patent law (manufacture, use, sale);
        2. the limitation:
            (*a*) of the manufacture of the patented product,
            (*b*) of the use of the patented process,
        to certain technical applications;
        3. the limitation of the quantity of products to be manufactured or of the number of acts constituting exploitation;
        4. the limitation of exploitation:
            (*a*) in time (a licence of shorter duration than the patent),
            (*b*) in space (a regional licence for part of the territory for which the patent is granted, or a licence limited to one place of exploitation or to a specific factory),
            (*c*) with regard to the person (limitation of the licensee's power of disposal, *e.g.* prohibiting him from assigning the licence or from granting sub-licences);
    B. Obligations whereby the licensee has to mark the product with an indication of the patent;
    C. Quality standards or obligations to procure supplies of certain products imposed on the licensee—in so far as they are indispensable for the technically perfect exploitation of the patent;
    D. Undertakings concerning the disclosure of experience gained in exploiting the invention or the grant of licences for inventions in the field of perfection or application; this however applies to undertakings entered into by the licensee only if those undertakings are not exclusive and if the licensor has entered into similar undertakings;
    E. Undertakings on the part of the licensor:
        1. not to authorise anyone else to exploit the invention;
        2. not to exploit the invention himself.

II. This announcement is without prejudice to the appraisal from a legal point of view of clauses other than those referred to at I (A) to (E).

Moreover a general appraisal does not appear possible for agreements relating to:

    1. joint ownership of patents,
    2. reciprocal licences,
    3. parallel multiple licences.

The appraisal of the clauses referred to at I (A) to (E) is confined to clauses of a duration not exceeding the period of validity of the patent.

III. The object of this announcement is to give enterprises some indication of the considerations by which the Commission will be guided in interpreting Article 85, paragraph (1), of the Treaty and in applying it to a number of clauses often found in certain patent licence contracts. So long as and in so far as such contracts do not contain restrictions other than those resulting from one or more of the clauses mentioned above, the Commission considers that they are not affected by the prohibition laid down in Article 85, paragraph (1). Generally speaking this specific information will remove the incentive for firms to obtain a negative clearance for the agreements in question, and will make it unnecessary to have the legal position established by an individual decision by the Commission; moreover there is no longer any need to notify agreements of this nature.

This announcement is without prejudice to any interpretation that may be made by other competent authorities and in particular by the courts.

A decision is to be made later on the question of the application of Article 85, paragraph (1), of the Treaty to clauses of the types mentioned above which are contained in contracts relating to joint ownership of patents, to the grant of reciprocal licences or parallel multiple licences, to agreements relating to the exploitation of other industrial property rights or of creative activities not protected by law and constituting technical improvements, and to any clauses other than those mentioned above.

This announcement is without prejudice to the interpretation of Article 4, paragraph (2), sub-paragraph (ii) (b) of Regulation 17.

IV. The undertakings listed at I (A) do not fall within the scope of the prohibition laid down in Article 85, paragraph (1), because they are covered by the patent. They only entail the partial maintenance of the right of prohibition contained in the patentee's exclusive right in relation to the licensee, who in other respects is authorised to exploit the invention. The list at I (A) is not an exhaustive definition of the rights conferred by the patent.

The obligation imposed on the licensee to mark the product with an indication of the patent (point I(B)) is in accordance with the patentee's legitimate interest in ensuring that the protected articles are clearly shown to owe their origin to the patented invention. Since the licensee may also make distinguishing marks of his own choice on the protected article, this provision has neither the object nor the effect of restricting competition.

The licensee's undertakings, mentioned at I (C), concerning the observance of certain quality standards for the protected products or for semi manufactures, raw materials or auxiliary materials, could not restrict competition which has to be protected (la concurrence à protéger) to the extent that they are intended to prevent the technically incorrect working of the invention. The undertaking to procure supplies of certain products can be left out of account, except when quality cannot be established by objective standards. In that case, such an undertaking has the same scope as quality standards.

The undertakings given by the licensee and mentioned at I (D) do not in any case have any restrictive effect on competition when the licensee retains the possibility of disclosing experience gained or of granting licences to third parties and is entitled to participate in the licensor's future acquisitions in the field of experience and inventions. With regard to undertakings given by the licensor concerning the disclosure of experience or the grant of a licence, as mentioned at I (D), these seem to be unexceptionable from the point of view of the law relating to competition, even without that limitation. Thus point I (D) only covers the obligation to disclose experience or to grant licences; this is without prejudice to the appraisal from a legal point of view of any restrictions imposed on the interested parties concerning the utilisation of such experience or inventions.

By the undertaking mentioned at I (E)—not to authorise the use of the invention by any other person—the licensor forfeits the right to make agreements with other applicants for a licence. Leaving out of account the controversial question whether such exclusive undertakings have the object or effect of restricting competition, they are not likely to affect trade between member states as things stand in the Community at present. The undertaking not to exploit the patented invention oneself is closely akin to an assignment of the right and accordingly does not seem to be open to objection.

Notice of July 29, 1968, on Co-operation Agreements

(J.O. 1968, C75/1)

Questions are frequently put to the Commission of the European Communities on the attitude it intends to take up, within the framework of the implementation of the competition rules contained in the Treaties of Rome and Paris, with regard to co-operation between enterprises. In this Notice, it endeavours to provide guidance which, though not exhaustive, could prove useful to enterprises in the correct interpretation of Article 85 (1) of the EEC Treaty and Article 65 (1) of the ECSC Treaty.

I. The Commission welcomes co-operation among small- and medium-sized enterprises where such co-operation enables them to work more rationally and increase their productivity and competitiveness on a larger market. The Commission considers that it is its task to facilitate co-operation among small- and medium-sized enterprises in particular. However, co-operation among large enterprises, too, can be economically justifiable without presenting difficulties from the angle of competition.

Article 85 (1) of the Treaty establishing the European Economic Community (EEC Treaty) and Article 65 (1) of the Treaty establishing the European Coal and Steel Community (ECSC Treaty) provide that all agreements, decisions and concerted practices (hereafter referred to as "agreements") which have as their object or result the prevention, restriction or distortion of competition (hereafter referred to as "restraints of competition") in the common market are incompatible with the common market and are forbidden; under Article 85 (1) of the EEC Treaty this applies, however, only if these agreements are liable to impair trade between the Member States.

The Commission feels that in the interests of the small- and medium-sized enterprises in particular it should make known the considerations by which it will be guided when interpreting Article 85 (1) of the EEC Treaty and Article 65 (1) of the ECSC Treaty and applying them to certain co-operation arrangements between enterprises, and indicate which of these arrangements in its opinion do not come under these provisions. This notice applies to all enterprises, irrespective of their size.

There may also be forms of co-operation between enterprises other than the forms of co-operation listed below which are not prohibited by Article 85 (1) of the EEC Treaty or Article 65 (1) of the ECSC Treaty. This applies in particular if the market position of the enterprises co-operating with each other is in the aggregate too weak as to lead, through the agreement between them, to an appreciable restraint of competition in the common market and—for Article 85 of the EEC Treaty—impair trade between the Member States.

It is also pointed out, in respect of other forms of co-operation between enterprises or agreements containing additional clauses, that where the rules of competition of the Treaties apply, such forms of co-operation or agreements can be exempted by virtue of Article 85 (3) of the EEC Treaty or be authorised by virtue of Article 65 (2) of the ECSC Treaty.

The Commission intends to establish rapidly, by means of suitable decisions in individual cases or by general notices, the status of the various forms of co-operation in relation with the provisions of the Treaty.

No general statement can be made at this stage on the application of Article 86 of the EEC Treaty on the abuse of dominant positions within the common market or within a part of it. The same applies to Article 66 (7) of the ECSC Treaty.

As a result of this notice, as a general rule, it will no longer be useful for enterprise to obtain negative clearance, as defined by Article 2 of Regulation 17, for the agreements listed, nor should it be necessary for the legal situation to be clarified through a Commission decision on an individual case; this also means that notification will no longer be necessary for agreements of this type. However, if it is doubtful whether in an individual case an agreement between enterprises restricts competition or if other forms of co-operation between enterprises which in the view of the enterprises do not restrict competition are not listed here, the enterprises are free to apply, where the matter comes under Article 85 (1) of the EEC Treaty, for negative clearance, or to file as a precautionary measure, where Article 65 (1) of the ECSC Treaty is the relevant clause, an application on the basis of Article 65 (2) of the ECSC Treaty.

This Notice does not prejudice interpretation by the Court of Justice of the European Communities.

II. The Commission takes the view that the following agreements do not restrict competition.

1. Agreements having as their sole object:
    (a) An exchange of opinion or experience,
    (b) Joint market research,
    (c) The joint carrying out of comparative studies of enterprises or industries,
    (d) The joint preparation of statistics and calculation models.

Agreements whose sole purpose is the joint procurement of information which the various enterprises need to determine their future market behaviour freely and independently, or the use by each of the enterprises of a joint advisory body, do not have as their object or result the restriction of competition. But if the scope of action of the enterprises is limited or if the market behaviour is co-ordinated either expressly or through concerted practices, there may be restraint of competition. This is in particular the case where concrete recommendations are made or where conclusions are given such a form that they induce at least some of the participating enterprises to behave in an identical manner on the market.

The exchange of information can take place between the enterprises themselves or through a body acting as an intermediary. It is, however, particularly difficult to distinguish between information which has no bearing on competition on the one hand and behaviour in restraint of competition on the other, if there are special bodies which have to register orders, turnover figures, investment figures, and prices, so that it can as a rule not be automatically assumed that Article 85 (1) of the EEC Treaty or Article 65 (1) of the ECSC Treaty do not apply to them. A restraint of competition may occur in particular on an oligopolist market for homogenous products.

In the absence of more far-reaching co-operation between the participating enterprises, joint market research and comparative studies of different enterprises and industries to collect information and ascertain facts and market conditions do not in themselves impair competition.

Other arrangements of this type, as for instance the joint establishment of economic and structural analyses, are so obviously not impairing competition that there is no need to mention them specifically.

Calculation models containing specified rates of calculations are to be regarded as recommendations that may lead to restraints of competition.

2. Agreements having as their sole object:
   (a) Co-operation in accounting matters,
   (b) Joint provision of credit guarantees,
   (c) Joint debt-collecting associations,
   (d) Joint business or tax consultant agencies.

These are cases of co-operation relating to fields that do not concern the supply of goods and services and the economic decisions of the enterprises involved, so that they cannot lead to restraints of competition.

Co-operating in accounting matters is neutral from the point of view of competition as it only serves for the technical handling of the accounting work. Nor is the creation of credit guarantee associations affected by the competition rules, since it does not modify the relationship between supply and demand.

Debt-collecting associations whose work is not confined to the collection of outstanding payments in line with the intentions and conditions of the participating enterprises, or which fix prices or exert in any other way an influence on price formation, may restrict competition. Application of uniform conditions by all participating firms may constitute a case of concerted practices, as may joint comparison of prices. In this connection, no objection can be raised against the use of standardised printed forms; their use must, however, not be combined with an understanding or tacit agreement on uniform prices, rebates or conditions of sale.

3. Agreements having as their sole object:
   (a) The joint implementation of research and development projects,
   (b) The joint placing of research and development contracts,
   (c) The sharing out of research and development projects among participating enterprises.

In the field of research, too, the mere exchange of experience and results serves for information only and does not restrict competition. It therefore need not be mentioned expressly.

Agreements on the joint execution of research work or the joint development of the results of research up to the stage of industrial application do not affect the competitive position of the parties. This also applies to the sharing of research fields and development work if the results are available to all participating enterprises. However, if the enterprises enter

346

into commitments which restrict their own research and development activity or the utilisation of the results of joint work so that they do not have a free hand with regard to their own research and development outside the joint projects, this can constitute an infringement of the rules of competition of the Treaties. Where firms do not carry out joint research work, contractual obligations or concerted practices binding them to refrain from research work of their own either completely or in certain sectors may result in a restraint of competition. The sharing out of sectors of research without an understanding providing for mutual access to the results is to be regarded as a case of specialisation that may restrict competition.

There may also be a restraint of competition if agreements are concluded or corresponding concerted practices applied with regard to the practical exploitation of the results of research and development work carried out jointly, particularly if the participating enterprises undertake or agree to manufacture only products or the types of products developed jointly or to share out future production among themselves.

It is of the essence of joint research that the results should be exploited by the participating enterprises in proportion to their participation. If the participation of certain enterprises is confined to a specific sector of the common research project or to the provision of only limited financial assistance, there is no restraint of competition so far as there has been any joint research at all—if the results of research are made available to these enterprises only in relation with the degree of their participation. There may, however, be a restraint of competition if certain participating enterprises are excluded from the exploitation of the results, either entirely or to an extent not commensurate with their participation.

If the granting of licences to third parties is expressly or tacitly excluded, there may be a restraint of competition; the fact that research is carried out jointly warrants, however, arrangements binding the enterprises to grant licences to third parties only by common agreement or by majority decision.

For the assessment of the compatibility of the agreement with the rules of competition, it does not matter what legal form the common research and development work takes.

4. Agreements which have as their only object the joint use of production facilities and storing and transport equipment.

These forms of co-operation do not restrict competition because they are confined to organisational and technical arrangements for the use of the facilities. There may be a restraint of competition if the enterprises involved do not bear the cost of utilisation of the installation or equipment themselves or if agreements are concluded or concerted practices applied regarding joint production or the sharing out of production or the establishment or running of a joint enterprise.

5. Agreements having as their sole object the setting up of working partnerships for the common execution of orders, where the participating enterprises do not compete with each other as regards the work to be done or where each of them by itself is unable to execute the orders.

Where enterprises do not compete with each other they cannot restrict

347

competition by setting up associations. This applies in particular to enterprises belonging to different industries but also to firms of the same industry to the extent that their contribution under the working partnership consist only of goods or services which cannot be supplied by the other participating enterprises. It is not a question of whether the enterprises compete with each other in other industries so much as whether in the light of the concrete circumstances of a particular case there is a possibility that in the foreseeable future they may compete with each other with regard to the products or services involved. If the absence of competition between the enterprises and the maintenance of this situation are based on agreements or concerted practices, there may be a restraint of competition.

But even in the case of [working partnerships] formed by enterprises which compete with each other there is no restraint of competition if the participating enterprises cannot execute the specific order by themselves. This applies in particular if, for lack of experience, specialised knowledge, capacity of financial resources these enterprises, when working alone, have no chance of success or cannot finish the work within the required time-limit or cannot bear the financial risk. Nor is there a restraint of competition if it is only by the setting up of an association that the enterprises are put in a position to make a promising offer. There may, however, be a restraint of competition if the enterprises undertake to work solely in the framework of an association.

AMENDMENTS
The words in square brackets were amended by the Commission corrigendum of August 28, 1968 (J.O. 1968, C84/14).

6. Agreements having as their sole object:
   (a) Joint selling arrangements,
   (b) Joint after-sales and repair service, provided the participating enterprises are not competitors with regard to the products or services covered by the agreement.

As already explained in detail under Section 5, co-operation between enterprises cannot restrict competition if the firms do not compete with each other.

Very often joint selling by small- or medium-sized enterprises—even if they are competing with each other—does not entail an appreciable restraint of competition; it is, however, impossible to establish in this Notice any general criteria or to specify what enterprises may be deemed "small- or medium-sized."

There is no joint after-sales and repair service if several manufacturers, without acting in concert with each other, arrange for an after-sales and repair service for their product to be provided by an enterprise which is independent. In such a case there is no restraint of competition, even if the manufacturers are competitors.

7. Agreements having as their sole object joint advertising.

Joint advertising is designed to draw the buyers' attention to the products of an industry or to a common brand; as such it does not restrict competition between the participating enterprises. However, if the participating enterprises are partly or wholly prevented, by agreements or concerted practices, from themselves advertising or if they are subjected to other restrictions, there may be a restraint of competition.

8. Agreements having as their sole object the use of a common label to designate a certain quality, where the label is available to all competitors on the same conditions.

Such associations for the joint use of a quality label do not restrict competition if other competitors, whose products objectively meet the stipulated quality requirements, can use the lable on the same conditions as the members. Nor do the obligations to accept quality control of the products provided with the label, to issue uniform instructions for use, or to use the label for the products meeting the quality standards constitute restraints of competition. But there may be restraint of competition if the right to use the lable is linked to obligations regarding production, marketing, price formations or obligations of any other type, as is for instance the case when the participating enterprises are obliged to manufacture or sell only products of guaranteed quality.

Notice of December 19, 1977, Concerning Agreements of Minor Importance which do not Fall under Article 85 (1) of the Treaty Establishing the European Economic Community

(O.J. 1977, C313/3)

I. On several occasions the Commission has made clear that it considers it important to promote co-operation between undertakings where such co-operation is economically desirable without presenting difficulties from the point of view of competition policy; in particular, it wishes to facilitate co-operation between small- and medium-sized undertakings. To this end it published the "Notice concerning agreements, decisions and concerted practices in the field of co-operation between undertakings" (J.O. 1968, C75/3) (hereinafter referred to as "agreements") listing a number of agreements that by their nature cannot be regarded as being restraints of competition. By issuing the present notice, the Commission is taking a further step towards defining the field of application of Article 85 (1) of the Treaty establishing the European Economic Community, in order to promote co-operation between small- and medium-sized undertakings.

In the Commission's opinion, agreements, whose effects on trade between Member States and on competition are negligible, do not fall within the prohibition on restrictive agreements in Article 85 (1) of the EEC Treaty. Only those agreements are prohibited which have an appreciable impact on market conditions, in that they appreciably alter the market position, *i.e.* the sales outlets and supply possibilities, of non-participating undertakings and of consumers.

In the present Notice the Commission has given a sufficiently concrete meaning to the term "appreciable" for undertakings to be able to judge for themselves whether the agreements they have concluded with other undertakings, being of minor importance, do not fall under Article 85 (1). The quantitative definition of "appreciable" given by the Commission is, however, no absolute yardstick; in fact, it is quite possible that, in individual cases, even agreements between undertakings which exceed the limits mentioned below may well have only a negligible effect on trade between Member States and on competition and are therefore not caught by Article 85 (1).

As a result of this notice, there should no longer be any point in undertakings obtaining negative clearance, as defined by Article 2 of Regulation 17 (J.O. 1962, 204), for the agreements covered, nor should it be necessary to have the legal position established through Commission decisions on individual cases; notification for this purpose will therefore no longer be necessary for agreements of this type. However, where it is doubtful whether in an individual case an agreement appreciably restricts trade between Member States or competition, the undertakings are free to apply for negative clearance or to notify the agreement.

This notice is without prejudice to any interpretation which may be given by the Court of Justice of the European Communities.

II. The Commission holds the view that agreements between undertakings engaged in the production or distribution of goods do not fall under the prohibition of Article 85 (1) of the EEC Treaty if:

—the products which are the subject of the agreement and other products of the participating undertakings considered by consumers to be similar by reason of their characteristics, price or use do not represent in a substantial part of the common market more than 5 per cent. of the total market for such products, and

—the aggregate annual turnover of the participating undertakings does not exceed 50 million units of account.

The Commission also holds the view that the said agreements do not fall within the prohibition of Article 85 (1) even if the above mentioned market share and turnover are exceeded by up to 10 per cent. within two successive financial years.

For the purposes of this notice the participating undertakings are:

1. The undertakings which are parties to the agreement.

2. Undertakings in which the undertakings which are parties to the agreement hold:

—at least 25 per cent. of the capital or of the working capital whether directly or indirectly, or

—at least half the voting rights, or

—the power to appoint at least half of the members of the supervisory board, the board of management or the bodies legally representing the undertaking, or

—the right to manage the affairs of the undertaking.

3. Undertakings which hold in an undertaking which is a party to the agreement:

—at least 25 per cent. of the capital or working capital whether directly or indirectly, or

—at least half of the voting rights, or

—the power to appoint at least half of the members of the supervisory board, the board of management or the bodies legally representing the undertaking party to the agreement, or

—the right to manage the affairs of the undertaking.

The aggregate turnover shall include the turnover in all goods and services achieved during the last financial year by the participating undertakings. The aggregate turnover shall not include dealings between undertakings which are parties to the agreement.

Notice of December 18, 1978, Concerning its Assessment of Certain Sub-contracting Agreements in Relation to Article 85 (1) of the EEC Treaty

(O.J. 1979, C1/2)

1. In this notice the Commission of the European Communities gives its view as to sub-contracting agreements in relation to Article 85 (1) of the Treaty establishing the European Economic Community. This class of agreement is at the present time a form of work distribution which concerns firms of all sizes, but which offers opportunities for development in particular to small- and medium-sized firms.

The Commission considers that agreements under which one firm, called "the contractor," whether or not in consequence of a prior order from a third party, entrusts to another, called "the sub-contractor," the manufacture of goods, the supply of services or the performance of work under the contractor's instructions, to be provided to the contractor or performed on his behalf, are not of themselves caught by the prohibition in Article 85 (1).

To carry out certain sub-contracting agreements in accordance with the contractor's instructions, the sub-contractor may have to make use of particular technology or equipment which the contractor will have to provide. In order to protect the economic value of such technology or equipment, the contractor may wish to restrict their use by the sub-contractor to whatever is necessary for the purpose of the agreement. The question arises whether such restrictions are caught by Article 85 (1). They are assessed in this notice with due regard to the purpose of such agreements, which distinguishes them from ordinary patent and know-how licensing agreements.

2. In the Commission's view, Article 85 (1) does not apply to clauses whereby:
— technology or equipment provided by the contractor may not be used except for the purposes of the sub-contracting agreement,
— technology or equipment provided by the contractor may not be made available to third parties,
— the goods, services or work resulting from the use of such technology or equipment may be supplied only to the contractor or performed on his behalf,

provided that and in so far as this technology or equipment is necessary to enable the sub-contractor under reasonable conditions to manufacture the goods, to supply the services or to carry out the work in accordance with the contractor's instructions. To that extent the sub-contractor is providing goods, services or work in respect of which he is not an independent supplier in the market.

The above proviso is satisfied where performance of the sub-contracting agreement makes necessary the use by the sub-contractor of:
—industrial property rights of the contractor or at his disposal, in the form of patents, utility models, designs protected by copyright, registered designs or other rights, or
—secret knowledge or manufacturing processes (know-how) of the contractor or at his disposal, or of
—studies, plans or documents accompanying the information given which have been prepared by or for the contractor, or
—dies, patterns or tools, and accessory equipment that are distinctively the contractor's,
which, even though not covered by industrial property rights nor containing any element of secrecy, permit the manufacture of goods which differ in form, function or composition from other goods manufactured or supplied on the market.

However, the restrictions mentioned above are not justifiable where the sub-contractor has at his disposal or could under reasonable conditions obtain access to the technology and equipment needed to produce the goods, provide the services or carry out the work. Generally, this is the case when the contractor provides no more than general information which merely describes the work to be done. In such circumstances the restrictions could deprive the sub-contractor of the possibility of developing his own business in the fields covered by the agreement.

3. The following restrictions in connection with the provision of technology by the contractor may in the Commission's view also be imposed by sub-contracting agreements without giving grounds for objection under Article 85 (1):
—an undertaking by either of the parties not to reveal manufacturing processes or other know-how of a secret character, or confidential information given by the other party during the negotiation and performance of the agreement, as long as the know-how or information in question has not become public knowledge,
—an undertaking by the sub-contractor not to make use, even after expiry of the agreement, of manufacturing processes or other know-how of a secret character received by him during the currency of the agreement, as long as they have not become public knowledge,
—an undertaking by the sub-contractor to pass on to the contractor on a non-exclusive basis any technical improvements which he has made during the currency of the agreement, or, where a patentable invention has been discovered by the sub-contractor, to grant non-exclusive licences in respect of inventions relating to improvements and new applications of the original invention to the contractor for the term of the patent held by the latter.
This undertaking by the sub-contractor may be exclusive in favour of the contractor in so far as improvements and inventions made by the sub-contractor during the currency of the agreement are incapable of being used independently of the contractor's secret know-how or patent, since this does not constitute an appreciable restriction of competition.

However, any undertaking by the sub-contractor regarding the right to dispose of the results of his own research and development work may restrain competition, where such results are capable of being used independently. In such circumstances, the sub-contracting relationship is not sufficient to displace the ordinary competition rules on the disposal of industrial property rights or secret know-how.

4. Where the sub-contractor is authorised by a sub-contracting agreement to use a specified trade mark, trade name or get up, the contractor may at the same time forbid such use by the sub-contractor in the case of goods, services or work which are not to be supplied to the contractor.

5. Although this notice should in general obviate the need for firms to obtain a ruling on the legal position by an individual Commission Decision, it does not affect the right of the firms concerned to apply for negative clearance as defined by Article 2 of Regulation 17 (J.O. 1962, 204) or to notify the agreement to the Commission under Article 4 (1) of that Regulation.

The 1968 notice on co-operation between enterprises (J.O. 1968, C75/3), which lists a number of agreements that by their nature are not to be regarded as anti-competitive, is thus supplemented in the sub-contracting field. The Commission also reminds firms that, in order to promote co-operation between small- and medium-sized businesses, it has published a notice concerning agreements of minor importance which do not fall under Article 85 (1) of the Treaty establishing the European Economic Community (O.J. 1977, C313/3).

This notice is without prejudice to the view that may be taken of sub-contracting agreements by the Court of Justice of the European Communities.

European Patent Convention

GENERAL PROVISIONS

ARTICLE 1

European Law for the Grant of Patents

A system of law, common to the Contracting States, for the grant of patents for invention is hereby established.

ARTICLE 2

European Patent

(1) Patents granted by virtue of this Convention shall be called European patents.

(2) The European patent shall, in each of the Contracting States for which it is granted, have the effect of and be subject to the same conditions as a national patent granted by that State, unless otherwise provided in this Convention.

ARTICLE 3

Territorial Effect

The grant of a European patent may be requested for one or more of the Contracting States.

EFFECTS OF THE EUROPEAN PATENT AND THE EUROPEAN PATENT APPLICATION

ARTICLE 64

Rights Conferred by a European Patent

(1) A European patent shall, subject to the provisions of paragraph 2, confer on its proprietor from the date of publication of the mention of its grant, in each Contracting State in respect of which it is granted, the same rights as would be conferred by a national patent granted in that State.

(2) If the subject-matter of the European patent is a process, the protection conferred by the patent shall extend to the products directly obtained by such process.

(3) Any infringement of a European patent shall be dealt with by national law.

FILING AND REQUIREMENTS OF THE EUROPEAN PATENT APPLICATION

ARTICLE 79

Designation of Contracting States

(1) The request for the grant of a European patent shall contain the designation of the Contracting State or States in which protection for the invention is desired.

(2) The designation of a Contracting State shall be subject to the payment of the designation fee. The designation fees shall be paid within twelve months after filing the European patent application or, if priority has been claimed, after the date of priority; in the latter case, payment may still be made up to the expiry of the period specified in Article 78, paragraph 2, if that period expires later.

(3) The designation of a Contracting State may be withdrawn at any time up to the grant of the European patent. Withdrawal of the designation of all the Contracting States shall be deemed to be a withdrawal of the European patent application. Designation fees shall not be refunded.

SPECIAL AGREEMENTS

ARTICLE 142

Unitary Patents

(1) Any group of Contracting States, which has provided by a special agreement that a European patent granted for those States has a unitary character throughout their territories, may provide that a European patent may only be granted jointly in respect of all those States.

(2) Where any group of Contracting States has availed itself of the authorisation given in paragraph 1, the provisions of this Part shall apply.

Community Patent Convention

GENERAL PROVISIONS

Article 1

Common System of Law for Patents

1. A system of law, common to the Contracting States, concerning patents for invention is hereby established.

2. The common system of law shall govern the European patents granted for the Contracting States in accordance with the Convention on the Grant of European Patents, hereinafter referred to as "the European Patent Convention", and the European patent applications in which such States are designated.

Article 2

Community Patent

1. European patents granted for the Contracting States shall be called Community patents.

2. Community patents shall have a unitary character. They shall have equal effect throughout the territories to which this Convention applies and may only be granted, transferred, revoked or allowed to lapse in respect of the whole of such territories. The same shall apply *mutatis mutandis* to applications for European patents in which the Contracting States are designated.

3. Community patents shall have an autonomous character. They shall be subject only to the provisions of this Convention and those provisions of the European Patent Convention which are binding upon every European patent and which shall consequently be deemed to be provisions of this Convention.

EFFECTS OF THE COMMUNITY PATENT AND THE EUROPEAN PATENT APPLICATION

Article 32

Exhaustion of the Rights Conferred by the Community Patent

The rights conferred by a Community patent shall not extend to acts concerning a product covered by that patent which are done within the

357

territories of the Contracting States after that product has been put on the market in one of these States by the proprietor of the patent or with his express consent, unless there are grounds which, under Community law, would justify the extension to such acts of the rights conferred by the patent.

THE COMMUNITY PATENT AS AN OBJECT OF PROPERTY

ARTICLE 43

Contractual Licensing

1. A Community patent may be licensed in whole or in part for the whole or part of the territories in which it is effective. A licence may be exclusive or non-exclusive.
2. The rights conferred by the Community patent may be invoked against a licensee who contravenes any restriction in his licence which is covered by paragraph 1.
3. Article 40 paragraphs 2 and 3 shall apply *mutatis mutandis* to the grant or transfer of a licence in respect of a Community patent.

IMPACT ON NATIONAL LAW

ARTICLE 81

Exhaustion of the Rights Conferred by a National Patent

1. The rights conferred by a national patent in a Contracting State shall not extend to acts concerning a product covered by that patent which are done within the territory of that Contracting State after that product has been put on the market in any Contracting State by the proprietor of the patent or with his express consent, unless there are grounds which, under Community law, would justify the extension to such acts of the rights conferred by the patent.
2. Paragraph 1 shall also apply with regard to a product put on the market by the proprietor of a national patent, granted for the same invention in another Contracting State, who has economic connections with the proprietor of the patent referred to in paragraph 1. For the purpose of this paragraph, two persons shall be deemed to have economic connections where one of them is in a position to exert a decisive influence on the other, directly or indirectly, with regard to the exploitation of a patent, or where a third party is in a position to exercise such an influence on both persons.
3. The preceding paragraphs shall not apply in the case of a product put on the market under a compulsory licence.

TRANSITIONAL PROVISIONS

ARTICLE 86

Option between a Community Patent and a European Patent

1. This Convention shall, subject to paragraph 3, not apply to a European patent application filed during a transitional period nor to any resulting European patent, provided that the request for grant contains a statement that the applicant does not wish to obtain a Community patent. This statement may not be withdrawn.

3. Articles 80 to 82 and 84 shall apply to a European patent as referred to in paragraph 1, the references in Articles 80 and 84 to a Community patent and the references in Articles 81 and 82 to a national patent being understood as references to such a European patent.

4. The transitional period referred to in paragraph 1 may be terminated by decision of the Council of the European Communities, acting on a proposal from the Commission of the European Communities or from a Contracting State.

FINAL PROVISIONS

ARTICLE 93

Precedence of the Provisions of the Treaty Establishing the European Economic Community

No provision of this Convention may be invoked against the application of any provision of the Treaty establishing the European Economic Community.

ARTICLE 95

Accession

1. This Convention shall be open to accession by States becoming Member States of the European Economic Community.

2. Instruments of accession to this Convention shall be deposited with the Secretary-General of the Council of the European Communities. Accession shall take effect on the first day of the third month following the deposit of the instrument of accession, provided that the ratification by the State concerned of the European Patent Convention or its accession thereto has become effective.

3. The Contracting States hereby recognize that any State which becomes a member of the European Economic Community must accede to this Convention.

4. A special agreement may be concluded between the Contracting States and the acceding State, to determine the details of application of this Convention necessitated by the accession of that State.

ARTICLE 98

Entry into Force

This Convention shall enter into force three months after the deposit of the instrument of ratification by the last signatory State to take this step; however, if the European Patent Convention enters into force with respect to the States signatories to this Convention at a later date, this Convention shall enter into force on the latter date.

APPENDIX 15

Draft Council Regulation on the Community Trade Mark

(COM(80) 635 final/2)

GENERAL PROVISIONS

ARTICLE 1

Community Trade Marks

(1) A trade mark for goods or services which conforms with the conditions contained in this regulation and is registered in manner herein provided is hereinafter referred to as a "Community trade mark."

(2) A Community trade mark shall have identical effect throughout the Community. No trade mark shall be registered as a Community trade mark otherwise than for the entire area of the Community; a Community trade mark shall not be transferred or surrendered or be the subject of a decision revoking the rights of the proprietor or declaring it invalid, nor shall its use be prohibited, save in respect of the entire area of the Community.

ARTICLE 2

Community Trade Marks Office

For the purposes of the application of this regulation a Community Trade Mark Office, hereinafter referred to as "the Office," is hereby established.

ARTICLE 5

Means Whereby the Rights in a Community Trade Mark are Obtained

The rights in a Community trade mark are obtained by registration.

ARTICLE 8

Rights Conferred by a Community Trade Mark

(1) A Community trade mark confers on the proprietor exclusive rights therein. The proprietor shall be entitled to prohibit any third party from using in the course of trade, save with his consent:

(a) any sign which is identical with or similar to the Community trade mark in relation to goods or services which are identical with or similar to those for which the Community trade mark is registered,

361

where such use involves a serious likelihood of confusion on the part of the public;

(*b*) any sign which is identical with or similar to the Community trade mark in relation to goods or services which are not similar to those for which the Community trade mark is registered, where the Community trade mark is of wide repute and use of that sign is detrimental to that repute.

(2) Use of the following kinds, *inter alia*, may be prohibited under paragraph (1):

(*a*) affixing the sign to the goods or to the packaging thereof;

(*b*) putting the goods on the market under that sign, or supplying services thereunder;

(*c*) using the sign on business correspondence or invoices.

(3) The rights conferred by a Community trade mark shall prevail against third parties from the date of publication of registration of the trade mark. Reasonable compensation may however be claimed in respect of matters arising after the date of publication of a Community trade mark application, which matters would, after publication of registration of the trade mark, be prohibited by virtue of that publication. The court seised of the case shall stay the proceedings until the registration has been published.

ARTICLE 11

Limits of the Rights Conferred by a Community Trade Mark

(1) A Community trade mark does not entitle the proprietor to prohibit its use in relation to goods which have been put on the market under that trade mark by the proprietor or with his consent.

(2) Paragraph (1) shall not apply:

(*a*) Where, the goods having been put on the market outside the Community, the proprietor is legally entitled to oppose their importation into the Community;

(*b*) Where the condition of the goods is changed or impaired after they have been put on the market;

(*c*) Where the goods are re-packaged by a third party; but this provision shall not apply where the third party proves that the use made of the trade mark by the proprietor, taking into consideration his system of marketing, tends to fragment the markets artificially and that the re-packaging could not affect the original condition of the goods, if the third party informs the proprietor beforehand that the re-packaged goods are to be put on the market and the new packaging indicates that the goods have been re-packaged by the third party.

Use of Community Trade Marks

ARTICLE 13

(1) A Community trade mark shall be put to serious use in the common market, consistently with the terms of this Regulation, in connection with

the goods or services in respect of which it is registered, unless there exist legitimate reasons for not doing so.

(2) Circumstances arising independently of the will of the proprietor of a Community trade mark are alone sufficient to constitute legitimate reasons for not using it.

(3) Use of a Community trade mark by a licensee or by a person who is associated economically with the proprietor shall be deemed to constitute use by the proprietor.

ARTICLE 16

Dealing with Community Trade Marks as National Trade Marks

(1) Unless Articles 17 to 22 otherwise provide, a Community trade mark as an object of property shall be regarded in all respects, including its geographical coverage of the entire area of the Community, as a trade mark registered in the Member State in which, according to the Register of Community trade marks, the applicant had his habitual residence or principal place of business or, failing either of these, a place of business, on the date of filing of the Community trade mark application.

(2) In cases which are not provided for by paragraph (1) the Member State referred to in that paragraph shall be the Member State in which the headquarters of the office is situated.

ARTICLE 17

Transfer

(1) A Community trade mark may be transferred, separately from any transfer of the undertaking, in respect of some or all of the goods or services for which it is registered.

(2) A transfer of the whole of the undertaking shall, unless some other intention appears, have effect to transfer any Community trade mark of the undertaking.

(3) Without prejudice to paragraph (2), an assignment of a Community trade mark shall be made in writing; otherwise it shall be void.

(4) Where it is clear from the transfer documents that because of the transfer the Community trade mark will mislead the public concerning the nature, quality or geographical origin of the goods or services in respect of which it is registered, the office shall not register the transfer.

(5) A transfer shall not affect rights acquired by third parties before the date of transfer.

(6) A transfer shall not take effect *vis-à-vis* the office or third parties until it has been registered, and then only to the extent that the transfer documents require. A transfer shall nevertheless take effect before registration *vis-à-vis* third parties who have acquired rights in the trade mark after the date of transfer but who knew of the transfer at the date on which they acquired those rights.

ARTICLE 21

Licensing

(1) Licences may be granted in respect of a Community trade mark for some or all of the goods or services for which it is registered.

(2) The rights conferred by a Community trade mark shall not be asserted *vis-à-vis* a licensee unless he operates his licence beyond the period of time for which it was granted or uses the trade mark in relation to goods or services for which it has not been registered or does not comply with the proprietor's instructions concerning the quality of the goods or services.

(3) The proprietor of a Community trade mark shall ensure that the quality of the goods manufactured or of the services provided by the licensee is the same as that of the goods manufactured or of the services provided by the proprietor.

(4) Paragraphs (5) and (6) of Article 17 apply to licences.

European Communities Act 1972

General Implementation of Treaties

2.—(1) All such rights, powers, liabilities, obligations and restrictions from time to time created or arising by or under the Treaties, and all such remedies and procedures from time to time provided for by or under the Treaties, as in accordance with the Treaties are without further enactment to be given legal effect or used in the United Kingdom shall be recognised and available in law, and be enforced, allowed and followed accordingly; and the expression "enforceable Community right" and similar expressions shall be read as referring to one to which this subsection applies.

(2) Subject to Schedule 2 to this Act, at any time after its passing Her Majesty may by Order in Council, and any designated Minister or department may by regulations, make provision—

(a) for the purpose of implementing any Community obligation of the United Kingdom, or enabling any such obligation to be implemented, or of enabling any rights enjoyed or to be enjoyed by the United Kingdom under or by virtue of the Treaties to be exercised; or

(b) for the purpose of dealing with matters arising out of or related to any such obligation or rights or the coming into force, or the operation from time to time, of subsection (1) above;

and in the exercise of any statutory power or duty, including any power to give directions or to legislate by means of orders, rules, regulations or other subordinate instrument, the person entrusted with the power or duty may have regard to the objects of the Communities and to any such obligation or rights as aforesaid.

In this subsection "designated Minister or department" means such Minister of the Crown or government department as may from time to time be designated by Order in Council in relation to any matter or for any purpose, but subject to such restrictions or conditions (if any) as may be specified by the Order in Council.

(3) There shall be charged on an issued out of the Consolidated Fund or, if so determined by the Treasury, the National Loans Fund the amounts required to meet any Community obligation to make payments to any of the Communities or member States, or any Community obligation in respect of contributions to the capital or reserves of the European Investment Bank or in respect of loans to the Bank, or to redeem any notes or obligations issued or created in respect of any such Community obligation; and, except as otherwise provided by or under any enactment,—

(a) any other expenses incurred under or by virtue of the Treaties or this Act by any Minister of the Crown or government department may be paid out of moneys provided by Parliament; and (*b*) any sums received under or by virtue of the Treaties or this Act by any Minister of the Crown or government department, save for such sums as may be required for disbursements permitted by any other enactment, shall be paid into the Consolidated Fund or, if so determined by the Treasury, the National Loans Fund.

(4) The provision that may be made under subsection (2) above includes, subject to Schedule 2 to this Act, any such provision (of any such extent) as might be made by Act of Parliament, and any enactment passed or to be passed, other than one contained in this Part of this Act, shall be construed and have effect subject to the foregoing provisions of this section; but, except as may be provided by any Act passed after this Act, Schedule 2 shall have effect in connection with the powers conferred by this and the following sections of this Act to make Orders in Council and regulations.

(5) [...]; and the references in that subsection to a Minister of the Crown or government department and to a statutory power or duty shall include a Minister or department of the Government of Northern Ireland and a power or duty arising under or by virtue of an Act of the Parliament of Northern Ireland.

(6) A law passed by the legislature of any of the Channel Islands or of the Isle of Man, or a colonial law (within the meaning of the Colonial Laws Validity Act 1865) passed or made for Gibraltar, if expressed to be passed or made in the implementation of the Treaties and of the obligations of the United Kingdom thereunder, shall not be void or inoperative by reason of any inconsistency with or repugnancy to an Act of Parliament, passed or to be passed, that extends to the Island or Gibraltar or any provision having the force and effect of an Act there (but not including this section), nor by reason of its having some operation outside the Island or Gibraltar; and any such Act or provision that extends to the Island or Gibraltar shall be construed and have effect subject to the provisions of any such law.

AMENDMENTS

In subs. (5) the words omitted were repealed by the Northern Ireland Constitution Act 1973 (c. 36), s. 41 and Sched. 6, Pt. I. The subsection referred to is subs. (2) of this section.

Decisions on, and proof of, Treaties and Community Instruments etc.

3.—(1) For the purposes of all legal proceedings any question as to the meaning or effect of any of the Treaties, or as to the validity, meaning or effect of any Community instrument, shall be treated as a question of law (and, if not referred to the European Court, be for determination as such in accordance with the principles laid down by and any relevant decision of the European Court).

(2) Judicial notice shall be taken of the Treaties, of the Official Journal of the Communities and of any decision of, or expression of opinion by, the European Court on any such question as aforesaid; and the Official Journal shall be admissible as evidence of any instrument or other act thereby communicated of any of the Communities or of any Community institution.

(3) Evidence of any instrument issued by a Community institution, including any judgment or order of the European Court, or of any document in the custody of a Community institution, or any entry in or extract from such a document, may be given in any legal proceedings by production of a copy certified as a true copy by an official of that institution; and any document purporting to be such a copy shall be received in evidence without proof of the official position or handwriting of the person signing the certificate.

(4) Evidence of any Community instrument may also be given in any legal proceedings—

(a) by production of a copy purporting to be printed by the Queen's Printer;

(b) where the instrument is in the custody of a government department (including a department of the Government of Northern Ireland), by production of a copy certified on behalf of the department to be a true copy by an officer of the department generally or specially authorised so to do;

and any document purporting to be such a copy as is mentioned in paragraph (b) above of an instrument in the custody of a department shall be received in evidence without proof of the official position or handwriting of the person signing the certificate, or of his authority to do so, or of the document being in the custody of the department.

(5) In any legal proceedings in Scotland evidence of any matter given in a manner authorised by this section shall be sufficient evidence of it.

INDEX

[References are to paragraph numbers]